Can Fiction Change the World?

# LEGENDA

LEGENDA is the Modern Humanities Research Association's book imprint for new research in the Humanities. Founded in 1995 by Malcolm Bowie and others within the University of Oxford, Legenda has always been a collaborative publishing enterprise, directly governed by scholars. The Modern Humanities Research Association (MHRA) joined this collaboration in 1998, became half-owner in 2004, in partnership with Maney Publishing and then Routledge, and has since 2016 been sole owner. Titles range from medieval texts to contemporary cinema and form a widely comparative view of the modern humanities, including works on Arabic, Catalan, English, French, German, Greek, Italian, Portuguese, Russian, Spanish, and Yiddish literature. Editorial boards and committees of more than 60 leading academic specialists work in collaboration with bodies such as the Society for French Studies, the British Comparative Literature Association and the Association of Hispanists of Great Britain & Ireland.

The MHRA encourages and promotes advanced study and research in the field of the modern humanities, especially modern European languages and literature, including English, and also cinema. It aims to break down the barriers between scholars working in different disciplines and to maintain the unity of humanistic scholarship. The Association fulfils this purpose through the publication of journals, bibliographies, monographs, critical editions, and the MHRA Style Guide, and by making grants in support of research. Membership is open to all who work in the Humanities, whether independent or in a University post, and the participation of younger colleagues entering the field is especially welcomed.

ALSO PUBLISHED BY THE ASSOCIATION

*Critical Texts*
*Tudor and Stuart Translations* • *New Translations* • *European Translations*
*MHRA Library of Medieval Welsh Literature*

*MHRA Bibliographies*
*Publications of the Modern Humanities Research Association*

*The Annual Bibliography of English Language & Literature*
*Austrian Studies*
*Modern Language Review*
*Portuguese Studies*
*The Slavonic and East European Review*
*Working Papers in the Humanities*
*The Yearbook of English Studies*

www.mhra.org.uk
www.legendabooks.com

# TRANSCRIPT

*Transcript* publishes books about all kinds of imagining across languages, media and cultures: translations and versions, inter-cultural and multi-lingual writing, illustrations and musical settings, adaptation for theatre, film, TV and new media, creative and critical responses. We are open to studies of any combination of languages and media, in any historical moments, and are keen to reach beyond Legenda's traditional focus on modern European languages to embrace anglophone and world cultures and the classics. We are interested in innovative critical approaches: we welcome not only the most rigorous scholarship and sharpest theory, but also modes of writing that stretch or cross the boundaries of those discourses.

*Editorial Committee*
Chair: Matthew Reynolds (Oxford)
Robin Kirkpatrick (Cambridge)
Patrick McGuinness (Oxford)
Ben Morgan (Oxford)
Mohamed-Salah Omri (Oxford)
Tanya Pollard (CUNY)
Yopie Prins (Michigan)

*Advisory Board*
Jason Gaiger (Oxford)
Alessandro Grilli (Pisa)
Marina Grishakova (Tartu)
Martyn Harry (Oxford)
Linda Hutcheon (Toronto)
Calin-Andrei Mihailescu (London, Ontario)
Wen-Chin Ouyang (SOAS)
Clive Scott (UEA)
Ali Smith
Marina Warner (Birkbeck)
Shane Weller (Kent)
Stefan Willer (Berlin)

*Managing Editor*
Dr Graham Nelson
41 Wellington Square, Oxford OX1 2JF, UK

www.legendabooks.com/series/transcript

# TRANSCRIPT

1. *Adapting the Canon: Mediation, Visualization, Interpretation*, edited by Ann Lewis and Silke Arnold-de Simine
2. *Adapted Voices: Transpositions of Céline's Voyage au bout de la nuit and Queneau's Zazie dans le métro*, by Armelle Blin-Rolland
3. *Zola and the Art of Television: Adaptation, Recreation, Translation*, by Kate Griffiths
4. *Comparative Encounters between Artaud, Michaux and the Zhuangzi: Rationality, Cosmology and Ethics*, by Xiaofan Amy Li
5. *Minding Borders: Resilient Divisions in Literature, the Body and the Academy*, edited by Nicola Gardini, Adriana Jacobs, Ben Morgan, Mohamed-Salah Omri and Matthew Reynolds
6. *Memory Across Borders: Nabokov, Perec, Chamoiseau*, by Sara-Louise Cooper
7. *Erotic Literature in Adaptation and Translation*, edited by Johannes D. Kaminski
8. *Translating Petrarch's Poetry: L'Aura del Petrarca from the Quattrocento to the 21st Century*, edited by Carole Birkan-Berz, Guillaume Coatalen and Thomas Vuong
9. *Making Masud Khan: Psychoanalysis, Empire and Modernist Culture*, by Benjamin Poore
10. *Prismatic Translation*, edited by Matthew Reynolds
11. *The Patient, the Impostor and the Seducer: Medieval European Literature in Hebrew*, by Tovi Bibring
12. *Reading Dante and Proust by Analogy*, by Julia Caterina Hartley
13. *The First English Translations of Molière: Drama in Flux 1663-1732*, by Suzanne Jones
14. *After Clarice: Reading Lispector's Legacy in the Twenty-First Century*, edited by Adriana X. Jacobs and Claire Williams
15. *Uruguayan Theatre in Translation: Theory and Practice*, by Sophie Stevens
16. *Hamlet Translations: Prisms of Cultural Encounters across the Globe*, edited by Márta Minier and Lily Kahn
17. *The Foreign Connection: Writings on Poetry, Art and Translation*, by Jamie McKendrick
18. *Poetics, Performance and Politics in French and Italian Renaissance Comedy*, by Lucy Rayfield

# Can Fiction Change the World?

Edited by
Alison James, Akihiro Kubo, and Françoise Lavocat

Transcript 29
Modern Humanities Research Association
2023

*Published by Legenda
an imprint of the Modern Humanities Research Association
Salisbury House, Station Road, Cambridge CB1 2LA*

*ISBN 978-1-83954-145-2 (HB)
ISBN 978-1-83954-146-9 (PB)*

*First published 2023*

*All rights reserved. No part of this publication may be reproduced or disseminated or transmitted in any form or by any means, electronic, mechanical, photocopying, recording or otherwise, or stored in any retrieval system, or otherwise used in any manner whatsoever without written permission of the copyright owner, except in accordance with the provisions of the Copyright, Designs and Patents Act 1988, or under the terms of a licence permitting restricted copying issued in the UK by the Copyright Licensing Agency Ltd, Saffron House, 6–10 Kirby Street, London EC1N 8TS, England, or in the USA by the Copyright Clearance Center, 222 Rosewood Drive, Danvers MA 01923. Application for the written permission of the copyright owner to reproduce any part of this publication must be made by email to legenda@mhra.org.uk.*

*Disclaimer: Statements of fact and opinion contained in this book are those of the author and not of the editors or the Modern Humanities Research Association. The publisher makes no representation, express or implied, in respect of the accuracy of the material in this book and cannot accept any legal responsibility or liability for any errors or omissions that may be made.*

*Trademark notice: Product or corporate names may be trademarks or registered trademarks, and are used only for identification and explanation without intent to infringe.*

*© Modern Humanities Research Association 2023*

*Copy-Editor: Dr Ellen Jones*

# CONTENTS

| | | |
|---|---|---|
| *Acknowledgements* | | ix |
| *Notes on the Contributors* | | x |
| Introduction | | 1 |
| ALISON JAMES, AKIHIRO KUBO, AND FRANÇOISE LAVOCAT | | |

PART I. CHANGING DEFINITIONS: FICTION ACROSS TIME, CULTURES, LANGUAGES, AND MEDIA

| | | |
|---|---|---|
| 1 | Poetic Forms of Narrative and Pragmatic Fiction: *Poiein* — *Plattein* — *Prattein* <br> CLAUDE CALAME | 17 |
| 2 | The Fiction of Factuality: Some Perspectives from Premodern Japan <br> JUDIT ÁROKAY | 31 |
| 3 | For a Theory of Fiction as *Show, Performance, Entertainment* <br> YASUSUKE OURA | 45 |

PART II. CHANGING MINDS: FICTION, BELIEFS, AND EMOTION

| | | |
|---|---|---|
| 4 | The Moral Problem of Fiction: Rethinking the Emotional Effects of Fictional Characters <br> MARIO SLUGAN | 55 |
| 5 | Lucianic Fictions and the Rise of Unbelief <br> NICOLAS CORREARD | 69 |
| 6 | Fiction and the Modelling of Chance <br> ANNE DUPRAT | 85 |
| 7 | Pygmalion's Virtual Doll: The Case of a Real Metalepsis? <br> NATHALIE KREMER | 97 |

PART III. CHANGING PRACTICES: POLITICAL USES AND EFFECTS OF FICTION

| | | |
|---|---|---|
| 8 | Etiquette to 'Change the World'? Fictional Time-Order and Imperial Power at the Court of Emperor Go-Daigo <br> SIMONE MÜLLER | 111 |
| 9 | The Construction of the Nation by Theatrical Fiction <br> CHARLOTTE KRAUSS | 129 |

| | | |
|---|---|---|
| 10 | Feminist Resistance and the Powers of Fiction<br>ANNE ISABELLE FRANÇOIS | 141 |
| 11 | Engagement and Enchantment: Political and Ethical Uses of Fantasy Fictions<br>ANNE BESSON | 155 |
| 12 | Fiction or Death: The Latin American Tradition of Nonfiction<br>ANNICK LOUIS | 165 |
| 13 | Fiction as Legal Authority? Orwell, Snowden, and State Cyber-Surveillance<br>HENRIETTE KORTHALS ALTES | 177 |
| 14 | Legal Revolutions as Fictions: Do they Change the World?<br>OTTO PFERSMANN | 191 |

PART IV. CHANGING FICTIONS: METAFICTIONAL EFFECTS

| | | |
|---|---|---|
| 15 | Quixotism as a Humorous Reflection on Fiction's Effects<br>YEN-MAI TRAN-GERVAT | 205 |
| 16 | Metafiction in Japanese and Western Literature: *Chô-kyokô* and Meta-Mystery<br>MASAHIRO IWAMATSU | 219 |
| 17 | Killing the Reader? On Some Unfortunate Side Effects of Reading<br>MAXIME DECOUT | 231 |
| 18 | When Fiction Changes the World... of Fiction<br>FRANK WAGNER | 241 |
| | *Chapter Abstracts* | 249 |
| | *Further Reading* | 257 |
| | *Index* | 259 |

# ACKNOWLEDGEMENTS

The point of departure for this volume was the founding colloquium of the International Society for Fiction and Fictionality Studies (ISFFS/SIRFF), held on November 28-30, 2019 at the EHESS, the Maison de la Recherche of the Université Sorbonne Nouvelle, and the University of Chicago Center in Paris. The editors thank the members of the ISFFS/SIRFF and the hosting institutions listed above, as well as the Institut Universitaire de France, the THALIM and CERC research groups, and the French section of the Department of Romance Languages and Literatures at the University of Chicago, for their generous support of this conference.

We are deeply indebted to the team of scholars who anonymously reviewed individual chapters and gave valuable feedback to the authors. We are also grateful to the anonymous peer reviewer for Legenda who offered useful suggestions on the whole volume. For their encouragement and expert guidance throughout the publication process, special thanks go to Graham Nelson at Legenda and to the Transcript series editor, Matthew Reynolds. Finally, we would like to acknowledge the careful copy-editing work done by Robert Gorman, Honi Pein, and Ellen Jones, and we thank Anna J. Davies for her preparation of the index.

# NOTES ON THE CONTRIBUTORS

After graduating from Eötvös Loránd University, Budapest, in German and English Language and Literature, **Judit Árokay** completed her M.A. and PhD in Japanese Studies at Hamburg University, then received her Habilitation from Freie Universität Berlin. Since 2007, she is full professor of Japanese Studies at the University of Heidelberg, specializing in pre-modern Japanese literature. Her special interests are *waka* poetry and poetic theory from the Middle Ages to the end of the Tokugawa period, ego-documents, and the rhetoric of literary and factual writing.

**Anne Besson** is Full Professor in Comparative Literature at the Université d'Artois (Arras). Author of *D'Asimov à Tolkien, cycles et séries dans la littérature de genre* (CNRS Editions, 2004), *La Fantasy* (Klincksieck, collection '50 questions', 2007), *Constellations* (CNRS Editions, 2015) and *Les Pouvoirs de l'enchantement* (2021), she has also edited some twenty collections including the *Dictionary of Fantasy* (2018). Her research fields include science fiction and fantasy genres (for children, teens, and adults), medievalism in contemporary culture, expansive fictional universes (literature and television), theories of fictionality, narratology, and the new media culture.

**Claude Calame** is Director of Studies at the École des Hautes Études en Sciences Sociales in Paris (Centre AnHiMA: Anthropologie et Histoire des Mondes Antiques). He has also taught at the Universities of Urbino and Lausanne, and at Yale University. His publications in English include *The Craft of Poetic Speech in Ancient Greece* (Cornell University Press, 1995), *The Poetics of Eros in Ancient Greece* (Princeton University Press, 1999), *Masks of Authority: Fiction and Pragmatics in Ancient Greek Poetics* (Cornell University Press, 2005), *Greek Mythology: Poetics, Pragmatics and Fiction* (Cambridge University Press, 2009), and most recently, forthcoming in English, *La tragédie chorale: Poésie grecque et rituel musical* (Les Belles Lettres, 2018).

**Nicolas Correard** is Assistant Professor (maître de conférences) in Comparative Literature at Nantes Université, currently Vice-Dean of the Faculty of Literature and the Humanities, and Associate Director of the research team LAMo. His research deals with early modern fiction and satire, particularly Lucianic and Menippean satire, imaginary voyages, and animal discourses, in their relationships with the history of ideas (philosophical, political, or religious criticism). He recently directed the volume *Lucien et la satire en prose* (issue of the journal *XVIIe siècle*, no. 286, 2020/1) and co-authored *Fictions animales* (Atlande, 2021).

MAXIME DECOUT is a professor at Sorbonne Université and a junior member of the IUF. He is the author of several essays, including *Albert Cohen: Les fictions de la judéité* (Classiques-Garnier, 2011), *Écrire la judéité* (Champ Vallon, 2015) and the *Album Romain Gary* (Bibliothèque de la Pléiade, 2019). He participated in the publication of Perec's works in the Bibliothèque de la Pléiade (2017). He has also published, at Éditions de Minuit, four essays that question the relationship between authenticity, lies, writing, and reading: *En toute mauvaise foi* (2015), *Qui a peur de l'imitation ?* (2017), *Pouvoirs de l'imposture* (2018), and *Éloge du mauvais lecteur* (2021).

Professor of Comparative Literature at the Université de Picardie-Jules Verne, ANNE DUPRAT is the author of recognized works on the theory of fiction and on the relationships between literature, cultural anthropology, and intellectual history. A member of the Institut Universitaire de France, her publications include *Vraisemblances: Poétique et théorie de la fiction* (Droz, 2009), *Fiction et cultures* (ed. with Françoise Lavocat, 2010), and *Histoires et savoirs: Anecdotes scientifiques et sérendipité aux XVI$^e$ et XVII$^e$ siècles* (ed. with Frédérique Aït-Touati, 2012). She is the principal director of the international Collaborative Research Project ANR-ALEA, *Figures of Chance* (2020–2023).

ANNE ISABELLE FRANÇOIS is Assistant Professor (maître de conférences) in Comparative Literature at the Université Sorbonne Nouvelle. After higher studies in France (École normale supérieure) and the UK (Cambridge), she completed her PhD (*summa cum laude*) at the École Pratique des Hautes Études (Paris) and the University of Dresden. Specialising in European literatures of the twentieth and twenty-first centuries, she pursues her research, crossing Comparative Literature and Gender and Cultural Studies, as a member of the *Centre d'Études et de Recherches Comparatistes*. She is the author of numerous publications, including 'Littérature comparée et *Gender*', *TRANS–* (Online), 2018 <https://doi.org/10.4000/trans.1828>.

Born in Fukuoka, Japan, MASAHIRO IWAMATSU completed a doctorate at the Université de Paris IV-Sorbonne, with a focus on literary theory. He is Professor in the School of Business Administration and the Graduate School of Language, Communication, and Culture, Kwansei Gakuin University (Nishinomiya, Japan). He has translated Marie-Laure Ryan's *Possible Worlds, Artificial Intelligence, and Narrative Theory* into Japanese. His essays under the pseudonym of Boshi Chino include *Why Do We Call for Narratives?*, *Do Stories Save Lives?* (both Chikuma Shobo), *An Immediate Introduction to Haiku* (NHK Publishing), and *How I Overcame my Prejudice against Unread Books* (Kadokawa Shoten).

ALISON JAMES is Professor of French at the University of Chicago. Her research interests include the Oulipo group, the contemporary novel, theories and representations of everyday life, and questions of fact and fiction. She is the author of *Constraining Chance: Georges Perec and the Oulipo* (Northwestern University Press, 2009) and *The Documentary Imagination in Twentieth-Century French Literature: Writing with Facts* (Oxford University Press, 2020). She has also edited volumes and journal issues on literary formalism, fieldwork literatures, and nonfiction across media.

HENRIETTE KORTHALS-ALTES is currently a research fellow at the Maison Française d'Oxford and teaches at Birkbeck College, University of London. Her research interests lie in contemporary French and comparative literature. More specifically, she has written on the cultural construction of melancholy in contemporary French fiction and thought. She also has a special interest in the intersections between literature and dance as well as literature and music, and has published on intermediality in the works of Roland Barthes and Pascal Quignard. Her current project looks at the writing and rewriting of history in relation to surveillance and self-surveillance.

CHARLOTTE KRAUSS is a professor of Comparative Literature at the Université de Poitiers (France) and director of the FoReLLIS research group. She is a specialist in cultural relations between Eastern and Western Europe as well as in the relationship between literature and politics, with a particular interest in the construction of the idea of the nation through fiction. She works on theatre and epic, as well as on intermediality, especially comics. Her book *La mise en scène de la nation: Les spectacles dans un fauteuil de l'Europe post-napoléonienne* was published in 2022 by Presses du Septentrion.

NATHALIE KREMER is Associate Professor (maître de conférences habilitée) at the Université Sorbonne Nouvelle and a member of the Institut Universitaire de France (IUF). She is a specialist in eighteenth-century literature and poetics. Since her doctoral thesis at the KU Leuven (Belgium) on literature and knowledge in the eighteenth century (*Vraisemblance et représentation au XVIII$^e$ siècle*, Champion, 2011), she has continued her work on art criticism (*Traverser la peinture: Diderot — Baudelaire*, Brill, 2018) and on the aesthetic relationship, or more specifically on the emotional and sensitive relationship between a work of art and the viewer.

AKIHIRO KUBO is Professor of French Literature at Kwansei Gakuin University. His research interests focus on twentieth-century French literature and theories of literature. He is the author of *Hyosho-no Kizu, Daiichiji Sekaitaisen kara miru Furansu Bungaku* [French literature and the First World War] (Jinbun Shoin, 2011) and the translator of Jean-Marie Schaeffer's *Pourquoi la fiction?* [*Naze-Fiction ka*] (Keio Gijuku Shuppan, 2019) and Gérard Genette's *Métalepse* [Metalepsis] (Jinbun Shoin, 2022).

FRANÇOISE LAVOCAT is Professor of Comparative Literature at the Université Sorbonne Nouvelle. She received an honorary doctorate in Humane Letters from the University of Chicago, and is a member of the Institut Universitaire de France and the Academia Europaea. Her publications include *Arcadies malheureuses* (Champion, 1997), *Usages et théories de la fiction* (ed. PUR, 2004), *La Syrinx au bûcher* (Droz, 2005), *La théorie littéraire des mondes possibles* (ed. CNRS, 2010), *Pestes, Incendies naufrages, Ecritures du désastre au XVIIe siècle* (ed. Brépols, 2010), *Fait et fiction: Pour une frontière* (Seuil, 2016, Del Vecchio, 2020), and *Les Personnages rêvent aussi* (Hermann, 2020). Since 2018, she has been president of the International Society for Fiction and Fictionality Studies.

Professor at the Université de Franche-Comté, **ANNICK LOUIS** graduated in Letters and Humanities from the University of Buenos Aires. She holds a PhD from the École des Hautes Études en Sciences Sociales (Paris) and a Habilitation à diriger des Recherches (HDR) from the same institution. She was a Visiting Professor at Yale (1999–2000), and a Fellow of the Alexander von Humboldt Foundation in Erlangen (2000–2002). She has published numerous essays on Latin American literature and intellectual history, as well as the following books: *Jorge Luis Borges: Œuvre et manœuvres* (L'Harmattan, 1997), *Enrique Pezzoni, lector de Borges* (Editorial Sudamericana, 1999), *Borges ante el fascismo* (Peter Lang, 2007), *L'invention de Troie. Les vies rêvées de Heinrich Schliemann*, (EHESS, 2020), *Sans objet: Pour une épistémologie du littéraire* (Hermann, 2021).

**SIMONE MÜLLER** is senior lecturer of Japanese studies at the University of Zurich. From 1992 to 1999, she studied Japanology, Sinology, and Philosophy at the University of Zurich, Tokyo University of Foreign Studies and Doshisha University (Kyoto), before completing her PhD (2003) and Habilitation (2012) in Japanese Studies at the University of Zurich. She has undertaken research stays at Sophia University (Tokyo), Kyoto University of Technology, and Cornell University. Her research interests are in Japanese literature and intellectual history. Her recent publications include 'The "Debate on the Literature of Action" and Its Legacy: Ideological Struggles in 1930s Japan and the "Rebirth" of the Intellectual' (*The Journal of Japanese Studies*, 2015), 'A Young Lady's Longing for a Lost Past: A Chronotopic Analysis of the Medieval Memoir "Utatane" ("Fitful Slumbers")' (BmE, 2020), and *Zeit in der vormodernen japanischen Literatur / Time in Premodern Japanese Literature* (de Gruyter, 2021).

**YASUSUKE OURA** is Professor emeritus at Kyoto University, Japan. His research focuses on French literature and literary theory. His publications include *Invitation to a Theory of Fiction: Literature, History, Play, Human Beings*, (2013; in Japanese) and *Japanese Literary Theories: An Anthology*, 2017 (in Japanese; an English version is forthcoming), as well as the edited volume *Fiction de l'Occident, fiction de l'Orient: Actes du colloque international* (Institute for Research in Humanities, Kyoto University, 2010).

**OTTO PFERSMANN** studied philosophy and law and is presently Professor in Legal Theory and Comparative Constitutional Law at the EHESS, Écoles des Hautes Études en Sciences Sociales (Paris). Otto Pfersmann has extensively published in Legal Philosophy and Comparative Constitutional Law (<http://lier.ehess.fr/index.php?1907>). His next book *Changement contre connaissance: Évolutions et révolutions juridiques* is due to appear with Éditions Vrin, Paris, 2022. Recent articles include: 'Legal Globalization as a Municipal American Problem', *Annuario di Diritto Comparato* (2017), pp. 475–98; 'Comparative Hermeneutics of Constitutional Revision Clauses and the Question of Structural Closure of Legal Systems', in *Cardozo Law Review* 40 (2019), p. 3191–3216; 'Le droit est-il narratif, la narrativité est-elle juridique?', in *Droit & Littérature*, 3, (2019), p. 169–80.

**MARIO SLUGAN** is Lecturer in Film Studies and Strategic Lecturer at the Institute of Humanities and Social Sciences, Queen Mary University of London. He is the author of three monographs including *Fiction and Imagination in Early Cinema* (Bloomsbury, 2019) and co-editor of four special issues including 'Documentaries and the Fiction/Nonfiction Divide', *Studies in Documentary Film* 14.2 (2019) and 'Fiction in Central and Eastern European Film Theory and Practice', *Apparatus* 8 (2019). He is Fellow of the Society for Cognitive Studies of the Moving Image and book reviews editor for *Early Popular Visual Culture*.

**YEN-MAI TRAN-GERVAT** is Assistant Professor (maître de conférences) in Comparative Literature at Université Sorbonne Nouvelle. Her research focuses on humour (particularly comic fiction) in early modern European literature (England, France, Spain) and on translations and adaptations of early modern works in later periods. Recent publications include: *Humour Studies et études littéraires: Vers une humoristique francophone*, co-edited with Bernard Andrès (2021) and 'Intercultural and Interartistic Transfers of Shandean Humour in the 20$^{th}$ and 21$^{st}$ Centuries' in *The Palgrave Handbook of Humour, History and Methodology*, ed. by Daniel Derrin and Hannah Burrows (2021).

**FRANK WAGNER** teaches contemporary French literature as an Assistant Professor (maître de conférences) at the Université Rennes 2. He is a member of *Vox-Poetica*'s editorial board, and co-director of *TheoCrit'* (a Peter Lang Verlag collection). His research deals with theory of literature (mostly narratology, poetics, and theory of fiction) and mutations in contemporary narratives. He has published more than one hundred articles in *Poétique, Protée, Les Cahiers de narratologie, Etudes littéraires, Fixxion, Roman 20–50*, etc. He has also edited or co-edited several books, notably *Lectures de Julien Gracq* (Presses Universitaires de Rennes, 2007), *Lectures de Robbe-Grillet* (Presses Universitaires de Rennes, 2010), and *Le Cinéma de la littérature* (Cécile Defaut, 2017).

# INTRODUCTION

*Alison James, Akihiro Kubo, and Françoise Lavocat*

University of Chicago, Kwansei Gakuin University, and
Université Sorbonne Nouvelle/Institut Universitaire de France

Does fiction change the world? Can it do so? This book examines a question that is often treated superficially and in contradictory ways, whether in common conceptions of fiction or by theorists of fiction: the question of the effects that reading or viewing fictional works can have on individuals and society at large. Even when such effects are not denied, they are often underestimated or presented in an unfavourable light.

Fictions themselves often offer a critical view of the confusion between fiction and reality, or of attempts to cross the ontological boundary between them. As far back as the eleventh century, the hero of Murasaki Shikibu's great novel, the *Genji Monogatari*, did not wish anyone to read sentimental novels to his daughter: they would supposedly lead her to believe that reality resembles fiction, exposing her to many disappointments.[1] The characters of Don Quixote or Madame Bovary have given lasting shape to the idea that reading novels makes those engaged in them incapable of understanding the world or of acting on it. The gap between the ideal world of Amadís or Walter Scott's heroes and the stratified society of the seventeenth or nineteenth centuries is judged to be unbridgeable and produces an inexhaustibly comic effect. Jane Austen's Catherine Morland, in *Northanger Abbey* (1817) habitually misreads the social world by applying interpretative frameworks from Gothic fiction. In the twentieth century, cinema explores the relationship between real and fictional worlds via the fantasy of crossing the screen.[2] In Buster Keaton's *Sherlock Jr.* (1924), a film projectionist becomes a fictional detective who solves a transposed version of the 'real' crime for which he has just been framed. Yet, on the level of the film's diegetic 'reality', it is his girlfriend who actually discovers the culprit, finding the stolen watch while he dreams. Woody Allen's *The Purple Rose of Cairo* (1985) reverses the trick by having the fictional character Tom Baxter (Jeff Daniels) emerge from the screen for the love of a spectator. However, he can have no impact on the unemployment and poverty of 1930s America; he cannot even modify the fate of an individual being, the unhappily married viewer (Cecilia, played by Mia Farrow) who falls in love with him. Alice or Dorothy, upon returning from Wonderland or Oz, find reality exactly as they left it. Numerous fictions that focus on the relationships between fiction and the real world emphasise their separation and incompatibility; they often mock those who exaggerate their attraction and powers and keep an unhappy or a ridiculous fate in store for them. At best, even if illusions do not lead to the downfall of those heroes who like fiction too much, fiction is presented as a mere space of projection, escapism, or wish-fulfilment.

However, is it really the case that these fictions have no effect at all on the real world — either as this world is represented in fictions, or as it exists outside of them? In the second part of *Don Quixote*, the Duke and Duchess who have avidly read the first part engage in games and disguises that transform their environment, for the pleasure of deceiving the hero, but above all that of becoming immersed alongside him in his universe of fictional chivalry. As for Emma Bovary's literary dreams, they at least incite Charles Bovary to transform himself after his wife's death, adopting her romantic ideas. Jane Austen intervenes in her narrative to criticise those who would mock her heroine Catherine by dismissing the knowledge brought by novels.[3] Buster Keaton's projectionist mimics the romantic gestures seen on screen as he successfully reunites with the heroine, while Cecilia, the spectator in *The Purple Rose of Cairo*, escapes, at least for a moment, her abusive husband. In real life, Don Quixote and Emma Bovary have become the paradigms and objects of identification for numerous readers and spectators. The demonstration of fiction's futility and its incapacity to change the world is thus reversed by the very strength of reader responses: these characters are inspiring enough to produce an '-ism' that extends their names — quixotism, *bovarysme* (see Baldick 2008) — to designate attitudes, ways of being and living in the real world. These fictions have allowed us to identify and name the effects of fictions on the world.

But are these effects limited to producing a few idealistic individuals who are unsuited to life in the real world? In fact, the dream of countless fictions — and perhaps of all fiction — is to modify or reinforce readers' beliefs, to convince them to embrace a cause, and even to make them take action. Whether fictions are celebrated, recommended, feared, or reviled, testimonies to such real effects abound. The very hostility that fiction arouses allows us to trace a cartography of its supposed effects — one that evolves according to time and genre, even if we can discern some continuities.

## 1. From Fiction to Reality

There is indeed no shortage of examples that show the influence of fictional universes on lives, identities, and social practices, today as in the past. The thousands of men and women who, between the sixteenth and eighteenth centuries in Europe, and even Brazil or Saint-Domingue, adopted the names of shepherds and shepherdesses in literary academies, are a good illustration of the large-scale impact of a fictional universe on society (Penge 2020: 223). Since the 1980s, the spread of theme parks inspired by the worlds of Disney and others have demonstrated the material inscription of fictions in the physical and economic world — to the point, according to Jean Baudrillard, of almost extending across the whole world, and even of replacing the real world with a simulation (Baudrillard 1981).

But above all, fictions are alleged to transform individuals by acting on emotions, beliefs, and feelings. The effect most often attributed to fiction is undoubtedly the incitement to love, whether it takes the form of a corruption of morals or a sentimental education. Leaving aside erotic books, which from the seventeenth century onward boast of making love to the reader via the eyes and ears (see Jeanneret 2003), the great novels of the same period, such as Honoré d'Urfé's *L'Astrée* (1607–1623), deliver models of discourse, behaviours, epistolary style and above all expression of feelings, to the point that readers signed their private letters with the name of Céladon, the hero of that novel (Denis and Lavocat 2008). Fictions, which are schools of feeling in the form of the great love and adventure novels of the seventeenth century, can also provide models of high virtues, inciting bravery and great endeavours; this is in any case the view of Pierre Fortin de la Hoguette (1648), who recommended in his will that his children read chivalric novels. Such a sympathetic view of fiction is far from being the rule, however, especially in that period: the Jansenist Pierre Nicole, and many other despisers of theatre, suspect that the evil passions expressed by the actor on stage might be contagious. Not only is the actor infected, but also the spectators and above all female spectators (for a long time, the presence of women on stage or in the theatre was not widely accepted). The emotions aroused by representations of fictional events were considered strong enough to provoke the most varied effects in the audience: men flee,[4] women miscarry, and people sometimes confess their crimes out loud when they recognise them on the stage (Lecercle 2012). We recall that Hamlet hopes in vain for this result when he stages a pantomime to remind Gertrude and Claudius of the crime they committed.

With the advent of Romanticism, new themes expand the repertoire of supposed effects and associated fears. The reality of the 'Werther Effect', which allegedly entailed an epidemic of suicides after the publication of Goethe's novel (1774), seemed sufficiently established for the Leipzig theological faculty to ban the work a year later (Siebers 1993). We also find that fiction influences public opinion enough to induce societal reforms or shape major political events. Fiction undoubtedly played a role in the emergence and spread of French anticlericalism; particularly, in the nineteenth century, in the denunciation of the Jesuits. The 554 performances of Molière's *Tartuffe* between 1801 and 1850, the dozens of re-editions of this play, and the novels that took up the character of the hypocritical and criminal Jesuit (including Eugène Sue's *Le Juif errant* of 1844), all indicate that fiction contributed powerfully to the formation of a liberal current of opinion (Leroy 1992). In the United States, a single book (along with its influential theatrical adaptations) was credited by both its admirers and opponents with changing minds and thus the world: Harriet Beecher Stowe's *Uncle Tom's Cabin* (1852), alleged to have sparked the Civil War. Written with an overt abolitionist aim, the bestselling book directly shaped political debates via its impact on public opinion. Nonfictional slave testimonies by Josiah Henson, Frederick Douglass, and others, also had an effect, of course — not least on Stowe herself who used them as a source of material for her novel (Reynolds 2011: 102–13). But the book's significant impact can be attributed in large part to the specific appeal of fiction — its ability to immerse readers in a story and create sympathy for characters (even among some contemporary readers who were unsympathetic to its politics).[5] Still, some later readers rejected what James Baldwin would call 'everybody's protest novel'; for Baldwin, it is a sentimental pamphlet that is both aesthetically and morally insufficient (Baldwin 1955). If Stowe's novel has a complicated afterlife, it is in part because of the very conventional elements that helped give its radical message mainstream success (its deployment of stereotypes, didacticism, and sentimentality), and in part due to the gradual transformation of its cultural meaning in light of new reading practices, especially among African American readers (Hochman 2011).

The twentieth century sees a continued concern with the effects of fiction, intensified by the influence of mass culture and its new media forms — even if the dominant genre of the novel often remains the focus of critical debates. Particular works of fiction are considered to have had a profound impact on public opinion. Henri Barbusse's *Le Feu* (*Under Fire*), a bestseller that won the Goncourt Prize in France in 1916, supposedly contributed to the rise of pacifism during the Great War. This example is all the more interesting since Barbusse did not originally conceive of this work as the pacifist novel that it would become thanks to its generic malleability and polyvocality (Pernot 2018: 147); moreover, the work is later accused of offering an inadequate documentary account by writers as different as Jean Norton Cru and André Breton.[6] In this case, the proximity of fiction to reality is a site of friction. After World War II, theories of literary engagement cast the novel as the privileged genre for both unveiling the world and acting upon it. This is not just a matter of realism (socialist or otherwise): thus, for Jean-Paul Sartre, the writer's free exercise of invention is understood to be inseparable from an appeal to the freedom of the reader (Sartre 1988: 139–40) — exceeding the real world in order to change it.

The rapidly changing media landscape of the late twentieth century, along with the emergence of new digital forms of fiction, brought new or intensified fears about the psychological consequences of immersion in fictional environments. Debates raged about the individual or social effects of television series and video games, with the latter in particular reviving the old Platonic notion of the victory of imitations over reality (see Schaeffer 2010: vii–xi). The rise of cyberculture, however, does not transfer all the (real or alleged) influence to interactive digital fictions. In the twenty-first century, Dan Brown's novel *The Da Vinci Code* (2003) caused such great concern to the Catholic Church that scholarly publications were produced to counter the idea that Jesus was married to Mary Magdalene (Ehrman 2004). While media representations are often accused of perpetuating stereotypes, they can also work against them; it has even been claimed that the TV series *24* contributed to the election of Barack Obama, via the so-called 'Palmer effect' that allowed viewers to become comfortable with the idea of an African American president (Yanes and Carter 2014: 73).

Lawsuits against writers illustrate the alleged effects of fiction from another perspective, while also pointing to the fragility of fiction's boundaries — especially when it borrows from reality. In France, charges of invasion of privacy have been brought against authors of autofiction such as Camille Laurens or Christine Angot (see Sapiro 2013); in Japan, when Yukio Mishima published *After the Banquet* (1960), the former minister of foreign affairs Hachiro Arita sued the novelist for allegedly breaching his privacy in this *roman à clef*.

## 2. Theories of Fictional Effects

Fictional worlds (i.e., mostly made up of imaginary and non-referential elements, even if we admit that most are ontologically hybrid) are often considered to be detached from the real world. John Searle describes fictional utterances as 'nonserious' utterances that do not commit authors to the truth of their propositions (1975: 320–21). How, then, can such non-truths affect us? In recent decades, philosophers and theorists have attempted to understand to what extent and by what means fictions shape our beliefs and actions. Some have taken seriously the ability of fiction to model emotions, feelings, and relationships (a question we return to in Part II of the present volume). The philosopher Stanley Cavell, for instance, argues that Hollywood 'comedies of remarriage' are a serious attempt to recreate marriage on the basis of the demand for acknowledgment and mutual freedom in the couple; cinematic fiction can thus have 'powers of instruction and redemption' (Cavell 1981: 7).

These accounts of the positive effects of fiction often hinge on the notion of empathy. Martha Nussbaum has explored fiction's ability to stimulate empathetic responses and develop the moral imagination (e.g., Nussbaum 1990 and 1995, making this point the centre of her larger defence of the role of the humanities in training democratic citizens (Nussbaum 2010). In the area of French literary studies, Alexandre Gefen has analysed the contemporary vogue for the idea of a consolatory fiction that heals intimate injuries and traumas (Gefen 2017). Our intuitive sense that fiction enlarges our capacity for empathy has also been put to the test scientifically. Seeking empirical evidence for the cognitive and moral benefits of fiction, psychologists have confirmed (to lesser or greater degrees) the influence of fiction on social cognition and skills associated with the theory of mind — in other words our capacity to discern the feelings and intentions and others (e.g., Mar, Oatley, and Peterson 2009; Dodell-Feder and Tamir 2018). Some work in literary studies then aims to bring insights from cognitive science back to literature (e.g., Zunshine 2006). While philosophical and cognitive approaches tend to focus on literary fiction (with some notable exceptions such as Cavell's attention to popular film), Sandra Laugier (2019) has recently shown how television series teach us to live, while a long-term sociological study by Sabine Chalvon-Demersay (2015) demonstrates how viewers of such series regularly mobilise fictional situations for the purposes of comparison, to help with decision-making. However, such claims for cognitive and moral benefits of fiction still have their sceptics; in his recent book *Imagining and Knowing* (2020), for instance, Gregory Currie casts doubt on whether we can really acquire much knowledge or empathy from fiction. James Dawes challenges the frequent claim that 'literature promotes empathy, and empathy promotes rights' (Dawes 2015: 427), suggesting furthermore that 'our collective conceptions of empathy are at best fractured and at worst incoherent' (429); that is, it may be the case that empathy does not take us beyond the reader to larger real-world effects. While arguing that fictions can be 'formative' in pragmatic terms and help us hone our mental capacities, Joshua Landy dismisses as 'wishful thinking' the prevalent affective and moralising understandings of fictional utility (Landy 2012: 9–10). The value of empathetic responses to fiction may also be questioned from another perspective: in Chapter 4 of this volume, for instance, Mario Slugan raises the possibility that the emotional effects of fiction may be ethically problematic. How can we justify caring about fictional characters, sometimes even more than we care about real-life people?

As this last point indicates, the effects of fiction are not always considered to be beneficial. Old worries about the psychological or social harm caused by fiction have not disappeared, even if they have taken new forms since Plato's criticism of poetic mimesis. Today, works of fiction are put on the hot seat for two main reasons. The first line of criticism, which primarily concerns role-playing games and video games, entails supposing that game-playing promotes aggression and violence; this idea remains widely accepted and is supported by some evidence, even if empirical studies remain inconclusive (Prescott, Sargent, and Hull 2018). Cinematographic fictions are also blamed for a number of crimes, since the perpetrators themselves sometimes invoke forms of imitation: the American serial killer Joel Rifkin claimed he had been inspired by Hitchcock's *Frenzy* (1972), the Norwegian terrorist Anders Behring Breivik by Lars Von Trier's *Dogville* (2003), the French spree killers Florence Rey and Audry Maupin by Oliver Stone's *Natural Born Killers* (1994), the Colorado mass shooter James Holmes by Batman comics and films. The online news media often emphasises these ties between fiction and murder (e.g., Ferenczi 2012; Marikar and Dola 2012). The second line of attack involves attempts to control fictions that implicitly or explicitly express contested values — whether this control is exercised through direct government censorship, through official organs such as the Conseil Supérieur de l'Audiovisuel in France, or simply through public pressure.

These debates have arguably grown more intense in the second and third decades of the twenty-first century, most recently with the impact of the #metoo movement and social justice movements such as Black Lives Matter. One widespread worry is that fictions do not simply represent, but also disseminate and perpetuate harmful stereotypes and behavioural norms regarding race, gender, or sexuality; or else that they offer an inadequate representation of women and minorities. The 'representation matters' slogan links questions of mimesis to questions of political representation. These tendencies do not necessarily lead to demands for suppression, however, but can also bring a useful recontextualisation and re-evaluation of popular fictions from the past, such as *Gone with the Wind* (see Stewart 2020).

In any case, both the attacks on and apologies for fiction, which belong to a long tradition even as they engage with changing social contexts, clearly rest on the same assumptions and are thus tinged with ambivalence. The effects of fiction are sometimes held to be beneficial (in terms of education, care, or the advancement of liberal freedoms) or harmful (the incitement of excessive passions and even violent acts, the diffusion of false or unpleasant images of the world, the legitimation and thus continuation of forms of social and political domination...). But all these claims are based on granting, perhaps to an exaggerated degree, the considerable power of fictions to influence minds, shape opinions, and change the course of events. The playful dimension of fiction seems to fall by the wayside in such debates. However, if the use of fiction is indeed a matter of 'shared ludic feint' — that is, of playful pretence, as Jean-Marie Schaeffer argues (2010: 138–39), how are we to measure its actual impact on our beliefs and our lives? This is the question we ask in this volume. The answer that we bring is a complex one. While communities of readers may well mobilise fictions for specific ends, and while fiction may also condition our norms and practices in more subtle ways, fictional works also resist this form of instrumentalisation and operate in a space of free imagination — a world without consequences. Fiction *can* change the world — but may do so less often than is generally believed. Still, fiction is constantly evaluated, sometimes too hastily or speculatively, in terms of its perceived social and moral influence. This is especially true in our current moment, which is witnessing an intensified (and perhaps excessive) anxiety about the effects of representation.

## 3. Fiction and Fictionality Studies: New Approaches

The question of the relative autonomy or effective power of fiction opens up varied research perspectives, a number of which are represented in this volume. The book presents selected papers from the founding colloquium of the International Society for Fiction and Fictionality Studies (ISFFS/SIRFF), held at the EHESS, the Université Sorbonne Nouvelle and the University of Chicago Center in Paris on 28–30 November 2019. Presenting a multi-disciplinary approach, it examines the question of fiction's effects from theoretical, sociological, historical, legal, and literary perspectives. Although it does not aim to be exhaustive, its case studies are drawn from varied periods and cultural traditions, including classical antiquity, medieval Japan, and the European Renaissance.

The Society aims to extend its research areas to as many cultural and linguistic spheres as possible; at this early stage, our membership has strengths in certain areas. The present volume is characterised by several contributions from Japan specialists (see Chapters 2, 8, and 16), as well as by Japanese scholars working on general issues in the theory of fictionality (Chapters 3 and 16). This relatively strong presence of Japanese culture and scholarship can be explained by two main factors. First, the Japanese context holds particular interest for fiction studies. From the particular form of self-writing known as the 'I-novel' (*watakushi-shôsetsu*) to *otaku* practices such as cosplay, many facets of Japanese culture allow us to investigate both the universality of fictional practices and their cultural specificities. Second, Japanese scholars have shown particular interest in Western theories of fiction. Major works translated into this language include Kendall Walton's *Mimesis as Make-Believe*

(1990), Marie-Laure Ryan's *Possible Worlds, Artificial Intelligence and Narrative Theory* (1991), and Jean-Marie Schaeffer's *Why Fiction? (Pourquoi la fiction?)* (1999/2010). These theories of fiction have also become a subject of reflection for Japanese scholars, as demonstrated by the philosopher Kunihiko Kiyozuka's work *Fikushon no Tetsugaku (The Philosophy of Fiction)* (2009/2017) and the collective volume edited by Yasusuke Oura, *Fiction de l'Occident, fiction de l'Orient (Fiction of the West, Fiction of the East)* (2010), which questions the scope of Western theory from a comparative perspective.

The authors of the chapters collected here agree for the most part on a definition of fiction as deriving from an attitude of 'shared ludic feint' (inspired by Searle [1975] and Schaeffer [2010]) and postulating non-referential states of affairs or 'possible worlds' (according to a semantic conception drawn from analytic philosophy). However, many contributions give greater emphasis to the pragmatic aspect of this definition. Claude Calame, a literary theorist and specialist in Ancient Greece, highlights the role of *plattein* or fabrication: the verbal and visual means which give fiction its pragmatic efficacy. More radically, Yasusuke Oura defines fiction in terms of performativity and performance. Furthermore, while most of our authors envisage fiction in the form of artistic artifacts, Otto Pfersmann follows Bentham, Kelsen, and Vaihinger in considering that laws and legal norms, and indeed the whole of the law, constitute fictions. These redefinitions indicate how the 'pretence' or make-believe of fiction can indeed be held to have real-world effects.

Our comparative and transhistorical approach highlights the varied understandings and impact of fiction in different contexts. While we have not neglected the debate on the emotional and behavioural effects of fiction on the individual level (see for example Chapter 4), our selection of papers has privileged approaches that evaluate the collective effects of fiction on communities of readers, whether from the point of view of intellectual history (Chapters 5 and 6), nation building and the consolidation of political power (Chapters 8 and 9); or, on the contrary, forms of activism that contest existing power structures (Chapters 10, 11, and 12). We also ask how technological change affects the ontological distinction between real and fictional entities (Chapter 7), and how legal reasoning may draw on fiction (Chapters 13 and 14). The question of the distinction between fact and fiction, a much-debated topic most recently explored by Lavocat (2016), Fludernik and Ryan (2019), and Fülöp (2021), has obvious relevance to the subject of this volume — whether we are considering the way fiction addresses those facts it wishes to change, or how it influences states of things in the world. Chapters 2 and 12 consider cases where the relationship between fiction and nonfiction is blurred for particular purposes, while Chapter 16 argues that self-referentiality in fiction takes on a transgressive force that it does not possess in nonfiction. The task we take on here is a broad reflection on a range of cases that bring to light fiction's many kinds of effect, and the different scales of these effects. The volume is also distinguished by its expansive treatment of the category of fiction, not limited to literary narratives but extending across a range of cultural forms: theatre and performance, fantasy fiction, digital simulations, and contemporary television series are among the domains considered.

Part I, 'Changing Definitions: Fiction Across Time, Cultures, Languages, and Media', offers a preliminary reflection on definitions of fiction — which does not mean the same thing in different times and places — and lays the groundwork for a pragmatic approach to the uses and effects of fiction. Examples drawn from East and West, and from Antiquity to the contemporary period, offer sites for exploring the scope and parameters of such a perspective. Claude Calame, in his contribution, turns to ancient Greek poetics to argue for an anthropological approach to fiction, which must be understood in relation to the historical and cultural context of its production; fiction refers to a world of shared representations, while its meaning is refigured through specific practices of interpretation and performance. Judit Árokay examines the continuity between fictionality and factuality in medieval Japan, in the case of texts that were read both for historical information and for entertainment, and which made use of conventional signs to establish the reliability of the narrator, frame the reading contract, and shape a community of reception. The connection of fiction to action and performance is the focus of Yasusuke Oura's chapter, which gives priority to the figure of the actor and explores the paradoxes of audience responses to embodied fictional enactments.

The second section, 'Changing Minds: Fiction, Belief, and Emotions', picks up this question of audience response in order to explore the cognitive and emotional effects of fiction as the privileged vector of its action on the world. This section also investigates the precise mechanisms by which fiction can contribute to shaping beliefs. These effects are not necessarily always positive, however: Mario Slugan uses examples from television and film to explore the philosophical and ethical problems posed by the effects of fiction on our emotions. How do we explain and justify our psychological investment in invented situations and characters? Even if the emotions provoked by fictional entities do not lead to real-life action, it remains troubling that we often respond more intensely to these characters than to real people. If this chapter asks whether we may believe too fully in fictional characters, in the following chapter Nicolas Correard explores the opposite possibility: that fiction may generate unbelief, exposing accepted notions and entities as inventions or constructions. The author investigates the underestimated contribution of Lucian of Samosata's novels to the spread of atheism in the early modern period. As an oblique form of expression, Lucianic fiction allows thinkers to envision what was still unthinkable: the fictional character of divine providence. Examining fiction's relationship to probabilistic models of prediction and projection, Anne Duprat explores the role of literary and artistic fiction in shaping our understanding of chance events. Fictions bridge the gap between the available scientific models for theorizing contingent probabilities and our understanding of the human meanings of chance, and may therefore offer a spur to effective action in the face of large-scale events, of varying degrees of unpredictability, such as the global pandemic or climate change. According to Nathalie Kremer, the real-life creation of androids and automatons may not exactly transgress the boundary between reality and fiction (as in a case of 'real' metalepsis), but it does operate a reversal of levels, whereby fiction can condition our daily practices and social norms.

While Part II moves from the individual effects to the larger-scale influences of fictional representations, Part III ('Changing Practices: Political Uses and Effects of Fiction') focuses more particularly on the instrumentalisation of fiction to construct public opinion, norms, and identities, whether in national or international contexts. Chapter 8, by Simone Müller, studies the case of the Japanese court in the fourteenth century: the court's rites and etiquette were codified in literary and semi-fictional form, creating an idealised regime that contributed to consolidating imperial power while allowing the emperor a degree of autonomy. Turning to nineteenth-century Europe, Charlotte Krauss studies the paradoxical role of theatre in the construction of national identities: on the one hand, playwrights develop an epic tendency in complex works that turn out to be unperformable; on the other, staged reinterpretations and reductions of these works allow a real social impact. Anne Isabelle François explores feminist engagements with works of fiction, showing in particular how the dystopian world of Margaret Atwood's *The Handmaid's Tale* (and its television adaptation) has inspired new modes of positive action. For Anne Besson, fantasy fictions such as *Game of Thrones* or the *Harry Potter* series are especially well-suited to forms of ethical and political appropriation, often engaging utopian thought precisely through the power of their dystopian imaginaries. In Chapter 12, Annick Louis shows how hybrid docufictional forms both draw on and challenge multiple kinds of discourse in the Latin American context, extending narrative possibilities to stage an unpredictable form of intervention into reality, and often exposing the insufficiency of legislation or legal discourse. This question of legal discourse and its relationship to fiction is a point of connection with the next two contributions, which address the impact of fiction on law from two distinct perspectives. Considering the case of Orwell's *Nineteen Eighty-Four*, Henriette Korthals Altes argues that reference to fiction can directly shape case law by articulating cultural norms in the absence of legal precedents, even if the legal debate does not fully grasp the complexities of Orwell's novel. Studying the role of founding documents in moments of historical revolution or rupture, Otto Pfersmann argues that changes to legal systems depend on fictional elements, with immense consequences for the course of history.

The fourth and final part ('Changing Fictions: Metafictional Effects') considers how humour, metalepsis, *mise en abyme*, and other metafictional techniques reveal or question the effects of fiction — on readers and on the world. As we have noted, these effects can be portrayed as harmful or beneficial. Varied responses are found in the many works inspired by *Don Quixote*, as Yen-Mai Tran-Gervat shows in her reconsideration of the 'Quixotic principle' as a mode of humorous self-reference. Connected to reflexivity and empathy rather than satire and parody, humour allows us to acknowledge our own susceptibility to the pleasures of fiction. Masahiro Iwamatsu takes a comparative approach to metafictional genres that emerged in the late twentieth century, exploring the different forms of self-reflexivity that are proposed in Japan, Europe, and the United States. By bringing narrative enunciation to the forefront, these paradoxical metafictions reveal what the reader expects of fictional communication. Asking just how far such communication can go, Maxime Decout's contribution studies the darker fantasy of the book that either kills its reader, or casts him or her as a murderer; these extreme situations, represented by various means in a number of twentieth-century works, at once stage and call into question the power that fictions hold. Frank Wagner's chapter concludes the volume by studying the propensity of fiction to represent, through techniques of *mise en abyme*, its own possible virtues and dangers.

This final section brings us full circle back to the world of fiction, and to a central dilemma: what can fiction tell us about its own effects? Does it grant itself a purely imaginary power? Whether fictional works make a *pro domo* case, or on the contrary portray the negative effects of fiction, or even dramatise their own lack of real purchase on the world, they set out the terms and the stakes of the question. However, it is another matter to measure, empirically, the ways in which fiction shapes both our understanding of the world and our actions in the world. As well as showing how fiction itself reflects on this problem, the varied chapters in this volume offer detailed studies of a range of cases where fiction can be said to have shaped attitudes, provoked responses, or to have been mobilised for various ends. They also point to directions for further study — in areas ranging from cognitive science to reception studies — in order to fully assess individual and collective responses to fiction.

Fiction, of course, is part of the world. Our initial question does not contest the fact that, as Jean-Marie Schaeffer points out, 'fiction is also a reality' (Schaeffer 2010: 186).[7] Indeed, it is hard to imagine a world without fiction. However, the specificity — and indeed the power — of fiction lies in the difference that it introduces between regimes of representation, and in its capacity to transform, transpose, or even leave behind the world of facts — even if it is never entirely cut off from reference. In this sense the real power of fiction is inseparable, paradoxically, from the very gesture of playful distancing that limits its direct efficacy. It is the various modalities of this indirect impact, which operates through the modelling, configuration, and reconfiguration of our relationship to reality, that the following essays address.

## References

ALLEN, WOODY (dir.). 1985. *The Purple Rose of Cairo* (Orion Pictures)
AUSTEN, JANE. [1817] 2003. *Northanger Abbey*, ed. by Marilyn Butler (London: Penguin)
BALDICK, CHRIS (ed.). 2008. *The Oxford Dictionary of Literary Terms*, 3$^{rd}$ edn <https://www.oxfordreference.com/view/10.1093/oi/authority.20110803095521412> [accessed 14 June 2021]
BALDWIN, JAMES. 1955. 'Everybody's Protest Novel', in *Notes of a Native Son* (Boston: Beacon Press), pp. 13–23
BAUDRILLARD, JEAN. 1981. *Simulacres et simulations* (Paris: Galilée)
BRETON, ANDRÉ. (1926) 1992. *Légitime défense*, in *Œuvres complètes*, ed. by Marguerite Bonnet, II (Paris: Gallimard, Bibliothèque de la Pléiade), pp. 282–96
CAVELL, STANLEY. 1981. *Pursuits of Happiness: The Hollywood Comedy of Remarriage* (Cambridge, MA: Harvard University Press)

CHALVON-DEMERSAY, SABINE. 2015. 'La part vivante des héros de série', in *Faire des sciences sociales, critiquer*, ed. by Pascale Haag and Cyril Lemieux (Paris: Éditions de l'EHESS), pp. 32–57

CRU, JEAN NORTON. 1929. *Témoins: Essai d'analyse et critique des souvenirs de combattants édités en français de 1915 à 1928* (Paris: Les Étincelles)

CURRIE, GREGORY. 2020. *Imagining and Knowing: The Shape of Fiction* (Oxford: Oxford University Press)

DAWES, JAMES. 2015. 'Human Rights, Literature, and Empathy', in *The Routledge Companion to Literature and Human Rights*, ed. by Sophia A. McClennen and Alexandra Schultheis (Abingdon: Routledge, 2015), pp. 427–32

DENIS, DELPHINE and FRANÇOISE LAVOCAT. 2008. 'L'Astrée, livre des jeux', in *Lire L'Astrée*, ed. by Delphine Denis (Paris: Presses Universitaires de Paris Sorbonne), pp. 273–86

DODELL-FEDER, DAVID, and DIANA I. TAMIR. 2018. 'Fiction Reading Has a Small Positive Impact on Social Cognition: A Meta-Analysis', *Journal of Experimental Psychology: General*, 147 (11): 1713–27 < https://doi.org/10.1037/xge0000395>

EHRMAN, BART D. 2004. *Truth and Fiction in 'The Da Vinci Code': A Historian Reveals What We Really Know about Jesus, Mary Magdalene, and Constantine* (Oxford: Oxford University Press)

FERENCZI, ALEXIS. 2012. 'Ces meurtriers qui se sont inspirés du cinéma pour tuer avant la fusillade dans le Colorado', *Huffington Post*, 20 July <https://www.huffingtonpost.fr/2012/07/20/meurtriers-inspiration-cinema-culture-crime-denver-colorado_n_1688700.html>

FORTIN DE LA HOGUETTE, PIERRE. 1648. *Testament, ou conseils fideles d'un bon pere à ses enfans. Où sont contenus plusieurs raisonnemens chrestiens, moraux & politiques* (Paris: Vitré)

FLUDERNIK, MONIKA, and MARIE-LAURE RYAN. 2019. *Narrative Factuality: A Handbook* (Berlin: de Gruyter)

FÜLÖP, ERIKA (ed.). 2021. *Fictionality, Factuality, and Reflexivity Across Discourses and Media*, Narratologia (Berlin: de Gruyter)

GEFEN, ALEXANDRE. 2017. *Réparer le monde. La littérature française face au XXI$^e$ siècle* (Paris: José Corti)

GENETTE, GÉRARD. 2004. *Métalepse: De la figure à la fiction* (Paris: Seuil)

HOCHMAN, BARBARA. 2011. *Uncle Tom's Cabin and the Reading Revolution: Race, Literacy, Childhood, and Fiction, 1851–1911* (Amherst: University of Massachusetts Press).

JEANNERET, MICHEL. 2003. *Eros rebelle* (Paris: PUF)

KEATON, BUSTON (dir.). 1924. *Sherlock Jr.* (Metro-Goldwyn Pictures).

KIYOZUKA, KUNIHIKO. (2009) 2017. *Fikushon no Tetsugaku [The Philosophy of Fiction]* (Tokyo: Keiso Shobo)

LAMARQUE, PETER, and STEIN HAUGOM OLSEN. 1994. *Truth, Fiction, and Literature: A Philosophical Perspective* (Oxford: Oxford University Press)

LANDY, JOSHUA. 2012. *How to Do Things with Fictions* (New York: Oxford University Press)

LAUGIER, SANDRA. 2019. *Nos vies en séries: Philosophie et morale d'une culture populaire* (Paris: Climats)

LAVOCAT, FRANÇOISE. 2016. *Fait et fiction: Pour une frontière* (Paris: Seuil)

LECERCLE, FRANÇOIS. 2012. 'Décontextualisation et réversibilité: L'usage de l'anecdote chez les polémistes', in *Anecdotes dramatiques, de la Renaissance aux Lumières*, ed. by François Lecercle, Sophie Marchand, and Zoé Schweitzer (Paris: Presses de l'Université de Paris-Sorbonne), pp. 109–24

LEROY, MICHEL. 1992. 'Les formes littéraires du mythe', in *Le Mythe jésuite* (Paris: PUF), pp. 259–28

MAR, RAYMOND A., KEITH OATLEY, and JORDAN B. PETERSON. 2009. 'Exploring the Link between Reading Fiction and Empathy: Ruling out Individual Differences and Examining Outcomes', *Communications*, 34 (4): 407–28 <https://doi.org/10.1515/COMM.2009.025>

MARCHAND, SOPHIE, FRANÇOIS LECERCLE and ZOÉ SCHWEITZER (eds.). 2012. *Anecdotes dramatiques, de la Renaissance aux Lumières* (Paris: Presses Universitaires de la Sorbonne)

MARIKAR, SHEILA, and KEVIN DOLAK. 2012. '9 Films and Shows that Inspired Real Crimes', *ABC News*, 23 July <https://abcnews.go.com/Entertainment/films-shows-inspired-real-crimes/story?id=16836535> [accessed 30 June 2022]

MURASAKI SHIKIBU. 2001. *The Tale of Genji*, trans. by Royall Tyler (London: Penguin Books)

'A New Objection.' 1852. *Ohio State Journal*, 28 December, online at Ohio History Collection <https://www.ohiomemory.org/digital/collection/p16007coll22/id/5976> [accessed 30 June 2022]

NUSSBAUM, MARTHA C. 1990. *Love's Knowledge: Essays on Philosophy and Literature* (Oxford and New York: Oxford University Press)

——. 1995. *Poetic Justice: The Literary Imagination and Public Life* (Boston: Beacon Press)

——. 2010. *Not for Profit: Why Democracy Needs the Humanities*. The Public Square Book Series (Princeton, NJ: Princeton University Press)

OURA, YASUSUKE (ed.). 2010. *Fiction de l'Occident, fiction de l'Orient: Actes du colloque international* (Kyoto: Institute for Research in Humanities, Kyoto University)

PENGE, LUCA. 2020. 'L'idea pastorale: Analogie, differenze e contatti fra l'Accademia dell'Arcadia e l'Ordine dei Fiori di Norimberga', in *Atti e Memorie dell'Arcadia*, 9: 221–50

PERNOT, DENIS. 2018. *Henri Barbusse: Les discours du 'Feu'* (Dijon: Presses Universitaires de Dijon)

PRESCOTT, ANNA T., JAMES D. SARGENT, and JAY G. HULL. 2018. 'Violent Video Games and Aggression Metaanalysis', *Proceedings of the National Academy of Sciences*, 115 (40): 9882–88 <doi: 10.1073/pnas.1611617114>

REYNOLDS, DAVID S. 2011. *Mightier than the Sword: Uncle Tom's Cabin and the Battle for America* (New York: W. W. Norton & Company)

RYAN, MARIE-LAURE. 1991. *Possible Worlds, Artificial Intelligence, and Narrative Theory* (Bloomington: Indiana University Press)

SAPIRO, GISÈLE. 2013. 'Droits et devoirs de la fiction littéraire en régime démocratique: Du réalisme à l'autofiction', *Revue critique de fixxion française contemporaine*, 6: 97–110

SARTRE, JEAN-PAUL. 1988. *What Is Literature? and Other Essays*, trans. by Steven Ungar (Cambridge, MA: Harvard University Press)

SCHAEFFER, JEAN-MARIE. 2010. *Why Fiction?*, trans. by Dorrit Cohn (Lincoln: University of Nebraska Press)

SEARLE, JOHN R. 1975. 'The Logical Status of Fictional Discourse', *New Literary History*, 6 (2): 319–32 <https://doi.org/10.2307/468422>

SIEBERS, TOBIN. 1993. 'The Werther Effect: The Esthetics of Suicide', *Mosaic: An Interdisciplinary Critical Journal*, 26 (1): 15–34 <https://www.jstor.org/stable/24780514>

STEWART, JACQUELINE. 2020. 'Why We Can't Turn Away from *Gone with the Wind*', University of Chicago Division of the Humanities, 13 June <https://humanities.uchicago.edu/articles/2020/06/why-we-cant-turn-away-gone-wind> [accessed 30 June 2022]

YANES, NICHOLAS A., and DERRAIS CARTER. 2014. *The Iconic Obama, 2007–2009: Essays on Media Representations of the Candidate and New President* (Jefferson, NC: McFarland)

ZUNSHINE, LISA. 2006. *Why We Read Fiction: Theory of Mind and the Novel* (Columbus: Ohio State University Press)

## Notes to the Introduction

1. '"Please do not read our young lady naughty tales like that," he said. "Not that a heroine secretly in love is likely to catch her interest, but she must not come to take it for granted that things like that really happen"' (Murasaki Shikibu 2001: 462).
2. On this form of metalepsis, which puts into play the relationship between the 'real' diegetic universe of the screening room and a metadiegetic filmic universe, see Genette (2004: 64).
3. 'Although our productions have afforded more extensive and unaffected pleasure than those of any other literary corporation in the world, no species of composition has been so much decried. From pride, ignorance, or fashion, our foes are almost as many as our readers. [...] "I am no novel-reader — I seldom look into novels — Do not imagine that I often read novels — It is really very well for a novel." Such is the common cant. "And what are you reading, Miss — ?" "Oh! It is only a novel!" replies the young lady, while she lays down her book with affected indifference, or momentary shame. "It is only Cecilia, or Camilla, or Belinda"; or, in short, only some work in which the greatest powers of the mind are displayed, in which the most thorough knowledge of human nature, the happiest delineation of its varieties, the liveliest effusions of wit and humour, are conveyed to the world in the best-chosen language' (Austen [1818] 2003: 36–37)
4. This is said to have been the effect provoked by the ghost of Hamlet's father at the beginning of Shakespeare's play (see Marchand, Lecercle and Schweitzer 2012).
5. For instance, a columnist for the Ohio State Journal responded to a reader who objected to a favourable review: 'It does not necessarily follow that we are in favor of running [slaves] off from their masters, to the very doubtful benefits of freedom in Canada, because we think 'Uncle Tom's Cabin' a readable book' ('A New Objection', 1852: 2).
6. The former, in his book on witness accounts of the Great War, accuses Barbusse of fictionalising and thus deforming the experience of soldiers (Cru 1929: 555–65); the latter sees in Barbusse's style a derivative naturalism that cannot compare to documentary film footage (Breton [1926] 1992: 286).
7. On this point see Frank Wagner's contribution to the present volume (Chapter 18).

PART I

# Changing Definitions: Fiction Across Time, Cultures, Languages, and Media

CHAPTER 1

# Poetic Forms of Narrative and Pragmatic Fiction: *Poiein* — *Plattein* — *Prattein*

*Claude Calame*

École des Hautes Études en Sciences Sociales (EHESS)

For a critic reading Yann Moix's *Orléans* (2019), the question inevitably arises: are we faced with 'fiction or reality', or more specifically, a 'nightmarish fiction or shock autobiography' (Vuillème 2019: 31)?[1] If we put aside the text's literary, 'poietic' qualities as an autobiographical narrative, and its use of the grammatical first person and past tenses which place us in the perspective of an adult looking back on his childhood, we find that Moix's novel is centred around a personal effort of recollection. It confronts us, in a narrative mode, with a certain brute reality: the moral and physical violence inflicted by parents who constantly torment their child, from the age of kindergarten through to senior year classes in mathematics. Their attitude of persistent denigration verges on sadism. Following a final ploy by his father to permanently remove him from a *hypokhâgne* class at a prestigious Paris *lycée* — the preparatory course leading to admission into the elite institutions of higher education — the author concludes: 'My last chance to be myself had just been crushed through the intervention of my father, who had not only destroyed my future, but had also left me in disgrace' (Moix 2019: 125). The text therefore presents us with a violent reality by means of a beautiful, self-reflexive writing style. Nonetheless, this fundamental reality seems to be largely contradicted by the testimony provided by the author's brother.[2]

Does this mean that the text, through its narrative and its literary use of language, stimulates the imagination to create a possible world with its own protagonists, values, and spatio-temporal framework, in a linguistic configuration lacking any relation to reality — that is, in other words, a fiction? But surely fiction, however 'poietic' it might be, must make some reference to lived reality if it is to at least capture the recipient's attention, let alone achieve the effect desired by the author and poet? This question must necessarily be framed in terms of fiction's own enunciative modes and their pragmatics, quite apart from the question of the capacity of language in general to refer to reality by means of its various discursive and enunciative forms.

From this point of view, it is essential for us to examine both the discursive productions of another culture and the reflections that these productions provoke within that culture. In this case, the confrontation with other narrative forms requires an anthropological approach. We need to apprehend the discursive manifestations that we could consider as fictions in terms of their own functioning and poetics, with an understanding of the pragmatics entailed by the historical and cultural context of their production, and taking into account the reflections that they provoke in terms of 'indigenous' categories. The productions and reflections in question will be those of ancient Greece, which are the most familiar to me, as I have devoted several works to Greek poetic manifestations that are situated between 'myth' and ritual performance. I propose, after this analysis, to return to cast a critical eye both on our own writings of fiction and on the definitions that we give to a concept that can only have an operative function.

These considerations led me to undertake the following study: we will start from two contemporary definitions of (narrative) fiction. We will then contrast them with the definition underlying Plato's reflections on the different forms of narrative and their moral, religious, and civic pragmatics, particularly in the *Republic*. Next, we shall consider Plato's criticism, particularly with regard to tragedy as a form of 'mimetic' narration. With this in mind, we shall test its application to one of Euripides's best-known tragedies, which will be examined in terms of its enunciative modes and its pragmatics with reference to its performance context. This journey through the tragic dramatisation of narrative that we commonly perceive as 'myth' will lead, finally, to some concluding critical remarks on the modern concept of fiction and its uses in the analysis of literary narration.

## 1. Two Comprehensive Definitions of Fiction

Let us address the question of definition in the terms set out by the title of this section of the present collection: 'Changing Definitions: Fiction across Time, Cultures, Languages, and Media'; in effect, we are concerned with the various signifiers and signifieds of fiction: fiction as an operative concept, as a tool for the analysis of narrative and literary creation, viewed, in this case, in terms of its pragmatic dimension. From this perspective, we shall refer briefly to two recent studies written in French, both of which encompass a vast corpus of principally literary works, and both of which lead to a broad definition of fiction.

First of all, Jean-Marie Schaeffer's study *Why Fiction?* argues that (narrative) fiction, whatever its form — literary, theatrical, or cinematographic — is attached to processes of pretending, and specifically a ludic feint, following the model of video games. In Schaeffer's view, fiction is implicitly grounded in action, and therefore in narrative, and can consequently be defined as a 'shared ludic feint' that is manifested in various different forms of immersion. He concludes that fiction does in fact maintain our relation to the world, and therefore to reality, to the factual, but it does so on the single condition that it provides pleasure, an 'aesthetic satisfaction': 'my hypothesis is that fiction has only a single immanent function and that this function is of an aesthetic order' (Schaeffer 2010: 301). This leads to the claim that 'a fiction is thus a game with representations or a ludic usage of representational activity' (Schaeffer 2010: 303). From a functional point of view, the aesthetic relation is therefore immanent to fiction, and as such it is the basis of fictional immersion.

Françoise Lavocat's essay *Fait et fiction: Pour une frontière*, similarly published in the 'Poétique' series of the Éditions du Seuil, returns to the underlying problem, which Schaeffer's remarkable essay had, in a sense, overlooked: 'fact or fiction?', or rather, as the title of Lavocat's work suggests, 'fact *and* fiction'. Lavocat argues that the relation between fact and fiction must be reframed in semantic terms of referentiality, or even in philosophical terms of ontology, and she approaches this question through the phenomenon of metalepsis. Metalepsis is understood here not as a variant of metonymy but rather as the staging of the narrator's or narratee's intervention in the narrative, or a slippage from the world that is narrated to the world in which the narrating takes place.[3] These two situations correspond respectively to the concepts of rhetorical metalepsis, functioning on the level of discourse and diegesis, and ontological metalepsis, functioning on the level of factuality. Some instances of metalepsis can, by transgressing the boundaries between reality and the constructed possible worlds of fiction, erase those very boundaries in the name of plurality. Other metalepses establish that 'in a fictional narrative, unlike in a factual narrative, the world that is narrated is ontologically dependent on the act of narration that produces it', as described by John Pier and Jean-Marie Schaeffer (2005: 14). Above all, these metalepses direct us towards the task of interpretation: 'we can say that fictions are possible worlds, but ones whose possibility (their accessibility) lies in wait, ready to be constructed by a reader, viewer, or internet user' (Lavocat 2016: 534). Fiction can be defined as a possible world, but it is a world whose possibility is in a sense a potentiality, and that therefore has to be interpreted.

If (narrative, 'literary') fiction requires interpretation, this is because it is constructed by means of language and discourse. The fictional narrative — just like the factual narrative — is a linguistic construction with its own narrative logic, with all the effects of meaning brought about by the polysemy of the words and statements that comprise it, with all the enunciative strategies that sustain it while instituting its own pragmatics, and with all the representations that it conveys and evokes in relation to the lived reality of its readers.

What, then, is (narrative) fiction? Does it have any distinctive features? In making one further attempt on the problem, I will adopt an anthropological and thus distanced perspective on another culture, in this case ancient Greek culture. I propose to shed an oblique, and therefore critical, light on some of our current problems around fiction by means of a comparative and differential approach. This approach can help us to self-reflexively reassess some of the concepts that we use to try to overcome the differences between our various definitions, in this case the concepts of (narrative) fiction as either a shared ludic feint, or fiction as the result of metalepses that create a possible world requiring interpretation.

## 2. Plato and the Crafting of Narrative

Before addressing a specific instance of fictional narrative, the scholar of ancient Greek poetics must necessarily begin their search, once again, with Plato's reflection in the *Republic* on those narratives that appear to be the very epitome of 'fictions'. These are the narratives that we, in our modern usage, classify under the anthropological concept of the 'myth', but as we shall see, the corresponding Greek term 'muthos' had a very different meaning in its various uses in its original contexts.

### 2.1. What to Narrate, and According to Which Criteria?

Let us recall the context of Plato's discussion of the role of narratives in the *Republic*. On the subject of the principle of justice that must apply in the ideal city, the question soon arises of the education of the future guardians of the city, elite citizen-soldiers. It will be based on the two pillars of traditional education, namely exercises in the gymnasium and the practice of the arts of the Muses (377a). With regard to the latter, the question of the stories told by the poets arises from the outset: what should be retained?

First of all, there are the stories ('muthoi', 377d) composed and told ('elegon') by Hesiod and Homer, as well as by other poets. These tales are as troublesome as they are 'deceitful' ('pseudeis'). It is necessary to avoid narrating ('mutologeteon', 378c) and depicting in painting both the battles of the giants and the many conflicts that pit deities against heroes and their relatives. This is followed by a series of proposals regarding the sort of narratives that would be capable of contributing to the good education of future guardians of the city — proposals that combine 'muthos' and 'logos' in a sense that we shall clarify below. At this point, the interlocutors in the dialogue, Socrates and the brothers Adeimantus and Glaucon, pick up the discussion of what one would be permitted to say and create ('legein kai poiein', 383a) on the subject of the gods in the new city. To begin with they discount, from among Homer's more praiseworthy narratives, the instance in which the epic poet presents Zeus instructing Agamemnon in a dream to take the city of Troy and bring misfortune to the Trojans (*Iliad* 2.1–34). Similarly they exclude the example in which Aeschylus, in an unknown tragedy (fr. 350 Radt), depicts Thetis condemning the god Apollo: the truthful oracle had sung the paean at her wedding celebrating long lives, but actually contributed to the death of her son Achilles. They take up the subject again, in relation to the topic of the existence of Hades and the horrifying way in which it is described, to determine how to supervise those who might attempt to relate ('legein', 386b) such narratives ('muthoi') as these. Through an implicit reference to the great poetic tradition of attributing praise and blame, Socrates's advice is to induce these storytellers not to draw a frightening portrait of things in Hades but rather to cast them in a positive light.[4] The criterion here is once again, in modern terms, one of a moral, even religious, nature.

Still on the subject of Hades, the interlocutors list a series of passages from the *Iliad* and the *Odyssey* that deserve to be censored, not for failing to be poetic and pleasurable for the listener, but rather because their poetic nature in itself makes it all the more important that they should not reach the ears of free men and their children. The same goes for Achilles, the son of a goddess, whom Homer represents (the verb used is 'poiein', 388a) in a state of languishing mourning. It is not seemly ('epitēdeion', 390c), either, to relate Hera consorting with Zeus, who is so overcome with desire that he forgets his own plans, nor to recount Aphrodite's affairs with Ares while she is married to Hephaestus. Similarly, episodes such as the slaughter of prisoners on Patrocles's funeral pyre or the abductions of women by Theseus (son of Poseidon) and Pirithous (son of Zeus) are declared to be 'not true' ('ouk alethē', 391b): they are deemed to be neither in conformity with human and divine law ('hosia', 391d), nor true ('alethē'). Again, the criteria for narrative truth are of a moral and religious nature.

As such, can we say that these are fictions? The fear of the protagonists of the *Republic* is actually that these narratives about gods, heroes, and those mortals who are now in Hades will make young people inclined to be wicked. This is therefore a question of the pragmatics of those narratives that appear to us to be fictions, and we shall soon return to this point.

From a terminological point of view, it should be noted that the narratives that provoke suspicion are variously termed 'muthoi' (391e), then 'logoi' (392a). We also find that the compound verb 'muthologeuein', constructed from the two terms mentioned above, is used twice in a single passage of the *Odyssey* (12.447–54) by Odysseus himself. Having reached the end of the long first-person narrative of his adventurous return journey, before finally being received at the court of Alcinous in Phaeacia, the hero uses this term to refer to the account that he gave on the previous day. This account related his stay with the nymph Calypso; as he had begun his narrative with this episode, he does not wish to repeat what he has already said ('eirēmena') clearly. The term 'muthologeuein' therefore refers to the narration of a narrative that is presented by its narrator as corresponding to a lived reality. In this passage from the *Odyssey* this compound verb is used in parallel with the verb 'mutheisthai', referring to a 'muthos' which, up until the classical period, denotes any type of developed and argued discourse, made to convince, notably by means of a narrative.[5] The use of these terms does not pertain to fiction, but rather to the effect on the addressee.

## 2.2. How to Narrate, and in Which Forms?

After considering what to narrate, we are next faced with the question of how those things should be told ('ha te lekteon kai hōs lekteon', 392c). We will therefore turn to poets and those 'creators of narratives' who illustrate different conceptions of justice: 'poiētai' and 'logopoioi' (392b) are all creators, artisans of 'poiein'. Between poetry and prose, singing ('aidein') and the telling of narratives ('muthologein'), how do poets and storytellers — so-called 'mythologues' ('muthologoi', 392d) — relate actions from the past, present, and future? This formulation brings to mind the talents of the nine Hesiodic Muses, as they are presented in the long proem to the *Theogony*:

> Come then, let us begin with the Muses who, through their songs,
> Gladden in his great understanding their father Zeus,
> Telling things that are, things that shall be, and things that were,
> With their voices in unison.[6]

The question is now no longer that of the actions that are related, but of the narration itself: 'hē diēgēsis' (392d), with its three modes — simple diegesis, diegesis 'dia mimēseōs', and the mixed mode. In diegesis 'dia mimēseōs' (through 'mimesis', representation), the poet delegates responsibility for what is said to the protagonists of the narrated action. Whereas Homeric poetry, through the introduction of dialogues into the narrative, mixes the two modes of narration, tragedy is entirely 'mimetic' (394b). This is why tragedy, an entirely mimetic form, along with the equally mimetic form of comedy, must be excluded from the ideal city, from the point of view of both creation ('poiēsis', 394c) and storytelling ('muthologia'). The objection here effectively relates to the reality effect produced by diegesis through representation, that is, through the dramatisation of the action that is being related.

We are therefore faced once again with the pragmatics of 'mythology'. The guardians of the city must do ('prattein', 395c) and represent ('mimeisthai') only that which contributes to the freedom of the city: they are the artisans of freedom. Owing to the exclusion of mimetic narrative modes, we are led to reject the narration and representation of past actions in favour of present, real action, but still viewed through a metaphor of artisanal creation. For this reason, the only poets or mythologues to be allowed in the city are those who draw their inspiration from models prescribed in law, with a concern only for social utility ('ōphelia', 398ab). This criterion of narrative choice had already been expressed by Xenophanes in certain elegiac verses, which we shall soon cite and comment upon briefly. The matter is taken up again at the conclusion of the *Republic*, where it is acknowledged that the poetic qualities of Homer, the educator of Greece, could lead us to allow poetry back into the city after all, particularly in the form of 'melos' (understood as a song performed with dancing and musical accompaniment; 607d): one could be seduced by the sweetness of poetry as long as it is useful ('ōphelimē') to political systems and simply to human life.[7] But with regard to the truth of this poetry, conceived not in terms of its factuality but rather in terms of its political and moral utility, Plato asserts that continued vigilance is necessary.

For poets, there remains the musical problem of the modes to be used for narrative poems in the form of songs. This is not only a matter of vocal expression, but also of (musical) harmony and (choreographic) rhythm. Beautiful rhythm and harmony will be determined by the word ('logos', 'eulogia'), since 'the beauty of the language, harmony, gesture, and rhythm are consequent upon one's character' (400d–400e). There is therefore a correspondence between the harmony that exists between the different elements of the song, considered as a musical performance combining both singing and dancing, and the harmony that exists between body and soul. This is another aspect of the poem's truth.

## 2.3. How to Craft the Narrative, and What are the Intended Effects?

We now have two verbs connected to the role of the poet: 'poiein', as the creation of a narrative in which the narrated action can be represented and dramatised in a 'mimetic' way, and can constitute a wicked act from the perspective of the wellbeing of the citizens; and 'prattein', which relates to the possible action that might be provoked by the narrated action in its poetic form, in a system of 'pragmatics' that must answer to the criterion of (social) utility. And what about fiction in all this? At this point we should return to the long development in the *Republic* with which we started. This discussion brings Book II of the *Republic* to a close while introducing the question that is addressed at the beginning of Book III as to which narratives ('muthoi', 386b) are capable of sustaining courage, with a concern for truth and utility ('alēthē', 'ōphelima').

The initial question is therefore that of the training to be given to the future guardians of the ideal city, which will be based on the two pillars of traditional education: gymnastics for the body and music for the soul. This starts with the arts of the Muses. Their educational power is centred around speeches ('logoi', 376e), and in the case of children, on narratives ('muthoi', 377a), including both true and untrue narratives. Insofar as it is a question of contributing to the 'crafting' ('plattetai', 377b) of young people by marking them with an imprint, it is necessary to regulate these crafted narratives ('plasthenthas') and those who make them ('hoi muthopoioi'!). To begin with, nursemaids and mothers will have to be convinced to tell only stories that have been chosen to craft ('plattein', 377c) the children's souls rather than to craft their bodies with their hands. Next, regulation will be applied to Homer, Hesiod, and other poets who compose false stories ('muthoi', 377d).[8] We therefore move from po(i)etic making and crafting to the further crafting that takes place as a consequence of these narratives.

This brings us to the need to establish 'models' ('tupoi', 379a) for speaking about the gods ('theologia'), whether these narratives are in the form of epic poetry, tragedy, or comedy. These models, determining what can be said and 'made' ('poiein', 383a) with regard to the gods, must be respected just as one must respect laws ('nomoi', 386c).

Poetic making, together with its practical effects, is therefore conceived as a crafting, as a fiction, in the primary and etymological sense of the Latin verb 'fingere'. This reflection on the virtues of 'crafting' also continues in other dialogues. In the *Laws* (671bc), the work of the blacksmith, conceived as 'plattein', illustrates the way in which a good legislator imparts education on young people. And in the *Phaedrus* (246c), speaking about the concept of the immortal in general, Socrates states that no reasoned discourse ('logos lelogismenos') can grasp it, but that without seeing it or conceiving of it, we 'craft' it ('plattomen') in the form of a god, an immortal being with a body and a soul.[9] Consequently, contrary to what we might have concluded on the basis of assertions from representatives of the First and Second Sophistics,[10] poetic 'plattein' does not necessarily refer to a deceptive discourse.

Admittedly, in his eulogy and defence of the beautiful and famous Helen, the rhetorician and sophist Gorgias asserts that many people try to convince, and indeed succeed in convincing, on countless subjects by crafting ('plasantes') a false discourse (*Encomium of Helen*, 11). This is really an effect of discourse ('logos') itself: even if everyone had the same memory of the past, the same perception of the present, and the same expectation for the future, their discourse would still differ according to varying opinion ('doxa'). It is worth recalling the memorable verses that Hesiod, in the *Theogony* (27–28), puts into the mouths of the Muses of Helicon, who have just initiated the poet: 'We know how to speak ['legein'] many lies that resemble reality; but we also know, if we so wish, how to utter ['gerusasthai'] truths.'[11] These verses have been commented upon at length,[12] but we shall highlight here only the insistence of the poet, inspired by the Muses, on relating a truth — a truth of a poetic nature, as we find in the *Theogony*, but also a truth of a practical nature, through the creation of the poem of the *Works and Days*, also in epic diction.

## 3. A Greek Example: Euripides's *Hippolytus*

By way of a transition towards examining a concrete example of classical Greek narrative, let us return to the concluding verses of Xenophanes's elegiac song, whose performance serves to inaugurate the ritual symposium (fr. 1, 19–22 Gentili-Prato):

> We must praise and hymn that man who, after drinking, reveals noble thoughts,
> So that the memory and spirit of virtue remain.
> We should not tell of the conflicts of the Titans, nor Giants, nor Centaurs,
> Fictions ['plasmata'] from our ancestors, nor of the strife of their battles:
> There is no use in these.

Two things are at stake: first, it is not the historicity of the actions recounted, but rather (and just as we see later in Plato) their civic and moral value that is the criterion of whether a narrative is true or untrue; the second important point is the form of the choral songs (referred to by the term 'molpē', v. 12) that are ritually offered up in the symposium at the peak of the festivities to celebrate the divinity (either Apollo or Dionysus) through 'respectful speech' ('euphēmois muthois', v. 14) and 'pure words' ('katharoisi logois').[13] Here we find Greek poetic narration understood as fiction, but now in the strict sense of the term; and this artisanal creation can only be conceived in the form of a musical performance that stages 'true' actions, that is to say, actions that are useful to the city.

Let us illustrate the point with a Greek tragedy. This is unquestionably a fiction from a modern perspective, both with regard to the action represented and the mode of representation, that is the creation by a poet of a narrated action in an entirely 'mimetic' mode, according to Plato's definition.

The plot of Euripides's *Hippolytus* is well known. In his exclusive and ultimately impious devotion to Artemis alone, the young Hippolytus provokes the wrath of Aphrodite. To take her revenge, Aphrodite makes use of Phaedra, wife of Theseus, the king of Athens, and kindles within her a violent passion for Hippolytus, her own stepson. Phaedra's nurse reveals to Hippolytus the incestuous love that Phaedra feels for him, and stung by Hippolytus's words, Phaedra, daughter of Pasiphaë, who was herself the mother of the Minotaur, commits suicide. When Theseus arrives in Troezen he finds his wife hanged and bearing on her wrist a written tablet accusing Hippolytus of having raped her. Theseus curses his son, who leaves in exile. Theseus's curse brings down on his son the vengeance of the god Poseidon, and the fleeing Hippolytus is attacked by a monstrous bull emerging from the sea. At this point the goddess Artemis herself appears and explains to a desolate Theseus the truth regarding his wife's written accusation. It only remains for the king of Athens to forgive and be reconciled with his son, in Hippolytus's dying moments. Up to this point — and especially with regard to the reference to a monster from the sea — we are in the midst of a full-blown fiction in the indigenous Greek sense of the term: 'plasmata tōn proterōn' ('fictions of old'), to use Xenophanes's expression for narratives depicting monstrous and violent beings such as centaurs.

But Artemis does not limit herself to revealing the truth by denouncing the divine will of Aphrodite and promising that she will take revenge on the goddess, nor is she satisfied with contributing to the reconciliation between the father and his dying son. Through a speech act executed in a form of performative future tense, she institutes a hero cult to honour Hippolytus:

> For you, oh unfortunate one, for the evils that you have endured,
> I shall establish ['dōsō'] the highest honours in the city of Troezen. (vv. 1423–24)

From now on, girls on the threshold of marriage will offer their hair to the young hero, accompanying their offering with tearful lamentations. Furthermore, Hippolytus, because of the love that Phaedra bore for him, will be celebrated so that the 'memory created by the Muses' ('mousopoios merimna', vv. 1428–29) will continue forever, maintained by the choral songs of the girls.

Therefore, the goddess Artemis is not only present, through the effect of dramatic mimesis as described by Plato, before the eyes of the spectators assembled in the theatre within the sanctuary of Dionysus Eleuthereus to celebrate the god in the musical contests, and especially the competition of the tragedies. But she also refers to the present ritual: in effect, the creation of the hero cult executed by the goddess within the theatrical fiction corresponds to the hero cult of Hippolytus that is actually being practised. As Pausanias tells us, in Troezen there was a 'mnēma', a tomb devoted to the hero, where girls did in fact used to dedicate their hair in the pre-marriage rite that, according to the tragic fiction, had been instituted by Artemis. This funerary monument was next to the tomb of Phaedra and the temple of Aphrodite Kataskopia, in the sanctuary from which the love-struck heroine used to watch the young man practising naked in his physical exercises. As for Athens, Pausanias states that on the route leading up to the Acropolis there is a funerary monument to Hippolytus, not far from the sanctuary of Themis. While recalling once again the existence of the tomb of Hippolytus in the city Troezen, the traveller Pausanias takes this opportunity to provide, in a mythographic form, the narrative belonging to the Troezenian tradition (which he refers to as a 'logos'). This 'myth' relates that Theseus, just before marrying Phaedra, had sent his son Hippolytus away, entrusting his care to Pittheus, king of Troezen; on a later occasion, when the king of Athens visited Troezen, Phaedra cast eyes on Hippolytus, who had by then become an adolescent, and fell in love with the young man, before bringing about his death. The existence of the monument devoted to Hippolytus in Athens is confirmed by a dedicatory inscription.[14]

This type of etiological conclusion, common in Athenian tragedies and especially those of Euripides, brings the dramatisation of the act of narrating, taking place in the time of heroes, back to the present time of the poet and of the play's spectators, that means to the present reality of their practice of religion and cults — in this case the Athens of Pericles at the time of the beginning of the Peloponnesian War. This is the same Athens whose tutelary gods were Pallas Athena and Poseidon Erechtheus, who reigned and were honoured on the Acropolis, at the foot of which stood the sanctuary-theatre dedicated to Dionysus the Liberator for the celebration of the festival of the Dionysia.[15] Furthermore, the final words of the *Hippolytus*, created by the poet Euripides and uttered by Theseus at the very moment of his son's death to recall the evils brought about by Cypris, are addressed to the territory of Athens and to Pallas Athena in a memorial speech act ('memnēsomai', v. 1461); the performative utterance 'I shall recall' brings to mind the monumental and narrative memorial role fulfilled by the hero's tomb ('mnēma') devoted to Hippolytus. Finally, the brief, concluding exodos sung by the chorus of Phaedra's followers, in the form of a threne (song of mourning), declares that a shared period of mourning is beginning for all the citizens ('politais', v. 1462):

> This grief is shared by all the citizens;
> It struck them without warning.
> Great will be the flow of tears.
> For the reputation of the mourning of great men
> Persists longer. (1462–66)

In this way, the heroic action represented in a mimetic and po(i)etic manner in another time and another place is connected, through a narrative memorial and ritual practice, to the present time and space of the city. The present civic time and space evoked here correspond specifically to the lived spatio-temporal references of the citizens participating in the representation as spectators, in the *hic et nunc* of the musical celebrations devoted to Dionysus Eleuthereus in his sanctuary-theatre. The pragmatics of the tragic representation on stage of the heroic and thus fictional action is also realised by means of the emotion felt by those witnessing it. Over the course of the successive 're-performances' of the tragedies of Euripides in particular,[16] these interpretative conditions of reception manifestly evolved in line with the development of the political, social, and religious context for each respective ritualised performance.

## 4. A Critical Review of Modern Definitions

Where do we stand, then, with regard to the conception of fiction as a shared ludic feint, grounded in the aesthetic satisfaction produced by the imagination, understood here as a faculty of mental modelling, as 'poietic imagination' (Jean-Marie Schaeffer borrows the term 'dichtende Einbildungskraft' from Kant (2010: 303–05))? Or again, with regard to fiction as a possible world of potentiality, constituted by the combination of 'rhetorical' metalepses of an enunciative nature and metalepses of an ontological nature, a world whose possibility is ultimately constructed by the receiver, through effects of 'hybridization with the factual' (Lavocat 2016: 522 and 532–34)? Should we opt for the cognitivist conception or a broadly hermeneutic one? Or should we consider all fiction that is based on a plot to be a narrative and poetic crafting in the sense of Plato's conception of diegesis and 'plattein'?

Certainly, Yann Moix is not Euripides and the autobiographical novel is not a Greek tragedy. And admittedly, the modern novel does not draw a strong connection, as some Greek tragedies do, between the act of narrating, delegated by the poet to their protagonists acting in a specific space and temporality, and the ritual practices in which the target audience is engaged in their own spatio-temporal framework. Furthermore, we must take into account the distinctions between enunciative modes, including the first-person narrative of the autobiographical novel and the third-person narrative of classical novels; the 'he' and 'she' of these novels are transformed into 'I' and 'you' when the narrative action is dramatised, either through the introduction of dialogues or through a theatrical performance, as Plato had already demonstrated in the passage of the *Republic* (394bc) where the diegetic modes of Homeric poetry are discussed alongside those of tragedy and comedy.

Nevertheless, following our critical consideration of Plato's *Republic* and a tragedy written and presumably directed by Euripides, we shall briefly make a case for a semio-narrative and pragmatic conception of fiction (in this case, only narrative fiction).

First of all, we would insist, like Plato, on the central role of diegesis, whether its enunciation is positively assumed by its author (as in Hesiod's *Theogony*) or whether, as in theatrical productions and particularly in Euripides's *Hippolytus*, the act of narrating is assumed by the protagonists of the action represented in a mimetic mode ('dia mimēseōs'), as described in the *Republic*. The important point to note is that this act of narrating has been the object of a process of emplotment and of discursive crafting. In this respect, it is essential to refer to Aristotle's reflections — which we have deliberately avoided citing until now — on epic poems and tragedies, in an essay on poetics in which he focuses on their narrative dimension. In Aristotle's *Poetics*, it is significant that 'muthos' is reduced to the technical sense of plot, but also that 'mimēsis' becomes the representation of action, whatever the narrative mode might be. We shall return to this point in a further stage of our research, which will be devoted to the concepts of prefiguration, configuration, refiguration, and narrative identity developed by Paul Ricœur with specific reference to the *Poetics*.[17]

What we shall therefore ultimately propose, in very general terms, is a semio-narrative anthropology of (narrative) fiction, a conception of fiction as the fictional rather than the fictitious. In an operative sense, the 'fictional' refers to the crafting — in this case linguistic craft — of a possible narrative world based on the reality of the poet (as 'poiētēs') and their audience, whereas the 'fictitious' relates to creations of the imagination.

Our starting point is therefore a semio-narrative approach that is sensitive to those very values that are invested by the poetic 'plattein' in the act of narrating, in its actors, and in the spatio-temporal framework in which that act and those actors develop. These values evolve according to semantic schemes or registers that are often intertwined with the effects of elaborate metaphors; these semantic values are often made manifest thanks to processes of 'enargeia', or revelation by means of images placed 'before the eyes' that stimulate the imagination (in the strict sense of the term).[18]

We then have recourse to a discursive approach, focused on the enunciative strategies of the 'poiein' that brings the fictional narrative to its public, notably through instances of metalepsis and often in a polyphonic mode, starting from the focal point of the instance of enunciation. This instance ultimately leads us back to the author who exists as a psycho-social individual acting in a particular historical and social context, and addressing a public who, at least initially, share that context.

Finally, we make use of an approach inspired by cultural and social anthropology in order to elucidate the social, political, institutional, and religious context in which the act of fictional narrating creates meaning, through forms of discourse that, as cultural practices ('prattein'), contribute to shaping and consequently making meaningful, in a shared semiotic system, a world of shared representations.

Leaving aside the cognitivist conception of fiction as playful pretending and immersion, and that of fiction as the consequence of metalepses, whether these are based on the convocation and real presence of the narrator or are alternatively instances of 'intrafictional' metalepsis (Lavocat 2016, 497–503), we are therefore faced with the question of reference, and consequently we are faced with the paradoxical concept of referential fiction, reference of a fictional nature.[19] Fiction, then, undoubtedly appears as the semantic 'configuration' of a world, but a configuration carried out using the polysemous resources offered by language;[20] and above all, through a plausibility achieved by linguistic effects, fiction seems to involve a reference not only to a perceived reality, but also to a world of shared representations. The reference is therefore twofold. On the one hand, it marks the act of poetic creation through the cultural competence of an author situated in the space and time of a particular social and cultural paradigm. On the other hand, it also necessarily relates to the work's reception and refiguration, which now principally takes place through the interpretative reading of the work of fiction, thereby involving the whole social and cultural encyclopaedia of the public in question.

In short, the approach to fiction that we propose, grounded in an analytic study, starts by identifying the markers of enunciation relating to the instance of discourse and to the author–creator (an exploration of the 'poiein'), then progresses to a survey of semio-narrative semantics (investigation of the 'plattein') based on indigenous representations and conceptual frameworks, and finally, by means of pragmatics (taking into account the 'prattein'), a study of fictional practices from the perspective of cultural and social anthropology.

*Translated from the French by Sam Ferguson*

## References

BORUTTI, SILVANA. 2003. 'Fiction et construction de l'objet en anthropologie', in *Figures de l'humain: Les représentations de l'anthropologie*, ed. by Francis Affergan, Silvana Borutti, Claude Calame, Ugo Fabietti, Mondher Kilani, and Francesco Remotti (Paris: Éditions de l'EHESS), pp. 75–99

BRISSON, LUC. 1994. *Platon, les mots et les mythes: Comment et pourquoi Platon nomma le mythe* (Paris: La Découverte)

CALAME, CLAUDE. 2006. *Pratiques poétiques de la mémoire: Représentations de l'espace-temps en Grèce ancienne* (Paris: La Découverte)

——. 2010. 'La pragmatique poétique des mythes grecs: Fiction référentielle et performance rituelle', in *Fiction et cultures*, ed. by Françoise Lavocat and Anne Duprat (Paris: Lucie éditions/SFLGC), pp. 33–56

——. 2011. *Mythe et histoire dans l'Antiquité grecque: La création symbolique d'une colonie* (Paris: Les Belles Lettres)

——. 2012. 'Vraisemblance référentielle, nécessité narrative, poétique de la vue: L'historiographie grecque classique entre factuel et fictif', *Annales: Histoire, Sciences sociales*, 67: 81–101

——. 2015. *Qu'est-ce que la mythologie grecque?* (Paris: Gallimard)

——. 2017. *La Tragédie chorale, Poésie grecque et rituel musical* (Paris: Les Belles Lettres)

CASSIN, BARBARA. 1995. *L'Effet sophistique* (Paris: Gallimard)

CERRI, GIOVANNI. 2015. *La Poétique de Platon*, trans. by Myrto Gondicas (Paris: Les Belles Lettres), first published as *La poetica di Platone* (Lecce: Argo, 2007)

DETIENNE, MARCEL. 1994. *Les Maîtres de vérité dans la Grèce archaïque* (Paris: Presses Pocket)

EKROTH, GUNNEL. 2002. *The Sacrificial Rituals of Greek Hero-Cults in the Archaic to the Early Hellenistic Periods* (Liège: CIERGA)

EVELYN-WHITE, HUGH G. TRANS. 1982. *Hesiod: The Homeric Hymns and Homerica* (Cambridge, MA: Harvard University Press)

GENETTE, GÉRARD. 1980. *Narrative Discourse: An Essay in Method*, trans. by Jane Lewin (Ithaca, NY: Cornell University Press)

——. 2004. *Métalepse: De la figure à la fiction* (Paris: Seuil)

LAMARI, ANNA A. 2017. *Reperforming Greek Tragedy: Theater, Politics, and Cultural Mobility in the Fifth and Fourth Centuries BC* (Berlin: De Gruyter)

LAVOCAT, FRANÇOISE. 2016. *Fait et fiction: Pour une frontière* (Paris: Seuil)

——, (ed.). 2010. *La Théorie littéraire des mondes possibles.* (Paris: CNRS Éditions)

——, and ANNE DUPRAT (eds.). 2010. *Fiction et cultures* (Paris: Lucie éditions/SFLGC)

MOIX, YANN. 2019. *Orléans* (Paris: Grasset)

MURRAY, PENELOPE. 1996. *Plato on Poetry* (Cambridge: Cambridge University Press)

NAGY, GREGORY. 1990. *Pindar's Homer. The Lyric Possession of an Epic Past* (Baltimore: Johns Hopkins University Press)

PIER, JOHN, and JEAN-MARIE SCHAEFFER. 2005. 'Introduction: La métalepse, aujourd'hui', in *Métalepses: Entorses au pacte de la représentation*, ed. by John Pier and Jean-Marie Schaeffer (Paris: Éditions de l'EHESS), pp. 7–17

PUCCI, PIETRO. 2007. *Inno alle Muse (Esiodo, Teogonia, 1–115)* (Pisa: Fabrizio Serra)

SCHAEFFER, JEAN-MARIE. 2010 [2005]. *Why Fiction?*, trans. by Dorrit Cohn (Lincoln: University of Nebraska Press), first published as *Pourquoi la fiction?* (Paris: Seuil)

——. 2005. 'Quelles vérités pour quelles fictions?', *L'Homme*, 175–76: 19–36

VUILLÈME, JEAN-BERNARD. 2019. 'Yann Moix revisite son enfance', in *Le Temps Week-end*, 28 August, p. 31

## Notes to Chapter 1

1. Translator's note: all translations from texts written in French are my own, except when stated otherwise.
2. In a letter published in *Le Parisien* (24 August 2019), Alexandre Moix claimed that Yann, not their parents, was the abusive one in the family. <https://www.leparisien.fr/culture-loisirs/mon-frere-ce-bourreau-la-lettre-d-alexandre-a-son-frere-yann-moix-24-08-2019-8138721.php>.
3. According to Gérard Genette's definition, metalepsis is 'any intrusion by the extradiegetic narrator or narratee into the diegetic universe (or by diegetic characters into a metadiegetic universe, etc.), or the inverse' (1980: 234–35).
4. On the subject of the dialectic of praise and blame as one of the foundations of Greek poetry, see especially Nagy (1990, 146–52 and 392–96).
5. For a survey of this 'indigenous' meaning of the term 'muthos' in its different uses almost up to the time of Plato, see Calame 2011, 42–49, and 2015, 23–30 (which also considers the term 'logos'); for the uses of the term and its compound forms in Plato, see Brisson (1994).
6. Hesiod, *Theogony* 36–39. These verses have been commented on extensively, but for the key points see Pucci (2007: 76–78).
7. On this long passage, see the commentary provided by Murray (2010: 230–34).
8. See the extensive commentary on this important passage by Cerri (2015: 37–55).
9. For other uses of the verb 'plattein' and the Greek idea of fiction as 'crafting', see Calame (2015: 78–86); on the notion of fabrication in Plato, see also Brisson (1994: 77-93).
10. See Cassin 1995: 470–80.
11. Translation from Evelyn-White 1982: 81.
12. See, in particular, the pages devoted to these verses by Pucci (2007: 54–69), alongside the critical remarks of Marcel Detienne (1994: 13–22).
13. On this subject, see Calame (2011: 47–49), as well as Cerri (2015: 57–68).
14. On Troezen, see Pausanias 2.32.3–4; on Athens, see Pausanias 1.22.1, as well as *IG* I² 324, 69 ff.; for the hero cult of Hippolytus in Troezen, see Calame (2015: 458–65); for Athens, see Ekroth (2002: 138–39).
15. For the historical and religious context of ritual representations in Attic tragedy, see Calame (2017: 65–88), which also provides extensive bibliographical references.
16. On this subject, see for example the recent study by Lamari (2017: 59–81).
17. In the meantime, with regard to the modes of representation, and especially the central concepts of the plausible, the possible, and the necessary, see Calame (2012). As for the use of the concept of configuration in this context, through the intermediary of narrative emplotment, see Calame (2006: 20–32).
18. This is the subject of Calame (2012).
19. As Lavocat observes, the question of reference is 'unavoidable' (2016: 525–25). On the concept of referential fiction, see, among others, my chapter 'La pragmatique poétique des mythes grecs' (Calame 2010).
20. This expression is derived from Silvana Borutti (2003: 93–97) in her reflection on the construction of the object through anthropological discourse, which is discussed critically by Jean-Marie Schaeffer (2005: 27–31).

CHAPTER 2

# The Fiction of Factuality: Some Perspectives from Premodern Japan

*Judit Árokay*

Heidelberg University

The title of this volume, 'Can Fiction Change the World?' takes us back to the question of how to define fiction, and how to distinguish fiction from non-fiction or factuality, especially if we consider a pre-modern age in a different culture. Perceptions of fictionality and factuality are highly variable across cultures and depend on literary traditions and conventions. In both cases, whether we are talking about fact or fiction, we have to consider the language, rhetoric, genre, style, and medium through which the 'stories' are transmitted. If we turn to a pre-modern period, such as the Japanese Middle Ages, which ranged from the twelfth to the sixteenth century, we are confronted with accounts and tales that sound highly fictitious to modern readers, yet, in fact, were read as historical accounts for many centuries.

The Middle Ages in Japan were a period in which new forms of storytelling emerged based on classical forms in the context of social and cultural upheaval (Komine 1988: 20–23). Now, how is it possible to delineate the factuality and fictionality of stories in a medieval setting? I would like to approach this question through the lens of the so-called *kagami* (mirror), referred to as historical tales (*rekishi monogatari*) in the modern age. I will re-contextualise this genre within the framework of literary and historical writing, and will try to show how the appearance of factuality was established and upheld in texts not only intended as historical writing but also recognised as such.

## 1. Fictional and Factual Narratives

Applying a modern nomenclature to pre-modern texts entails several problems. Even though there are differences between the two languages, the Japanese term for literature (*bungaku*) has become synonymous with fiction or fictional writing, similarly to English, but if we look at the Middle Ages or even the Early Modern period, there was no comparable demarcation between fictional and factual literature. In modern literary and historical studies, however, texts that are of literary value (belonging to the wider category of *kotenseki* 古典籍) and historical documents (*shiryō* 史料 or *komonjo* 古文書) are treated separately, a division which is based on the notion of the referentiality of the texts. On the side of the historians, there is an aversion to examining texts that include literary or poetic elements such as topoi, lyrical expression, quotations from literary texts, or explicitly narrative embellishment. On the other hand, in literary studies, seemingly factual accounts such as diaries, biographies, or historical narratives are excluded from the field for their lack of aesthetic embellishment.[1] This division of labour between the disciplines has led to the exclusion of texts from both sides, and consequently to one-sided judgements concerning the 'quality' of texts.

The question is whether and how the modern-day opposites, fiction and factual accounts, were conceptualised in a pre-modern setting. As we will see, a number of terms existed to differentiate between factual texts and fictional narratives. For factual stories we have expressions like *ki* 記 (record, account), *den* 伝 (tradition, legend), *denki* 伝記 (biography), *nikki* 日記 (diary), *shō* 抄 (extract, selection). These texts were not, however, perceived as a distinct group of historical accounts (*rekishisho* 歴史書) as they would have been under the modern approach. While these expressions did refer to genre and gave a kind of formal orientation, they were not genre categories in a strict sense. Normally, they were included in the title of the texts; however, many texts had alternative titles, which means that the titles entailed no concrete genre restrictions.

On the other hand, there are terms referring to the fictionality of texts, such as 虚言 (*soragoto* or *munashiki koto*), and 偽り (*itsuwari*), meaning lie, deception, falsehood, illusion, fabrication. The texts themselves are referred to as *tsukuribanashi* (made-up story), *monogatari* (tale), *e-monogatari* (illustrated tale). The terms we use today for these fictional narratives are *tsukuri monogatari* (made-up narrative), *kyokō* (fiction), or *fikushon*, a calque from the English.

Historiographical texts, topographies, and diaries are classified as containing *shinjitsu* (truth, veracity, authenticity), *makoto* (truth, honesty), and *mi no ue no hanashi* (stories about oneself, things the narrator has witnessed). The difference between fact and fiction was definitely perceived: for certain texts, the reader expected that they were true, that they transmitted facts, and for others, it did not matter whether they contained fictional elements as long as they were entertaining. There is no doubt that *Taketori monogatari*, *Ochikubo monogatari*, *Sumiyoshi monogatari*, and *Genji monogatari* were in their times considered what we would now call 'fikushon'. Nevertheless, these stories could also serve as a material basis for learning about court manners and etiquette. Such an example is the *Genji monogatari* that became an official sourcebook for imperial etiquette a few decades after its appearance.

On the other hand, there is a long-standing tradition of historiographical writing starting with the *Nihonshoki* (720), which was the first of six imperially commanded histories of Japan (*Rikkokushi* 六国史) devised after Chinese models. These histories were referred to as *seishi* (正史), official histories, as opposed to *haishi* (稗史), collections of non-official narratives and of rumours. On the factual side of the opposition, there were also diaries of court officials and official diaries of court life (*nikki*). Due to the factual details and their lack of embellishment, these texts were considered as recording historical facts. But these are only the extremes. With most texts, it is hard to discern to what extent they are truthful and authentic. As we will see, it is evident that there was no clear-cut delineation between factual and fictional writing.

In an attempt to bring some order into a huge corpus of texts that addressed historical matters and were, until his time, consulted for their factual value, the historian Tsuda Sōkichi[2] distinguished five possible sorts of *rekishi bungaku* (historical account/literature). The first were texts recording temporal, and thus historical, change in a detailed manner;[3] second were those recording historical events with descriptions, embellished according to the conventions of the day, which aimed at conveying the emotions of the protagonists to the audience. His third category comprised historical novels that take a historical person or event as the starting point, before introducing fictional protagonists or placing them in a fictional setting to show the universal aspects of history (in the sense of historia magistra vitae est);[4] fourth are legends and mythologies; and fifth, completely fictional narratives set in the past (Tsuda 1973: 15). This is a scale referring to the fictional content of texts; the question is, however, how the audiences in classical and medieval times perceived these differences. Aileen Gatten has analysed the Heian epistolary tale *Tōnomine shōshō monogatari* (961–68; alternative title *Takamitsu nikki*)[5] and comes to the following conclusion with respect to the perception of classical and medieval audiences:

> In other words, in the Heian and Kamakura periods there seems to have been no perceived need for categories as historical fiction, fictional biography or other combinations of historical facts and fictionalized characters. Fiction concerned imaginary people and nonfiction, real people. Narihira was a historical figure whose family line, career, and poetry were well known to Heian readers. *Ise monogatari* tells of the life of a Narihira-like figure. Therefore, Heian readers accepted the story as factual. [...] If factual accuracy, in our sense, meant less to Heian kana writers than to modern biographers and historians, affective considerations meant considerably more. [...] This quality, rather than a capacity to inform or instruct, seems to have constituted the primary appeal of nonfiction in the Heian sense. (Gatten 1998: 190–91)

For medieval audiences, the factuality of the protagonists seemed to have mattered more than the factuality of the details that served to illustrate their lives and actions. Embellishment was not, per se, perceived as fiction, but it was a strategy to convince audiences of the plausibility of the story and the credibility of the narration, as will be demonstrated by the textual strategies of *Ōkagami*.

## 2. The Textual Context of Historical Tales

Before, however, turning to the historical accounts/tales (*rekishi monogatari*) and the *Ōkagami* in detail, I would like to outline the context in which these histories were read. There are several famous texts, which are part of the canon of classical literature today, that either discuss the possibilities of fictionality and factuality or play with this dichotomy.

The often cited first instance is the *Tosa nikki*, a poetic diary of the courtier and poet Ki no Tsurayuki (872–945), dating from the 930s, which relates his return as official governor from his province Tosa to the capital (Ki no Tsurayuki 1981). As can be gathered from historical sources, the voyage itself and many of its details are factual. The author, however, has chosen a female narrator to tell the story. The events that occur on the way to the capital, the feelings of the governor, and the poems recited, are narrated from the perspective of a female persona. A text that, on the basis of its title and the historicity of the protagonist, would be associated with facticity, is fictionalised by the figure of the narrator.

The author of the diary *Kagerō nikki* from the end of the tenth century, in an attempt to set herself apart from fictional writing and tell nothing but the truth, emphasised the difference between *monogatari* and *nikki* in the preface to her work, which is more like an autobiography than a diary in the strict sense (Fujiwara no Michitsuna no haha 1997). She deplores that the ancient tales contain all kinds of falsehoods and inventions, and in opposition to those, she would like to give an authentic account of herself, of her own life as the wife of an influential aristocrat. She puts forward the argument that her life story should be exceptional enough to be told and to be of interest to the (admittedly rather intimate) public audience of the court. Even if many details of the story are told in a factual manner, the narrator uses several elements that are normally associated with fictional narratives: conversations are rendered in direct speech, a number of poems are integrated into the text, the narration takes on an omniscient mode, and there are ellipses of months and years, while longer passages of time are summarised.

In the next well-known example, the *Genji monogatari* (1008), the opposition of fact and fiction is the topic of the chapter Hotaru (Fireflies) (Murasaki Shikibu [1008] 2001). Hikaru Genji deplores that the women in his palace are mainly occupied with reading and copying fictional stories; they are perfectly absorbed, neglecting even their appearance. Tamakazura, the main figure of the chapter, counters and defends the tales against the accusation of being simply lies. Hikaru Genji gives in and admits that it is only through fictional stories that one has access to the reality of everyday life, and thereby to history. He comes to the conclusion that fictitious narratives have the function — beyond dispersing ennui — to provide examples for positive and negative behaviour, for virtue and sin, and to present a description of everyday life that is much more detailed than in the official histories (Murasaki Shikibu [1008] 2001: 460–61).

A contemporary of the *Genji monogatari*, the *Izumi Shikibu nikki*, a diary, covers one year in the life of a court lady (Izumi Shikibu 1969). Judging from the title, and analogous to the *Kagerō nikki*, the reader could assume that the text is factual but, quite to the contrary, it poses several problems. In a diary, we assume with Lejeune and his definition of the autobiographical pact that the author is identical to the narrator and the protagonist. However, it is highly problematic to try to apply this modern definition to pre-modern texts, especially those from a different cultural and linguistic sphere. In Japanese, it is not obligatory to place a subject in a sentence because there are other means to indicate the subject, such as deictic pronouns or honorific language. These means allow for the frequent change of subject, but also for an indecision with regard to the grammatical person. It is feasible, on the basis of the grammatical structure of the text, to read the *Izumi Shikibu nikki* as a diary in the first person; however, a few times, the protagonist is referred to as 'the woman', giving the impression that we are confronted with a third person narrative. On these grounds, Western translations that cannot do without a specific subject have opted for a third person narrative. In Japanese, on the other hand, it is possible to leave this question unresolved. As a consequence, in the Middle Ages, this question remained undecided even for the Japanese readership: the text was passed on under the title of *Izumi Shikibu nikki* as well as of *Izumi Shikibu monogatari*.[6]

Thus, the opposition of *monogatari* versus *nikki* — as it was formulated in the *Kagerō nikki* — is far from being unambiguous, even in the context of classical court literature.

Historiographic or topographic texts, on the other hand, also contain many fictitious elements, myths, legends, and all sorts of oral forms of transmission and poetry as they try to integrate the sources at their disposal to reconstruct the past of the empire. Most of the Japanese histories, especially the first six official histories (*Rikkokushi*), follow Chinese models, whose structure was established with the first Annals dating back to the fifth century BCE, and the *Shiji* (Records of the Grand Historian by Sima Qian and Sima Tan) in the first century BCE. They include purely historiographic sources such as annals, genealogies of emperors, and chronicles of aristocratic houses, but also model biographies of important men and sometimes of women, anecdotes, and legends. Although they aim for an official history, they allow for a certain polyvocality as they integrate alternative versions of the same event told in different regions of the land or in text variants. The tradition of imperial histories that began in Japan with the *Nihonshoki* in 720 came to an end in 901, but by then a model for writing history had been established. These official histories were followed by a different type of historical account, written in Japanese, in a narrative style with fewer formal restrictions.

## 3. The Mirror as History

The term *rekishi monogatari* was introduced in 1899 by Haga Yaichi, professor of Japanese literature, who referred to the historical accounts written after the *Rikkokushi*, the six official imperial histories, as historical tales (Haga 1899: 123).[7]

Prior to this categorisation, Japan saw a quite intensive surge in the development of historiography as a discipline. From the 1870s, an instrumental view on history developed, which saw the function of writing history as affirming the authority and legitimacy of the emperor. In this respect, the aims of 'modern' history were no different from the first histories written in Japan in the eighth century, the *Nihonshoki* and *Kojiki*. Under the influence of Western historiography, new models of historical writing emerged during the 1880s and 1890s, and the discipline became multifaceted. On the basis of philological enquiry, textual scholarship, and archaeology, long established myths and facts came to be scrutinised, among them the veracity of historical tales that had been previously accepted as truthful records of the past (Brownlee 2014: 86–90).[8]

In Haga's view, the *rekishi monogatari* were similar to the made-up narratives (*tsukuri monogatari*) of the Heian period, especially in their language, as they were written in Japanese and not in *kanbun*. Instead of a chronological account, they retold history along the structural model of the official histories in a narrative manner with many details and rhetorical embellishment. Four of the historical tales are known under the title 'mirror' (*kagami*, *kagamimono*), the first among them *Ōkagami* (The Great Mirror), written at the beginning of the twelfth century.[9]

The title 'mirror' reminds us of the genre of 'speculum' within the European medieval context: texts that were often didactic in their intent while encompassing encyclopaedic, historical, political, or moral texts. Thus, the term speculum is rather vague for a European reader, but *kagami* in a Japanese historiographical context was quite explicit: mirror as a metaphor refers to history itself, as it reflects ages past. This was already the meaning of the term in China, beginning in the second century BCE, and subsequently in Japan. *Kagami* refers to a mirror that reflects things gone by. The story told by the main narrator, Yotsugi, is commented as: 'Your descriptions of all those Emperors have been just like reflections in a mirror. [...] When I listen to you, I feel as I do when I catch a glimpse of my face in a bright, shiny mirror - it is embarrassing to see what I really look like, but the reflection is amazingly true to life' (McCullough 1980: 85). Throughout the text, the metaphor allows for different instances of word play with mirrors that have become dull or are, on the contrary, exceptionally clear. The narrator of *Ōkagami* draws a comparison between the genius of the historiographer and the mirror, which reflects things precisely as they are, without altering or falsifying them. He says of himself: 'I am a plain old-fashioned mirror from a bygone age, made of good white metal that stays clear without being polished' (McCullough 1980: 86).

Readers accustomed to the six official histories might have expected from a 'kagami' an official chronological history. In fact, the name of the narrator also points to this direction as it is revealed to be Ōyake no Yotsugi, meaning 'official account of generations'. As a matter of fact, *yotsugi* or *yotsugi monogatari* was a contemporary term for accounts on subsequent generations.

The *Ōkagami* was written around 1100 — according to leading historians, between 1085 and 1105 — by an unknown author. I want to introduce this text here as an example, as it has several unique features that were copied by later 'mirrors', although never fully reproduced. The account covers the period of 850 to 1025, which corresponds to the golden era of the Fujiwara family with Fujiwara no Michinaga (966–1028) as its most influential representative. Under Michinaga, the imperial court was completely dominated by Fujiwara interests — daughters of Michinaga were married to emperors and themselves produced princes and future emperors, the cultural life of the court was administered by the extended Fujiwara family, and they maintained the especially important courtly salons where poetry and narrative literature flourished. The *Ōkagami* takes up and partially repeats the contents of the *Eiga monogatari*, a historical tale written by the important female poets of the courtly salons, notably Akazome Emon (956–1041), which centres around the person of Michinaga and gives an account of his splendid reign in elegant Japanese. *Eiga monogatari* itself was already a novel form for writing history after the tradition of the six official histories (*Rikkokushi*) had been discontinued in 901, which is the reason why Haga Yaichi defines it as the first *rekishi monogatari*. While the *Rikkokushi* had been written in Chinese (*kanbun*) and were strictly chronological, the *Eiga monogatari* takes up the narrative tradition of court literature (*monogatari*) and applies it to a historical subject. Instead of a chronicle of political events, a detailed description of Michinaga's personality and merits, courtly life, and ceremonies are at the centre of the narrative. Given the status of the author(s), the eulogy on Michinaga is understandable, but it throws serious doubts on the veracity of the account: in a system of patronage, written by dependent insiders who are part of the system, many minute details are recorded but no objectivity can be expected (Gatten 1998, 192).

With the *Ōkagami*, however, a completely new perspective appears, an ambulatory history that is characterised by polyvocality, to borrow David Bialock's terminology. Wandering reciters take over from court scholars (Bialock 2007: 156–74). The *Ōkagami* subverts the tradition of court literature by moving the perspective away from an insider of the court writing for readers (an audience) who are similarly insiders, to multiple narrators who have witnessed the events they are reporting but from a more detached perspective. Their account is directed towards an audience that comprises the new military class gaining influence from the beginning of the twelfth century. The aim of the narration is as Yotsugi states: '"I have only one thing of importance on my mind," he went on, "and that is to describe Lord Michinaga's unprecedented successes to all of you here, clergy and laity of both sexes"' (McCullough 1980: 68).

Still, the narration maintains a critical distance from the protagonist, and the mode of presentation has a dramatic structure that is an expression of the period of change and the emergence of the medieval feudal system.[10] The portrait of Michinaga, whose merits are the main topic of the *Ōkagami*, is positive but is constantly scrutinised by the audience, contrary to the *Eiga monogatari*.

## 4. Giving Credibility to the Narration

The narrative begins at the temple Urin-in where a crowd is waiting for the arrival of a priest and the commencement of a Buddhist ceremony, the exegesis of the *Lotus Sutra*. The unnamed narrator of the meta-narrative appears and reports that while waiting, he becomes witness to a conversation between two extremely old men. One of them is Ōyake no Yotsugi who turns out to be 190 years old; the other, Natsuyama no Shigeki is 180 years of age. The wife of Shigeki, without an active role in the story, is also among the crowd and extremely old.[11] But what might be the reason for introducing such improbable narrators from the beginning?

Yotsugi, as his name already implies, relates the history of fourteen generations of *tennō*, beginning with his own birth in 876 during the era of Emperor Seiwa, until Goichijō in 1025. His account comprises some original elements, and he reports things as he has witnessed them in a captivating manner. His age might not be plausible, but it is the very element that is supposed to render his account absolutely reliable: he has been an (eye-)witness to all the things he reports. This establishes his credibility in the first line for the medieval audience. For those passages that he evidently cannot have been an eyewitness for, e.g., the events in the Fujiwara family before his own birth, there is an explanation for his credibility: Shigeki characterises him as somebody who has a frightening capacity for memorising everything he has heard, and Yotsugi himself says: 'I am an old man who has kept his eyes open and remembered every single thing. [...] Listen quietly, everyone. There is nothing I have not seen or heard' (McCullough 1980: 86–87). At the end of the story, the question about his incredible longevity arises, and he explains it with reference to his mission to proclaim the glory of Fujiwara no Michinaga among subsequent generations.

The form of Ōkagami has also some innovative aspects for relating history: between the two old men, a dialogue ensues, utilising a form that is referred to as *mondōtai*. Although this conversation is completely dominated by Yotsugi, this gives room for questions by the audience, and for alternative renderings of the same event. The polyvocality that sets the *Ōkagami* apart from the *Eiga monogatari* is due to the fact that Yotsugi's account, which is centred on the official side of Michinaga, is interrupted by insights from Shigeki, who refers to more private details. On the other hand, the young samurai who takes part in the conversation also gives occasional glimpses into the political consequences of Fujiwara policy when he refers to those dispossessed in the process of the Fujiwara ascent (Bialock 2007: 158–59), adding a critical tone to the eulogy on Michinaga.

The dialogue form (*mondōtai*) is characteristic of Buddhist and Confucian texts for instruction, and thus is well known to the audience. Here it is recast in a group conversation (*zadan keishiki*), like a *mise en scène*. Instead of a chronological account of events, the dialogue allows for the presentation of multiple versions, or at least different aspects, of an event, while the presence of an audience allows for questions and even criticism of the narrator. This framing is unique to the *Ōkagami* among historical accounts and tales, and even among the *kagami*. The other *kagami* start with an introduction in dialogue form — taking up the motif of the mythically aged narrator — but soon revert to the usual chronological presentation of events and lack the dramatic framing that characterises the *Ōkagami*.

Yotsugi and Shigeki arrive at the scene of the Urin-in without any explanation, and at the end of the story, they disappear into the crowd. Their appearance reminds the reader of the tradition of itinerant professional storytellers in medieval Japan who told the history of the war between the Taira and the Minamoto, especially during the twelfth and thirteenth centuries. The *Heike monogatari* came into being in its current form through continuous application of the oral tradition. It was not a homogenous text that existed before it was told, but was created by oral embellishment of written accounts that again were based on contemporary diaries and chronicles. It is characterised by formulaic speech that might arouse our suspicion about the veracity of the content, but in the Middle Ages, this was exactly what the audience expected. If the details were only probable, they were accepted, even if they were not provable. As Kenneth D. Butler has pointed out with reference to the recitation of the *Heike monogatari*: 'The singer establishes a special rapport to the audience which is drawn into the story and made to believe they are listening to an accurate account of actual historical events' (Butler 1969: 104–05). By being specific and detailed, the narrator gives an authenticity to his account; by his physical presence, he lures the audience into believing his story to be true.

The mythically ancient itinerant storytellers of the *Ōkagami*, referred to as *okina* (old man), are the clue to the credibility of the narration. Even granting the possibility that the motif was not taken at face value, the very old people who appear by chance and vanish without a trace after the ceremony are not only associated with itinerant storytellers, but also possibly with divine visitors in disguise. As pointed out by the famous ethnographer Orikuchi Shinobu (1887-1953), there are links to different cults of very old people, as in Taoism or in shamanistic practices (*marebito*), that were conveyed as living practice in rituals and in the Nō-theatre. The so-called *okina* plays were traditionally a part of seasonal agricultural ritual and were later integrated into the framework of the Nō theatre. The *okina* plays or dances are highly ritualised, performed by three actors playing two very old people in masks (*okina* and *sanbasō*) and a younger person (*senzai*). Several days before the performance, the main character *okina* enters a phase of ritual cleansing which is kept up until the performance. During the play, in the scene, he puts on his mask (*okina* mask) which signifies his transformation into a deity. Now, these *okina* plays seem to reach back to the shamanistic belief in *marebito*, divine visitors, possibly ancestral spirits, bringing luck and wealth; they appear in human guise equipped for a journey. This belief contributed to a culture of hospitality towards visitors from afar like itinerant monks, artists, or healers, as they were held for possible divine visitors.[12] With this background, the motif of the mythically old storytellers appears in a different light: instead of fictionalising their account, it emphasises its credibility.

In this sense, Yotsugi is situated in plural settings that serve to enhance his credibility: his account is put into the context of the exegesis of holy texts and the tradition of the Chronicles of Japan:

> 'I am going to discuss serious matters now. Pay close attention, everyone. Just as you must look at today's exposition of holy writ as an aid to enlightenment, so you should think, as you listen to me, you are hearing the Chronicles of Japan.' [...] 'We have heard plenty of sutra expositions and sermons, but nobody has ever told us such marvellous things', said the monks and laymen. Ancient nuns and monks touched their hands to their foreheads and sat listening with pious fervour. (McCullough 1980: 86)

Finally, the place of this historical performance should be mentioned as it adds to the credibility and validity of its content. The Buddhist framing, as well as the congregation waiting for a Buddhist priest, enhances the authority of the presentation. As the story is being told at a temple famous for its religious ceremony of *bodaikō* (the exegesis of the *Lotus Sutra* [*Saddharma Puṇḍarīka Sūtra*]), a parallel is drawn to historical account as exegesis of the truth of bygone ages. In the same way as the *Lotus Sutra* was supposed to tell stories of enlightenment in order to lead its readers to enlightenment, Yotsugi is revealing the truth about Michinaga and his unique capacity as a political figure, but also as a spiritual leader. If we further take into account that the *Lotus Sutra* is known as the text that develops a famous apology of fictionality and delusion, we have an additional argument for the reliability of the account.

It was well known that Buddhist texts, especially the *Lotus Sutra*, contained fictional accounts. A well-known example is the allegorical story of the wealthy man whose sons are playing in a burning house and, as they are absorbed, the father is unable to lure them out. He reverts to an expedient means, deceit, to persuade his children to come out. The justification is that as far as lies, deceit, and delusion serve to lead the ignorant minds to spiritual revelation, they are tolerable means. Only the right intention is important. In this reading, fiction doesn't correspond to deceit but, on the contrary, it becomes a *hōben*, an expedient means to lead the unconscious to spiritual revelation according to their needs and possibilities. In the Buddhist context where language itself was seen as a fraudulent means, it was exactly the delusion produced by fiction which offered the possibility of touching upon reality.

On the level of the narrative, Yotsugi is emphasising the truthfulness of his account by calling on the buddhas: 'if you think I have intentionally added a single falsehood, may the buddhas of this temple bear witness on my behalf, and also the buddhas and bodhisattvas invoked by the preceptor at today's service. Of all the ten commandments, the prohibition against falsehood is the one I have observed most carefully ever since my youth, which is precisely why I have been able to live so long. I certainly would not come and violate that commandment today at the site of a service where a special point is to be made of administering it' (McCullough 1980: 235).

## 5. Conclusions

For the pre-modern, we have to assume a different approach to fact and fiction than the one we take for granted nowadays on the basis of the referentiality of texts. There seems to be a certain continuity between fictionality and factuality, as the texts were supposed to be read (or listened to) for the historical information they contained, as well as for entertainment. The idea of history as something different from literature is rather new, in Europe as well as in Japan. In Europe, historiography developed as a science during the nineteenth century, parallel to the golden age of the historical novel. We can truthfully say that the first historical accounts were historical novels. Philology in the nineteenth century developed as a critique of fictional writing, with the aim of separating fact from fiction on the basis of scientific criteria.

In Japan, the development of historiography at the end of the nineteenth century was connected to the process of nation building and the need for a national identity constructed, among other means, on the basis of a national history that was to be written. At the same time, European historians teaching at Japanese universities introduced new methods and approaches to historical texts and artifacts, which gave rise to the critique of the political appropriation of history. This was the first time that the veracity of official histories, historical accounts, and tales was seriously questioned and scrutinised.[13]

As the perception of fiction is relative to the time and culture of the perceiver, we have to keep in mind the possible 'contracts' between author and reader. For medieval readers, there existed a group of conventional signs in the texts that helped them to discern whether a text claimed to be fictional or factual. These were: the title and genre of the text, the person of the narrator, certain attitudes of the narrator, and conventional structures and models for presenting/telling history. These criteria would help the reader understand how to approach the text, but were not at all decisive in terms of the factuality or the fictionality of the text in a modern sense. But, if it is not the difference between fact and fiction that counts, what mattered for the medieval period? Much more important seems to be the reliability of the narrator, which is established through different means, as we have seen in the case of the Ōkagami.

To return to the topic of this volume: even if historical accounts and *monogatari* (tales) are considered fiction nowadays, they managed to create a community of the aristocracy or of certain families/clans and their descendants, and to serve as a kind of encyclopaedia of imperial rites and manners. In this sense, then, these accounts definitely contributed to changing the world.

## References

BIALOCK, DAVID T. 2007. *Eccentric Spaces, Hidden Histories: Narrative, Ritual, and Royal Authority from 'The Chronicles of Japan' to the 'Tale of the Heike'* (Stanford, CA: Stanford University Press)

BROWNLEE, JOHN S. 2014. *Japanese Historians and the National Myths, 1600–1945: The Age of the Gods and Emperor Jinmu* (Vancouver: UBC Press)

BUTLER, KENNETH D. 1969. 'The *Heike monogatari* and The Japanese Warrior Ethic', *Harvard Journal of Asiatic Studies*, 29: 93–108

*Eiga monogatari, Ōkagami*. 1971. *Rekishi monogatari*, 1 (Tokyo: Yūseidō shuppan)

FUJIWARA NO MICHITSUNA NO HAHA. 1997. *The Kagerō Diary: A Woman's Autobiographical Text from Tenth-Century Japan*, trans. by Sonja Arntzen, Michigan Monographs in Japanese Studies, XIX (Ann Arbor: Center for Japanese Studies, University of Michigan)

FUKUDA, YASUNORI. 2016. *Igakusho no naka no 'bungaku': Edo no igaku to bungaku ga tsukuriageta sekai* ['Literature' in Medical Texts: The World of Edo Period Medicine and Literature] (Tokyo: Kasama shoin)

GATTEN, AILEEN. 1998. 'Fact, Fiction, and Heian Literary Prose: Epistolary Narration in Tōnomine Shōshō Monogatari', *Monumenta Nipponica* 53 (2): 153–95

GOMI, FUMIHIKO. 2015. *Bungaku de yomu Nihon no rekishi: Koten bungaku hen* [The History of Japan as we Read it in Literature: Classical Literature] (Tokyo: Yamakawa shuppansha)

HAGA, YAICHI. 1899. *Kokubungakushi jikkō* [Ten Lectures on National Literature] (Tokyo: Fuzanbō)

*Imakagami, Mizukagami, Masukagami, Akitsushima monogatari*. 1973. *Rekishi monogatari*, II (Tokyo: Yūseidō shuppan)

Izumi Shikibu. 1969. *Diary: A Romance of the Heian Court*, trans. by Edwin A. Cranston (Cambridge, MA: Harvard University Press)

Ki no Tsurayuki. 1981. *The Tosa Diary*, trans. by William N. Porter (Rutland: C.E. Tuttle)

Komine, Kazuaki. 1988. 'Ōkagami no katari: Katarite to hikkisha no isō' [Narration in the *Ōkagami*: The Registers of the Reciter and the Scribe], *Nihon bungaku*, 37 (1): 20-32

McCullough, Helen C., trans. 1980. *Ōkagami: The Great Mirror; Fujiwara Michinaga (966–1027) and His Times* (Princeton, NJ: Princeton University Press)

Mehl, Margaret. 1988. *History and the State in Nineteenth-Century Japan* (London: Macmillan)

Müller, Simone. 2009. 'Fiktivität und Fiktionalität im *Izumi Shikibu nikki*: Narratologische Bestimmung eines heian-zeitlichen 'Frauentagebuches', *Asiatische Studien* 63 (3): 515–52

Murasaki Shikibu. [1008] 2001. *The Tale of Genji*, trans. by Royall Tyler (New York: Viking)

*Ōkagami*. 1985. Vol. xx of *Nihon koten bungaku zenshū* [Complete Works of Classical Japanese Literature] (Tokyo: Shōgakukan)

*Ōkagami*. 1967. Vol. xxi of *Nihon koten bungaku taikei* [Compendium of Classical Japanese Literature] (Tokyo: Iwanami shoten)

Tsuda, Sōkichi. 1973. 'Nihon no bungakushi ni okeru rekishi bungaku' [Historical Literature in the Framework of Japanese Literary History], in *Rekishi monogatari*, ii: *Imakagami, Mizukagami, Masukagami, Akitsushima monogatari* (Tokyo: Yūseidō shuppan), pp. 15–20

## Notes to Chapter 2

1. There are exceptions to the rule such as Gomi Fumihiko who tries to extract historical information from literary sources (Gomi 2015), and the even more original Fukuda Yasunori who reads medical treatises from the early modern for their literary components (Fukuda 2016).
2. 1873–1961. Tsuda was a historian of the Taishō and Shōwa eras who belonged to those few who, in the 1910s and '20s, questioned the factuality and veracity of the first Japanese histories, *Kojiki* (712) and *Nihonshoki* (720). This *lèse-majesté* caused him serious trouble; he was even imprisoned for a short time. His view on the ancient myths and legends of Japan became the mainstream view after the Pacific War.
3. This sort of text is quite rare in Japan, but *Ōkagami* belongs to this group, according to Tsuda, as a text that has no models in Chinese historical writing. Rai San'yō's *Nihon gaishi* (1827) would be another example (Tsuda 1973: 15).
4. The *Genji monogatari* was also read as a *roman à clef*: even if the protagonists were fictitious the first instinct of readers was to identify the historical figures that were allegedly hidden behind them.
5. The text records the seclusion of Fujiwara no Takamitsu in a prose tale that is built on the poems exchanged in letters between Takamitsu, his wife, and his sister. Fujiwara no Takamitsu is reputed to have left his family all of a sudden to take refuge from his court life in the temple Enryakuji, on Mount Hiei. The historical figure Takamitsu is well documented as he belonged to the court elite, but it is the construction of the tale that makes his story for the first time significant and is the reason for its survival.
6. For a detailed discussion of the fictionality issue see Müller (2009).
7. Haga Yaichi used the term for the first time in the fifth of his 'Ten lectures on national literature'. He identified eight such tales: *Eiga monogatari* (eleventh century), four texts with the word *kagami* (mirror) in the title (*Ōkagami, Mizu kagami, Masu kagami, Ima kagami*), and three other texts up to the fourteenth century: *Akitsushima monogatari, Iya yotsugi, Iya masukagami*. There exist also alternative categorisations for the medieval sequels. In the Early Modern period, the prolific female poet and writer Arakida Reijo (1732–1806) wrote the sequel up to the beginning of the Tokugawa shogunate; that is, the beginning of the seventeenth century: *Ike no mokuzu* and *Tsuki no yukue* (both 1771).

8. Several historical tales like the *Heike monogatari*, the *Taiheiki*, from the thirteenth to the fourteenth century were used as sources of Japanese history and quoted in subsequent early modern histories of Japan like the *Dai nihonshi* (a monumental history ordered by the shogunate, compiled from between seventeenth and the end of the nineteenth century) or the *Nihon gaishi* (by Rai San'yō, 1827, printed 1829).
9. The fact that *rekishi monogatari* in the sense of historical 'tale' or 'fictional narrative' was not used until modern times shows that the concept of tale was not associated with the texts called 'mirror'.
10. Komine has elaborated on the narrative aspects of this transition analysing the lingual strategies of the scribe/narrator in the *Ōkagami* (Komine 1988).
11. In the popular version of the *Ōkagami* (*rufubon*) the age of the participants is reduced but still mythical: Yotsugi is 150, Shigeki 140, even the young samurai who is 30 in the manuscript is 20 in these versions.
12. A further link can be established to Taoist beliefs and practices that aim at longevity, i.e., extending one's life ideally to the point of immortality.
13. For a detailed account see Mehl (1998).

CHAPTER 3

# For a Theory of Fiction as *Show, Performance, Entertainment*

*Yasusuke Oura*

*Kyoto University*

## 1. Show, Performance, Entertainment

To start with, I would like to clear up any misunderstanding that may arise from the title of this article — a misunderstanding that is linked, unfortunately, to the term 'performance'. What I mean by this word is not the performative aspect of language, which we refer to when we define fiction as a speech act (an implicit speech act, in a way); that is, when we adopt a communicational or pragmatic approach to fiction. I don't reject this usage; on the contrary. However, the performance I consider here is quite different. The juxtaposition of three terms in my title — *show, performance*, and *entertainment* — clearly expresses what I have in mind. Performance, here, is used in a sense close to that of 'performing arts': theatre, dance, musical performance, etc.

It is no doubt necessary to explain the choice of these three terms, often used in their English form in many languages, including Japanese, without too much semantic deviation. I confess that I chose them without much reflection, but realised afterwards that this choice had a certain internal logic. *Show* relates above all to the object of the show, precisely the object to be *shown*, made seen, while also involving the one who shows, makes something seen. We probably spontaneously think of certain forms of stage performance, but the medium in closest affinity with the *show* today is surely television; the *TV show* is, at least in its American usage, quite simply synonymous with a television programme, whether fictional (as in the case of television series or TV films) or non-fictional (news, variety shows, etc.).

*Performance* is primarily related to the quality of execution of an artistic or even sports programme in which the body plays a major role. We appreciate the finesse of a game, the speed of a movement, the beauty of a body. As for *entertainment*, it is the business or production side that is emphasised here. The will to divert, to amuse, to 'entertain' the public is evident; this is precisely the goal of the producer. The case of cinema is obvious because it is an 'industry'. As we know, the names of American film production companies (or their divisions), are often accompanied by this term, such as Warner Bros. Entertainment, Sony Pictures Entertainment, and so on.

Thus, we can doubtless affirm that *show, performance*, and *entertainment* correspond roughly, and with an obvious overlap, to the three aspects of a show: product, productivity, production (or producer). However, the point I would like to insist on is rather the following: these three terms together designate the existence of a very broad category of stage or film performances, whether fictional or non-fictional (often fictional *and* non-fictional). I propose here to take this category into account when rethinking fiction and fictionality.

## 2. Decentring Debates on Fiction

It is a fact that most contemporary fiction theorists have taken the novel, or the written fictional narrative, as their central object. Despite this, theatre has not been excluded from their field of inquiry; it even occupies a constant place among 'literary fictions', but the fictionality of theatre is often derived from that of the novel; it is the status of the *text* of the play that is investigated. Even if staging or the actor's performance is taken into consideration, it seems to me that the underlying model is modern theatre, in its more or less realistic form — that is to say, fictionally stable, with its famous 'fourth wall' clearly separating stage and hall, the imaginary world of the work and the real world of the audience. As far as I know, little attention is paid to shows and performances where precisely this separation is far from obvious.

Above all, I would like to shift the debate on fiction and fictionality by giving priority to fictions based on visual, non-written representation, whether staged or filmed: theatre, cinema, television series, etc. For I am, if not convinced, at least inclined to believe that the fictionality of theatre is fundamentally different from and, in a certain sense, more 'basic' than that of the novel. I will not be able to develop this argument fully here, but it seems to me in some ways simple and effective to use theatrical fiction as a model. My vision of basic fictionality is simple: a flesh-and-blood being pretends, 'playfully' of course, to be an imaginary character: Laurence Olivier playing Hamlet, Johnny Depp playing Jack Sparrow. Everything starts from there. For me, the Schaefferian term 'feintise' (Schaeffer 2010), the Searlian term 'pretense' (Searle 1975) or even the Waltonian 'make-believe' (Walton 1990) only take on their proper meaning when applied to acting. As far as cinema and TV series are concerned, I therefore give priority to live-action movies over animated films. In a word, my theory of fiction is a theory of the *actor*. My interest in performance is evidently not unrelated to this position.

Of course, it remains to be seen how the fictionality of the novel can be explained on this basis — no easy task. Leaving the question open, I will simply say this: the novel is a *written* fiction and, as such, it seems to me, fundamentally resistant to the mimetic theory of fiction. We observe in the work of a well-known Japanese literary critic, Shigehiko Hasumi (2007), a total rejection of theories of fiction from Searle to Schaeffer, and this rejection is significant in more than one respect (Oura 2019). Hasumi is one of the proponents of the thesis that *writing does not imitate anything*. Those who hold this view also tend to confuse fictionality with literarity. Although I do not follow them in this, we should not underestimate the scriptural specificity of the novel. Indeed, we might find here one reason why the theory of fiction is still not fully established.

Why, moreover, need we seek at all costs a definition that is valid for all kinds of fiction? There is a multitude of fictions, different in form and nature. Perhaps it is time to give up the search for an irreducible and homogenous essence of fiction and accept its plurality for good.

## 3. *Shows* and Panfictionalism

Let us return to the show and to performance. *Show*-type performances are everywhere. Some have a long tradition: ballet; Commedia dell'Arte; opera; Indian classical theatre; shadow or puppet theatre from Asia, Near East, Africa; Japanese Nō theatre; Kabuki; Peking opera; to mention only the best known. Others are more intimate and popular: street shows, fairgrounds, cabaret, circus, magic shows, etc. I have already briefly discussed the latest avatars of the *show* on television. Today, these shows are proliferating on a planetary scale thanks to new technologies in computing and telecommunications.

If we seem to see a rampant panfictionalism nowadays, this can probably be attributed not only to postmodern ideology, or even to the abundance of films, cartoons, TV series, video games, manga, etc. that declare themselves to be more or less fictional, but also, and above all, to the ubiquity of shows of all kinds that invade large and small screens, those of the computer and the smartphone. A glance at YouTube allows us to gauge the extent of this phenomenon. These are shows that are not clearly fictional or nonfictional — we don't even know whether they are public or private, professional or amateur: they often fall somewhere in between. It is precisely this ambivalence that interests the audience. Today's audience is both too distrustful to naively believe the truth of an allegedly true or factual discourse, and too jaded to enjoy a classical, realistic fictional technique. Think, for example, of the 'reality show' especially those television programmes that are constantly multiplying, from *Big Brother* to *Love Island*. The somewhat paradoxical name of the genre speaks for itself: the two terms 'reality' and 'show' form an inseparable couple, one of which needs the other. It is as if we want 'reality' to be even more real, by means of a certain staging called 'show'. This is before we even consider *docufiction, docudrama, docucomedy, mockumentary, pseudo-documentary* or anything else of this ilk. In any case, I would argue that even if this deliberate destabilisation of the boundaries between fact and fiction does not annihilate these boundaries (I agree with Françoise Lavocat [2016] on this point), its muddying of the waters nevertheless contributes greatly to the spread of panfictionalistic ideas.

If the show has existed in one form or another from time immemorial, it is because it is no doubt a response to humankind's fundamental desire to see a performance — a feat of voice and body, speech and mind — and to the pleasure, wonder, and laughter that this performance provokes. The circus show is typical in a way. We can also think of those one-man shows by actors, comedians, or humourists who, on a dinner-theatre stage or a television set, tell stories, perform skits, imitate celebrities. What we go to see is their performance. Performance is the basis of all shows, whether fictional or nonfictional; their 'artistic' quality depends on it. It is in itself fiction-neutral, just as dance and music are; fictionality 'grafts' itself onto performance, so to speak, in the case of fictional shows. By what means? Through the introduction of a narrative framework, a *story*, even if the latter alone is not enough to ensure fictionality (since there are 'true stories').

Perhaps we can say that performance is to shows what style is to writing: just as there is no show without performance, there is no writing without style. And the 'literary' character of writing depends on it, as Genette said (with respect to non-fictional prose) (Genette 1993: 28).

My aim is not to study the *show* as such, but rather to examine performative elements within fictional shows, and in particular to see how performativity and fictionality intersect in these shows.

## 4. Performativity and Fictionality

It must be noted that there are degrees of performativity in fictional shows. Opera and musical drama are more performative than realistic theatre; musical film is also more performative than other types of fiction film. We see that music and dance are the most salient performative elements, but they are not the only ones. Let us take the example of cinema. We can say that some films, even if they are not musicals, are more performative, *showier* than others. These are films in which one finds, for example, a strong stylisation, a concern for composition, symmetry, an unusual scenography, a playful spirit, humour, quotations, etc., which are all signs of detachment with respect to narrativity. One can think of certain films by Wes Anderson (*Moonrise Kingdom*, *The Grand Budapest Hotel*, etc.) or François Ozon (*Huit femmes*, *Swimming Pool*, etc.), or, in terms of colour and design, perhaps even by Pedro Almodóvar. Thus, a consideration of cinematographic performativity can provide us with an elementary screening criterion for all fictional films.

Fiction is the realm of *approximation*. It is a patchwork of narrative blocks whose succession is perceived as a causal continuity. Moreover, its relation to referents, that is to say, its resemblance to reality, is also approximate; this is what Jean-Marie Schaeffer calls a relation of 'global analogy' (Schaeffer 2010: 189). This fundamental horizontal and vertical discontinuity (so to speak) of fiction is not exactly the same for all semiotic media. In the case of the novel, the discontinuity is symbolic, since it makes use of written natural language, whereas in the case of performances by actors, it is both iconic and corporeal. Let's look, for example, at how languages are treated in English-language films, i.e., the majority of films. No one is shocked to see a presumed Parisian character speaking perfect English (in the original version of the film), with the occasional 'Bonjour' or 'Mademoiselle', or if necessary, a slight 'typical' French accent. This applies not only to languages but also to cultures. An Asian person in a Western film is an Asian without a precise identity, often an amalgam of Chinese, Japanese, Vietnamese, Thai, etc. See the curious character named Ra's al Ghul in *Batman Begins*, played by the Japanese actor Ken Watanabe: he is a martial arts master, lives in the Himalayas, speaks an incomprehensible language, and is at the head of an army of ninjas (the 'League of Shadows') wearing the pseudo-armour of ancient Japanese warriors. The examples are countless. The signs scattered here do not refer to any referent, but are intended to *signify* cultural stereotypes. This is, without a doubt, one way of being fictional.

In the case of highly performative shows such as opera or musical film, what is most visible is narrative discontinuity. We often have a succession of several nodes or large scenes in the story, wherein the narrative thread is sometimes even cut off altogether to make way for an almost pure performance; the extreme and somewhat caricatural example would be 'Bollywood' productions where the characters suddenly start dancing together in the middle of the film, often independently of any narrative context. It's a moment of celebration.

In performative shows, fictionality is displayed and exhibited to the detriment of narrative continuity and ordinary verisimilitude. A fiction always sets in motion two opposing movements: one towards concealing fictionality in order to reinforce the referential illusion, to 'make it real'; another towards revealing fictionality in order to signal that this is, after all, a fiction, an artifact or a work of art. Performance moves in the second direction (while this tendency may sometimes have an ethical motive, aiming to ward off criticism of fiction as a lie, this motive is inoperative in the case of performance).

Performance concerns actors, or actors–singers–dancers: real people, in any case, not the fictional characters they play. The public admires their finesse, dexterity, and art, as well as their name — or the extent to which their performative art is worthy of their name or acting troupe, house, or school. Does performance work against the 'fictional immersion' of the audience? Not at all, at least in a show of high quality. This is the great paradox of fiction.

## 5. Bunraku and Fictional Immersion

Let's take a closer look. In a fictional show, the 'actorial' instance, so to speak, far from being a transparent relay that would allow the audience to come into direct contact with the fictional world, takes on a physical, corporeal density that is itself a source of pleasure. On the one hand, there is the actor and his performance, and on the other, the character and the world of the story. The two cohabit in the same person, but this cohabitation is not always self-evident. I believe that traditionally, it is often the mask that has assumed the function of intermediary, of transition. The mask represents an eminently fictional figure, while at the same time pointing to its own fictionality. Think, for example, of the masks of the Commedia dell'Arte or Nō theatre. The mask is there, as it were, to stabilise the relationship and the fragile equilibrium between the two movements I mentioned earlier: between concealing and unveiling fictionality. From this point of view, a show without a mask entails a certain emancipation, since without the mask, fictionality asserts itself more frankly, in a more autonomous way.

Another example from Japanese traditional theatre is that of Bunraku (more exactly, *Ningyô Jôruri*). This is a form of puppet theatre that originated in Osaka in the seventeenth century. This is admittedly not an ideal example, because the actor as such is not present, but it is in many ways revealing. In Bunraku, the character is embodied by a puppet, and the puppeteers who manipulate it stand behind it. In general, a puppet is moved by three puppeteers who share the task: two apprentices, so to speak, wearing a black habit and headgear (*kurogo*), and a master, often dressed 'normally', face uncovered. What is extraordinary in Bunraku is the fact that, apparently, the very visible presence of these manipulators, even that of the main puppeteer (*omozukai*) with the visibly impassive face of a sixty-year-old, moving with the puppet while making it express itself in a thousand subtle and pathetic ways, does not hinder in any way the fictional immersion of the audience. I do not rule out the possibility of contrary reactions (there are sometimes polemics about the relevance of this *dezukai* or 'revealed manipulation'), but it seems that, more often than not, the audience is easily fascinated by the imploring gesture of a desperate lover or the courageous act of an indignant warrior. Moreover, the artifice is also visible through the presence of the reciter (*tayû*) and the *shamisen* player who, seated on a side stage, are in charge of the vocal and musical component of the performance. In particular, the work of the *tayû* is important: all alone, he recites, sings, utters the words of all the characters, women, men, children, old people, each time with a tremolo, broken intonations, complaints, tears, etc., while still telling the story in the third person. In short, he speaks the whole text (he has his book in front of him, on a desk); it is a rhythmic, controlled, but exalted reading. A true performance.

## 6. Pleasure Above All

The example of Bunraku prompts us to make two points. Firstly, in this type of show, the artifice is obvious and yet, as we have seen, immersion can work — even work very well. What does this mean? It means that we spectators have an extraordinary ability to *see only what we want to see*. This is a will similar to that expressed in Coleridge's famous '*willing* suspension of disbelief'. Moreover, this will is not only 'poetic'; it is also economic in nature: since we pay a good deal for admission, we want to 'get our money's worth', to be rewarded with an equivalent amount of pleasure. Such is the law of the entertainment market.

But does the Bunraku audience really strive to see only the puppets? Do they avoid looking at the puppeteers — especially the one who reveals the face of an old man with thirty or forty years of the profession behind him — for fear of fictional disenchantment? Not necessarily. In fact, we know that some fans even go specifically to see the master puppeteer's performance, especially when his name is Minosuke Yoshida or Tamao Yoshida. (These are the prestigious names of master puppeteers, passed on from generation to generation. Hence the current Minosuke Yoshida (1933– ), a national living treasure, is the third to bear this name, and the current Tamao Yoshida (1953– ) is the second.) We need to look for another answer, probably a deeper and more complex one. We have to see not only a happy 'cohabitation' between the performativity and fictionality of this type of performance, but also a kind of interdependence. The relationship is not symmetrical, however, because there can be performance without fiction, but there can be no fictionality without performance. It would appear, however, that on the one hand the audience can enjoy and appreciate the performance at leisure above all in cases where fictionality is assured, where there is no possibility of deception (after all, the puppet is itself, like the mask I mentioned earlier, a clear signpost of fictionality), and that, on the other hand, the intensity of fictional immersion seems to depend on the quality of the performance. Still, it is difficult to distinguish between admiration for a performance and fictional immersion, that is to say, empathy for a fictional character.

The second remark that can be drawn from the Bunraku example, which is closely related to the first, is that *very little is needed* for fictional immersion to function. Immersion can be triggered by a slight leaning of the character-puppet's head, or the jerky to-and-fro of his porcelain hand, or a painful twist of his kimono-clad body — all these movements ingeniously arranged by the puppeteer and signifying doubt, fear, or terrible suffering for the poor character. The occasions are often fragmentary and sporadic, but this is enough. Do we find it distracting? Why not? Distraction or entertainment, it depends on the perspective. In the past, Japanese audiences liked to eat and drink while watching Kabuki shows, chatting as well, until the advent of the Western norm that imposed silence. In fact, we are well prepared even before the curtain rises. It is like opera. You know the story by heart; you wait for the right moments to fully invest in this mental role-playing and feel united with the heroine or hero. And once again, there is a good deal to be said for this response. It leaves the eye well rinsed and the belly filled.

## 6. In Conclusion: Fiction and the Body

Performance is related above all to the actor's body. If I propose here a broad sweep of the field of shows and performances in order to rethink fiction and fictionality, it is ultimately in order to highlight this corporeality of fiction, because I wonder if we tend to neglect it in our theories of fiction. We need to start from, and return from time to time to, the *homo fingens*: a human being in possession of a body that plays, wants to play or to pretend, in order to entertain or be admired, to make people laugh, cry, or live another life. It is worth remembering that the use of fiction can be as simple as this.

Fiction with a human face, or rather with a human body, imposes a certain number of limits that condition both the making and receiving of fictional creations. For example, a character may die in a stage or film show, but the actor who plays him does not; we know that his motionless body means death, but that in fact he is only pretending to be dead. This much is obvious. But we should note that this duplicity (dead character/live actor) does not exist in the novel, because the actorial instance is missing. In 'paper' fiction, *everything is taken on symbolically* (the same is true of manga and cartoons, but to a lesser degree). In other words, in the novel, the death of a character does not require any physical effort on the part of the actor (voluntary cessation of breathing, etc.), nor any special effects such as we see in so many films today. This is one of the sources of the audience's admiration, or even wonder. Mock death is just one small example. Consider too the invisible man, or the man flying through the air. The audience is fond of such 'acrobatics', which challenge human physical and intellectual limits.

An actor is not only a biological being but also a social being, with a name and reputation. Hiring an actor influences audience expectations, sometimes determining the very course of the story. If Brad Pitt appears at the beginning of a film, we can be sure that the character he plays will not die soon. This simple fact reveals the insufficiency of intratextual analysis for this kind of fiction. Employing children or animals requires special precautions, especially ethical ones. Furthermore, corporeality is linked to sexuality. In this area, fictions based on visual representations are much less free than written fictions. Thus, via the body of the actor, problems of freedom of expression and censorship take a vivid and concrete form. These are also problems of fiction.

A reconsideration of fiction in the light of *show*, *performance*, and *entertainment* therefore allows us to broaden our view of fiction, enrich our theoretical research, and regain ground that we may tend to neglect.

*Translated from the French by Alison James*

## References

GENETTE, GÉRARD. 1993. *Fiction and Diction*, trans. by Catherine Porter (Ithaca, NY: Cornell University Press)

HASUMI, SHIGEHIKO. 2007. *Aka no Yūwaku* [Red Temptation] (Tokyo: Shinchōsha)

LAVOCAT, FRANÇOISE. 2016. *Fait et fiction: Pour une frontière* (Paris: Seuil)

OURA, YASUSUKE. 2019. 'Some Recent Reflections on Fiction' [in Japanese], in *Le fictif, ou le réel: Mélanges offerts à Yasusuke Oura*, ed. by Akihiro Kubo, Manabu Kawada, and Masahiro Iwamatsu (Kyoto: Yasusuke Oura Retirement Papers Editorial Committee), pp. 233–49

SCHAEFFER, JEAN-MARIE. 2010. *Why Fiction?*, trans. by Dorrit Cohn (Lincoln: University of Nebraska Press)

SEARLE, JOHN R. 1975. 'The Logical Status of Fictional Discourse', *New Literary History* 6 (2): 319–32 <https://doi.org/10.2307/468422>

WALTON, KENDALL L. 1990. *Mimesis as Make-Believe: On the Foundations of the Representational Arts* (Cambridge, MA: Harvard University Press)

PART II

# Changing Minds: Fiction, Beliefs, and Emotion

CHAPTER 4

# The Moral Problem of Fiction: Rethinking the Emotional Effects of Fictional Characters

*Mario Slugan*

*Queen Mary University of London*

Building on the discussion of the paradox of fiction as initially introduced by Colin Radford (1975) and Kendall Walton (1978), this chapter proposes that the existing debates overlook the paradox's moral dimension.[1] Focusing either on its descriptive or normative aspects, commentators have had little to say about why consumers of fiction are regularly more emotionally involved with or care more for fictional characters than for real-life people. Formulated in this way, the moral problem of fiction is linked to the paradox of fiction insofar as they both assume that fictional entities cause genuine emotions. Building on (counter)factualist solutions to the paradox of fiction, and contrary to the jointly most commonly accepted proposals involving quasi-emotions (Walton 1978) or thought theory (Carroll 1990), I suggest that the best way to proceed is to deny (in most but not all cases) the assumption that *fictional entities* are the cause of emotions (be they genuine or quasi). Where I part ways from (counter)factualists, however, is in identifying the objects and causes of emotions. Whereas (counter)factualists claim that we react emotionally to entities who are or could be like the fictional entities depicted, I suggest that we emotionally react to real-life structures such as implausible yet logical possibilities, appearance, representational techniques, investment, and expectations. I conclude with a proposal that there are some emotions that fictional entities do cause — viz. sympathy and antipathy — but that these emotions are characterized by the absence of clearly associated actions.

As originally formulated, the paradox of fiction involves three assertions. Separately they all appear intuitively correct but taken together they cannot hold simultaneously: (1) fictional entities (characters, objects, events, etc.) cause genuine emotions, (2) only entities which we believe truly exist can cause genuine emotions, (3) we do not believe that fictional entities truly exist.[2] The dominant view is that the paradox is not really a paradox, i.e., the proposition (2) is seen as false (Stecker 2011; Friend 2017; Konrad, Petraschka, and Werner 2018; Kroon and Voltolini 2018).

In other words, the generally accepted solution — dubbed the 'thought theory' — is that there are numerous objects and events in whose existence we do not believe but which do cause genuine emotions (Carroll 1990; Gendler 2008). One example includes sexual fantasies which lead to actual emotional arousal. In the case of horror, then, we actually fear the fictional monster lurking in the shadows.

There are, of course, other ways to defuse the paradox.[3] Some scholars deny (3). Samuel Taylor Coleridge (1817) proposed that consumers willingly suspend their disbelief when engaging fictional entities. More recently, David B. Suits (2006) has argued that because it is ordinarily possible to believe both $p$ and not-$p$ it is also possible to believe in fictional objects and events while at the same time also not believing in them. A larger minority reject (1). Walton (1978, 1990, 1997), most notably, maintains that fictional objects and events cause only make-believe or quasi emotions which should be characterized as distinct from emotions that we experience in real-life situations. Regardless of the solution to the paradox, the underlying concern for most of those engaged in the debate is that in our engagement with fiction the fictional entities (whether we believe them or not) do cause emotions of one type or another (genuine or quasi). But what if, as the (counter)factualists have suggested, it is not fictional entities that cause these emotions, or, at the very least they do so in far more limited cases than previously thought? And, even more importantly, what if the focus on the epistemological aspect of the paradox precludes us from recognizing its more pressing moral dimension?

## 1. The Moral Dimension of the Paradox

It is undeniable that morality comes into play in discussions of puzzles and paradoxes of imagination and the arts. The puzzle of imaginative resistance often revolves around the difficulty to imagine 'morally deviant' fictional worlds such as the one in which murdering people is the right thing to do if they are causing a traffic jam (Hume 1857; Weatherson 2004, 1). There also exists a large literature on the role of imagination and the arts in moral persuasion (for overviews see Eaton 2015; Liao and Gendler 2019). The reasons why we sympathize with morally otiose characters such as Tony Soprano (James Gandolfini) from *The Sopranos* (HBO, 1999–2007) when in real-life such characters would be deplored have also been discussed at length (Carroll 2004; Smith 2011; Slugan 2019). But when it comes to the paradox of fiction, scholars identify only its descriptive and normative dimension (cf. Friend 2017). Whereas the descriptive question asks whether emotions induced by fictional entities are of the same type as those elicited by real-life structures, the normative concern relates to whether emotions induced by fictional entities are somehow inappropriate.

Importantly, neither the descriptive nor the normative question has a moral dimension. Descriptive concerns, clearly, deal only with categorization. But even the normative question understands the (in)appropriateness in terms of subjective rationality or justification (Radford 1975), rather than morality. Under this framework, an emotion is justified if it is appropriate to the evidence of the situation. If I have good reason to believe that my friend has betrayed me, my anger is justified. But if it turns out that there was no betrayal, I would no longer be justified in being angry at her. Similarly, if a colleague tells me a tragic story of his sister and elicits my pity, but then reveals that in fact he does not have a sister, I would be unjustified in pitying his sister because she does not exist. According to Radford, emotions induced by fictional entities are precisely of this type — unjustified — because they do not have an appropriate object.

I propose that there is a moral dimension to the paradox which has garnered virtually no attention in these discussions. I refer to the phenomenon where consumers of fictions appear to care about fictional entities far more deeply than about real-life people and events. A cursory online search of the subject reveals numerous threads on online fora such as Quora or Reddit which tackle questions such as 'why do I prefer fictional characters over real people?', 'why do I have no empathy for real people only fictional characters?', and 'does anyone else feel empathy for fictional characters but practically zero for people?'[4] The widely reported teen infatuation with the vampire protagonist of *The Twilight Saga* (2008–2012), Edward Cullen (Robert Pattinson), also fits this bill.

To get a better understanding of how deep these emotions can run and how much more involving they can be than engagement with real-life tragedies, I wish to first offer my own experience of watching *Game of Thrones* (HBO, 2011–2019) as anecdotal evidence.[5] In episode 8 of season 4 — 'Mountain and the Viper' — Tyrion Lannister (Peter Dinklage) awaits trial by combat after Oberyn Martell, known as the Viper (Pedro Pascal), has volunteered to serve as his champion against Lord Gregor, the titular Mountain (Hafþór Júlíus Björnsson). Oberyn has the upper hand throughout the combat but, once he knocks out Gregor, instead of finishing him off he demands a confession for a previous crime. Gregor uses this opportunity to get a hold of Oberyn and crushes Oberyn's skull with his bare hands. Tyrion, in turn, is sentenced to death and the episode ends.

I remember I was so upset about this that I could not come to grips with what had happened for a whole week (until the next episode when the narrative took a different turn). And I recollect trying to come to terms with how shaken up I was — for I could not recall the last time something had unnerved me this much. Crucially, this 'something' involved real-life events. Certainly, not even reports about Daesh's war crimes at the time of the episode's original screening — the summer of 2014 — came close to disturbing me as much. In this context the problem is surely primarily moral rather than epistemological — how can I be so disturbed by this fictional event and yet care so little about factual contemporary atrocities by comparison?

Now, the example is clearly anecdotal and could be dismissed merely as evidence of an antisocial personality disorder. Yet, I would argue that being afflicted by the suffering of fictional characters more than by that of flesh and blood people is a regular occurrence. Consider the fate of your favourite fictional character and compare the intensity of your resulting emotion to what you feel when you, say, meet a homeless person on the street. Or think of how often you have cried about some news report as opposed to when watching your favourite melodrama. That you have cried even once over a fictional fate such as the perishing of Lee's (Casey Affleck) children in a fire due to his negligence in *Manchester by the Sea* (Kenneth Lonergan, 2016) while having not cried at least one time when you see reports of real-life tragic losses of life in the Mediterranean Sea or Syria should be enough to raise the moral dimension of the paradox. It should also discount the talk of antisocial personality disorder in my anecdotal case or, alternatively, indicate that all who standardly engage with fiction suffer from it.

Phrased in a more formal way and building on premise 1): x) most consumers of fiction have at least once had an intensive emotional response (hatred, infatuation, crying, etc.) to a fictional entity, y) most consumers of fiction have at least once *not* had an intensive emotional response to real-life people facing tragedies, z) it follows that some consumers of fiction are more emotionally involved with fictional entities than with real-life people.

The problem which I dub the moral problem of fiction (MPF henceforth) can be formulated as follows:

> (A) We should be more emotionally invested in real-life entities than fictional ones.
>
> (B) We are regularly more emotionally invested in fictional entities than real-life ones.

As we can see the MPF takes a different slant than the normative aspect of the paradox of fiction. The MPF is not about the justification of emotions but about the comparison to real-life emotional responses. Whereas in the discussion of normativity the emotional response appears to be irrational, in the MPF the emotion's intensity trumps what would be fitting for an emotional response to a real-life entity. In the MPF it is not that the emotional response is inappropriate in Radford's sense but that it is scandalous that there is an emotional response for a fictional entity (Lee's children) when there is little or none for a comparable real-life entity (actual child victims of fires).[6] In other words, to defuse this problem it will not help us to argue contra Radford by identifying how emotional responses to fictional entities might be rational after all or how different justifications might apply to fictional as opposed to real-life emotions (for overviews see Friend 2017; Liao and Gendler 2019). Rather, I propose that the solution is to deny (B). Allow me to sketch out the idea on the *Game of Thrones* example first.

It was clear to me that I was not concerned with Oberyn's fate: it was the effect that his death had on Tyrion — the fact that this amounts to his death sentence — that had me all up in knots. But then I started wondering: is it really Tyrion that I fear for, or is something else bothering me here? Tyrion was clearly my favourite character in the show and with him out of the picture I would no longer enjoy the show nearly as much. His jokes and cynical remarks, such as 'All dwarfs are bastards in their fathers' eyes', were a constant source of delight and amusement. From this perspective, what is really making an emotional effect on me is the possibility that I will no longer derive pleasure from the show — for there will no longer be a vehicle for delivering lines of the above type — rather than fretting for a fictional character's life. Similarly, I have also invested a substantial amount of time in the show for it not to keep paying off. The fact that I have recast my emotional engagement in this way — as an investment of time and an expectation of a specific type of pleasure — disarms the MPF because I am not actually emotionally involved with the fictional Tyrion, but with real-life structures.

The general idea of this paper, then, is that it is possible to take the above line of reasoning and apply it to the paradox of fiction. In other words, it is possible to circumvent the classic solution to the paradox of fiction — denying (2) — in such a way that what our emotions pertain to are not fictional characters but real-life structures, including the investment of time or narrative expectations. Moreover, once we recognize the existence of the MPF we have a novel (and more pressing) incentive to solve the paradox of fiction which goes beyond epistemological concerns. At the same time, my position differs from that of the (counter)factualists who claim that there are no occasions when we emotionally engage fictional entities (Weston 1975; Paskins 1977; Charlton 1984, 1986; McCormick 1988). In other words, what I do claim is that numerous classic examples in these discussions can be rearticulated as pertaining to different real-life structures. In other words, this is more about arguing that the paradox of fiction can oftentimes be sidestepped than about arguing what the solution to the paradox is. Put in yet another way, I am more interested in trying to articulate the phenomenological experience of the varied causes and objects of emotions in engaging fiction and the accompanying moral problem (after all, the personal anecdotal evidence I return to so much has been the original impetus for this piece), than in proceeding by way of eliminating specific premises constituting the paradox of fiction (1, 2, or 3).

## 2. Not Fearing Fictions

Kendall Walton's slime and Charles, its fearful spectator, offers itself as the first case-study on which to test the idea.[7] According to Walton's famous example, when Charles, a stand-in for the standard spectator, watches a horror film and is faced with a green slime on screen, he fears the monster: 'His muscles are tensed, he clutches his chair, his pulse quickens, his adrenalin flows. Let us call this physiological/psychological state "quasi-fear"' (1978: 6). The fact that Walton speaks of quasi-emotions, as explained above, and denies (1) rather than (2), should not worry us because the point here is to sidestep the paradox rather than to probe its standard solutions. In other words, I propose that Charles does not fear the slime at all (genuinely or quasi) but a real-life structure instead. Interestingly, Walton briefly addresses the possibility that Charles' fear is about real-life matters and not of the slime:

> If Charles is a child, the movie may make him wonder whether there might not be real slimes or other exotic horrors like the one depicted in the movie, even if he fully realizes that the movie-slime itself is not real. Charles may well fear these suspected actual dangers; he might have nightmares about them for days afterwards (*Jaws* caused a lot of people to fear sharks which they thought might

really exist. But whether they were afraid of the fictional sharks in the movie is another question). (Walton 1978: 10)

This is his only reference to the solution and Walton dismisses the option as quickly as he introduces it. I, however, do not think that he is right in eliminating the explanation as a fringe phenomenon. In fact, it seems to me that standard monster horror films, the subgenre from which Walton takes his example, hinge precisely on this type of reaction for their emotional effects. Consider the subgenre's typical bipartite structure — before and after the monster's full reveal — and the three broad ways — suspense, surprise, and appearance — in which the fear of the monster may be generated.[8]

The structural pivot around which most monster horrors revolve is usually what Carroll (1990) refers to as onset while I prefer to call it the full reveal of the monster.[9] The first part usually rests on building up suspense and fearful expectations in preparation for the revelation of the monster by showing the signs of the monster here and there. This can be done by a range of techniques — use of negative space, character blocking, underexposure, shadows, atypical movement, tight framing, camera movement, shot prolongation, ominous sounds and music, infrasound, etc. Crucially, the monster will eventually be revealed in full. As guides for writing horror films suggest (Blake and Bailey 2014; Bell 2020), once the monster has finally fully revealed itself, precisely because the spectator now knows what the monster she was fearing is and how it looks and sounds, the general fear levels seem to drop off and different fear-inducing strategies need to be deployed in the subsequent part of the film. Building suspense at this point can only go so far and strategies usually change to eliciting fear by surprise or by appearance (visual and audio alike).[10]

To flesh out this bipartite structure and the threefold fear-inducing strategy, let us briefly consider the short film *Lights Out* (David F. Sandberg, 2013).[11] In the first part of the film, the protagonist turns the light on and off a couple of times because each time it is off a silhouette appears at the end of her corridor. She stops this when, in a partially revealing jump scare (followed by a discordant sound to keep the unease), the being abruptly appears only a foot away from her but now with its back turned to the camera. Once the protagonist retires to bed (with her corridor and bed light on), the suspense continues with the play of approaching off-screen sounds, the switching off of the light in the corridor, her bedroom doors creaking, and her bed light slowly losing power. Trembling, she manages to fix the bed light, the light returns to the corridor as well, and she sighs with relief, but it is all just to make the finale more potent — a jump scare cut to a close-up of the fully revealed monster with the light switch in its fingers. Again, the discordant sound plays, and the light goes out...

I propose that until the full reveal, the fear elicited is not of some fictional monster partially visible only in the dark but rather of an implausible yet logical possibility that something like this might be lurking somewhere in the real world. That monsters might indeed exist. That something horrendous like this might happen. That one day we might be in a situation of this sort. What films of this type do is, I suggest, to tap into a scientifically irrational, but strictly speaking not illogical fear that there are dark stones left unturned. Suspense of the reveal, then, is really about the miniscule possibility that the world is not free of monsters after all. In the end, there is no logical reason why something like the being from *Lights Out* could not exist in the real world. Perhaps we have simply not come across it hitherto.

Once the monster in *Lights Out* is fully revealed, the object of fear is again better described as one of real-life structures rather than that of the fictional monster. First, the reveal itself is frightening precisely because it hinges on the representational suddenness of the jump scare rather than on the nature of the fictional being. There is a loud noise, something jumps onto the screen. As numerous horrors demonstrate, the subject of the jump scare need not be frightening in itself. So long as it is unexpected it will work. This is the shock quality of the manner of representation rather than of what is represented.

Of course, in this particular instance the shot is a reveal of the monster — the camera lingers on for a moment and allows us to take in its visual appearance, a woman-like figure with blank eyes where pupil and iris should be, wide open mouth, and sharp teeth. As such, it is precisely what Walton had in mind when discussing the slime — the moment the spectator faces the frightful being. But again, there is no reason to say that what is frightening is the fictional monster. Rather, we can say that what is frightening is primarily what Walton (1990) would call the prop in the game of make-believe that is fiction. We are afraid of the *appearance* of the person made up to look like they have blank eyes and sharp-looking teeth — the prop — rather than of the make-believe monster who is about to murder its victim. In this case, our fear arises from the uneasy feeling that something is almost human but not quite (certainly the case in contemporary zombie films). Many times, fictions can also capitalize on other hardwired phobias such as those of snakes and spiders or, in the audio domain, of shrieking sounds.

What is the upshot of arguing that we fear real-life structures rather than fictional entities beyond sidestepping the paradox of fiction and not running afoul of the MPF? First, the offered explanation deals with at least three types of the *fear of* in monster horrors — what is coming next (suspense), jump scares (surprise), and props (appearance). By contrast, Walton (and most of the participants in the debate) tackle only the appearance type of *fear of*. (In fact, as can be seen from the discussion of Tyrion, my explanation also covers *fear for* a fictional character.) Moreover, Walton would not deny that the jump scares work on the level of how something is represented rather than what is represented. And there are also techniques such as shrieking sounds which elicit immediate fear responses. So, if there is at least one type of *fear of* in monster horrors which is undeniably due to real-life structures, I propose that an account which rests solely on real-life structures is theoretically simpler and more elegant than the one which needs to deal with fictional entities.

Admittedly, I have explained the suspense type of *fear of* with recourse to implausible yet logical hypotheticals — what if something like the depicted monster actually exists? Although I have referred to this in terms of real-life structures, hypotheticals are imaginings as much as imaginings involved in fictional engagement. In other words, why prefer one solution over the other if both involve imaginings? Because this is a better description of what the phenomenological experience of the object of fear is in monster horror than the one offered by Walton. This brings me to the second upshot of this analysis. It reveals that the essence of monster horrors is not the fear of fictional monsters but the irrational fear for oneself. Irrational here is meant not in Radford's sense of normativity, but in the sense that contrary to standard evidence we still cling on to the implausible yet logical possibility, dramatized by horrors, that monsters might exist and that we might encounter them. After all, why are people afraid to turn the lights off even after the monster film has ended? They must be afraid of some horrific real-life possibility rather than the fictional monster from the film.

The last upshot of this account is that it explains the structure of the monster horror genre. If we feared the monster because of its fictional nature rather than its prop-like qualities, then once the monster is fully revealed — as a slime, ghost nun, zombie, etc. — it is reasonable to assume that we should fear it even more given that now we know its horrifying nature and what it is capable of. But that does not seem to be the case. Usually, the moment of unveiling is as anticlimactic as it is climactic precisely because thereafter, we know what it is that we were anticipating. Once the focus shifts from the monster to the protagonist after the full reveal, and what Carroll refers to as confrontation is being set up, we do not fear the monster during that period. But arguably, we are still supposed to imagine a monster on the loose and, given its nature, we should still be afraid of it even if the film is presently not focused either on it or its signs. If it were the nature of the monster that frightens us, simply entertaining in imagination that it has proved itself threatening should keep us scared. But in the absence of screen time, i.e., where fear-generating strategies are missing, make-believing the monster alone does not suffice to scare us. This demonstrates that it is not the fictional entity that we fear but real-life structures evoked by the aforementioned strategies.[12] This is also why looking away and shutting our eyes during the projection temporarily rids us of fear.

It is worth pausing here for a moment and fleshing this out further with the help of Carroll's definition of art-horror. According to him, we are art-horrified by a monster if and only if our state of agitation has been caused by the thought that the monster is possible and that it is threatening and impure (Carroll 1990: 27). Given that art-horror is different from fear for Carroll and that for horror impurity plays a vital role, we can bracket off the notions of art-horror and impurity. This allows us to say that we fear a fictional monster if and only if our state of agitation has been caused by the thought that the monster is possible and that it is threatening. My point is that following the full reveal we keep imagining (a subset of thinking) the monster's possibility and its threatening nature, yet this does not cause us to fear. This suggests that it is not the fictional monster that is scaring us but the fear-inducing strategies. Crucially, these strategies — suspense, surprise, and appearance — all boil down to real-life structures.

We can formalize the argument as follows:

1) The fictional monster in horror is a specific content of imagination,

2) The fictional monster in horror either causes quasi-fear (Walton 1978) or fear (Carroll 1990),

3) From 1) and 2) it follows that in horror it is the specific content of imagination that causes either quasi-fear or fear,

4) Yet, in horror, the specific content of imagination on its own neither causes quasi-fear nor fear,

5) From 3) and 4) it follows that the fictional monster in horror neither causes quasi-fear nor fear,

6) Yet, horror causes either quasi-fear or fear,

7) In horror it is either the fictional monster that causes quasi-fear or fear or it is the real-life structures (suspense, surprise, and appearance) that cause fear,

8) From 6), 7), and 8) it follows that in horror it is the real-life structures that cause fear.

## 3. Generalizations

Can these claims about real-life structures as both causes and objects of emotions be applied more generally outside of horror and the emotion of fear?

The example that has commanded the most attention in discussions of this sort is, of course, Anna Karenina. Although the majority view today is that we do feel for the fictional character Anna, in the past it has been argued that we feel for some real-life structures instead. Barrie Paskins (1977) and William Charlton (1984, 1986) proposed that we have feelings towards people who are or could be like Anna. Michael Weston (1975) and Peter McCormick (1988) suggested variants of the view that feelings are due to general truths about life that issue from the works. These views purport to be general solutions to the paradox of fiction so only one counterexample is enough to disqualify them (cf. Yanal 1999). Indeed, sympathy with Tony Soprano undermines Paskins's and Charlton's position because were there somebody like Tony Soprano in real life, we would not sympathize with him. The issue here is that the emotions towards the fictional Tony and the hypothetical real-life Tony are quite different — sympathy and opprobrium, respectively. Sympathy for the fictional Tony is also a problem for Weston and McCormick because this sympathy can hardly be because of some general truth *The Sopranos* convey, whatever that might be. In fact, my analysis of fear also presents a challenge to their formulations. Fearing surprises like jump scares and appearances like props are neither to do with people who are or could be like the green slime, nor about general truths. And fearing for Tyrion is about something else altogether: expectations and time investment.

Although (counter)factualists' claims cannot be generalized to all fictional emotions, this does not mean that (counter)factualists are incorrect when it comes to examples like Anna. Radford's insistence that it is *her* that we pity and not somebody else (who might be) like her is not a problem because, under Paskins' account, to pity *Anna* is precisely to pity somebody (who might be) like her.

At the same time, we should be careful with somewhat different examples. I have already mentioned the infatuation with Edward Cullen. Being smitten by a character like Edward Cullen, I propose, is better described as obsessing about, however far-fetched, the possibility that somebody as good-looking and gentle, yet at the same time exciting and dangerous might come into our teenage life. But this is neither about a real-life truth nor about an actual person like Edward.[13] Unlike with horror where all consumers are supposed to fear the monster, all audiences are merely supposed to sympathize with Edward, rather than be infatuated with him. Infatuation is only a reaction common to one subsection of the audience — teenage girls. In other words, neither (counter)factualist nor other solutions of the paradox of fiction, have much to say about reactions which are not intended for all, but constitute fairly typical reactions for subsections of the audience (e.g., teenage girls).

## 4. Conclusion

Despite my best efforts to the contrary, it remains the case that it is difficult to deny (1) completely. Sympathy or antipathy towards fictional characters are emotions which are difficult to rearticulate as real-life structures. In other words, on top of wise-cracking remarks which can be enjoyed on the level of their non-fictional content, as demonstrated by their publication in an illustrated book form as *The Wit & Wisdom of Tyrion Lannister*, I think it is correct to say that I was genuinely harbouring positive emotional dispositions towards Tyrion as a fictional character, i.e., as a make-believe structure. Although I was not genuinely afraid *for* Tyrion or upset that *he* might die, I think it is fair to say that I like *Tyrion*. Although we have provided a more precise account of the object of emotions in Charles's and some other key cases, the paradox of fiction appears to persist.

But this does not mean there has not been any headway on the matter. There is something in common among the emotions whose objects we have identified as real-life structures as opposed to the ones whose objects remain fictional entities — the existence of clearly associated actions, i.e., behavioural responses. In real-life contexts, whereas emotions regularly involve objects (cf. Friend 2010), only some emotions entail typical actions.[14] Fear, for instance, entails flight (from the object) or fight (with the object). Pitying somebody regularly generates helping him or her. Aggressive behaviour towards the object typically accompanies hatred. Standard action accompanying infatuation is seeking closeness to the object. By contrast, sympathy and antipathy lack clearly associated actions. The emotions entail feeling generally positively or negatively inclined towards the object, respectively, but do not specify a clear action issuing therefrom. We may give a person who we sympathize with a thumbs up or frown at the person we feel antipathy for, but these are hardly clearly defined action types as above. Moreover, in cases of sympathy and empathy no action at all is also a perfectly typical behavioural response.

We might say, then, that the emotions elicited by real-life structure, unlike the ones induced by fictional entities, have a strong and clear action potential insofar they have a clearly associated behavioural reaction with them. This chimes well with one of the main traits of fictional entities — their general dissociation from behavioural effects. If fictional entities generally do not have behavioural effects, it is reasonable that fictional entities would only generate emotions which have no clearly associated actions. Conversely, it would also make sense that fictional entities do not generate emotions which have clearly associated actions. Similarly, only real-life structures should generate emotions which have clear behavioural reactions (although they can also generate emotions without clearly associated actions).[15] And this is precisely the result that the above analysis of fictional monsters and characters produces. In other words, we could hypothesize that fictions generate only a subclass of emotions related to real-life structures — those without clearly associated actions.

What remains is the status of the MPF. The emotions elicited by real-life structures identified here — fear, infatuation, hatred, pity — are also of higher intensity than those elicited by fictional entities — sympathy and antipathy. This looks promising for the MPF for it is how *much* we care that is at stake. At the same time, both sympathy and antipathy might be said to cause the MPF if emotions towards real-life people are of lower intensity or non-existent. It is possible to have more sympathy for Tyrion than for, say, a deserving local troubled youngster. In this case we might want to say that the problem is not really MPF but a *pathological* issue in the sense that our normal reaction to *real-life people* should be stronger. The MPF is really about the fact that even when we *normally* react to real-life structures, it is still the case that the *normal* reaction to fiction is more intense than to real-life structures, which seems scandalous. Whatever its solution might be, I hope this article has demonstrated that the MPF is ripe for exploration and that it may also help us rethink the paradox of fiction.

# References

BELL, NEAL. 2020. *How to Write a Horror Movie* (New York: Routledge)

BLAKE, MARC, and SARA BAILEY. 2013. *Writing the Horror Movie* (London: Bloomsbury)

CARROLL, NOËL. 1990. *The Philosophy of Horror: Or, Paradoxes of the Heart* (New York: Routledge)

———. 2004. 'Sympathy for the Devil', in *The Sopranos and Philosophy*, ed. by Richard Greene and Peter Vernezze (Chicago: Open Court), pp. 121–36

CHARLTON, WILLIAM. 1984. 'Feeling for the Fictitious', *The British Journal of Aesthetics* 24 (3): 206–16

———. 1986. 'Radford and Allen on Being Moved by Fiction: A Rejoinder', *The British Journal of Aesthetics*, 26.4: 39–394

COLERIDGE, SAMUEL TAYLOR. 1817. *Biographiae Litteraria; Or Biographical Sketches of My Literary Life and Opinions* (London: S. Curtis)

EATON, ANNE WESCOTT. 2015. 'Literature and Morality', in *The Routledge Companion to Philosophy of Literature*, ed. by Noël Carroll and John Gibson (New York: Routledge), pp. 433–50

FRIEND, STACIE. 2017. 'Fiction and Emotion', in *The Routledge Handbook of Philosophy of Imagination*, ed. by Amy Kind (New York: Routledge), pp. 217–29

GENDLER, TAMAR SZABÓ. 2008. 'Alief in Action (and Reaction)', *Mind and Language* 23(5): 552–85

HUME, DAVID. 1757. 'Of the Standard of Taste', in *The Philosophical Works of David Hume*, ed. by T. H. Green and T. H. Grose, 4 vols (London: Longman, Green), vol. 4, pp. 1874–75

KONRAD, EVA-MARIA, THOMAS PETRASCHKA, and CHRISTIANA WERNER. 2018. 'The

Paradox of Fiction — A Brief Introduction into Recent Developments, Open Questions, and Current Areas of Research, including a Comprehensive Bibliography from 1975 to 2018', *Journal of Literary Theory*, 12 (2): 193–203

KROON, FRED and ALBERTO VOLTOLINI. 2019. 'Fiction', in *The Stanford Encyclopedia of Philosophy*, ed. by Edward N. Zalta. Accessed 11 June 2022. <https://plato.stanford.edu/archives/win2019/entries/fiction>

LIAO, SHEN-YI and GENDLER, TAMAR. 2019. 'Imagination', *The Stanford Encyclopedia of Philosophy*, ed. by Edward N. Zalta. Accessed 11 June 2022. <https://plato.stanford.edu/archives/win2019/entries/imagination/>

LEVINSON, JERROLD. 1997. 'Emotion in Response to Art: A Survey of the Terrain', in *Emotion and the Arts*, ed. by Mette Hjort and Sue Laver (Oxford: Oxford University Press), pp. 20–34

McCORMICK, PETER J. 1988. *Fictions, Philosophies, and the Problems of Poetics* (Ithaca, NY: Cornell University Press)

PASKINS, BARRIE. 1977. 'On Being Moved by Anna Karenina and *Anna Karenina*', *Philosophy*, 52 (201): 344–47

RADFORD, COLIN. 1975. 'How Can We Be Moved by the Fate of Anna Karenina?', *Proceedings of the Aristotelian Society, Supplementary Volumes*, 49: 67–80

SLUGAN, MARIO. 2019. *Noël Carroll and Film: A Philosophy of Art and Popular Culture* (London: Bloomsbury)

SMITH, MURRAY. 2011. 'Just What Is It That Makes Tony Soprano Such an Appealing, Attractive Murderer?', in *Ethics at the Cinema*, ed. by Ward Jones and Samantha Vice (Oxford: Oxford University Press), pp. 66–90

STECKER, ROBERT. 2011. 'Should We Still Care about the Paradox of Fiction?', *The British Journal of Aesthetics*, 51 (3): 295–308

SUITS, DAVID B. 2006. 'Really Believing in Fiction', *Pacific Philosophical Quarterly*, 87 (3): 369–86

WALTON, KENDALL L. 1978. 'Fearing Fictions', *The Journal of Philosophy*, 75 (1): 5–27

———. 1990. *Mimesis as Make-Believe: On the Foundations of the Representational Arts* (Cambridge, MA: Harvard University Press)

———. 1997. 'Spelunking, Simulation, and Slime', in *Emotion and the Arts*, ed. by Mette Hjort and Sue Laver (Oxford: Oxford University Press) pp. 37–49

WEATHERSON, BRIAN. 2004. 'Morality, Fiction, and Possibility', *Philosophers' Imprint* 4 (3): 1–27

WESTON, MICHAEL. 1975. 'How Can We Be Moved by the Fate of Anna Karenina?', *Proceedings of the Aristotelian Society, Supplementary Volumes*, 49: 81–93

YANAL, ROBERT J. 1999. *Paradoxes of Emotion and Fiction* (University Park, PA: Penn State Press)

## Notes to Chapter 4

1. This work has been supported in part by the Croatian Science Foundation under the project UIP-2020-02-1309.
2. I distinguish between fiction (which I use as a shorthand for a fictional work of art) and fictional entities. In this sense, fiction is a real-life material object part of the content of which are fictional entities.
3. For a more detailed overview going beyond the tripartite taxonomy of which the premise is denied see Levinson (1997).
4. <https://www.quora.com/Why-do-I-have-no-empathy-for-real-people-only-fictional-characters>; <https://www.quora.com/Why-do-I-prefer-fictional-characters-over-real-people>; <https://wrongplanet.net/forums/viewtopic.php?t=166190>; <https://www.reddit.com/r/sociopath/comments/6pawqo/does_anyone_else_feel_empathy_for_fictional/>.

5. The point is to illustrate the problem with one (personal) example and then draw attention to the fact that this experience is quite common. After all, the discussion of the paradox of fiction in terms of its three premises also starts from what we *personally* experience as intuitively correct. The personal example could have easily been transformed into a third person account such as Walton's 'Charles', but this merely clothes what are regularly arguments starting from personal intuitions into academically more acceptable frames.
6. It is undeniable that the presentation of these entities is crucial for actual effects on media consumers as opposed to what they ought to be. But this does not disarm the underlying *moral* demand: irrespective of how somebody's suffering is presented, the *fact* of somebody's suffering *should* suffice for strong emotional involvement. To focus briefly on two nonfictional representations, whether we are watching a ninety-minute documentary focusing on a single person or a five-second report citing death statistics, both presentations give sufficient information about suffering which *should* bring about the same level of emotional involvement. The *moral* paradox is that they do not appear to do so. To get to the moral paradox of fiction, we simply need to replace a documentary with a fiction film in this example.
7. The other obvious example is the pity for Anna Karenina which I discuss in the following section.
8. The other important fear in horror films is fear *for* the protagonist. I have already discussed how fear for fictional characters can be articulated when discussing the example of Tyrion so will not address it further.
9. The reason is that whereas his interest is primarily in the plot structure, mine is in the relation of the plot and the fear-inducing strategies.
10. To discuss suspense as one way of inducing fear and horror is coherent with Carroll's view (1990) that suspense on its own is a different emotion than horror.
11. <https://www.youtube.com/watch?v=FUQhNGEu2KA>. Accessed 11 July 2022.
12. I believe this also explains why the horror genre is among the most challenging to execute successfully. So much of its effect rests on the revelation of the monster but once it is revealed, it is difficult to keep the audience afraid.
13. For Yanal this is because no real-life person could be a vampire. Under my irrational hypotheticals framework, the fact that not all fictional characters have real counterparts does not pose a problem.
14. I would like to thank Anna Abraham for drawing my attention to this.
15. That there is a clear associated action does not mean that the action has to be executed, just that there is a potential for one. Under this framework, frequenting instead of running away from horror films is no more mysterious than riding roller coasters instead of avoiding them — they both present fear-inducing real-life structures.

CHAPTER 5

# Luscianic Fictions and the Rise of Unbelief

*Nicolas Correard*

Université de Nantes

This article relies on the following assumption: that there is a strong relationship between 'interpreting' the world and 'changing' it, contrary to what Karl Marx implied in his famous eleventh *Thesis on Feuerbach*: 'The philosophers have only interpreted the world in various ways; the point, however, is to change it.' To use Marx himself as an example, Marxism's new interpretation of work did, in fact, contribute greatly to changing and improving the conditions of work in the nineteenth and twentieth centuries.[1] Now that his theories are quite neglected, we can feel the difference, and can assess the link between certain ideas and 'realities', between the fortune and decline of some intellectual trends and the state of contemporary social forces, whatever the cause and the effect may be. Not that Marxist philosophy was true *per se* — in fact, its materialistic framework was somewhat misleading. The point is rather that by showing the mechanism of social domination underpinning capitalist economy, it caused major shifts in the world's political balance. But should we extend this idea from the intellectual world, and theories in general, to 'fictions' as giving 'versions of the world' (to quote Nelson Goodman's expression [1978]), and more especially to *literary fictions*?

The case is complex because the cultural weight of literary fiction has always been relative: it is no longer what it used to be before the rise of mass media, cinematographic fictions, or Internet culture. This may account for the fact that we do not believe *any more* in the power of *literary* fictions to change the world. It is, however, worth noting that the cultural weight of literary fiction was also quite limited during the period predating the American and French Revolutions, and not only because of the limits of literacy. Contrary to more established genres, novels were generally considered mere *pastimes* by serious voices, including humanist intellectuals, and they were considered as such in all recognised poetics of the time — if they were mentioned at all. 'Invented to entertain the lazy ones', the *fainéants* ('do-nothings'), judged Furetière, though a novelist himself, when he wrote the entry 'Roman' ('novel') of his *Dictionnaire universel* (1690: 283). How could literary fictions change the world by any means in the time of *Don Quixote*, which seems to deride idealistic postures? Literary fictions may give a special type of pleasure, they may answer a deep and natural anthropological need to feed the imagination, as Pierre-Daniel Huet reckoned in his *Traité de l'origine des romans* (1678); but precisely so because they drive their readers out of the world, enabling them to escape from reality. This would be the common-sense answer. We may add that the idea of *changing* the world was quite alien to *Ancien Régime* mentalities; and when occurrences can be found, they are not positive ones, generally speaking. Changing the world was not something to wish for in the politics and political thought of pre-democratic societies, and when reforms were pleaded for (we might think for instance of religious Reforms), it was generally on behalf of a 'return' to original purity (for instance to the purity of the primitive Church that had been corrupted).

Yet, we will uphold the paradox that some types of literary fictions, though read by a limited number of people, *did matter* in some world changes that occurred from the Renaissance to the Enlightenment. But we need to put forth a methodological *caveat*: causal relationships between social forces and cultural products, particularly fictions, are not easy to trace, because there is much more than a dual relationship at stake; it is rather an interaction in which nothing like a mechanistic causality can be expected. Of course, it is not *because* young desperate men read *Werther* that they committed suicide, even though there is a probable relationship between the fiction of suicide and the epidemic thereof. Similarly, any criteria about what mattered *more* are very elusive. What mattered more in the change in women's status and behaviours in French society between the world wars and in the post-war period? The employment of women in the workforce during World War I, the advent of washing machines in the 1950s, changes in the legal system, or the novels of Colette and Sagan? Are fictions just *signs* of a transformation, or are they a significant *force* in a conundrum, if not a driving one? And who are we to judge? This is the task of the historian, not of the literary critic.

But, as literary critics, we have to recognise that fictions are embedded in cultural *and* social change in a way that is very difficult to track, like the interaction between particles at a subatomic scale. Nobody would doubt that Black American jazz musicians and artists, as much as Black American athletes, changed the image of Black people in twentieth-century North America, undermining old stereotypes about the *negro*. But shall we say that Toni Morrison mattered as much for the Black cause as Martin Luther King, or Michael Jackson, or Barack Obama? Fictions probably play a subtler role, a more complex one. Their effects may be *invisible* but real, absolutely *unspectacular* but deep. It would be naïve to think that in order to avoid global warming, it is more urgent to produce eco-fictions and post-apocalyptic novels, than to enforce new fiscal policies. But it would be equally naïve to think that new fiscal policies could be enforced without a deep change in representations. The case of the global ecological disaster looming is even more difficult to envision because we do not even know if eco-fiction and eco-friendly fiscal policies combined may still change anything at this stage — but we have no other choice than to believe it and to act accordingly.

## 1. The Reception of Lucian and the History of Ideas: A Connection to be Made

We shall now turn to what might be considered a matter of sheer literary erudition, but which in fact involves a major cultural change in early modern Europe. We will argue that the rediscovery of an Ancient Greek author of fictions, Lucian of Samosata (c.125–80 CE), the main representative of a specific brand of satire called Menippean satire, was an important phenomenon supporting the rise of religious unbelief in Renaissance Europe, and throughout early modern times. Lucian was both extremely popular and polemical during early modern times. Polemical, because as the Byzantine compilation known as *Suda* puts it, 'he spared neither gods nor men'. The question of his influence has long been raised, but most studies remain short-sighted (particularly Lauvergnat Gagnière 1988). Because various sectors of Lucianic literature have been studied independently, recurrence remains in the shadows and certain connections are still waiting to be made. And this is all the truer of the connections between literary texts and the history of ideas. While literary studies focus on reception and imitation without paying much attention to the historical context, historians of ideas have largely neglected texts which do not fit with what we expect from a philosophical debate (i.e., argumentation, logic, transparency).[2] Even if the history of irreligion has recently taken a hermeneutical turn, resorting to the analysis of veiled meaning (Staquet 2013) in the wake of Jean-Pierre Cavaillé's research on the practice of dis/simulation and the limits of acceptable discourse (see for instance Cavaillé 2016), the specific contribution of complex literary forms remains largely understated.[3]

Lucian was generally considered the arch-enemy of religious superstition in Antiquity, and the prototype of the *atheon*:[4] he derided the pantheon in his burlesque Olympian fictions (notably *Zeus Tragedian; Zeus Refuted; The Assembly of Gods*), in which a ridiculous Zeus proves unable to manage the rabble of gods and cannot even answer men's questions, thus ruining the idea of divine providence. Lucian poked fun at the belief in the underworld in his *Dialogues of the Dead*, while he parodied literary *katabasis*, necromantic rituals and mystery cults in other narratives of travels below. He laughed at those who believed in ghosts, resurrections, and supernatural events in his *Philopseudes*; he carped at religious cults in some declamatory pieces (*On Sacrifices* and *Of Mourning*), pointing to the vanity of prayers; he wrote two fictional biographies of real religious leaders (the *Alexander* and the *Peregrinus*), in order to expose their imposture. At some point in his picaresque life, Peregrinus the quack converts himself to a new sect of ignorant folk believing in some 'crucified Sophist', a short passage sanctioned by a *damnatio memoriae* which lasted about a millennium. The Byzantine *Suda* thus asserts that Lucian was justly chastised with an infamous ending: he was eaten by dogs, and would go to hell with Satan.

Yet some Italian humanists of the *Quattrocento* found his manuscripts and translated them. The taste for his works was such that he became one of the most translated, edited, read, commented, and imitated among the Ancients — certainly more than Homer or Plato among the Greeks.[5] Of course, his 'fictions of unbelief', as we may call them, were not the only factor at stake: there are other stylistic, moral, and epistemological reasons accounting for his success. He was a model of Attic style and a model in the art of associating jest and earnestness. He was the perfect mouthpiece for humanists blaming vices such as the arrogance of intellectuals, the cupidity of rich men, or the ambition of princes. Towards philosophical doctrines, he showed the example of a wise detachment that appeared as a safe haven for sceptics in raging intellectual controversies (Correard 2008). As for his religious incredulity, it could generate embarrassment, or even dismay. Of course, Lucian had derided the Pagan gods, and some Fathers of the Church had espoused his irony and even used some of his devices (Baldwin 1982). Virtually all commentators would make this point in the Renaissance so that Lucian was, in some measure, 'christened' (Zappala 1990).

Yet his most lucid commentators understood that his irony was unredeemable. As the German humanist Obsopoeus pointed out in the notes preceding his Latin translation of the *Zeus refuted*, published in the complete *Luciani Samosatensis Opera* directed by Moltzer (Mycillus), Lucian proves an atheist by insisting on the fact that the notion of God's omnipotence and the notion of his benevolence are incompatible, considering his tolerance of Evil in the world. Maybe Jupiter does not exist at all for Lucian, and it is nothing more than a *figment*, a mythological and fictional character. But what would come of the world without the fear of a divine punishment? asks Obsopoeus, echoing general *angst* about the social and moral consequences of unbelief (Lucian 1538: 200v°). Erasmus, one of the main translators, editors, and imitators of the Greek satirist, and moreover one of the main proponents of a profound reformation of the Church, repeatedly commented that Lucian could help fight against *some* superstitions which had invaded modern religion. But he remained silent on Lucian's alleged atheism, or downplayed it, while applying Lucianic irony to the theological debates of the time. If Lucian was to be ignored, then what about Pliny? he asked in a humanistic appeal to hermeneutical and philological tolerance of Pagans. Yet Erasmus, 'the Dutch Lucian', was a sincere Christian, as were Rabelais and various evangelical imitators of Lucian. The case is different with some other imitators, ranging from Leon Battista Alberti to Voltaire, as well as Giordano Bruno and Cyrano de Bergerac (to quote the most famous) who mustered Lucianic fiction in their dismantling of Christian creeds. So, there is not *one* ideology common to all imitators of Lucian in the modern age, but various uses, and various extents of the satire. In some cases, *bad* creeds are exposed as fictions; in others, *all* religious creeds may be exposed as fictions. In all cases, though, the use of *fiction* as a model to understand religious beliefs was the distinct mark of Lucianic writings.

## 2. Fictions of Atheism in the *Quattrocento*?

Let us now consider some concrete instances of Lucianic fictions, starting with the most frontal challenge addressed to the belief in the existence of a God who interacts with humans. Negating the *intervention* of some divine principle in the world was considered as the most common definition of atheism in the Renaissance (more than the absolute negation of the existence of some divine principle). By this standard, the *Momus*, composed around 1450 by Leon Battista Alberti, one of the leading figures of Florentine humanism, was the first major atheist fiction in Europe.[6] A friend of several of the first translators of Lucian from Greek to Latin, such as Maffeo Vegio or Poggio Bracciolini, Alberti imitated Lucian's Olympian dialogues, which carry strong sceptical, cynical, and epicurean insights in matters of religion. In Lucian's *Zeus tragedian*, the gods complain that men do not pay sacrifice to them anymore and may cease to address prayers to them, as they doubt the capacity of the immortals to help those who live on earth. The gods then hearken to a controversy launched down below by a Stoic philosopher, Timocles, who believes in the existence of a divine order, and an Epicurean opponent, Damis, who denies it. They are stunned to see that the theistic arguments voiced by Timocles prove completely ineffective and contradictory, while Damis calmly maintains that the universe is ruled by chance.

In Alberti's Book I, Momus, the God of Blame, criticises the behaviour of Jupiter who acted cruelly by creating men only to inflict plagues on them. Rejected from heaven because of his inclination towards free speech, Momus descends among men to preach that Jupiter is powerless, that he is submitted to Destiny, and that nature follows its own laws, without the will of any divinity running it (Alberti 2019: 22–25). When the gods realise that it might be more dangerous for them to let Momus spread atheism on earth than to bear his presence in the skies, as he vents the secret of their powerlessness to men, they readmit him to Olympus. In Book II, understanding he has no other choice in order to survive, Momus converts to hypocrisy and pleases the immortals by blaming men who challenge their authority, attributing atheistic discourses to some mortal philosopher he does not name, and from whom he distances himself out of prudence, in an episode at the very heart of the story (Alberti 2019: 120–27).

Obviously, Momus is a figure of the intellectual, of Alberti himself, who writes daringly but prudently, attributing his views to fictional doubles in a jocular tone, exactly as Momus attributes his own views to a prop in the fiction. This is an intellectual who fantasises through his character about a sad destiny for himself, should his book be correctly deciphered: once his double discourse is unmasked, Momus is castrated and tied to a stake in the Ocean at the end of book IV, in a Promethean punishment which also evokes a parody of the crucifixion. Momus dies for having prophesied that Jupiter's days were counted, that his imposture would be revealed, and that he would be replaced (Alberti 2019: 24–25). The Momus–Jupiter allegory is complex and has been interpreted in several ways. Reducing it to an image of the relationships between Alberti and Popes Eugen IV or Nicolas V, for whom he worked as a secretary in Rome, would be missing the point. Momus is to Alberti what Zarathustra is to Nietzsche: the figure of an Antichrist, a lonely prophet of the doom of the Christian age, because Jupiter, if we follow the allegory coherently, stands for God. The Renaissance scholar Stephen Greenblatt has recently argued in his bestseller *The Swerve* (2011) that Poggio Bracciolini changed the world in 1417 when he discovered a manuscript of the *De Rerum Natura*. Yet Lucretius was scarcely imitated and it is difficult to find a real expression of philosophical atheism before the clandestine manuscript of the *Theophrastus redivivus* of 1659 (Gengoux 2014); whereas Lucian's Epicurean fictions begot offspring — and more than one, as we shall see — as soon as they were read.

Why fiction? Because it is an oblique means of expression, of course. We should not forget that Alberti's life was at stake. The allegorical *montage* is actually so complex and so puzzling that modern historians of ideas have completely overlooked such a text. But this reading of fiction-as-a-mask may still beg the question, as the book of *Momus* develops a deeper insight into cults as religious fictions and into men as creatures who prolong their lives through fictions — Book IV would support this claim but would require too much analysis to be dealt with in this paper. More generally, fiction stands as a device to think what was still unthinkable: that gods, and not only the Pagan ones, are merely fictions.

Exceptional as it is, Alberti's book was not without influence: it was published long after Alberti's death, in 1520 in Rome, but it circulated in manuscript form and inspired a strong undercurrent of Lucianic fictions in which humanists expressed their doubts about Providence. Another prominent figure, the Neapolitan Giovanni Pontano, staged Gods discussing the disorders at the surface of the earth and railing at human superstitions and prayers in his *Charon* (Pontano 2012). Antonio de Ferraris, known as Galateo, imagined the soul of a hermit who closely resembles its creator, barred from access to heaven after his death. The soul of the hermit vainly claims for his sincerity and right deeds, while lamenting that God's Providence seems to reward the wrong ones. He is condemned by Peter and other characters of iniquitous Biblical figures and cynical saints for his liberty of speaking: 'learn to stay silent, or you'll be punished', commands the character of saint Thomas (Ferrariis 2009: 84). The hermit's Job-like complaint echoes Galateo's religious doubts, expressed in other writings. Antonio Cammelli staged his own soul going down to hell after death, again questioning divine providence and asking forbidden questions until he is told to stop: either these questions should not be asked, or they cannot be answered; in any case, Jupiter's thunder is to be feared, the soul learns (Cammelli 2005: 39). These last two texts remained in manuscript form, their authors expressing through fiction their awareness of the threat of censorship and the necessity of self-censorship (Correard 2020).

## 3. The Significance of Literary *Imitatio* in a Time of Religious Troubles and Censorship

*Quattrocento* fictions of unbelief did not change the world, indeed, because they remained a clandestine literature. When others were printed during the sixteenth century, amidst open religious quarrels, they appeared all the more dangerous when written in vulgar languages, thus capable of reaching a wider audience, so that they were immediately quenched. In 1537, an anonymous French author composed a Lucianic piece entitled *Cymbalum mundi* in which Mercurius, sent down to earth, carries with him Jupiter's book, where everything that happened, is happening, and will happen is supposed to be written. Unfortunately, he is robbed of the book and the robbers poke fun at the fact that Jupiter did not foresee the theft. Something must be wrong with the book (the Bible?), acknowledges Mercurius (*Cymbalum mundi* 1983: 24). While Lutherans and other Reformed theologians were waging theological wars about providence and free will, and gathering political support with real wars in view, this little comical fiction appeared intolerable: the Parliament of Paris ordered its suppression, and it survived only in two copies (for a recent reappraisal, see Mothu 2016). The Italian writer Niccolò Franco fancied a double, Sannio, going to heaven and sharing his feeling of scandal with Jupiter: how could the God of the gods bear so many evils and injustices in this world, even letting corrupt clergymen stain his name by using it to reinforce their power? Ironically, Jupiter sends back Sannio to the earth with a financial reward, in exchange for his promise to keep silent and to adorn temples (Franco 1541: XXXIX r°–v°). Niccolò Franco finished his life in jail a decade later, persecuted by the Inquisition. Again, a literary imitator had dared express in a supposedly jocular fiction a deeply irreligious insight, not far from Machiavelli's, on religion as a fiction supported by political interests.

The sole fact that religious and political authorities took this type of satirical fictions so seriously, although they had little in common with reformist pamphlets or any clear political agenda, shows that they gave them great importance. Giordano Bruno also privileged Lucianic satire to express his anti-Christian stance. While he was first and foremost a philosopher, Bruno had followed Alberti's path in composing the fiction of the *Spaccio della bestia trionfante* (1585), where Momus and Jupiter discuss ways to reform the world. Momus advocates a radical purge, pointing to religious impostors such as Orio, who pretended to accomplish miracles and walk on waters, or the Centaurus Chiron, a chimera supposedly half man and half God, who never existed except in the imagination of those who dared affirm that the impossible is possible (Bruno 2000: 196–97 and 210–11). These allusions to Christ *as a fiction* were noted as particularly blasphemous by the Inquisitors who prosecuted Bruno, and they apparently counted in the decision to send him to the stake. Significantly, the first burst of a frankly atheistic discourse among the French *libertins* did not occur with the *Theophrastus redivivus*, but a couple of years earlier, in Cyrano de Bergerac's Lucianic fiction *Les États et Empires de la Lune* (1656), where the key discourse of a shadowy figure, le '*jeune fils de l'hôte*', sketches all the lines of an anti-Christian, materialistic understanding of the world negating the main religious dogmas (the Creation of the world, the existence of spiritual entities and the immortality of the soul, the existence of a divine will, of retribution after death). This leads us to a retrospective interpretation of the fictional journey, designed as a complex puzzle. As is the case with Alberti, the complete image of Cyrano's thought in *Les États et Empires* is revealed not to the dull reader, but only to the clever one, able to reconstruct a coherent interpretation in a narrative chaos (Cavaillé 2004). Cyrano's ideas were largely borrowed from such thinkers as the scandalous Vanini, who had pushed to the extreme post-Aristotelian naturalistic philosophy, or from the rediscovery of Epicurean sources, but significantly, they were staged much more forcefully in his Lucianic fiction, where Genesis is openly parodied and exposed as a fiction in a key section, than in most contemporary clandestine philosophical treatises.

It is no wonder then, that even before Cyrano and Bruno, '*Lucianici*' had become one of the most damning categories used by sixteenth-century religious polemicists, who often made it a synonym of *epicureans* or *libertines* or *atheists* (see Lauvergnat Gagnière 1988: 133–96), as we can see by the famous treatise *De scandalis* written by Calvin. Calvin included in this category those who 'raise doubt everywhere', 'rail at everything', even the Bible, and treat religions as 'figments of the human brain' (Calvin 1550: 70–71). Cornelius Agrippa, one of the most eminent of these 'railers' listed by Calvin, had included in his serio-comical declamation against false knowledge not only religions, whose laws have no other ground than the 'credulity of men' (Agrippa 1531: f. LII v°), but all kinds of theology, including biblical theology, as he questioned the authenticity of the Scriptures. '[Agrippa] casts doubt on all religions', stated cardinal Giovio (Giovio 1546: f. 63v°–64 r°). Confronted with the censorship of the theology faculties of Leuven and the Sorbonne, Agrippa pleaded in a later *Apologia* that a declamation is but a 'fiction' of discourse, a joke (Van der Poel 1997: 168). Most Renaissance Lucianic literature was nevertheless put on the Index from 1559 onwards, along with books of doctrine containing explicit heretical statements. Again, repression directed against fictions proves that they were far from innocuous, and that by proposing different interpretations of the world, they had, at least, the power to change representations.

## 4. From the Closet of Humanistic Erudition to the Modern Novel: A Secularisation of Incredulity?

We might object at this stage that Lucianic fictions never changed the world because they were severely repressed, so that this kind of high-brow incredulous gaze at religious creeds and practices, new to some humanists and far from widespread in their *milieu* (as the vast majority of intellectuals would still define themselves as Christians), ultimately stayed confined to the (happy) few. Up to now, we have indeed dealt with underground works and forgotten masterpieces. But there were also the mainstream ones, of a softer kind, which nevertheless propagated incredulity as a fashionable literary attitude that could have some influence *outside* fiction — because they were intended as such. Erasmus, the 'Batavian Lucian' as he was called by his detractors, not only put forth a general satire against the follies of humanity in his *Moriae Encomium*, he also invented a more specific way to target religious impostures, of which he was impatient to rid Christianity. He drew inspiration from Lucian in some of his *Colloquia familiarum* such as the *The Religious Pilgrimage*, where he stages an ironic interlocutor who raises doubt, in the manner of Lucian's Tychiades, about the miracles that a pilgrim claims to have witnessed, such as a statue of the Virgin lactating (Erasmus 1878, vol. II: 1–37). Erasmus proves a master at inventing situations which enhance the absurdity and irrationality underlying the fabric of saints and miracles. His literary jokes were not only perceived as anticatholic. That he was a 'Lucian' *redivivus* was among the harshest epithets thrown at his face by Luther during their famous polemic, which marked the divorce between an adventurous Humanist thinker and a new Christian prophet.[7]

Rabelais was not far behind. His ironic use of the evangelical motto *quod vidimus testamur* in the first chapter of *Pantagruel* introduced an unsettling game where the limits between the sacred and the profane, Evangelical inspiration and satirical fiction were blurred in an unsettling Menippean hotchpot. Narrating a biblical genealogy in the manner of Lucian's *True Stories* at the opening of Pantagruel was a most daring gesture: was Rabelais poking fun at the *massoreths*, the bad commentators of the Bible? Or was he poking fun at the Old Testament, fraught with fables according to Cornelius Agrippa, one of Rabelais's favourite readings? In either case, he never ceased to teach the reader how to distance himself from literalism, and to turn to interpretation, allegory, irony, because, as Erasmus had already realised in his commentaries of the Bible, spontaneous adhesion to the Word fuels fanaticism, while freeing interpretation is the key to toleration — hermeneutics, ethics, politics, and religion being solidly bound. This opposition lies at the very heart of the *Quart livre* (Correard 2012). Idolaters believe in their fictions, unaware that they are products of human fantasy. One should not forget that Rabelais, despite his wide reception, was considered the schoolmaster of the *libertins*, as the Père Garasse insisted in his *Rabelais réformé* and *Doctrine curieuse*, calling him a buffoon 'who wreaks more havoc with his drolleries than Calvin did with his new doctrines' (Garasse 1624: 1026). He therefore became dubious reading in France by the time of the Revocation of the Edict of Nantes.

Similarly, the founding text of picaresque literature, *Lazarillo de Tormes*, published in 1554, is just the visible surface of a rich Spanish vein of Lucianic literature in the sixteenth century, a clandestine one as recent research has shown (Vian Herrero 2005). '*Lucianus, Apuleyus, Lazarillus*', writes a commentator of the time (Lollio 1558: 502), who clearly perceived the link between ancient and modern literary unbelief. The whole montage was more astute in this case, the satire being attributed to an innocent fool supposedly writing his autobiography. But as readers learn how to decipher the world, they can discern the traps and lies of the clergy, and they will encounter plentiful ironical allusions to dogmas. In the *Lazarillo*, Lucianic inspiration thus joined with another type of fiction of unbelief invented in the Middle Ages by Boccacio, in some stories of his *Decameron* about religious impostors.[8] Most works of this kind, like the *Crotalón*, remained manuscripts, while *Lazarillo* saw the light and made its way into the world, though not easily: the book was censored and rewritten in 1572 by Inquisitor López de Velasco, who put into circulation an alternative version which did not entirely succeed in suppressing the memory of the original, known at least through English and French early translations. A copy of the original version in Spanish, the so-called Barcarotta copy, was found in 1992 walled in an old house which had belonged to a Jewish landlord of the time, who hid it as best he could. The book we now hold as the landmark of an aesthetic revolution, the forerunner of the modern, realistic, Balzac-like 'novel', was in its time a smuggled product, a challenging piece in a complex game of powers around Christian beliefs. Its author had turned the fictional art of make-believe into a lesson of doubt for his reader.

The case of demonological scenes gives a good example of how some patterns of comical fiction provided a sharp tool to inquire into the fictionality of belief. Through his character Tychiades, Lucian had poked fun in his *Philopseudes* at gullible philosophers who believed ghost stories, anecdotes about magic tricks, and supernatural influences. Erasmus imitated him in staging a fake possession case in his *Exorcism*, pointing to the way cunning clerics could manipulate credulous worshipers to reap some profit (Erasmus 1878, vol. I: 391–401). *Lazarillo de Tormes* included a similar scene in its Tratado V, which gave rise to a literary *topos*. In Spain, picaresque authors such as Cervantes or Espinel; in France, authors of Menippean satires and *histoires comiques* such as Barclay, Viau, Sorel, or Claireville; in England, Nashe or Butler: all would use fiction as a way of triggering the interest of readers in strange, fantastic events before deluding them and edifying them with laughter (Correard 2016). It has often been said that narrative literature and fictional anecdotes fed the 'realistic' theses of people who believed in the existence of witchcraft and possessions, while critics of demonology were mainly philosophers and physicians. Some of them were actually fiction writers, conscious that Lucianic irony could offer an antidote against naïve belief. While authors of *histoires tragiques* would try to hide the fictionality of their ghost narratives in order to have the reader believe it was real, the *histoires comiques* exhibited fictionality as a way of understanding what was at stake in a collective hallucination. It did not imply heterodoxy as such: the belief in supernatural phenomena such as possessions or apparitions was held to be dubious by a significant part of the catholic clergy, and by most Reformed theologians. But it is an example of the way in which Lucian's irony, once the privilege of some humanistic minds, passed from elite circles to a more widespread type of literature. Without necessarily promoting the most radical irreligious views of an Alberti, a Bruno, or a Cyrano, it contributed to spreading a secularised and rationalistic, matter-of-fact representation of the world in popular novelistic forms.

## 5. Did Lucianic Irony Survive the Enlightenment? On the Use of Fiction in a Time of Cultural Conflict

As we have seen, the success of Lucianic fiction in the Renaissance owed a lot to the longing for *parrhêsia*, or free speech, and it was fostered by the necessity of oblique discourse in a time of repression. Even if the practice of *imitatio* progressively lost its prestige by the time of the Quarrel of Ancients and Moderns, Menippean satire kept some appeal in the context of a wider cultural conflict between secularised views and the authority of religious voices and institutions. Fiction remained a convenient, most appropriate means of dis/simulation, if only because censorial constraints were merely loosened, not abolished, in most parts of Europe. Treasured by an early religious sceptic like La Mothe Le Vayer (Roche 2020), the ambiguous nature of Lucianic irony (Christian or not?) burst forth some generations later in Enlightenment England with the most scandalous *A Tale of a Tub* (1707), published anonymously by the 'English Lucian' and Dean of the Cathedral of Saint-Patrick in Dublin. Inspired by Rabelais and Erasmus, Swift derided the main Christian confessions in the central tale of the three brothers Peter, Martin, and Jack (i.e., Catholicism, Lutheranism, and Calvinism). His best commentators still remain divided as to whether his radical irony spares some moderate Anglican position (as Martin seems relatively spared), or if the 'lashes of the whip were so long that they went up to the father', to quote Voltaire's judgement about the *Tale* in his *Lettres philosophiques* (chap. 22), an opinion shared by many a Christian polemist who condemned this little comic fiction (Weinbrot 2005: 116–64).

We might pile up examples of the way Lucianic fictions inspired ever more literary versions of the religious impostor, much more than modern literary critics generally grant. But one will suffice. One of the most scandalous aspects of Lucian's works, his satirical biographies of Peregrinus and Alexander the Prophet, had resurfaced and mirrored the developments of Biblical criticism. Exposing the tricks of religious leaders and exploring the psychology of their followers, Lucian had shown how quacks could pass as prophets. Some readers were puzzled by the fact that Peregrinus's or Alexander's 'miracles' evoked others more familiar to Christians, and the parallel with J. C. was quickly drawn, sometimes through the mediation of a third character, the Pagan saint Apollonius of Tyana depicted by Philostratus. Couldn't Lucianic irony, a useful touchstone for detecting frauds, be applied to the narrative of the Gospels? To make a long story short (see Correard 2017), we might jump to its end, when the 'German Lucian' Christoph Martin Wieland wrote a two thousand page-long version of his own of the story of Peregrinus. Lucian had missed some parts of his life, which are added by the 'German Voltaire', as the alternative epithet for Wieland goes: in a central section of his *Geheime Geschichte des Philosophen Peregrinus Proteus* (Wieland 1791), Peregrinus becomes a zealot of the Galilean sect, following a small-scale Jesus who accomplishes fake resurrections in a proselyte campaign which has no other purpose than to build his power. The work encompasses some long historical digressions on the formidable success of Christianity, inspired by Edward Gibbon, the controversial historian of the last centuries of the Roman Empire. In the end, the unmistakable but disturbing parallels between Christ, Apollonius, and Peregrinus lead to a bold rewriting of the gospels, in a Lucianic fiction which stands now as one of the most sophisticated productions of the Enlightenment. After decades of open polemics on miracles between the *philosophes* and *antiphilosophes*, Lucianic fiction still appeared a relevant model to the former in order to stage a decisive view: Wieland's point is not only to debunk imposture, but to account for the persuasive power of religious fictions over the mind. And only a fiction may account for it, a fiction presented through a complex *montage*, since this new, complete novel of Peregrinus is told by the character of Peregrinus himself to the character of Lucian, with whom he converses in Hell.

This example leads us to a last corpus which deserves scrutiny, as it shows why Enlightenment thinkers did not favour only pamphlets or philosophical treatises in order to propel a rationalistic understanding of religious creeds, but also, again and again, fictions. Dialogues of the dead enjoyed considerable success in the eighteenth century, and it is no wonder that Voltaire wrote *Conversation dans les Champs-Elysées* (1765) where he brought together Lucian, Erasmus, and Rabelais to inveigh against religious fanatics and joke about how to bypass censorship. While Fontenelle, a definite, although discreet heir of the *libertins érudits*, had started a new vogue with his 1684 *Nouveaux dialogues des morts*, he had carefully avoided religious topics, and reduced the Hells of satire to a most conventional fictional frame. Yet, numerous dialogues of the dead were later issued by French exiles who enjoyed freedom of printing in the Netherlands, and along with philosophical treatises written by freethinkers, they formed part of the vast clandestine literature which helped to propagate the ideas of a (more or less) radical Enlightenment. Some of them, by such authors as Gueudeville (*Dialogues des morts d'un tour nouveau*, 1709) or Jean-Frédéric Bernard (*Dialogues critiques et philosophiques*, 1730), reverted to Lucian's irony with new targets in sight, starring as the main characters of the satire Christian martyrs and saints, or prophets like Mahomet — a codename for Christ in much Enlightenment literature — all avowing their impostures in Hell. The same tendency can be found in England, though more sparingly, with authors like Fleetwood Sheppard (*Calendar Reformed*, 1704), Matthew Prior ('A Dialogue between Thomas More and the Vicar of Bray', c. 1712) or John Sheffield ('A Conversation between Mahomet and the Duc de Guise', *Works*, 1723). The genre was so popular that it prompted a reaction from the orthodox camp. Could the ludicrous and satirical hells of Lucianic literature not be Christianised *a posteriori*, and turned against the new Lucians of the age?

The anti-Christian literary propaganda of Lucianic writers was thus paralleled by a Christian counter-offensive which strove to give credibility to the idea that Hell is a *real* place, as some freethinker characters realise too late. Anonymous pamphlets staged Spinoza, Bayle, Hobbes, Voltaire, or David Hume as dead characters surprised to still be there in the world beyond, acknowledging too late that death does not mean complete extinction, and that they were wrong to deem Hell a mere fiction... To quote but one example, in the anonymous *Moses and Bolingbroke; A Dialogue* (attributed to Pye, 1754), a prominent figure of English freethinking who had suggested that Genesis was a sheer collection of 'poetical creations' is confronted by the prophet Moses, who was still considered the real writer of Genesis and the Pentateuch by sound Christian doctrines. God's spokesman forces the freethinker to repent. In the end, libertine Bolingbroke suffers horrible torments, the last page being full of his gasps as if he were dying again in Hell — a quaint scene, indeed. Readers may remain unconvinced. Showing very poor literary qualities, these dialogues totally lack Lucianic verve and insight. They ran the risk of appearing ridiculous. Dante's *Inferno* has always remained quite unique in its literary attempt at representing the Hell of Thomist theology. Christian dialogues of the dead? The oxymoron was difficult to bear. Using fiction as a tool to maintain that Hell is no fiction was a rather slippery device for Christian propagandists, and it could hardly dissipate doubts.

An anecdote sums up the situation very well. At his death, David Hume rapidly became a character in many dialogues of the dead (some portraying him rather favourably, some as an evil or inconsistent *provocateur*). A tale circulated in the public about the agony of this arch-sceptic, who is supposed to have shed his doubts at the hour of truth and repented for his irreligious views. Yet Hume's close friend, Adam Smith, tells a very different story in his correspondence (Baier 2006). Visiting Hume a couple of days before his death, he found him lying down, calmly reading Lucian's *Dialogues of the Dead* and jesting at the prospect of his own demise, wondering if he would have money enough to pay Charon the fee for the passage… Hume did not write dialogues of the dead, but at the hour of truth, the philosopher opted for comical fiction.

## Conclusion

Can we conclude that Lucianic fictions changed the world? Let us go back to our general culturalist perspective, and to the problem of the role of fictions as bringing new representations in the context of broader cultural change (we might think of the parallels we raised in the introduction with twentieth-century fictions of social progress). It is difficult to say whether Menippean satires should be considered as a historical *avant-garde*, or just as a side effect of early modern unbelief. We would not dare to say that they mattered more in the rise of unbelief than early modern developments of Biblical criticism, for instance. They certainly mattered less than the broad historical phenomenon of confessional divisions in Europe resulting from religious reforms, which definitely unsettled theological and religious authority. Dialogues of the dead may even appear as marginal to historians of ideas in comparison with the vast number of philosophical treatises enrolled in the Enlightenment campaign for change. But the latter were largely predated by some complex humanistic fictions which described nature as self-governing, God's providence as inexistent, and widely shared beliefs as pure constructions — *social fictions*, as is the case in Alberti's *Momus*. Definitely, they were much more than mere *signs* of a change.

Taken as a whole, Lucianic fictions played a role which ought not to be underestimated, for the two major reasons mentioned above in the case of Alberti. In societies where public expression, especially printing, was governed by multiple (and more or less effective) instances of censorship, and where expression of unbelief could be severely punished (atheism being considered as the ultimate heresy), *fiction* was probably the best means available to convey unorthodox ideas — because it is a very indirect and complex one, all the more so since allegory and irony were generally inserted in order to veil meaning. Even if they were correctly deciphered by censors, these fictions remained more acceptable, thanks to their obliquity. Their hermeneutic complexity also accounts for the fact that modern literary critics — when they interpret them at all — have generally studied them independently, without really connecting them. Or else, those reception studies that have considered Lucianic literature as a whole have done so at the cost of interpretation, as they remained blind to the intellectual context.

But fiction was also a philosophical tool, as authors manipulating it were highly conscious of the creative power of the human mind. It is not easy to assess which comes first between the philosophical intent and the literary practice. A lot of early modern intellectuals may have experienced a shock when they read Lucian and perhaps this helped change their minds, prompting the temptation to adapt Lucianic irony, while they were still immersed in a multi-layered, millenarian Christian culture. Fictions may of course change the reader in the first place, and the general conclusions we might draw from the recent 'ethical turn' in literary studies may here acquire a specific relevance. Literary imitation was not only an affair of stylistic imitation. It meant adopting a new type of intellectual attitude, daring an iconoclastic gesture which first pertained to a small elite (or even to a small number of persons in the intellectual elites), but which had become widely shared by the dawn of the French Revolution.

## References

AGRIPPA, HEINRICH CORNELIUS. 1531. *De incertitudine et vanitate scientiarum artiumque declamatio invectiva* (Cologne: n. pub.)

ALBERTI, LEON BATTISTA. 2019. *Momus*, ed. by P. Laurens (Paris: Les Belles Lettres)

BAIER, ANETTE, 2006. 'A Tale of Three Letters: Hume's Readings on his Deathbed', *Hume Studies*, 32 (2): 347–56

BALDWIN, BARRY. 1982. 'The Church Fathers and Lucian', *Studia Patristica*, 17: 626–30

BERRIOT, FRANÇOIS. 1984. *Athéismes et athéistes au XVI$^e$ siècle en France*, 2 vols (Paris: Cerf)

BRUNO, GIORDANO. 2000. *Spaccio della bestia trionfante*, ed. by M. Ciliberto (Milan: Einaudi)

CALVIN, JEAN. 1550. *Des scandales* (Geneva: J. Crespin)

CAMMELLI, ANTONIO. 2005. *Dialogo*, in *Sonnetti Faceti* (Pistoia: Libraria dell'Orso)

CASTER, MARCEL. 1937. *Lucien et la pensée religieuse de son temps* (Paris: Les Belles Lettres)

CAVAILLÉ, JEAN-PIERRE. 2004. '"Qu'il y ait un Dieu je vous le nie tout à plat." Contexte théorique et enjeux pratiques des arguments athéistes du Fils de l'hôte', *Littératures classiques*, 53: 65–74

——. 2016. 'Les frontières de l'inacceptable. Pour un réexamen de l'histoire de l'incrédulité', in 'Les dossiers de Jean-Pierre Cavaillé, Les limites de l'acceptable', special issue, *Les Dossiers du Grihl* <http://journals.openedition.org/dossiersgrihl/4746> [accessed 12 July 2022]

CORREARD, NICOLAS. 2008. '"Rire et douter": Lucianisme, scepticisme(s) et pré-histoire du roman (xv$^e$–xviii$^e$ siècle)' (unpublished doctoral thesis, Université Paris Diderot — Paris 7)

——. 2012. 'Les "histoires véritables" du "Lucien français": De la poétique de l'incrédulité au regard moraliste du *Quart Livre*', 'Bouquet I — Rabelais, *Gargantua/Le Quart Livre*', special issue, *Le Verger*, 1 <http://cornucopia16.com/blog/2014/07/21/janvier-2012-nicolas-correard-u-nantes-les-histoires-vraies-du-lucien-francais-de-la-poetique-de-lincredulite-au-regard-moraliste-du-quart-livre/> [accessed 30 June 2022]

——. 2016. 'Criti-Comic Demonology. Picaresque Novels, *Histoires Comiques* and the Supernatural', in *Seventeenth-Century Fiction: Text & Transmission*, ed. by J. Glomski and I. Moreau (Oxford: Oxford University Press), pp. 64–80

——. 2017. 'Apollonius, Peregrinus et les imposteurs religieux: Lecture policière et critique créative à l'âge classique', *Acta fabula*, colloques en ligne (online symposia) <https://www.fabula.org/colloques/document4831.php> [accessed 30 June 2022]

——. 2020. 'Littérature sério-comique et discours oblique à la Renaissance', *L'Oblique et le crypté : TransversALL*, 3: 17–54

——. 2021. 'Du scandale du Mal au scandale de la Providence : Lucien de Samosate et l'"athéisme" dans l'Europe humaniste', *Nouvelle revue du Seizième siècle*, 17 (3): 29–65

*Cymbalum mundi*. 1983. Ed. by P. H. Nurse (Geneva: Droz)

ERASMUS, DESIDERIUS. 1878. *The Colloquies*, trans. by N. Bailey. 2 vols (London: Reeves & Turner)
FERRARIIS, ANTONIO DE (Galateo). 2009. *Eremita*, ed. by S. Valerio (Rome: Edizioni di Storia e Letteratura)
FRANCO, NICCOLÒ. 1541. *Dialogi piacevoli* (Venice: Giolito di Ferrarii)
FURETIÈRE. 1690. *Dictionnaire universel*, III (The Hague: Arnout & Reinier Leers)
GARASSE, FRANÇOIS. 1624. *La Doctrine curieuse des beaux esprits* (Paris: S. Chappelet)
GENGOUX, NICOLE. 2014. *Un athéisme philosophique à l'âge classique* (Paris: Champion)
GIOVIO, PAULO. 1546. *Elogia viris clarorum* (Venice: M. Tramezinus)
GOODMAN, NELSON. 1978. *Ways of Worldmaking* (Indianapolis: Hackett)
GREENBLATT, STEPHEN. 2011. *The Swerve* (New York: Norton)
HOBSBAWM, ERIC. 2011. *How to Change the World: Tales of Marx and Marxism* (London: Little, Brown Books)
HOBSBAWM, ERIC. 2014. *Et le monde changea: Réflexions sur Marx et le marxisme, de 1840 à nos jours*, trans. Frédéric Joly (Arles: Actes Sud)
HUET, PIERRE DANIEL. 1678. *Lettre de M$^r$ Huer à M$^r$ de Segrais de l'origine des romans* (Paris : n. pub.)
HUNTER, MICHAEL and WOOTON DAVID (eds.). 1992. *Atheism from the Reformation to the Enlightenment* (Oxford: Clarendon Press)
LAUVERGNAT GAGNIÈRE, CHRISTIANE. 1988. *Lucien de Samosate et le lucianisme en France au XVI$^e$ siècle : Athéisme et polémique* (Geneva: Droz)
LOLLIO, ANTONIO. 1558. *De Oratione* (Basel: J. Oporinus)
LUCIAN OF SAMOSATA. 1538. *Luciani Samosatensis opera*, ed. by J. Moltzer (Frankfurt: Egenolphus)
———. 1913–1967. *Lucian of Samosata, Complete Works*, 8 vol., trans. by H. Harmon, H. Kilburn and M. D. McLeod (London: Heineman)
LUTHER, MARTIN. 1823. *On the Bondage of Free Will*, trans. by H. Cole (London: Bensley)
MARSH, DAVID. 1998. *Lucian and the Latins. Humor and Humanism in the Early Renaissance* (Ann Arbor: University of Michigan Press)
MCCLURE, GEORGES. 2018. *Doubting the Divine in Early Modern Europe. The Revival of Momus, the Agnostic God* (Cambridge: Cambridge University Press)
MOTHU, ALAIN. 2016. 'Le livre de Jupiter. L'athéologie du *Cymbalum mundi*', *Bibliothèque d'Humanisme et de Renaissance*, 78 (2): 333–61
PANIZZA, LETIZIA. 2001. 'La ricezione di Luciano da Samosata nel Rinascimento italiano: "coripheus atheorum o filosofo morale"', in *Sources antiques de l'irréligion moderne: Le relais italien*, ed. by Jean-Pierre Cavaillé and Foucault Didier (Toulouse: Presses Universitaires du Mirail), pp. 119–37
[PYE, SAMUEL]. 1765. *Moses and Bolingbroke; A Dialogue* (London: Sandby)
PONTANO, GIOVANNI. 2012. *Charon*, in *Dialogues*, trans. by J. H. Gaisser (Cambridge, MA: Harvard University Press)
ROBINSON, CHRISTOPHER. 1979. *Lucian and His Influence in Europe* (Chapel Hill: University of North Carolina Press)
ROCHE, BRUNO. 2020. 'La Mothe le Vayer à l'école du "gentil Lucien"', *XVII$^e$ siècle*, 286: 49–61
SIDWELL, KEITH. 1974. 'Lucian of Samosata in the Italian Quattrocento' (unpublished doctoral thesis, University of Cambridge)
STAQUET, ANNE (ed.). 2013. *Athéisme voilé/dévoilé aux temps modernes* (Brussels: Académie Royale de Belgique)
VAN DER POEL, MARC. 1997. *Cornelius Agrippa, the Humanist Theologian and his Declamation* (Leiden: Brill)

Vian Herrero, Ana. 2005. 'El diálogo lucianesco en el Renacimiento español', in *El Diálogo renacentista en la península ibérica/Der Renaissancedialog auf der Iberischen Halbinsel*, ed. by Ana Vian Herrero, et al. (Stuttgart: Franz Steiner Verlag), pp. 51–56

Weinbrot, Howard. 2005. *Menippean Satire Reconsidered: From Antiquity to the Eighteenth-Century* (Baltimore: The John Hopkins University Press)

Wieland, Cristoph Martin. 1791. *Geheime Geschichte des Philosophen Peregrinus Proteus* (Leipzig: Göschen)

Zappala, Michael. 1990. *Lucian of Samosata in the Two Hesperias: An Essay in Cultural and Literary Transmission* (Potomac, MD: Scripta Humanistica)

## Notes to Chapter 5

1. Significantly, the title of the last book of the great historian of the communist movement, Eric Hobsbawm, was altered by its French translation from *How to Change the World: Tales from Marx and Marxism, 1840–2011* (2011) to *Et le monde changea: Réflexions sur Marx et le marxisme, de 1840 à nos jours* (*And the World Changed: Reflections on Marx and Marxism from 1840 to Today*, 2014). Translation is no absolute treason here, as Hobsbawm's point is precisely to show that Marx's ideas *did* change the world.
2. Some exceptions need to be made: besides Alain Mothu's recent study on the *Cymbalum mundi* (2016) and Georges McClure's on the character of Momus (2018), discussed below, see for instance Panizza (2001).
3. We may note their absence, for instance, in the collective work on early modern atheism edited by Hunter and Wooton (1992). Similarly, François Berriot hardly mentions Lucian's influence in his reference work on early modern atheism (1984).
4. Lucian's attitude towards religion was tackled in Caster's landmark study (1937).
5. The bibliography on Lucian's reception is particularly rich. Suffice it to refer here to Sidwell (1974), Robinson (1979), and Marsh (1998).
6. The claim was at the heart of a research talk in June 2017 in Nantes (seminar 'Le scandale', organised by Karine Durin and Anne Rolet). A revised and enlarged version of this paper has been published (Correard 2021). Meanwhile, Georges McClure published his important *Doubting the Divine in Early Modern Europe: The Revival of Momus, the Agnostic God* (2018), which pinpoints the link between the character of Momus and the fortune of agnosticism.
7. Levelling the charge of 'scepticism' at Erasmus's praise of doubt as a commendable attitude in religious controversy, Luther equated it with a lack of faith in his *Table Talk* or in *The Bondage of Free Will* ('you hug in your heart a Lucian, or some other of the swinish tribe of the Epicureans; who, because he does not believe there is a God himself, secretly laughs at all those who do believe and confess it. Allow us to be assertors', section 2 [Luther 1823: 12]). Believing implies asserting according to Luther, while the sceptics toy with their 'fables' in a Lucianic mindset (section 40).
8. Many stories in Boccacio play on belief and the art of make-believe, but we may think of the subtler ones, which allude to Christian dogmas on Hell (the story of Ferondo, III, 8) or angels (the story of friar Alberto, IV, 2).

# CHAPTER 6

# Fiction and the Modelling of Chance

*Anne Duprat*

*Université de Picardie Jules Verne/Institut Universitaire de France*

What role is there for fiction in a changing world? If the question is not new, recently two major phenomena have drastically modified our way of asking it. The first is the sudden, unprecedented acceleration of the changes we face, especially apparent in the effects of climate change; the second is the newly visible influence which decisions, both individual and collective, may have on it — an influence starkly outlined by the health crisis afflicting the whole world since January 2020. These recent modifications have lent new urgency, if not a new meaning, to an ancient question: does fiction, insofar as it models our vision of the world and affects our behaviour, render us more or less able to react to a complex and evolving situation?[1] By questioning the specific relation between fiction and chance — that is, between fiction and the (indeterminate) future — the present contribution begins to respond to this question. To do so, it must first return to the capacity of fictions to function like models, in the special case of chance as a phenomenon representable only within a human experience of reality. Subsequently, the question will be refined by asking how the particular efficacy of such modelling should be attributed to fiction as such — rather than to narrative, on the one hand, or thought experiment, on the other.

## Fictions and Models: The Case of the Representation of Chance

The profound crisis currently affecting our belief in the capacity of societies and individuals to foresee future events also affects the very structure of our representation of the world, insofar as this relies on models.

We know the importance that models possess in the adoption of public policies. Measuring climate change, estimating terrorist risk or the consequences of population migration, predicting health risks — all these processes are constantly being modelled to provide the basis of decisions. This is notably the *raison d'être* of the probabilistic models of Bayesian networks. The Covid-19 pandemic has seen both an increase in the amplitude of the phenomena being modelled — now on the scale of all humanity — and an unprecedented compression of the temporal delay before the projections are validated or corrected. These two developments naturally influence the way we judge the credibility of such models — in terms of the nature and the extent of acceptance received from researchers, on the one hand, and from the public, on the other. With responses ranging from complete rejection to measured scepticism, from theoretical acceptance of the probability of a fact such as climate change to complete adherence to its implications (adopting a politics of ecology, modifying individual behaviour in the face of an epidemic), today the power of models and of modelling is unavoidably the focus of questioning.

Models, however, are neither theories (they cannot be proven wrong or refuted by experience) nor representations (they do not reproduce an existing state of things). What they propose is a range of possible projections based on a set of initial data, formulated in a hybrid vocabulary between that of ordinary language and that of science. This range of possibilities makes it possible to proceed towards actions and decisions because it presents, for a given situation, a useful schematising of the subsequent situations that may result from the current one.

Modelling is a fiction to the extent that it delineates the structures of a hypothetical world, which takes the place neither of a theory composed of scientific propositions nor of a complete possible representation of this world. Certainly, models are distinct from fictions in that they are made to serve as a basis for a decision — a function much more difficult to assign to fictions produced by art, for which the question of the autotelic is ever-present. Nevertheless, the two kinds of design share the same mode of functioning, if not the same function: they project, in a way that cannot be verified, the structure of a credible, though currently non-existent, world.

When we question the credibility of these models, what we test is therefore not only the validity of the hypothesis that organises them but also the heuristic reach and pragmatic value of the world that they create. When we try to measure the influence of the scenarios transformed into images by Al Gore's documentary film *An Inconvenient Truth* (2006) on Americans' attitudes and actions towards reducing greenhouse gases, we naturally seek to know to what degree the public has adopted the reasoning promoted by the film — i.e., 'If nothing is done, here is what will logically happen.' But we also ask what role the credibility of the world represented in it has played in eliciting the emotional, ethical, and pragmatic assent of the spectators.

In the strictly pragmatic terms of the effects produced by representations on our beliefs, the question is fundamentally the same one that presents itself when we question the capacity of fictions openly presented as such, and notably 'non-realistic' fictions — for example, the 3D science-fiction film *Wall-E* (A. Stanton, 2008) — to function as credible models of an indeterminate future, and as a result to trigger behaviour in the hope of modifying this future.

Does fiction — literary fiction in particular — propose models for conceiving the unforeseeable? In other words, do fictions model the role played by contingency in the course of events? The question may have two meanings, one critical and the other more heuristic. On the one hand, the issue is to understand to what extent fictional processes *actually* intervene in our understanding of chance as a form of event in the world — even if their intervention only serves to skew this understanding. To identify that intervention and denounce the errors and illusions that it entails is the traditional objective of critical analysis of fictional discourses and practices; to start with, we recall the necessity of such criticism for an approach to the cognitive biases associated with the representation of chance. On the other hand, our examination may also expose the conditions in which fiction *may* lend form and existence to this intervention of chance in the course of events, and thereby contribute in a legitimate way to shaping our attitudes and modes of behaviour in the face of the future, the site of the indeterminate.

## 1. What World(s)?

In posing the question of whether fiction changes the world, we of course mean primarily the world as it is conditioned by thought, knowledge, affect, and representations. In our domain it has long been well known that fiction proposes models for understanding our relation to chance as a subjective form of apprehending the real.[2] This understanding translates into modes of behaviour and attitudes which in turn change and remodel the world. That is why literary fiction, seconded by audio-visual forms (cinema and serial fiction) and video games, has always been the privileged domain of the representation of chance and its effects, whether prospectively — in our attitudes towards the unexpected, the indeterminate and the unforeseeable — or retrospectively, in our ways of interpreting and understanding events, and the different systems of causality that had the power to make them appear, and make them what they are (Köhler 1973; Richardson 1997; Meiner 2008; Lyons 2011).

Since fictional scenarios authorise free manipulation of cause-and-effect connections, they have always functioned as a testing ground for artificial representation, and hence for moral interpretation of the expected outcome of modes of conduct, thoughts, and actions. From the epic to the *histoire tragique*, from classical comedy to the philosophical tale and the sentimental novel, fictional narrative is the testing ground for human behaviour. Far from impairing the signifying capacity of the forms of behaviour represented, the incursion of unexpected events, improbable encounters and coincidences punctuating the itineraries of characters only draws out their meaning, since the framework of events functions as an echo chamber for the logical processes engaged by their actions and reactions. A misfortune — a messenger arriving too late, a handkerchief forgotten, and thereby precipitating the deaths of the lovers of Verona or of Desdemona — is merely the concrete form assumed by the actual causes of their downfall: that is, the hate or jealousy that operates through the chance event. Similarly, in the novels of Victor Hugo or Jules Verne, chance is present only to highlight the hero's power of action, as he triumphs over all the obstacles posed by the passive resistance of the world. Thus, in spite of fate, Michel Strogoff constantly succeeds in finding new means of crossing Siberia, in order to put into the hands of the czar's brother at Irkutsk the message he has been ordered to deliver. Likewise, when Jean Valjean, determined to rescue an innocent man condemned in his place, tries desperately to reach the court of Arras in the night, fate seems at first to thwart his journey, and thereby to second his all-too-human wish to renounce this terrible sacrifice. Despite all his efforts, he can find no carriage able to get him there in time. Impossible, however, to escape his destiny: at the last moment, chance intervenes again — was there any doubt? — and puts in his way the vehicle permitting to fulfil his heroic destiny, whether he wants to or not. In the same way, the American cinema of Fritz Lang, like that of Hitchcock in the 1950s, makes use in opening sequences of shots showing railway tracks separating, then joining again, like the careers of the heroes whom the story is bound to unite (*Human Desire*, 1954). Still more directly, the introductory sequence of *Strangers on a Train* (1951) alternately follows the apparently independent steps of each of the two main characters in New York's Grand Central Station, up to the moment when the shoe of one of them, knocking against the other's in the car where both are seated, triggers the apparently fortuitous dialogue which will initiate the entire plot: the proposition of an exchange of murders between two perfect strangers depends wholly on the falsely coincidental nature of their encounter.[3]

In all these examples, which illustrate the classic use of chance as a device for manipulating scenarios, fictional techniques model the intervention of occurrences by proposing structures (scenarios, rituals, methods, attitudes) permitting us to understand our own experience of chance, in a way that differs from thought experiment. It is indeed in the complete environment of an unfolding narrative that our encounter with chance takes shape and becomes the object of an experience that is lived, incarnated, given meanings and values. We should recall that in ordinary language chance is always figured as the result of the experience we make of it. Almost all the terms that designate chance in the natural languages of the West present the notion, not as an inert or neutral phenomenon, but rather already modalised, captured in its interaction with a human trajectory. They all engage something in the realm of meaning, value, or action; indeed, the mobility of these attributions in the different European languages, or their historical evolution in a single one, makes one of the most fascinating objects for a diachronic or comparative study of the vocabulary of chance. Whatever the discourse in which one finds it, the vocabulary of chance always designates that which happens to someone, which falls upon or comes to encounter him or her — that which is desired, feared, mistaken, or recognised. As the linguist Jean-Claude Milner reminds us, even the syntactic presentation of chance phenomena is never neutral: it seems, he says, 'that languages are always led, when they put a series of phenomena in relation, to colour the encounter, whether in terms of causality or [...] in terms of contrasts'.[4]

This pre-information of chance, first by linguistic usage then by incorporation into a plot, does not make it exceptional from the point of view of a phenomenology of perception: insofar as it affects the course of human lives, chance is conditioned by language, narrative, and fiction in the same way as other aspects of life. By contrast, its essentially constructed nature poses an obvious obstacle to describing it outside human perception and experience — in mathematics, physics, astronomy, or biology. How might a fiction present chance in the world of facts, as opposed to that of representations, if the latter is the only context in which it is *actually* presented? In this domain, fiction indeed changes the world. It modifies the world to the point of rendering it unrecognizable by the scientists who observe, calculate, or theorise it — increasingly so since the 1920s, when physics, more recently followed by cybernetics, began to widen the gap between an exact science and a human science of the world.

An initial response to this problem, that of epistemological criticism, consists in applying here, as elsewhere, a general analysis of the errors and illusions imported into the language of the sciences by natural language.[5] Such analysis aims especially to identify the effects produced by the metaphorical processes at work, with a view to ridding such descriptions of the biases of representation and culturally determined interpretation which affect them. Certainly, since the de-Christianisation of the language of science in the West, the arrival of things, and states of things, in the world is no longer systematically attributed to God acting upon the universe. Subsequent modern and post-modern discourses concerning chance have nevertheless not rid themselves of the biases of agency, anthropomorphic or otherwise, or of the narrative effects which belief in a divine Providence had installed in conceptions of contingency. Personifications and narrativisations, borrowed from the spheres of human action, plastic creation and/or the functioning of artificial universes, are still employed to characterise the play of chance in the world. If the principle of causality is no longer ascribed to the continual action of a demiurge on the world, the evolution of an organism continues to be described as its history or destiny, and the behaviour of a system capable of emergence and self-organisation — if not as the result of a project, at least as a signifying and interpretable activity emanating from a more or less collective subject.

An epistemological criticism of the fictional processes at work in our apprehension of contingency, as it figures in the real universe, identifies these biases of representation, these habits of language and these metaphors. This may lead to an analysis of the role which they have historically played, and still play today, in constituting the scientific paradigms which have successively founded each episteme and structured its relation to knowledge.

However, the limits of such a procedure are soon encountered in the particular case of chance when we highlight the role that fiction plays in our representation of the future as being subject to contingency and indeterminacy. The epistemological approach simply extends to the domain of fiction the fundamental critique of language mounted by analytic philosophy. But the representation of chance entails a specific paradox which sets it apart. On the one hand, the contingent nature of an event (which means that it might or might not occur) cannot be presented independently of a narrative or plot. On the other hand, what the incorporation into a plot suspends or erases is precisely all those determinants that make the event contingent: its singularity, its raw character, its occurrence in a series of discrete elements whose outcome cannot be predicted because the series cannot be summarised and its principle cannot be calculated by any formula. All these characteristics are suppressed by the integration of an event into a narrative (however illogical or absurd), as by its appearance in a fictional universe (even one that is counter-intuitive or unrealistic). To understand how our representations of chance function, therefore, we must question more precisely the analogy, the parallelism of functions, which governs relations between contingency as a possible object of knowledge (the way things happen and arrange themselves in the world outside language) and contingency as fictions present it, and as the users of fictional worlds experience it — above all, in that familiar model of chance presented *in vitro*, the narrative.

## 2. From the Critique of Fiction to Fiction as Critique

This is where the extent of the comparison proposed at the outset between fiction and modelling can be specified. Models, as was recalled above, have in common with fictions the fact that they are neither theories nor complete representations, but hybrid constructions combining simplified schematisation and rigorous scientific description. They both make use of ordinary language to describe complex phenomena — urban traffic flows, a river's flood level, the properties of a substance — and are intended to be useful in concrete social situations by presenting different possible ways in which they may develop.

But in this respect, Nicolas Bouleau's reflections (2002 and 2005) on the social utility and political efficacy of probability-dependent modelling (following Hans Jonas) can shed light on the different functioning of abstract models, like the ones engineers employ, and of fictions. From this point of view, Bouleau affirms that the critique formulated by epistemologists — from Ernst Mach to Gaston Bachelard and Paul Feyerabend — of models as projections that are part scientific, part technological, misses its mark. We all know that models are under-determined: a number of models may coexist without being invalidated, and experimentation is not sufficient to refute them. It is their pragmatic effectiveness, and not their logical or scientific status, that we need to analyse to understand why, even when projections relying on probabilities are considered credible, they can fail to persuade individuals and collectivities to assume responsibility in the face of the risk that they measure.

Now, in analysing this effectiveness, 'one runs up against a philosophical problem: the antinomy or incompatibility between the idea of an "event that can be probabilized" and that of an "event that signifies", whether as an element of language or as a phenomenon that is interpretable within an affective and cultural symbolic structure'.[6] The primary effect of the abstraction necessary for calculating the probability that an effect will occur is to suppress the human meanings that attach themselves to the data being used. This suppression was strikingly evident in the case of the successive modellings on which various states needed urgently to rely during the Covid-19 pandemic in order to take decisions concerning health and economic policy — notably the most consequential one involving the lockdown of populations. Every model had to cross at least two sets of data that were flagrantly heterogeneous in their implications, and hence morally incompatible — those bearing on human and on economic losses.

It is only after producing calculations that a model relying on abstract probabilities once more produces intelligibility, but this time on the scale of the global structure that it describes. This is what is proposed for interpretation. 'On the one hand', as Bouleau explains, 'this is the historical origin of statistics: they efface signifieds to free up ratios. On the other hand, they create new signifiers by causing the emergence, on the basis of raw data, of tendencies, correlations, and "factors" taking account mainly of observed phenomena, which cause meaning to appear.'[7]

The chief obstacle to adopting the responsible attitudes which these models ought to prescribe resides, then, in the very complexity which the intervention of probability creates in them. The more rigorous the modelling, the more it renders visible the random and multi-determined character of the tendencies it reveals — and the less legible it becomes, actually inducing fatalism in the community for which it is destined.[8]

It is on this point that fictions, both literary and ludic, appear as more effective kinds of models than the others when it comes to their treatment of random situations, in that they gain in semantic density what they lose in rigor. Indeed, the human meanings which find themselves effaced when a situation is probabilised by a technological or physical model are typically those that accompany the presentation of chance in literary fiction, where the cognitive biases of common perception are amplified and aesthetically valorised. This is evident in the classic example of semantic bias in the perception of chance given by Cournot in 1843: to describe as 'rare' a tossing of coins that produces 'tails' ten times in a row, then 'heads' ten times, depends on a social, human interpretation of the event.[9] This description, erroneous from the mathematical point of view, is suppressed by the direct expression of the situation in terms of probabilities; by contrast, it will be integrated, valorised and developed by fiction. Thus, baroque and Romantic aesthetics privilege the extraordinary stroke of chance that corresponds to occurrences felt to be rare. But ordinary, day-to-day chance, which all the realisms since the nineteenth century have aimed to represent, corresponds by the same token to a representation of a doxic kind, perceived as such based on each epoch's idea of a statistically representative distribution of possible occurrences. Indeed, the fictional invention of chance (narrative, poetic, ludic) is founded on the detailed development of worlds constructed on the basis of the biases — not only cognitive, but also cultural and social — which preside over the human perception of chance.

These reflections call for two remarks. On the one hand, the fictional modelling of chance extends, exceeds, and thereby discloses the meaningful effects introduced into language by the treatment of chance. It deploys completely, to the point of paradox or absurdity, the worlds implied by the hypotheses that the language concerning contingency produces. In doing so, it further reveals the gulf separating the world as it is formalised and calculated by science from the non-rigorous descriptions currently imparted by natural language. It has thus been possible, since the 1920s, to use the fictional experience itself to provide an epistemological critique of models. This is the case with some of the fictions utilised by scientific discourses, notably those which were produced following the development of quantum physics in the early twentieth century — that is, from the moment when scientific discourse regarding the world began to diverge significantly from the representations of it in ordinary language. The micro-stories or parables which emerged in scientific discussions at the crucial moments when these discussions encountered the public debate about science — for example, the Einstein-Bergson debate during the 1922 Conference of Paris or the Einstein-Bohr controversy at the Solvay Councils of 1927 and 1930 — were then typically the object of competing interpretations, because their function was to show that one cannot, or can no longer, represent in ordinary language the behaviour of matter, time, or space as the new sciences understand them. In the new languages of science, they are no longer objects of possible human experience.

It is in the fictional status that must be attributed to those well-known paradoxical anecdotes — the story of Einstein's twins, the 'experiment' of Schrödinger's cat, the problem of Maxwell's demon — that their critical function lies, a function that, once again, thought experiment handles differently. The exact meaning of each of the situations evoked becomes apparent only from the moment when the hypothesis is not only articulated as micro-story (narrativity) but also developed in a possible word (fictionality), then confronted with a possible experience of the real. Science fiction, a literary genre dedicated to the thorough development of these micro-stories, only accentuates the demonstration: the scenarios it develops run up against this limit of the realistic representation of abstract theoretical propositions on the behaviour of space-time, universal relativity, or the coexistence of possible worlds — as is shown, for example, in the cinema of Christopher Nolan (*Inception* 2010, *Interstellar* 2014). When it is a question of creating and furnishing, on the basis of a counterintuitive hypothesis, a world that is actually inhabitable, in which a narrative unfolds in an actually liveable time, the diegetic treatment of that world necessarily distances itself from the rigor of the hypothesis.[10] Demonstration of this gap between theory and representation of the world thus appears more as the positive result of a critical function frankly taken on by the fiction itself than as the failure of truthfulness that epistemological analysis of fictional discourse is traditionally eager to expose.

Furthermore — and this is the second point that can be gleaned from the special relationship of fiction to chance — fictions not only serve to show the limits of possible representations of the world outside natural language. By returning to the problem of the incompatibility between the ideas of a 'probabilisable event' and a 'meaningful event' in the context of a search for the predictive function of representations, one can show that it is both an intrinsic quality and an objective of a fictional system to manage the interconnection between the probability of the event and its capacity to signify. That capacity largely explains the pragmatic effectiveness particular to those dense modellings of future situations which comprise fictions.

## 3. Fictions of Chance — Between Narrative and Thought Experiment

We have seen that a special link unites chance and narrative, since insertion into a plot in itself constitutes a model for conceiving the dynamic relation between events. To understand how things occur and give order to our attitudes towards those which may arrive in the future, we produce and make use of scenarios. Relying on a simple division of the conceptions of plot in narratology — here we will make use of the account proposed by K. Kukkonen in the *Living Handbook of Narratology* — one sees that each of them serves as a framework for one of the fundamental aspects of our relation to chance. If we understand plot above all as the result of a plan imagined and applied by an author (Kukkonen 2014, para. 5), we again find one of the major determining characteristics of some fictional modellings of chance — those which show its effects to be the product of a superior intentionality and the sign of an authorial plan at work in the world (destiny, providence, fortune, determinism). By contrast, by considering the plot as a progressive structuration (Kukkonen 2014, para. 4) and focusing on the fashion in which readers will perceive, as they become aware of it, the link between the events, the motivations of the characters engaged in them and the consequences of their actions, we recognise the temporal model permitting us to consider how events arrive over the duration. Here the relation between events is understood as what happens to *us*, the surging up of things perceived at the moment when they acquire meaning and existence by crossing a human path. We emphasised earlier the importance of this intersection in the naming and syntactic treatment of chance in natural languages. There, contingency is pre-understood as a process in which chance appears at the moment of an encounter between two independent causal chains; that encounter arrives in a privileged way in the unfolding of a story. Finally, if we consider plot in its overall form, as a fixed structure (Kukkonen 2014, para. 3), and concentrate synthetically and spatially on the way all the events are organised and configured among themselves within a narrative, we realise that this framework is the one used today to understand and explain most of the forms of 'objective' chance as it manifests itself in the physical world, especially in the theory of systems and the epistemologies of complexity. Indeed, chance in this context is no longer thought of in the linear form of the intervention of unforeseen occurrences along a temporal continuum, but in non-linear form, according to an essentially spatialised model.

It is not, of course, beside the point to note that these three different conceptions of plot, which encompass all the possible figurations of chance and demand recognition as the only possible forms of representing how things may occur, have been successively privileged in the history of such representations. The worlds of Antiquity and the Middle Ages, dominated by the authorial/providential view of chance, have been succeeded first by the de-Christianisation of the modern world and a material perception, individually experienced, of event-relations, then by the emergence of a post-Newtonian physics which, by transforming the relations among space, time, and matter, now imposes an essentially global and systemic concept of contingency.[11]

Narrativity, then, constitutes the essential framework of every possible representation of what may happen; but it is fictionality, as a logical, rhetorical, and doxic mode of enunciation, which figures as responsible for the effectiveness of the representations produced. Since a model is under-determined, as N. Bouleau reminds us, it can be critiqued only by proposing other alternative models, which in turn cause the emergence of what Jean-Marc Lévy-Leblond (1996) calls 'co-vérités' (*co-truths*).[12] The emergence of these co-truths alerts the imagination to the limits of any model's scientific claim, whatever it may be; but it also permits imagination to inhabit as a site of possible experience those models which show themselves most convincing by arousing both a rational and an emotional attachment to the alternative representation proposed.

Now, this function is characteristic of fictional practices, not in that they make use of narrative, but in that they project coherent states of things: possible worlds. Literary, visual, or ludic fiction entails a complete deployment of alternative worlds which, in practice, goes beyond the development of a hypothesis; the latter certainly ensures the veracity of the thought experiment, but limits its pragmatic reach. Insofar as it proposes inhabitable worlds, even when they are counterintuitive or devoid of characters, fiction operates in a medium that involves the subject emotionally, has a known cognitive reach, and functions effectively in this respect as a possible experimental field for all the situations and states of things accessible from a given situation. Certainly, it is this density of fiction that distances the representation it produces from the rigor which the exact illustration of a scientific theory ought to impose — as every expert engaged as a technical counsellor on the making of a science-fiction film finds out at his or her expense. But this is also what allows the novels, films, and series in question to furnish dense and complex models for conceiving a dense and complex reality in the milieu where we encounter it: that of experience. Moreover, and beyond this pragmatic value of fictions which combine the construction of narratives with the production of worlds, fictions possess the inherent capacity to project states of things not found in other manifestations of language, primarily in poetry, or in the sensual form realised by the visual and auditory arts. Since the end of the nineteenth century, from Mallarmé to André Breton, post-symbolist and surrealist poetry has been the type of creation in which this capacity of the arts to present chance — instead of *re*-presenting it — has imposed itself most clearly. The same applies to the different currents of aleatory creation in the plastic arts, to the extent that they also employ fictional processes (James 2012). Finally, the ludic and video-ludic arts, notably relying on computer-generated pseudo-chance, have appeared since the 1980s as the latest development of this attempt to manifest random structures of the world in the sphere of human activity.

Fiction thus appears as the mechanism which best permits us to manage the paradox linked to an intelligible representation of the absence of causality, not because it makes it possible to conceive this absence in itself, but because it provides an experience of it which constantly exceeds the aporias of its rigorous scientific formulation. This is doubtless what lends the fictional figurations of chance their own heuristic value — and in this sense their capacity to change the world through the representation we make of it, which serves as the basis for the decisions we make.

*Translated from the French by Richard Hillman*

## References

BOULEAU, NICOLAS. 2002. *La Règle, le divan et le compas* (Paris: Seuil)
——. 2005. 'Hasard, modélisation et pensée critique', in *Le Hasard: Une idée, un concept, un outil*, ed. by Jean-Paul Delahaye (Paris: L'Harmattan), pp. 79–90
COURNOT, ANTOINE-AUGUSTIN. 1843. *Exposition de la théorie des chances et des probabilités* (Paris: Hachette)
CURRIE, GREGORY. 1990. *The Nature of Fiction* (Cambridge: Cambridge University Press)
——. 2020. *Imagining and Knowing: The Shape of Fiction* (Oxford: Oxford University Press)
DUPRAT, ANNE. 2020A. 'Fiction et crise du prévisible', in *Reflections on Culture in the Age of Confinement*. Accessed 12 June 2022. <https://bcla.org/culture-and-confinement/>; trans. by John DeWitt as 'Fiction and the Crisis of the Predictable'. <https://hasard.hypotheses.org/3446> [accessed 12 June 2022]
——. 2020B. 'L'œuvre, la peur et le temps: Pour une saisie du risque par la littérature', in *Narratives of Fear and Safety*, ed. by Kaisa Kaukiainen et al. (Tampere: Tampere University Press). Trans. by Francis Guèvremont as 'Fear, Time and the Literary Work: Towards an Artistic Apprehension of Risk'. <https://www.academia.edu/42630151/Loeuvre_la_peur_et_le_temps._Pour_une_saisie_du_risque_par_la_litt%C3%A9rature> [accessed 12 June 2022]
— ET AL. (ed). [forthcoming]. *Figures of Chance I & II* (London: Routledge)
DUPUY, JEAN-PIERRE. 2004. *Pour un catastrophisme éclairé: Quand l'impossible est certain* (Paris: Seuil)
GAUVRIT, NICOLAS. 2009. *Vous avez dit hasard? Entre mathématiques et psychologie* (Paris: Belin)
JAMES, ALISON. 2012. 'Aleatory Poetics', in *Princeton Encyclopedia of Poetry and Poetics*, ed. by Roland Greene (Princeton, NJ: Princeton University Press), pp. 31–32
JONAS, HANS. (1979) 1984. *Das Prinzip Verantwortung: Versuch einer Ethik für die technologische Zivilisation* (Frankfurt: Neuauflage als Suhrkamp Taschenbuch)
KÖHLER, ERICH. 1973. *Der literarische Zufall, das Mögliche und die Notwendigkeit* (Munich: Fink)
KUKKONEN, KARIN. 2014. 'Plot', in *The Living Handbook of Narratology*, ed. by Peter Hühn et al. (Hamburg: Hamburg University) <http://www.lhn.uni-hamburg.de/article/plot> [accessed 12 June 2022]
LAVOCAT, FRANÇOISE. 2016. *Fait et fiction: Pour une frontière* (Paris: Seuil)
LÉVY-LEBLOND, JEAN-MARC. 1996. *Aux contraires (l'exercice de la pensée et la pratique de la science)* (Paris: Gallimard)
LYONS, JOHN D. 2011. *The Phantom of Chance, From Fortune to Randomness in Seventeenth-Century French Literature* (Edinburgh: Edinburgh University Press)
MATHERON, GEORGE. 1989. *Estimating and Choosing: An Essay on Probability in Practice* (Berlin: Springer)
MEILLASSOUX, QUENTIN. 2013. *Métaphysique et fiction des mondes hors-science* (Paris: Aux Forges de Vulcain); trans. by Alyosha Edelbi as *Science Fiction and Extro-Science Fiction* (Minneapolis, MN: Univocal, 2015).
MEINER, CARSTEN. 2008. *Le Carrosse littéraire et l'invention du hasard* (Paris: PUF)
MILNER, JEAN-CLAUDE. 1991. 'Hasard et langage', in *Le Hasard aujourd'hui*, ed. by Henri Barreau et al. (Paris: Seuil), pp. 43–53
MONOD, JACQUES. 1970. *Le Hasard et la Nécessité: Essai sur la philosophie naturelle de la biologie moderne* (Paris: Seuil)
PAVEL, THOMAS. 1986. *Fictional Worlds* (Cambridge, MA: Harvard University Press)
RICHARDSON, BRIAN. 1997. *Unlikely Stories: Causality and the Nature of Modern Narrative* (Newark: University of Delaware Press)

Schaeffer, Jean-Marie. 2010. *Why Fiction?*, trans. by Dorrit Cohn (Lincoln: University of Nebraska Press)

## Notes to Chapter 6

1. On the specific relation of fiction to the pandemic as a collective phenomenon, see Duprat (2020a and 2020b).
2. On this, see the considerable network formed in the last twenty years by 'pragmatic' theories of fiction and by the discussions they have prompted on the specific effects of fictional works and practices, from Jean-Marie-Schaeffer's *Why Fiction?* ([1999] 2010) to Françoise Lavocat's *Fait et fiction* (2016).
3. It should be recalled that both films were adapted from novels, and that their new treatment notably accentuates the role initially assigned to chance: *Human Desire* was a new adaptation of Jean Renoir's *La Bête humaine* (1938), itself adapted from the novel by Emile Zola; *Strangers on a Train* was partly drawn from the novel by Patricia Highsmith (1950).
4. 'Il semble que les langues soient toujours amenées quand elles mettent en rapport des séries de phénomènes, à colorer la rencontre, soit en termes de relations causales, soit [...] en termes de contrastes' (Milner 1991: 50).
5. On the consequences of this critique for a theory of fiction, see Currie (1990 and 2020) and Pavel (1986).
6. 'On se heurte à un problème philosophique: l'antinomie ou la non-compatibilité entre l'idée d' "événement probabilisable" et celle d' "événement ayant une signification", soit comme élément de langage soit comme phénomène interprétable dans une symbolique affective et culturelle' (Bouleau 2005, 85). See also the discussion by the mathematician George Matheron, to which N. Bouleau refers, or Jacques Monod's ground-breaking thesis on the role of chance in biology (Matheron 1989; Monod 1970).
7. 'D'un côté c'est l'origine historique des statistiques, elles effacent des signifiés pour dégager des ratios. D'un autre côté elles créent de nouveaux signifiants en faisant émerger, à partir de données brutes, des tendances, des corrélations, des "facteurs" rendant compte principalement des phénomènes observés, qui font apparaître du sens' (Bouleau 2005: 86).
8. An analysis of the causes of this fatalism and the forms it may take is developed at length in the works of Jean-Pierre Dupuy, whose conclusions also rely on the theories of Hans Jonas (Dupuy 2004; Jonas [1979] 1984).
9. In the same way that someone asked to give a sequence of figures at random will rarely propose the same one ten times in a row; for an overall view of these cognitive biases in the ordinary representation of chance, see Gauvrit (2009).
10. Hence, noted Q. Meillassoux (2013), the fact that most works of science fiction do not suspend the very conditions of the possibility of science. One may add that even those that do so, such as the novel *Ravages*, by René Barjavel, install their extra-scientific scenario in a world, and unfold their diegesis along a temporal thread, that both remain perfectly realistic. The same applies to the counterintuitive or metaleptic novel-systems of John Barth or Andrew Crumey.
11. On the relation between literary treatments and theories of chance in the West, see A. Duprat et al. (ed.), *Figures of Chance I & II*, forthcoming.
12. N. Bouleau, calling for modelling to become 'le moyen d'une pensée critique' (the means of critical thinking), sees in it 'un appel indispensable à l'imagination et une ouverture vers des choix, une politisation au bon sens du terme des causes réelles de l'avenir' (an indispensable call to the imagination and an opening up to choices, a politicisation in the positive sense of the term of the real causes of the future) (2005: 88).

CHAPTER 7

# Pygmalion's Virtual Doll: The Case of a Real Metalepsis?

*Nathalie Kremer*

Université Sorbonne Nouvelle/Institut Universitaire de France

## 1. An Incongruous Marriage

Licentious frolics can lead to the most serious of relationships. On 9 January 2019 the French newspaper *Libération* published a blog post announcing the marriage in Tokyo, on 4 November 2018, of Kondô Akihiko and the virtual singer Hatsune Miku (Giard 2019).[1] In an interview, the happy groom tells the story of his love:

> *When did you fall in love with Hatsune Miku?*
> We first met in 2007, on the Internet, but the first feelings appeared in May 2008 with the song *Miracle Point* [composed for Hatsune by Oster project]. Listening to this song several times, watching the video, *I felt a connection to her*.
> [...]
> *In what ways do you love her?*
> At first, she was a vocaloid [a text-to-speech software, appearing as the Hatsune Miku figure, a humanoid avatar], so I listened to the songs and watched the videos online. Then I bought the little rag doll that I could cuddle and sleep with. In 2016, I bought the PSP VR [playstation with virtual reality headset] so I could play with Hatsune in virtual reality, and all of a sudden she appeared in front of me, close by, and it was really exciting. In February 2018, I bought the Gatebox,[2] and then... Miku — in the form of a hologram — became interactive! Thanks to the Gatebox my life with Miku has taken on more colour: in the morning she wakes me up saying 'Good morning', in the evening she greets me kindly when I come home from work. If I stay awake too long, she tells me it's time to go to bed. Her presence has become much more palpable. *She crossed the screen.* I'm waiting for the next versions, the ones that will allow Miku to materialise freely in our world. I'm also waiting for us to give her an artificial intelligence so we can really talk to each other. (Giard 2019; emphasis added)

Hatsune Miku is a cultural icon in Japan, massively popularised on the Internet, but her name does not refer to any existing real person: she is a fictional image that can take the form of a virtual figure in video games, or can appear as a hologram, i.e., as a three-dimensional image appearing suspended in the air in a Gatebox. By claiming to feel a love connection with the virtual doll, the young man seems to operate with a metonymic confusion between the pragmatic situation (that of establishing a virtual connection with the image), and the ontological effect, which is that of non-reciprocal feeling, since there is no 'reality' or real entity 'behind' the appearance of this figure he worships. The beloved woman does not exist; the marital bond, on the other hand, does exist in reality... at least in the eyes of the young man. Indeed, the so-called 'marriage' has no legal value, because the singer does not really exist: the marriage certificate has not been delivered by the civil authorities, but by the Gatebox. The marriage therefore consists of a form of *shared ludic feint*, in the sense that Jean-Marie Schaeffer defined it (Schaeffer 2010: 138–39), but it is a playful pretence in which the game is taken very seriously. The young man conceives himself as really married to his fictional beloved, and the game does not end in due course, and is therefore no longer bounded by reality since it has replaced it definitively. This incongruous marriage of Akihiko and Hatsune is certainly not the first example of objectophilia, the practice of which has intensified in the last decade, with objecto-sexual marriages becoming more and more widespread and mediatised.[3] However, when sexual desire relates not to a real object but to a virtual object — a fictional — can we say that we are confronted with the intrusion of fiction into reality?

In other words, can we say that virtual reality as a medium for fiction changes the very nature of fiction itself, ie., by allowing it to intervene in reality? Would this incongruous marriage between Akihiko and Miku then form, through the interference of the means of virtual reality, a marriage between reality and fiction, i.e., a case of real metalepsis? The answer to this question is inseparable from an answer to the present volume's animating question: *'Does fiction change the world?'* Indeed, as Françoise Lavocat perfectly puts the point in *Fait et fiction*:

> From the real world to fiction (immersion, interaction), from fiction to the real world (modelling behaviour through fiction, dressing up as characters, theme parks and derived products), there are many ways of appropriating fictions, ways of accessing them, playing with them and extending our acquaintance with them. There are old and new methods of doing so. Still, needless to say, writing or reading a book has never made it possible to be part of it, except, precisely, for the fictional characters who are readers, writers, or mangaka created by Tom Holt, Jasper Fford or Hajime Katsuragi. Watching a film has never allowed us to cross over to the other side of the screen, except in a novel by Haruki Murakami or a film by Woody Allen. (Lavocat 2016, 484–85; my translation)

The thesis Françoise Lavocat puts forward lucidly in the chapter 'Borders of Fiction and Metalepsis' is that *'real metalepsis does not exist'* (Lavocat 2016: 520; my emphasis): that metalepsis, in other words, only exists within fiction as a possible privileged power of the latter. Now, if a virtual technology helps make possible marriage between a real human being and a fictional entity, can we infer the existence of real metalepsis, and conclude that fiction not only changes the world, but that in doing so, it transgresses the boundary between it and the world?

For Akihiko, this statement is certainly true: he says, as we have seen, that his beloved 'has crossed the screen'. This image of a crossing of the screen has become emblematic of metalepsis since 1985, when the character Tom Baxter crosses the cinema screen in Woody Allen's *The Purple Rose of Cairo*.[4] For Akihiko, there is therefore real metalepsis. However, if this phenomenon takes place from his viewpoint, it is entirely his own doing: the young man had to buy the necessary equipment to be able to enter into 'virtual' contact with his fiancée. The link between 'real' and 'virtual' is based entirely on technological progress, as Akihiko himself attests by detailing the phases of his 'relationship' with the idol: first, a games console, then a virtual image, all with the expectation that this image will finally be equipped with artificial intelligence, 'so that we can really exchange.' The term '*really*' emphasises that this is less a reciprocal relationship than Akihiko's own feelings projected onto the holographic doll; let's not forget that all the doll's reactions are of course pre-programmed.

The marriage between reality and fiction, as posed in this example, is therefore based on two necessary conditions: on the one hand, technological development, which confronts us with the question: can we put the doll or hologram and their intermediate phase, the moving robot, on the same footing? And on the other hand, the illusion, in which the receiver is lulled into thinking that there is an interaction between him and the figurine, which leads us to wonder about the relationship between consciousness and immersion. These two questions lead us to two essential aspects of an old story told by Ovid, about the dream that human beings have had since the dawn of time: that of seeing inanimate objects come to life.

## 2. Pygmalion's Desire

Akihiko testified that he 'bought the little doll' representing Miku, which he can 'cuddle' and 'sleep with.' This detail allows us to link his story directly to the fable of Pygmalion as told by Ovid in Book X of *Metamorphoses*, where the eponymous sculptor, having fallen in love with the statue he created, caresses his idol and sleeps with her, dreaming that she will become a real woman:

> Again and again his hands moved over his work to explore it.
> Flesh or ivory? No, it couldn't be ivory now!
> He kissed it and thought it was kissing him too. He talked it, held it,
> imagined his fingers sinking into the limbs he was touching,
> [...]
> He'd whisper sweet nothings or bring his idol the gifts which give pleasure to girls,
> [...]
> He even dressed it in clothes, put rings on the fingers and necklaces round the throat,
> hung jewels from the ears and girdled the breasts with elegant bands.
> (Ovid 2004: x, lines 254–65)

The myth of Pygmalion is the fundamental paradigm of the desire to animate fiction, i.e., the becoming-true of a fictional image that seems to have inhabited man's dreams since antiquity. This paradigm has seen several moments of resurgence throughout the history of European culture, resurgences that always appear to be linked to accelerations in philosophical and scientific developments. Thus, we can distinguish two great periods of revival of the Pygmalionian dream. The first takes place in the Enlightenment, when philosophical materialism and empiricism spread as an epistemological mainstream. The motif of the animated statue in fact lends itself well to the materialist thesis that all matter is alive, endowed with energy, and capable of mutations in a movement of continuous transformation.[5]

This step is accompanied in the history of Pygmalion's rewritings by the eradication of divine intervention in order to privilege a materialistic or technological explanation for the metamorphosis of the statue. The myth of Pygmalion then joins that of Prometheus in the celebration of his skill and creative powers (Geisler-Szmulewicz 1999).[6] Considering that this transition was prepared during the Enlightenment, the novel *L'Ève future* by Villiers de l'Isle-Adam, published in 1868, is certainly the most accomplished example. Here, the marvellous mythology is removed, only to reappear in another form. Indeed, the android creature made by Edison, named Hadaly, is meticulously described as the supreme achievement of the knowledge and genius of its creator, yet it is endowed with a soul (referred to as Sowana in the novel) that has mysteriously passed from a real woman to the android — whereby the latter incorporates a form of the fantastic in place of the marvel he had banished. As Gwenhaël Ponnau summarises in his essay on *L'Ève future*:

> Though he is so prolific in scientific explanations and justifications — explanations, justifications, theoretical and almost technological discourses which abundantly nourish the matter of the book — Edison, whom the young lord calls his 'dear sorcerer', must admit that he is overwhelmed by the enigma of the creature born of his inventor's genius. (Ponnau 2000: 9)

As Victor Stoichita puts it in his study *The Pygmalion Effect* (2006), today the fable is experiencing a second moment of revival, which differs from that which took place in the eighteenth century in that it is no longer marked by an ideal of *mimesis*-imitation, but by that of a *technesis*-transformation. Indeed, in the classical age, the dream of animation was still conceived as transition from the inanimate *to* the living, animation coming after a first phase of creation, through a divine or material instance, similarly to its incarnation in Ovid's stories. This phase of the Pygmalionian dream was based on the ideal of the robot or technical being perfectly resembling the human model, which could come to life according to an (impossible) ideal of resemblance-duplication. Frankenstein can be seen here as the negative image of the Pygmalion, in his functioning as a hinge between the two moments of the myth, *mimèsis*-imitation and *technesis*-transformation.

Today, this dream of transforming the moving-statue or robot into a living being seems to have become that of a *simultaneity* between art and life, according to an ideal of coincidence between the technical work of art and life, i.e., the semblance of life that we would like to endow it with through artificial intelligence. Stoichita rightly points out that, thanks to advances in technology, the simulacra imagined and created today look more alive, and therefore better promote illusion or what he calls the '*pygmalion effect.*'

For example, Professor Hiroshi Ishiguro, Director of the *Intelligent Robotics Laboratory* at the University of Osaka, has become world-renowned for his ability to build his robots so that they look perfectly human, with an artificial intelligence system that allows them to interact with humans in a way that seems so natural[7] that they can create an illusion of life — even, as Ishiguro admits, 'if only for a brief period' (Whitehouse 2005). His best-known robot, the Geminoid HI, built about ten years ago, thus forms a third stage in the development of the Pygmalionian dream, one that marks the transition from fiction to reality. The Geminoid HI is indeed a kind of Hadaly, but real: the robot is a technological clone of its creator Ishiguro, that not only looks like him but has even been modelled on him, by receiving injections of Ishiguro's skin cells and hair implants. For Ishiguro, the robot even has a soul: it is not a machine object, but has a form of 'living' presence.

Did Ishiguro make Pygmalion's dream come true, and create a form of fiction-become-reality? Are the androids created by Ishiguro and his team the 'real' accomplishment of the virtual figures like Hatsune Miku? The difference is reminiscent of that between the traditional arts of sculpture and painting: they are two forms of inanimate figures, which can induce an illusion of reality, but one visual, one spatial in form. Their degree of illusion varies,[8] but they are two cases of non-animated figures that found a fictitious representation (either of a robot professor Ishiguro simulating an exam with students, or of a fictitious popstar that is married) and, in doing so, intrude into our reality. Have today's technological and computer advances made real metalepsis possible?

## 3. Definition of Metalepsis

To answer this question, we must first return to the definition of metalepsis which, it must be acknowledged, has been subject to both evolution and fluctuation. Many studies have already recalled the stages of its redefinition over the last half-century. Its first instance is a narratological definition, which can be found in 1972 in Genette's *Figures III* as a transgression of narrative levels, as in 'any intrusion by the extradiegetic narrator or narratee into the diegetic universe (or by diegetic characters into a metadiegetic universe, etc.), or the inverse' (Genette 1972: 244, my translation).[9]

In 2004, Genette took up the question of metalepsis again in an essay that generalises the figure to fiction (Genette 2004), where metalepsis is defined as the transgression of a boundary, whatever it may be, between two universes, as long as one of them can be perceived as represented. Genette's essay follows his contribution to a collective work on the 'breaches of the representational pact' published by John Pier and Jean-Marie Schaeffer in 2005. This volume also includes an influential article by Marie-Laure Ryan wherein she distinguishes between rhetorical metalepsis, as a fact of narrative, and ontological metalepsis, as the interpenetration of two ontologically separate worlds (Ryan 2005).

I agree with the current pleas of fiction theorists for a broader definition of fiction that is not restricted to the narrative novel nor even to language, and whose pragmatic use must be considered.[10] This automatically implies considering metalepsis in an ontological sense (which, moreover, is only a more elaborate form of rhetorical metalepsis[11]). The question is whether ontological metalepsis can actually exist or not. To this end, I'd like to draw on Lavocat's perfectly argued study in *Fait et fiction* (Fact and Fiction) to consider metalepsis from the point of view of its definition (1), its characteristic (2) and its stake (3):

> 1. Metalepsis is defined as a 'meeting of entities and worlds of different statuses' (Lavocat 2016: 518).[12]
>
> 2. Metalepsis is characterised by the transgression of a boundary between two worlds. Indeed, according to Lavocat, 'transgression is a defining element of metalepsis, even if it has become so frequent that it could become dull and blunt' (2016: 518). The 'idea of transgressing and crossing a level, a limit, in a word a border' (2016: 474), is indeed central.
>
> 3. Finally, the challenge of metalepsis is to show the frontier while transgressing it: in this sense, it does not cancel or merge worlds, but paradoxically maintains 'an ontologically heterogeneous space' (Lavocat 2016: 489).[13]

In short, metalepsis consists of presenting two ontologically different worlds together, in their paradoxical heterogeneity.[14] Given these defining traits, can we consider the examples of Geminoid HI and virtual singer Hatsune Miku as real metalepses? These examples seem to fit well within the definition of metalepsis (1 and 3), but we cannot find characteristic (2), metalepsis as a boundary transgression, in them. Indeed, as regards the definition of metalepsis as a factor in the creation of 'an ontologically heterogeneous space' (Lavocat 2016: 489), as well as the challenge of maintaining these two worlds together in the same universe, we can affirm that there is indeed the coexistence of two different ontological worlds within our examples: the fictional (in its robotic or virtual form) on the one hand, and the living on the other. One is programmed and inanimate, the other free and animate, and the two cannot merge or be confounded, but only coexist. Proof of this is that virtual creatures can regret the ontological limits of their cybernetic existence, as in Guillaume Béguin's play *Titre à jamais provisoire* (created in 2018), in which the spectator witnesses the laments of a perfectly autonomous and lively android woman who deplores the impossibility of her having children, since her creators had not thought of providing her with a uterus and a female hormonal cycle!

The Pygmalions of the cybernetic age lead us to reconsider the relationship between fiction and reality from the point of view of what Markus Gabriel calls a 'new realism' (Gabriel 2020),[15] in which the world is seen not in opposition to the mind, as different ontological substances, but according to an ontological pluralism. Within this theory, mathematical numbers, norms, galaxies, and fictional dolls are forms of reality in the same way as living beings, objects, and human or natural actions (see also Gabriel 2015). Reality is therefore plural, in which different 'fields of meaning' are distinguished (fictional meaning, moral meaning, technological meaning, and so on), all of which are 'real' and can interfere with each other.

Ontological pluralism can thus be observed concretely today through the fictional use of Ishiguro's robots, or the game with virtual avatars resembling us. In the case of Geminoid HI, there is no question of an ontological transgression of boundaries: the avatar and the professor are side by side in the same space (the laboratory, the examination room, the stage in front of the camera), without the robot having to transgress any separating 'screen.' In the case of Kondô Akihiko and his virtual singer Hatsune Miku, although the former claimed that she 'crossed the screen', can we seriously consider her to have left the Gatebox to move freely in interior space? No, of course not, she is dependent on and even a prisoner of the Gatebox, and despite the fact that the holder is convinced that a love link exists between them, she will never leave her glass case.

## 4. Transgressing the Border

It is necessary to linger on the question of transgression as a characteristic of metalepsis, and to ask, frankly: is the transgression of a frontier necessary for metalepsis? And what kind of boundary are we talking about?

Let us take a third example, while remaining in Japan: an attack took place on 21 May 2016 against the Japanese 'idol'[16] Mayu Tomita. She was stabbed by a young man who declared that Tomita had betrayed him by refusing to accept a gift he wanted to give her, and by no longer responding to his messages on social networks, even though he alleged that they were intimate. The *otaku* (i.e., the fanatical admirer) was sentenced to fourteen years and six months in prison for attempted murder, while the victim can no longer practice her profession as an idol because the attack left her disabled. The acts and consequences here are very real, and one would be tempted to consider this an example of a real metalepsis. However, it is possible to question that definition. Indeed, the example is reminiscent of Stendhal's soldier attacking an actor on the stage during a performance of *Othello* in Baltimore in 1822, an example given by Genette as a case of real metalepsis, as opposed to the fictitious metalepsis of Don Quixote attacking the cardboard puppets of Master Pierre (Genette 2004: 50–51). There is, in all these cases, 'metaleptic conduct' that entails the crossing, albeit 'illusory', of the border between fiction and reality, as Genette and several other theorists have reasoned; the crossings are illusory 'since [they] in no way reach the characters they aim at but only the actors, of flesh or cardboard, who embody them' (2004: 51).

Now, to speak of *real* metalepsis nevertheless seems contradictory if one considers the crossing of the border as *illusory*. This is the position defended by Lavocat, contrary to Marie-Laure Ryan's position (2006: 226) on the rare existence of real metalepsis in cases such as the American spectator of Othello, or our Japanese aggressor. Those who attack actors, Lavocat argues, do not have to cross any real 'wall':

> These assaults, which explode any form of fictional contract (such as Don Quixote tearing to pieces Don Pedro's puppets), are not [...] a matter of metalepsis [...]. While for all other media the obstacle of the page or screen is impassable, there is none between stage and room, neither material nor ontological. (Lavocat 2016: 486–87)

In other words, there is, in all these cases, confusion between illusion and reality, but not metalepsis. On the contrary, in order to be able to function, the receiver must be in a split mental state, as defined by Jean-Marie Schaeffer (2010: 190)[17]; that is to say, they do not really *believe* in the fictional illusion. Only the paradoxical recognition of the coexistence of the two distinct ontological worlds makes it possible to keep them together: otherwise, one of them will necessarily be destroyed. Metalepsis, on the contrary, does not break the representation but maintains it in a form of paradoxical logic. The ontological pluralism defended by Markus Gabriel (2015, 2020) precisely allows us to think of metalepsis as really possible, in the sense that several realities coexist and interfere in a perfect recognition and awareness of their difference. For Kondô Akihiko, the singer really exists, even if she does not exist in the same way as humans, in flesh and blood.

However, the question of transgression arises not only in the nature of metalepsis, but also in its form. Indeed, metalepsis is usually equated with the violence of an assault or assassination. Nevertheless, not all metalepses are subversive, as Lavocat points out:

> As a paradox, metalepsis induces a singular cognitive response, of variable amplitude, which probably stems from the blockage of understanding caused by any paradox, but which is not resolved by it. [...] At the very least, it can be said that the idea of a cognitive disruption is consubstantial with metalepsis. (Lavocat 2016: 519)

Transgression is therefore not a necessary condition for metalepsis; it is not even a sufficient condition, since I can really cross the curtain of a stage and not commit real metalepsis by this transgressive gesture. I will therefore insist that it is rather the idea of a *passing* or *crossing*[18] that is essential in the appearance of metalepsis, but that this crossing-over can very well take place for us without confusion on our part — after all, it is the logical consequence of the split mental state, which allows the recognition of the existence of two different universes at the same time. This is perfectly possible, particularly from the point of view of the new realism as defined by Gabriel (2015, 2020). Moreover, the traversing does not imply the annulment of the original universe; this is the paradox.

## 5. Real or Fictional Metalepsis?

How then can we conceive of this passing of a frontier? One cannot really cross the screen of a cinema nor really enter a book, of course: this privilege belongs to fiction, as Lavocat has clearly demonstrated. And so, the story of Pygmalion seems to be only the story of an illusion, of a Pygmalion-effect, but not of a metalepsis: for that to happen, Ishiguro's robots would have had to come straight out of the pages of Villiers de l'Isle-Adam's novel, which is, of course, impossible. It should also be pointed out that in the Ovidian fable and its traditional rewritings, there is no question of seeing a metalepsis in the metamorphosis of the statue because it is, after all, only a transformation of matter that belongs to the same fictional universe as Pygmalion.[19] The transition from the inanimate to the living therefore does not imply a passage, a crossing from one universe (or one reality, in Gabriel's words) to another.

However, when students in Osaka pass an exam thanks to the training given by the Geminoïd HI in simulation experiments, which create a fictitious exam space, or when a Pygmalion-Akihiko spends two million yen on a wedding ceremony, we do observe a change in the 'real' world, under the impulse of a 'fictional' world, that can be described as metaleptic. The metaleptic passage does not consist in the becoming-living or becoming-reality of fiction, but in fiction's crossing of the frontiers of representation that reality has drawn around itself. If one remembers that the crossed frontier is one between worlds of different *statuses*, i.e., of unequal *level*,[20] one can consider as metaleptic those moments when fiction creates a tangible change out *in* the world.[21]

Indeed, as a product of the real world (whether through the act of artistic, literary, or technological know-how), fiction is an enclave in the world, certainly with unlimited potential, but embedded in the real world that produces it, thinks it, and plays with it. At the moment when the fictional product directs our actions in the world and becomes the source of a change in behaviour and know-how, the world becomes the product driven by what it has itself generated. From a simple enclave in the world, fiction becomes a way of rewriting the world map by remodelling our beliefs, knowledge, and behaviour.

Yves Citton's analyses in *Mythocratie* support this idea when he asserts that any form of exposure to fiction produces a 'metaleptic scriptwriting activity' ('activité de scénarisation métaleptique' (Citton 2010: 86), insofar as it influences our acts even though it is the product of our acts. Seen from this angle, the marriage of Kondô Akihiko and Hatsune Miku may reasonably be qualified as metaleptic; and if the transgression — Hatsune's removal from her glass bulb — is impossible, it is even important that it *cannot* take place, insofar as this separation maintains precisely the delimitation, and thus the paradoxical coexistence, between fiction and reality. Metalepsis is thus less about the meeting and mixing of two forms of being (in this case, virtual fiction and human reality) — a sort of 'thematic' approach to metalepsis, which is of course impossible and which would form a denial of the ontological pluralism of reality — than about the pragmatic modification of an order of things or behaviours in a world, under the effect of an action produced from a different world than this one. Ontological pluralism allows us, precisely, to admit that reversals of levels are possible and real.

Also, if Françoise Lavocat is right to say that there is no real metalepsis possible between reality and fiction, this point concerns the thematic plane, so to speak, of an intrusion of characters, figures, or imaginary objects from one (fictional) world into another (non-fictional) one. But on a pragmatic level, we can indeed observe a reversal of levels between reality and fiction, when fiction leads reality by conditioning our uses.

# References

CAÏRA, OLIVIER. 2011. *Définir la fiction* (Paris: Éd. de l'EHESS)
CITTON, YVES. 2010. *Mythocratie : Storytelling et imaginaire de gauche* (Paris: Éditions Amsterdam)
DENEYS-TUNNEY, ANNE. 1999. 'Le roman de la matière dans *Pigmalion ou la statue animée* (1741) d'A.-F. Boureau-Deslandes', in *Être matérialiste à l'âge des Lumières : Hommage offert à Roland Desné*, ed. by Béatrice Fink and Gerhardt Stenger (Paris: PUF)

GABRIEL, MARKUS. 2015. *Why the World Does Not Exist*, trans. by Gregory Moss (Cambridge: Polity)
——. 2020. *Propos réalistes* (Paris: Vrin)
GEISLER-SZMULEWICZ, ANNE. 1999. *Le Mythe de Pygmalion au xix$^e$ siècle: Pour une approche de la coalescence des mythes* (Paris: Honoré Champion)
GENETTE, GÉRARD. 1972. *Figures III* (Paris, Seuil)
——. 2004. *Métalepse: De la figure à la fiction* (Paris: Seuil)
GIARD, AGNÈS. 2019. 'Pourquoi épouser une femme fictive?', *Libération*, 1 September <http://sexes.blogs.liberation.fr/2019/01/09/pourquoi-epouser-une-femme-fictive/>
HOBSON, MARIAN. 1982. *The Object of Art: The Theory of Illusion in Eighteenth-Century France* (Cambridge: Cambridge University Press)
LEDIT, GUILLAUME. 2017. 'Hiroshi Ishiguro, l'homme androïde(s)', in *Usbek et Rica*, 25 October <https://usbeketrica.com/article/hiroshi-ishiguro-robots-homme-androide> [accessed 22 June 2022]
LAVOCAT, FRANÇOISE. 2016. *Fait et fiction: Pour une frontière*, Poétique (Paris: Seuil)
MARSH, AMY. 2010. 'Love Among the Objectum Sexuals', *Electronic Journal of Human Sexuality* 13 (1 March) < http://www.ejhs.org/volume13/ObjSexuals.htm> [accessed 19 June 2020]
OVID. 2004. 'Pygmalion', in *Metamorphoses*, trans. by David Raeburn, revised edn (London: Penguin Classics)
PAVEL, THOMAS. 1986. *Fictional Worlds* (Cambridge, MA: Harvard University Press)
PIER, JOHN, and JEAN-MARIE SCHAEFFER (eds.). 2005. *Métalepses: Entorses au pacte de la représentation* (Paris: Éd. de l'EHESS)
PONNAU, GWENHAËL. 2000. *L'Ève future ou l'œuvre en question* (Paris: PUF)
RYAN, MARIE-LAURE. 2005. 'Logique culturelle de la métalepse, ou la métalepse dans tous ses états', in *Métalepses: Entorses au pacte de la représentation*, ed. by John Pier and Jean-Marie Schaeffer (Paris: Éd. de l'EHESS), pp. 201–33
SCHAEFFER, JEAN-MARIE. 2010. *Why Fiction?*, trans. by Dorrit Cohn (Lincoln: University of Nebraska Press)
STOICHITA, VICTOR. 2006. *The Pygmalion Effect: Towards a Historical Anthropology of Simulacra* (Chicago: University of Chicago Press)
WAYTZ, ADAM, NICHOLAS EPLEY, and JOHN T. CACIOPPO. 2010. 'Social Cognition Unbound: Insights into Anthropomorphism and Dehumanization', *Current Directions in Psychological Science*, 19 (1): 58–62 <doi:10.1177/0963721409359302>
WHITEHOUSE, DAVID, 'Japanese Develop "Female" Android', *BBC News*, 27 July 2005, <http://news.bbc.co.uk/2/hi/science/nature/4714135.stm#:~:text=Japanese%20scientists%20have%20unveiled%20the,in%20a%20human%2Dlike%20manner>, accessed 16 July 2022

## Notes to Chapter 7

1. The interview was covered by many media outlets during 2019. Translations are mine.
2. As Agnès Giard explains: 'the Gatebox is a personal assistant coupled with a home automation system with a holographic interface. To put it more clearly: it is a cylindrical glass bulb in which evolves a holographic creature capable of interacting with its owner, turning off the light, turning on the TV and eventually checking the contents of the fridge and placing orders for deliveries on the Internet. The creature (currently provided in two forms: Hikari Azuma and Hatsune Miku) can talk to its owner, understand his orders, exchange e-mails and SMS messages with him and act as an alarm clock' (Giard 2019).
3. The most famous cases are those of Lee Jin-gjyu, who married his manga cushion in 2010, and of Erika Eiffel, who married the Eiffel tower. See Marsh (2010); Waytz, Epley, and Cacioppo (2010).

4. See the discussion of this example in the editors' Introduction to this volume.
5. A materialist version of Pygmalion is given by Boureau-Deslandes in 1741 (Deneys-Tunney 1999: 93–108).
6. Note that originally, in the fables about Pygmalion before Ovid, Pygmalion was not the creator of the statue with which he fell in love.
7. 'In Nara at the *Advanced Telecommunications Research Institute International* and the *Intelligent Robotics Laboratory* at the University of Osaka, Hiroshi Ishiguro is pursuing his goal: to create a robot *"that looks, moves, and really talks like a human"*' (Ledit 2017; my translation) ('Du côté de Nara au sein du *Advanced Telecommunications Research Institute International* et du *Intelligent Robotics Laboratory* à l'université d'Osaka, Hiroshi Ishiguro poursuit son objectif: créer un robot *"qui ressemble, bouge, et parle réellement comme un humain"*').
8. In the case of the Ishiguro androids, we are dealing with the Pygmalion effect, what Marian Hobson calls a 'total' or 'bipolar' illusion ('Bipolar illusion insists that the consumer makes a mistake about what he sees, be it only momentarily. [...] A mistake about the nature of what is seen must totally exclude awareness and thus pleasure too'. Hobson 1982: 49).
9. For more on these kinds of narrative metalepsis, see part IV, Chapters 16 and 17 of the present volume.
10. On fiction and narrative, see Caïra (2011: 30–31): 'Many theorists, as different as Peter Lamarque and Stein Olsen, Margaret Macdonald, Kendall Walton, Gregory Currie, or David Lewis, make narrative the elementary substratum of the fictional experience. To define fiction as a particular form of narrative, or as a result of the desire to tell stories, is to preclude the examination of certain fictions because they are not narrative' (my translation). Like Lavocat, I 'understand here by "use" ways of thinking, of doing, of appropriating fictions through play, interpretation, re-creation' (Lavocat 2016: 12n2; my translation).
11. As Lavocat argues: 'The distinction between rhetorical metalepsis and ontological metalepsis must first of all be requalified in terms of degree; for all metalepsis is ontological in the sense that it produces effects linked to an impossibility caused by the encounter of entities and worlds of different statuses' (Lavocat 2016: 518, my translation).
12. We should specify that it is not the meeting that is impossible, but rather that it is judged as such and in this sense often produces very varied effects of shock or pleasure.
13. See also Lavocat (2016: 480): 'The fusion of worlds does not take place, because the very stake of all metaleptic works is to play with the frontier, to manifest it by simulating its crossing. This passage does not have the effect of abolishing it, on the contrary, it aims to make it perceptible — conceivable, visible, imaginably palpable: this experience of thought is the privilege of fiction, and we are apparently more fond of it than ever before'; and Lavocat (2016: 479): 'The concept of metalepsis is logically incompatible with the concept of fusion of worlds.'
14. This definition of metalepsis is dependent on Thomas Pavel's conception of fiction (Pavel 1986).
15. See especially the introduction and the chapter on neutral realism (Gabriel 2020: 103–34).
16. The *idols* are young artists, often highly mediatized, with a cheerful innocent image. They play the roles of singer, actor, animator, and model, under contract for a limited period of a few months or years. They have been produced in large numbers by the entertainment industry in Japan since the 1960s. The example I am referring to here concerns the idol Mayu Tomita, who was assaulted by Tomohiro Iwazaki.
17. We find this (non-metaleptic) illusion in Ovid, who clearly indicates that Pygmalion deludes himself voluntarily in his relationship with the statue ('No, it couldn't be ivory now!' and 'imagined his fingers sinking into the limbs he was touching' [Ovid 2004: x, lines 255, 267]).
18. Lavocat also emphasises in the conclusion of her book that the verb 'to pass' is more neutral than the term 'to transgress' (Lavocat 2016: 522n1).
19. Even the intervention of Venus cannot be considered as metaleptic since it also belongs to the fictional universe of Pygmalion and its statue, where the marvellous is possible.
20. Cf. metalepsis as 'crossing a level, a limit, in a word, a boundary' (Lavocat 2016: 474).
21. In a similar way, perhaps — but inversely — we can consider as metaleptic the moments that we call 'cameo effect' in fiction: Lavocat recalls the example of Alfred Hitchcock appearing fleetingly in his films, not as a character but as a real person, producing a 'cameo effect' or an

intrusion of reality into the fictional world: 'these metalepses consist of small events, salient glimpses of reality, sufficiently circumscribed and autonomous not to crack the fictional world and to highlight, to give a taste of the incongruity of presences coming from another world, the world outside fiction' (Lavocat 2016: 491).

PART III

# Changing Practices: Political Uses and Effects of Fiction

CHAPTER 8

❖

# Etiquette to 'Change the World'? Fictional Time-Order and Imperial Power at the Court of Emperor Go-Daigo

*Simone Müller*

*University of Zurich*

## 1. Introduction

This chapter discusses whether, and to what extent, temporal regimes of etiquette at the imperial court of medieval Japan were fictionalised or idealised for political purposes.¹ To probe this question, I examine two works known as *Kenmu nitchjū gyōji* 建武日中行事 (Daily observances of the Kenmu era) and *Kenmu nenjū gyōji* 建武年中行事 (Annual observances of the Kenmu era), attributed to Emperor Go-Daigo 後醍醐天皇 (1288–1339, r. 1318–1339). They describe the reputed daily and annual routine at the court of Emperor Go-Daigo at the beginning of the fourteenth century.²

In the following, I will argue that *Kenmu nitchū gyōji* and *Kenmu nenjū gyōji* may be considered semi-fictitious narratives that aim to create an idealised 'temporal regime' of court routine in order to reinstall and consolidate imperial power and thus to change the world through a literary text. By describing the court as a refined and integral temporal mechanism — similar to a clock — the emperor is integrated into a regular, functioning system, in which he evolves as a symbol of social and political order and thus as an authoritative ideal. Order, in the form of a temporal model, figures the emperor's 'purity' or clockwise 'perfection', thus legitimising his claim to rule. The two works under investigation may, therefore, be considered narratives of 'inner-imperial' order. Moreover, I will argue that the two texts express the wish for an intrinsically 'Go-Daigo-like' clockwork that safeguards for the emperor some measure of both autonomy and sovereignty.

## 2. Content and Structure of *Kenmu nitchū gyōji* and *Kenmu nenjū gyōji*

*Kenmu nitchū gyōji* and *Kenmu nenjū gyōji* form part of a specific genre called *yūsoku kojitsu* 有職故実 (knowledge about old matters), manuals describing court ceremonies and etiquette. The genre developed from *kanbun nikki* 漢文日記, sinographic diaries written by male aristocrats (cf. Matsuzono and Kondō 2017: 5). Subgenres of *yūsoku kojitsu* are *nitchū gyōji* 日中行事 (daily observances) and *nenjū gyōji* 年中行事 (annual observances) that emerged in the ninth century (Matsuzono and Kondō 2017: 6).

*Kenmu nitchū gyōji* purportedly records the daily procedures at the court of Emperor Go-Daigo, starting in the early morning at the hour of the hare (c. 5–7 am),[3] with the raising of the lattice shutters and the palace's morning cleaning, thereafter describing chronologically various daily observances: imperial washing and prayer at the Lime Altar (*ishibaidan*) at the hour of the dragon (c. 7–9 am); breakfast and working rapport at the hour of the snake (c. 9–11 am), formal morning meal at the hour of the horse (c. 11 am — 1 pm); formal evening meal at the hour of the monkey (c. 3–5 pm); lightening of the palace and storing of the duty board (*nikkyū no fuda* 日給の簡[4]) when the daily observances are finished — which roughly corresponds to the hour of the rooster (c. 5–7 pm); and lowering of the lattice shutters and officials' name calling at the hour of the boar (c. 9–11 pm). The day ends when the emperor goes to sleep with the lighting of the royal bedroom using oil lamps. The work closes with a brief description of relevant monthly observances at the court such as the report of the officials' working hours to the emperor on the third day of every month, or the memorial service to Kannon (*Kannon*-gu 観音供) on the eighteenth day.

*Kenmu nenjū gyōji* on the other hand, describes, also in a chronological order, eighty-six ceremonies at the imperial court, beginning with the first annual activities — the Imperial New Year's Ceremony *Shihōhai* 四方拝 (salutations to the four directions) and the Imperial Reception on New Year's Day (*Ganjitsu no sechie* 元日の節会), followed by many festivities such as the Kasuga Festival (*Kasuga no matsuri* 春日の祭) on the upper day of the monkey in the second month, the Kamo Festival (*Kamo no matsuri* 賀茂の祭) on the middle day of the rooster in the fourth month, the Gion Festival (*Gion'e* 祇園会) on the fourteenth day of the sixth month, the Niinae Festival (*Niinae no matsuri* 新嘗祭) on the twenty-third day of the eleventh month, and ending with the cleansing ceremony *Yo'ori* 節折 (break of the season) at the end of the twelfth month, according to the lunar calendar. The traditional view dates the text between 1334 and 1336 — at the beginning of the so-called Kenmu Restoration (Kenmu no shinsei 建武の新政, 1333-1336), an attempt by Emperor Go-Daigo to overthrow the shogunate and restore imperial rule (cf. Blümmel 1979: 12; Wada 1989: 417; Satō 2015: 6–7; Matsuzono and Kondō 2017: 61). However, some textual evidence (cf. Blümmel 1979: 12–13) suggests that the work may also have been written earlier, around 1327.[5]

It is still open to discussion whether the two documents were written on the command of Emperor Go-Daigo or by Emperor Go-Daigo himself. The uncertainty of authorship does not change the texts' aim, however. They can be considered part of Go-Daigo's reform ambitions (Blümmel 1979: 12), an attempt to revive discarded court ceremonies from the Heian period. The two documents thus have an important political function: they aim to confirm the emperor's authority and the 'excellency of his reign' (Matsuzono and Kondō 2017: 61) to posterity as well as prescribing court etiquette for future generations. This raises the question of to what extent these prescriptive and politically motivated texts correspond to court reality. Were they followed strictly at the time, or did they rather have a symbolic and political function? Did they reflect court reality or an ideal?

## 3. Historical Background: Emperor Go-Daigo and the Will to Restore Imperial Order in a Time of Chaos

To answer these questions, it is vital to contextualise the historical moment of text production. At the end of the twelfth century, power shifted from the court in Kyōto to the military government in Kamakura, first led by the Minamoto and later by the Hōjō clan. The takeover of power by the warrior aristocracy gradually weakened the political impact and economic situation of the court, eventually scaling it down to a mere ceremonial institution. Two attempts to restore imperial power were undertaken. The first was the Jōkyū Rebellion in 1221 led by retired Emperor Go-Toba 後鳥羽 (1180–1239, r. 1183–1198) and his sons.[6] The political force behind the second, known as the Kenmu Restoration, was Emperor Go-Daigo. In 1333 he overturned the Kamakura shogunate ruled by the Hōjō clan with the assistance of the Ashikaga clan. In 1336 however, the Ashikaga turned against Go-Daigo and established the so-called Muromachi bakufu in Kyoto by enthroning Emperor Kōmyō 光明天皇 (1322–1380, r. 1336–1348). Subsequently, the court split into a southern court ruled by Emperor Go-Daigo and a northern court ruled by Emperor Kōmyō. This era is known as one of the bloodiest periods in Japanese history. *Kenmu nitchū gyōji* and *Kenmu nenjū gyōji* were thus produced in a time of political, economic, and social chaos.

In this context the very name of Emperor Go-Daigo appears to be meaningful. Go-Daigo was named after Emperor Daigo 醍醐天皇 (885–930, r. 897–930) who endeavored to abolish the regency government (*sekkan seiji* 摂関政治) of the Fujwara clan, reinstate direct imperial rule (*shinsei* 親政), and revive court rituals of the Ritsuryō legal system from the eighth century. By casting himself as an emperor of etiquette like his forerunner, Go-Daigo positioned himself as an emperor who represents cultural refinement and re-establishes order. As Matsuzono and Kondō (2017: 69) point out, Go-Daigo's ambitions not only reflect personal ideals, however, but also the court aristocracy's 'Zeitgeist.' The idealisation of the Engi-era (901–23), when Emperor Daigo ruled over Japan, exhibit a nostalgia for the courtly past that was spurred by the political dominance of the warrior aristocracy. As a consequence, since the thirteenth century, national ceremonies came to be understood as a form of art (*geinō* 芸能) and etiquette was considered an important part of cultural education (Satō 2003, 249–63; Matsuzono and Kondō 2017: 71).

Donald Polkinghorne (2005: 13), in 'Narrative Psychology and Historical Consciousness', claims that 'narrative processing is triggered when cultural canons are violated and routines are breached.' This holds true notably for the time of Emperor Go-Daigo, characterised by Andrew Goble (1996: xi) as 'a distinct era when past orders and practices were violently repudiated.' We may therefore argue that *Kenmu nitchū gyōji* and *Kenmu nenjū gyōji* are narratives that aimed at restoring social and cultural order and stabilising power by reviving court etiquette.

## 4. Evidence of Fictionality on the Level of *Histoire*

In its preface, which I will quote below, *Kenmu nenjū gyōji* claims to describe imperial observances over the previous twenty years (traditionally interpreted as the time since Go-Daigo's enthronement) with the aim of making them the model for future generations. Conventional views therefore hold that the work provides a truthful report of ceremonies practised at the court of emperor Go-Daigo (cf. Matsuzono and Kondō 2017: 61–62). However, the text almost entirely lacks reference to contemporary political events. Although there are numerous laments about the degeneration of ceremonies, the text as a whole provides a picture of an almost perfectly functioning sacred place, removed from the turmoils of the secular world. It may thus be argued that the document is set in a historical vacuum in order to provide an ideal image of courtly order.

Considering the turbulent political times, it is doubtful that all the observances described in *Kenmu nenjū gyōji* were practised at the time.[7] This doubt is supported by the narrator's numerous interwoven questions concerning the procedure of some rituals. The entry on the Imperial Reception of the Green Horses (*Aouma no sechie*) on the seventh day of the first month, to give just one example, states that there are many obscurities regarding the ceremony's operation (Wada 1989: 128; Blümmel 1979: 49). It is therefore likely that the agenda of some ceremonies described in *Kenmu nenjū gyōji* were reconstructed with the help of former *nenju gyōji* and other documents from the Heian period and that they were not practised in such minute detail as the text suggests.[8] Comparisons with diary entries seem to support this assumption. For instance, in *Hanazono tennō shinki* 花園天皇宸記 (Diary of Emperor Hanazono, 1310–1332), written around the same time as *Kenmu nenjū gyōji*, the Reception of the Green Horses (*Aouma no sechie* 白馬節会) taking place on the seventh day of the first month is as a rule mentioned only briefly (e.g., the years 1311, 1312, 1313, 1324, 1332). Moreover, in some years the reception is not mentioned (e.g., 1320, 1331) or conducted (e.g., 1325.) at all. Sometimes the entry for the seventh day of the first month is actually missing (e.g., 1323) (cf. *Hanazono Tennō shinki* 1975). Also in *Fushimi tennō shinki* 伏見天皇宸記 (Diary of Emperor Fushimi, 1287–1311), sometimes the entry for the seventh day of the first month is omitted (e.g., 1389) (cf. *Fushimi Tennō shinki* 1975). Although this is not proof that the ceremony was performed in an abbreviated manner, it may indicate that it had no major importance at the time. An even more concise example is the Repast in the Presence of a Kami (*Jinkonjiki* 神今食) taking place on the eleventh day of the sixth and the twelfth month, which is described in great detail in Kenmu nenju gyōji (italics), but which appears to have been out of use by the time of Emperor Go-Daigo. Satō (2003: 201, 211) therefore argues that the description of the rite does not rely on real experience, but rather reflects nostalgia for court etiquette in the past. Moreover, even though the emperor is described as an integral part of minutely structured court activity, there is some doubt over the rigidity with which the emperor followed all these rules. The following analysis demonstrates the gap between textually documented and practised court etiquette at the time by way of imperial meals.

In *Kenmu nitchū gyōji*, three meals are minutely described, reporting the various procedures, movements, and collaboration of servants, dishes, and tableware:

> 1) The breakfast (*asagarei no omono* 朝餉の御膳), a light, informal meal taken in the morning (*asa no hodo*), presumably at the hour of the snake (c. 9–11 am),[9] at the Breakfast Room (*asagarei no ma*). It was prepared by the palace kitchen office Mizushidokoro and served by ladies-in-waiting.
>
> 2) The morning meal (*asagozen* 朝御膳[10]), a formal meal taken at the hour of the horse (c. 11 am to 1 pm) at the *daishōji* 大床子, a special dais in the emperor's daily living quarters (*hinoomashi* 昼御座). It was prepared by the office in charge of the emperor's meals, Naizenshi, and the offerings office, Shinmotsudokoro, and served by male courtiers.
>
> 3) The evening meal (*yūgozen* 夕御膳), a formal meal at the hour of the rooster (c. 5–7 pm), also served at the dais. It was prepared by the Naizenshi and Shinmotsudokoro offices and served by male courtiers.

In quantity, the descriptions of the imperial meals cover almost half of the document, attesting to the importance that they were given within the daily observances at the imperial court. To give an impression of the procedure, here is a text passage describing the morning meal *asagozen*:

> First, the four spices [miso, salt, vinegar, and sake] are brought. They are placed on the first tray (*ban*). The servant at the royal table (*baizen*) comes forward and places them left of the horse-face-shaped plate. Next, the food in the plate with a cap (*gaiban*) is placed north of the horse face-shaped plate. […]. Or it is placed at the northern rim of the four spices. Next, the third tray: one oak basket with offerings for the gods (*kubotsuki*) and four bowls with rice and vegetables piled up to the edge (*hiramori*) are placed in the middle of the second dining table. The bowls with rice and vegetables are placed on the left and right sides of the oak basket. The fourth tray: one oak basket is placed *vis-à-vis* the former oak basket. Two bowls with rice and vegetables are placed at the left and right end of the former [oak basket]. The [bowls with] soup are lined up at the northern end of the second dining table. Fifth tray: A sake cup is placed within the eastern rim of the second dining table. The cover is not taken away. The sixth tray: a bowl with water is placed on the northern rim of the first dining table. The earthenware bowl (*amagatsu*) [for the protection against misfortunes] is placed within the four spices (or at the rim in the north of the four spices, or before the horse face-shaped plate in line with the four spices). When the Emperor does not come [to the meal], the *yakusō* [servant who hands over the food from the servant at the royal table] is ordered to place the food on the second dining table. When the servant at the royal table stands in front of the first dining table, he receives a sign. The first and second dining tables arrive […]. Then, one plate with highly piled up bowls (*takamori*) and one plate with flame-broiled food is ordered to be brought. It is carried and served by the Chamberlain (*kurōdo*). The servant at the royal table takes it and places it in two rows on the right side of the horse face-shaped plate (highly piled-up bowls). At the southeastern rim, both earthenware bowls with flame-broiled food are placed. The servant at the royal table retreats to the round sitting mat. The Chamberlain places his hands on the balustrade of the Table Room's (*daibandokoro*) drainboard and announces to the Emperor, 'the meal arrives' (or 'it has arrived'). The sovereign comes to the dais (*daishōji*). He puts his knees on the end of the dais, ascends, crawls

forward, and sits gracefully on the round sitting mat. The servant at the royal table heralds his arrival at the round sitting mat by bowing his knees.[11] (*Kenmu nitchū gyōji* 1989: 385; 389, trans. Müller 2021: 115–16)[12]

The two formal meals at the dais are in accordance with the Ritsuryō legal system that was modeled after the meal etiquette of the Chinese Sui and Tang courts (Yoshinouchi 2013: 248; 250, see also Okuno 2004: 160–61), except for the circumstance that, initially, the official meals at the dais were served by ladies-in-waiting and not by male officials.[13] The informal meal at the Breakfast Room was presumably introduced in the late ninth century (cf. Yoshinouchi 2013: 248; 257). These three meals correspond to entries in other *nitchū gyōji* documents between the ninth and eleventh centuries such as *Saikyūki* 西宮記 (Diary of Nishinomiya Sadaijin Minamoto no Takaakira, ca. 969), or *Higashiyama gobunkobon 'nitchū gyōji'* 東山御文庫本『日中行事』 (Daily observances from the Higashiyama library), presumably written at the beginning of the eleventh century (cf. Nishimoto 2012). However, from various court records and research (Yoshinouchi 2013, 2014; Satō 2008; Nagata 1990; Morita 2005), we know for certain that the information provided by *nitchu gyōji* do not accurately reflect court reality. Documents attest that during the Heian period the two formal meals at the dais degenerated to a formal skeleton and were gradually replaced by the informal meal at the Breakfast Room. This becomes notably clear through various officials' diaries, whose function was not primarily to document idealized etiquette but rather to describe court practice. According to Morita Tei (2005, quoted in Yoshinouchi 2013: 248), these shifts were due to signs of the waning influence of the emperor's court government: the morning and evening meals initially took place after completion of governmental affairs; therefore, they were set at the hour of the horse (c. 11 am–1 pm) and the hour of the monkey (c. 3–5 pm). As a consequence of the government's degeneration, starting at the time of Emperor Saga 嵯峨天皇 (786–842, r. 809–23), the morning meal was moved forward to the hour of the snake (c. 9–11 am). It was henceforward gradually replaced by the meal at the Breakfast Room that had been introduced at the end of the ninth century due to changes in the meal culture. Satō Masatoshi (2008) sets these changes in imperial meal practices historically between the end of the ninth and the beginning of the tenth century. According to the extant research (Nagata 1990; Morita 2005; Satō 2008; Yoshinouchi 2013: 248; 257) it seems therefore likely that by the tenth century the meal at the Breakfast Room gradually had superseded the formal meals at the dais and by the eleventh century had replaced the meal at the dais as the emperor's practiced meal for good. Instead, at the dais, chopsticks were placed symbolically, or the emperor's everyday robe (*nōshi*) was put on his seat. A small amount of each untouched dish, called *saba* 佐波, was put in an earthenware pot and placed on the roof of the palace in order to offer it to the gods and spirits (Okuno 2004: 161). The document *Kinpishō* 禁秘抄 (Annotations of court secrets, 1221) states:

> At the meal at the dais, sometimes, the Emperor must attend. Its etiquette: when the Chamberlain announces the imperial meal, the Emperor arrives at the dais from behind the curtain, dressed in a *nōshi* garment (he sits down on

> his knees, eastward). The servant at the royal table attends him. Before, this was eaten formally. In recent times only the chopsticks are placed. The *saba*-dish [for the offering to the gods] is taken, and the chopsticks are placed. The servant at the royal table takes these chopsticks, takes other chopsticks, places them, breaks them, and presents [the dishes]. [...]. The sovereign does not come [to the meal] in recent times. When he does not come, a *nōshi* garment is put on the Emperor's seat [on his behalf]. [The meal] is served at the seat of the Breakfast Room.[14] (*Kinpishō* 1971: 379, my translation)

This quotation from *Kinpishō* thus attests to the fact that in the thirteenth century, the official meal at the dais had become a purely formal and empty etiquette.[15]

In the thirteenth century, other major shifts appear to have taken place pertaining to imperial meal practices. According to *Kinpishō*, the formal meal at the dais had been simplified to one meal a day.[16] The informal meal at the Breakfast Room that had been in the interim amplified from one to two, and eventually three meals a day, was also concentrated in one meal. Moreover, neither of these two meal customs seems to have been in practice at the beginning of the thirteenth century but had been replaced by simple meals taken three times a day. The entry in *Kinpishō* states as follows:

> Generally, the imperial meals are the meals taken at the dais (in ancient times in the morning and the evening, in recent times it is served one time [a day]) and the meal in the Breakfast Room (served in the morning, evening, and at night).[17] They are all served once. In recent times, the sovereign does not participate in these meals. There is also a simple meal [taken] three times [a day]. From this, the lady-in-waiting only takes the *saba*-dish [for the offering to the gods]. It is informally called the small imperial dish. At this meal which is the responsibility of the wet nurse, [the Emperor] must participate[18] three times.[19] (*Kinpishō* 1971: 378, my translation)

Since the Heian period, the timing of the meals had gradually shifted as well. Documents testify that from the eleventh century onwards, when the meals at the Breakfast Room began to be served three times a day, they were set at the hour of the snake (c. 9–11 am), the hour of the horse (1–3 pm), and the beginning of the night (cf. Okuno 2004: 161). Regarding the meal at the Breakfast Room, *Kinpishō* states:

> According to *Kanpyō no goyuikai* (Last caution of the Kanpyō era, 897),[20] the morning meal was served at the hour of the snake [c. 9–11 am]. The evening meal was served at the hour of the monkey [c. 3–5 pm]. However, as it is served three times [a day] in recent times, lunch is at the hour of the sheep [c. 1–3 pm]. The evening meal is at the beginning of the night, I think.[21] (*Kinpishō* 1971: 379–80, my translation)

Moreover, as *Higashiyama gobunkobon 'nitchū gyōji'* attests, the official evening meal at the dais seems to have been postponed from the hour of the monkey (c. 3–5 pm) to the hour of the rooster (c. 5–7 pm) by the beginning of the eleventh century (cf. Yoshinouchi 2013: 239; 250).

The fall into disuse of the formal meal at the dais is also confirmed by *Kenmu nitchū gyōji* itself:

> When the Emperor attends from the beginning, the servant at the royal table at the round sitting mat announces the meal. He is supposed to eat properly, but recently he comes only for the sake of formality. Sometimes he eats rice soaked in water. The servant at the royal table arrives, distributes the dishes, and when he puts it into the vessel for hot water and serves it, a Chamberlain brings the rice soaked in water. When the meal is finished, he places the chopsticks and leaves. When he does not eat properly, the *saba*-dish [for the offering to the gods] is taken, put in an earthenware bowl [for the protection against misfortunes] and offered.[22] (*Kenmu nitchū gyōji* 1989: 389–90, trans. Müller 2021: 116–17)

From the explanations above, it seems likely that the meals described in extensive detail in *Kenmu nitchū gyōji* may not correspond to court reality at the time. Moreover, the following quotation from *Kenmu nitchū gyōji* bears witness to the emperor's freedom of choice over whether he in fact wanted to take the meal in the Breakfast Room formally or not, thus providing him with some measure of autonomy:

> The breakfast is served. A *tokusen* [lady-in-waiting working at the palace kitchen office Mizushidokoro], takes the food tablets (*midai*), goes to the Table Room, and puts them on the meal shelf (*omonodana*). Imperial objects are not placed directly on the dining table (*daiban*). The lady-in-waiting that serves at the royal table waits at the mats at the end of the Breakfast Room. Middle-ranked ladies-in-waiting wait at both sides of the kitchen's sliding door. Low-ranked ladies-in-waiting stand behind. The breakfast is brought as usual. If [the Emperor] does not eat properly, the servant at the royal table places the chopsticks, breaks the end and serves [the food]. She returns three times. We do not know the meaning of this, but now it is a custom. The second time her hair is lifted.[23] (*Kenmu nitchū gyōji* 1989: 374–75, trans. Müller 2021: 112)

If the meals described in *Kenmu nitchū gyōji* probably do not reflect the practiced meal etiquette at the time (which needs to be further confirmed by comparison with other documents), why, then, we may wonder, are the formal meals in *Kenmu nitchū gyōji* described in such detail, and why do the hours correspond to those of the Ritsuryō system, reflecting a practice from the distant past? With respect to *Higashiyama gobunkobon 'nitchū gyōji'*, which also reflects the meal conventions of the Ritsuryō system, Yoshinouchi (2013: 267) argues that the practice of the emperor's meals took some time to be reflected in *nitchū gyōji* documents. She ascribes this to the fact that *nitchū gyōji*, as a rule, were written by male courtiers who omitted to record informal meals such as the breakfasts that were served by ladies-in-waiting. Moreover, she stresses that the meals at the dais were supposed to be accentuated as the formal meals of the emperor in the Ritsuryō genealogy (2013: 266–67). We may, therefore, infer that *Kenmu nitchū gyōji*, which may well have been modeled after *Higashiyama gobunkobon 'nitchū gyōji'*, seems to have included fictitious elements in order to copy the etiquette of the Ritsuryō system, with the aim of providing an image of a well-structured temporal order and thus of continuity at court. The emperor himself, as a symbol of higher authority and, judging by his political ambitions, in his narcissistic and power-driven personality, claims to follow etiquette but does not need to actually do so. Nevertheless, he is always present in the imperial temporal order, be it only by way of chopsticks.

The fictional character of *Kenmu nenju gyōji* on the level of *histoire* is also stressed by Matsuzono and Kondō (2017: 66–67). Whereas in medieval documents the focus is traditionally on well-established examples, omitting new ceremonies that do not have precedent, they argue that *Kenmu nenjū gyōji* contains many unconventional entries. Via the example of ceremonies that were already in decay at the time such as the Salutations to the Four Directions, as well as other observances like the Iwashimizu Interim Festival (*Iwashimizu rinjisai* 石清水臨時歳) they demonstrate that *Kenmu nenjū gyōji* contains numerous inconsistencies pertaining to spatiotemporal procedures and etiquette. Matsuzono and Kondō attribute this to the author's ignorance and arbitrary mixing of sinographic sources. They deduce that Emperor Go-Daigo did not record his own experiences and that many ceremonies described in *Kenmu nenjū gyōji* do not reflect courtly observances practised at the time. They therefore consider *Kenmu nenjū gyōji* to be a 'fictitious work' (*kyokō no sakuhin* 虚構の作品) (Matsuzono and Kondō 2017: 67) that pictures a holy time in which the world is in order (Matsuzono and Kondō 2017: 69), and that, on the basis of a fictitious setting that pretends to report real court practice at the time, aims at presenting to the world the self-image of an ideal emperor (Matsuzono and Kondō 2017: 73).

## 5. Evidence of Fictionality on the Level of *Discours*

In order to carve out the two texts' higher-ranking function on the level of *discours*, it is helpful to compare them with other similar documents. In terms of chronography, *nitchū gyōji* and *nenjū gyōji* differ considerably from Sinitic diaries. Although they are also structured chronologically, they do not represent a linear temporal order within 'fully relational' historical time with an implicitly open end, but rather a prototypical daily or annual cycle within 'absolute' (cf. Steineck 2018: 175) — or in Roland Harweg's (2009) terminology — 'mythographic' time. Structurally, they thus represent a kind of ideal in which chronological sequences are identically repeated on a diurnal and annual level. This cyclically composed time structure reflects the text's political function as it symbolises a timeless divine order of the imperial court.

*Kenmu nitchū gyōji* and *Kenmu nenjū gyōji* are also peculiar in terms of language. In contrast to previous similar works that are, as a rule, written in Chinese, such as *Shinsen nenjū gyōji* 新撰年中行事 (Newly edited annual observances by Fujiwara no Yukinari (972-1027)), *Saikyūki* 西宮記 (Records from the Western Palace, 969) and *Higashiyama gobunkobon 'nitchū gyōji'*, the two texts under investigation are written in vernacular Japanese (*kana majiri-bun* 仮名交じり文). This seems to be meaningful. By describing court etiquette in the native language, the imperial court is presented as an explicitly 'native' place of divine order. Language thus affects a sense of vicinity and identification alike, consolidating the emperor's claim to power.

Moreover, partly due to the use of the native language that allows for a more diversified expression of tense, aspect, and mood, the two texts possess a higher degree of narrativity and poeticity than their Chinese predecessors. Their fictional character becomes most pronounced in the preface of *Kenmu nenchū gyōji*. Apart from the fact that other *nenjū gyōji*, as a rule, do not have prefaces at all but directly begin with descriptions of the imperial New Year's ceremony, the preface of *Kenmu nitchū gyōji* is written in a highly refined poetic style:

> In the imperial palace, more than twenty springs and autumns have passed. Observances from the past seem not to be unclear, and if I write them down now, *I have the feeling* that they are not uncommon. However, the public ceremonies, that are held once in a while may, although they may not become a mirror for the future, become a reference point for tales that in the world [of emperor Go-Daigo] it was like this.[24] (*Kenmu nenjū gyōji* 1989: 20, emphasis added, my translation)

The preface makes clear — albeit in a deliberately modest way — the text's function: it shall give testimony of ceremonial etiquette at the court of emperor Go-Daigo in order to be remembered and serve as a model for future court etiquette.

Previous research equated the work's narrator with Emperor Go-Daigo. Matsuzono and Kondō (2017: 61), however, consider the work's narrator to be a fictional emperor. The foreword's high degree of narrativity seems to support this view. By stressing that the document will become the source of 'tales' (*monogatari* 物語) about the past in the future, the preface introduces a 'narrative' of annual ceremonies, by rhetorically fictionalising it. Satō (2003: 7-8, 212) argues similarly: by the example of the work's introduction and the aforementioned Repast in the Presence of a Kami she claims that *Kenmu nenjū gyōji* is written in a tale-like tone (*katari kuchō* 語り口調) with a fictitious perspective (*kakō sareta shiten* 仮構された視点) that stages the emperor as the protagonist of a court tale. Fiction thus aims at stabilising and strengthening court power and becomes a tool to achieve immortality. The text's narrativity is stressed by various subjective expressions, such as 'I have the feeling' (*kokochi suredo* 心ちすれど). Similar insertions continue throughout the whole document. In the following quotation describing the New Year ceremony Salutations to the Four Directions, the highlighted expressions provide the text with a subjective and narrative character as well:

> At the welcoming of spring, there are notably numerous public events at the imperial palace, and *it is difficult [to decide]*, which of them comes first. The ladies-in-waiting of the palace provisions office Tonomori [Tsukasa] and the housekeeping office Kamori [Tsukasa] *busily and hurriedly* prepare the decoration here and there. [At dawn], when the banishment of evil spirits of the previous year (*tsuina*) is finished, and the lights at the stone path under the porch *are only dimly visible*, the decoration of the New Year festivities are *hurried along*. The voices of the Chamberlains and their servants that perform affairs *are notably loud*, and due to the [important] occasion, *they make proud faces*.[25] (*Kenmu nenjū gyōji* 1989: 22, emphasis added, my translation)

All these subjective comments (e.g. 'difficult to decide', 'busily', 'hurriedly', etc.) provide the observances with some measure of singularity and concreteness, again rendering the text more narrative than its generic predecessors. The following are two Sinitic examples for comparison: the first is the beginning of *Kamo ujibito*

*Yasutaka nenjū gyōji* 賀茂氏人保隆年中行事 (Annual observances of Yasutaka from the Kamo clan, ?) and the second from *Gōke shidai* 江家次第 (Course of events of the Ōe family, 1111) written by Ōe no Masafusa 大江匡房 (1041–1111):

> After the banishment of evil spirits of the previous year, the Chamberlains order the various offices [to make the] decoration. The [servants of the] housekeeping office Kamori Tsukasa place *hagomo* drainboards at the third bay of the eastern court of the [Emperor's residential palace] Seiryōden, approximately twenty centimeters behind the stone stairs. On them, they spread long straw mats, in the direction of south and north. On top, they place eight folding screens in Song-style. Inside, at three places, they place seats for nobles. [...] At the hour of the tiger [c. 3–5 am], the Emperor arrives.[26] (*Kamo ujibito Yasutaka nenjū gyōji* 1971: 153).
>
> After the banishment of evil spirits of the previous year, the [servants of the] palace provisions office Tonomori Tsukasa offer water for the imperial washing [...]. At the hour of the cock-crowing [hour of the ox, c. 1–3 am] [servants of the] housekeeping office Kamori Tsukasa make the decorations. At the eastern court of the Seiryōden Palace, they first spread *hagomo* drainboards. On top of them they spread long straw mats (in the direction of the southern and northern doors), and on top of them they place eight folding screens. [...]. At three places seats for nobles are set up.[27] (*Gōke shidai* 1991: 12)

Compared to *Kamo ujibito Yasutaka nenjū gyōji* and *Gōke shidai*, which describe the various procedures at court in a deadpan style, *Kenmu nenjū gyōji* exhibits a most interesting interplay between universality and singularity: the order at court is reasserted by way of the text's chronographical structure, implying cyclical recurrence. At the same time, the situational descriptions generate a vivid image of singularity and intimacy.

In *Kenmu nenchū gyōji*, the temporal order of Go-Daigo's court is also stressed by pointing out incorrect etiquette in the past that has been corrected at the court of Emperor Go-Daigo, as well as by various comments by the narrator. These express the aim of restoring the order of the past Ritsuryō legal system:

> The bamboo blinds of the emperor's daily quarters at the southern edge and of the northern vestibule (*gakunoma*) are lowered (in old times court ladies of the Shōkyōden Palace [back-court] have attended in this room, I think) [...].
>
> Recently, in the Satodairi-Palace [Tominokōji Palace], [the bamboo blinds] in the middle of the first bay were raised only half. This is a mistake. Nowadays, according to proper ritual, they are, as in usual times, raised to the ropes of the holding hook.[28] (*Kenmu nenjū gyōji* 1989: 31–32, my translation)

*Kenmu nitchū gyōji* includes narrative sequences as well. Unlike its predecessors, such as *Higashiyama gobunkobon* '*nitchū gyōji*', the daily observances are written in a vibrant, subjective, and personal style. This becomes evident in the work's very opening:

> At the hour of the hare [c. 5–7 am], the Chamberlains *stir at* the sound of the morning cleaning by the [custodians of the] palace provisions office Tonomori no Tsukasa, and raise the lattice shutters (*kōji*) of the Seiryōden Palace. [A Chamberlain] *tries to push open* [the door in the] second bay (*ma*) to the south. *As it is still locked*, he enters from the Demon Room (*oninoma*) [...].[29] (*Kenmu nitchū gyōji* 1989: 358, emphasis added, trans. Müller 2021: 107)

The text's peculiarity becomes distinct by comparing the opening of *Kenmu nitchū gyōji* with that of *Higashiyama gobunkobon 'nitchū gyōji'*:

> At the hour of the hare [c. 5–7 am], the [servants from the] palace provisions office, Tonomori Tsukasa, do the morning cleaning. [...] The lattice shutters are raised. One Chamberlain enters from the Demon Room and releases the wooden [bolt] in the emperor's daily chamber. The other Chamberlains enter from the eastern door of the Courtiers' Hall (*tenjō*) and start from the second bay to the south [...].[30] (*Higashiyama gobunkobon 'nitchū gyōji'* 2008: 51–52, my translation)

Whereas *Higashiyama gobunkobon 'nitchū gyōji'* has a decidedly documentary character, centring on the observances as such by avoiding any subjective and personal descriptions, the focus in *Kenmu nitchū gyōji* is more on the situational actions of the players. This becomes apparent in expressions such as 'stir at' (*odorokite* おどろきて), 'tries to push open' (*oshite miru* をして見る), or 'as it is still locked' (*imada sashitareba* いまださしたれば).

Another critical difference between *Kenmu nitchū gyōji* and its generic predecessors is some measure of temporal vagueness concerning the daily observances. Whereas *Higashiyama gobunkobon 'nitchū gyōji'* states the exact hour of each activity, *Kenmu nitchū gyōji* sometimes mentions only approximate times:

> *In the morning* [...] the daily attendance reports take place. [...] *When the daily affairs are finished*, [...] the [duty] board of the Courtiers' Hall is stored (i.e., put back into the bag).[31] (*Kenmu nitchū gyōji* 1989: 377, 383, 400, emphasis added, trans. Müller 2021: 114; 119)

> At the hour of the dragon [c. 7–9 am] the daily attendance reports of the court officials take place (from the third month to the eight month it is at the *hour of the dragon*, but from the ninth month to the second month it is at the *hour of the snake*). [...] At the *hour of the sheep* [c. 1–3 pm], the board is stored in the emperor's habitual residence.[32] (*Higashiyama gobunkobon 'nitchū gyōji'* 2008: 51, my translation, emphasis added)

The temporal order of Go-Daigo's court is ensured, but nevertheless supplies the emperor and his entourage with some discretion pertaining to the organisation of their schedule. The court appears as a perfectly functioning but, at the same time, somewhat less rigid space, that provides its members with some measure of temporal freedom. This observation receives support from a statement by Matsuzono and Kondō (2017: 63). They point out that in *Kenmu nenjū gyōji* the descriptions of the observances are focused equally on the emperor, the senior nobles (*kugyō*) and the privy gentlemen (*tenjōbito*), high ranked officials who had access to the emperor's residential palace Seiryōden, by giving neither of them specific priority. *Kenmu nenjū gyōji* therefore 'provides the picture of an organism in which the courtiers mutually perform etiquette in the form of an inner circle' (Matsuzono and Kondō 2017: 68), aloof from politics. By way of this technique, the emperor presents himself as standing on a horizontal hierarchical line with the upper strata of his entourage. However, at a closer look the emperor's supremacy is still maintained, if only by the fact that his actions are described before those of his subordinates, and by the work's overall focus on the perspective of the emperor.

Matsuzono and Kondō's observations also relate the text's fictionality pertaining to the temporal level of 'order' (cf. Genette 1980): it appears that *Kenmu nenjū gyōji* exhibits a different chronology than traditional *nenjū gyōji*. In analogy to Satō (2015: 15–16) they argue that the purpose of the record is not to picture a specific ritual as a whole; rather the focus is clearly on the temporal sequence of etiquette (*sahō no rensa* 作法の連鎖) (Matsuzono and Kondō 2017: 63) of the emperor and his entourage, notably senior nobles and privy gentlemen, by combining them at the discretion of the author. Via a textual comparison of the Ceremony of Investiture (*joyi* 叙位) in the first month of the year with *Gōke shidai*, they work out how the author of *Kenmu nenjū gyōji* ruptures the procedure's chronology through analepses and prolepses as well as various ellipses (Matsuzono and Kondō 2017: 64–65). Therefore, the arrangement of the procedures on the level of *discours* does not reflect the chronological order of the respective ritual on the level of *histoire*. These temporal shifts may be considered further indicators of the text's fictionality.

## 6. Summary: Fiction to Change the World?

To sum up, we may conclude that, firstly, by way of a cyclically framed chronographical structure and temporally shaped etiquette, *Kenmu nitchū gyōji* and *Kenmu nenjū gyōji* provide a sort of courtly screenplay for an emperor who wishes to represent a guarantor and symbol of divine order and continuity in times of unrest. Minutely structured court etiquette, running like clockwork, provides the fiction of an ideal and timelessly recurring world order that will be remembered in the future, thus guaranteeing Emperor Go-Daigo's immortality. Thus, illusiveness becomes the very source of persuasiveness.

Secondly, even though the emperor is pictured as an integrated part of a detailed, temporally structured divine order, he still emerges as an individual with some measure of autonomy. This is achieved by references to his not always acting according to the prescribed etiquette, as well as by interspersed subjective descriptions, providing the text with some measure of narrativity and immediacy. Moreover, by loosening the observance's temporal rigidity, the imperial court appears as a space with a slightly less strict schedule in comparison with predecessors of the genre. The implementation of a unique temporal ordering of the player's actions that at some instances provides the illusion of a flat hierarchy among the upper strata of court aristocracy creates a more communal and poetic space of social order and pictures the emperor as a ruler close to his entourage. This is accentuated by the use of vernacular instead of Sinitic language, which stages Go-Daigo as an intrinsically 'Japanese' emperor and allows for identification with him. By equipping the emperor with specifically subjective and human traits, and by integrating him into the court's temporal order, he is painted as a model of ethical behaviour and identification.

Through all these textual techniques, the court is pictured as a divine and ideal place of stability and a secular space of identification alike. The emperor exhibits his almightiness, divinity, and self-elevation by way of integration into an almost perfect temporal clockwork, while signifying at the same time — by not appearing at certain meals — that this temporal integration is highly symbolic. The two texts thus exhibit a narrative subordination under a temporal dictate with a decidedly political aim, which is to consolidate imperial power by temporally ordering the world.

## References

BLÜMMEL, MARIA-VERENA. 1979. *Hofzeremonien im japanischen Mittelalter: Eine Untersuchung zu den Jahresbräuchen des Kaisers Go-Daigo (Kemmu-nenjūgyōji)* (Wiesbaden: Harrassowitz)

*Fushimi tennō shinki* [伏見天皇宸記; Diary of Emperor Fushimi]. 1975 [1965]. Ed. by Rinsen Shoten Shiryō Taisei [臨川書店史料大成], Rinsen Shoten Shiryō Taisei 3, vol. 2, 247–329 (Kyoto: Rinsen Shoten)

GENETTE, GÉRARD. 1980. *Narrative Discourse: An Essay in Method*, trans. by Jane Lewin (Ithaca, NY: Cornell University Press)

GOBLE, ANDREW EDMUND. 1996. *Kenmu: Go-Daigo's Revolution* (Cambridge, MA: Council on East Asian Studies, Harvard University)

*Gōke Shidai* [江家次第; Course of events of the Ōe family (Ōe Masafusa 大江匡房)]. 1991. Watanabe Naohiko [渡辺直彦] (ed.), Shintō taikei 4 (Tokyo: Shintō Taikei Hensankai)

*Hanazono tennō shinki* [花園宸記; Diary of Emperor Hanazono]. 1975 [1965]. Ed. by Rinsen Shoten Shiryō Taisei [臨川書店史料大成], Rinsen Shoten Shiryō Taisei 3, vol. 1, vol. 2: 1–246 (Kyoto: Rinsen Shoten)

HARWEG, ROLAND. 2009. *Zeit in Mythos und Geschichte: Weltweite Untersuchungen zu mythographischer und historiographischer Chronographie vom Altertum bis zur Gegenwart. Chronographie im Orient vom Altertum bis zur Gegenwart*, III (Berlin: LIT)

*Higashiyama gobunkobon 'nitchū gyōji'* [東山御文庫本日中行事; Daily observances from the Higashiyama library]. 2013. In Yoshinouchi Kei [芳之内圭], *Nihon kodai no dairi no un'ei kikō* [日本古代の内裏の運営機構; Administration mechanism at the Imperial Palace in ancient Japan], 232–45 (Tokyo: Hanawa Shobō)

*Jichū gunyō* [侍中群要; Cornerstones of Jichū officials]. 1985. Commentary by Mezaki Tokuei [目崎徳衛] (Tokyo: Yoshikawa Kōbunkan)

KAWAKAMI, MITSUGU [川上貢]. 2002. *Nihon chūsei jūtaku no kenkyū* [日本中世住宅の研究; Study of medieval Japanese residences] (Tokyo: Chūō Chōron Bijutsu Shuppan)

*Kamo ujibito Yasutaka nenjū gyōji* [賀茂氏人保隆所伝; Annual observances of Yasutaka from the Kamo clan]. 1958. In *Zoku gunsho ruijū* [続群書類従; Continued collection of writings sorted by type] 10 (jō), ed. by Hanawa Hokiichi [塙保己一] and Ōta Tōshirō [太田藤四郎], 153–87 (Tokyo: Zoku Gunsho Ruijū Kanseikai)

*Kenmu nenjū gyōji* [建武年中行事; Annual observances of the Kenmu era]. 1989. In *Shintei Kenmu nenjū gyōji chūkai* [新訂建武年中行事註解; New annotations of Annual observancs of the Kenmu Era], ed. and comm. by Wada Hidematsu [和田英松], 20–356 (Tokyo: Kōdansha)

*Kenmu nitchū gyōji* [日中行事; Daily observances of the Kenmu era]. 1989. In *Shintei Kenmu nenjū gyōji chūkai* [新訂建武年中行事註解; New annotations of Annual observances of the Kenmu era], ed. and comm. by Wada Hidematsu [和田英松], 357–414 (Tokyo: Kōdansha)

*Kinpishō* [禁秘抄; Annotations of court secrets]. 1971. In *Gunsho ruijū* [群書類従; Collection of writings sorted by type] 26, ed. by Hanawa Hokiichi [塙保己一], 367–418 (Tokyo: Zoku Gunsho Ruijū Kanseikai)

MATSUZONO, HITOSHI [松薗斉], and KONDŌ YASUKAZU [近藤好和]. 2017. *Chūsei nikki no sekai* [中世日記の世界] [The world of medieval diaries] (Tokyo: Mineruba Shobō)

MORITA, TEI [森田悌]. 2005 [1999]. *Ōchō seiji to zaichi shakai* [王朝政治と在地社会; Court politics and countryside society] (Tokyo: Yoshikawa Kōbunkan)

MÜLLER, SIMONE. 2021. 'Temporal Regimes in *Kenmu nitchū gyōji* (Daily Observances of the Kenmu Era), with annotated translation', In *Zeit in der vormodernen japanischen Literatur / Time in Premodern Japanese Literature,* ed. by Raji Steineck, Simone Müller, and Sebastian Balmes. Berlin: de Gruyter (=*Asiatische Studien / Études Asiatiques,* 75 (1): 89–129)

NAGATA, KAZUYA [永田和也]. 1990. 'Shinmotsudokoro to Mizushidokoro [進物所と御厨子所; The palace kitchen offices Shinmotsudokoro and Mizushidokoro]', *Fūzoku,* 29 (1): 34–51

NISHIMOTO, MASAHIRO [西本昌弘] (ed.). 2010. *Shinsen nenjū gyōji* [新撰年中行事; Newly edited annual observances] (Tokyo: Yagi Shoten)

NISHIMOTO, MASAHIRO [西本昌弘]. 2012 [2008]. 'Higashiyama gobunkobon "nitchū gyōji" ni tsuite [東山御文庫本『日中行事』について; On the *Higashiyama gobunkobon "nitchū gyōji"*]', in *Nihon kodai no nenjū gyōji-sho to shinshiryō* [日本古代の年中行事書と新資料; Ancient Japanese books on annual observances and new documents], 139–61 (Tokyo: Yoshikawa Kōbunkan)

OKUNO, TAKAHIRO [奥野高広]. 2004. *Sengoku jidai kyūtei seikatsu* [戦国時代の宮廷生活; Court life during the Warring States period] (Tokyo: Yagi Shoten)

ŌTA, SEIROKU [太田静六]. 2010. *Shindenzukuri no kenkyū* [寝殿造の研究; Study of palace architecture] (Tokyo: Yoshikawa Kōbunkan)

POLKINGHORNE, DONALD. 2005. 'Narrative Psychology and Historical Consciousness', in *Narration, Identity, and Historical Consciousness,* ed. by Jürgen Straub, 3–22 (New York: Berghahn Books)

*Saikyūki* [西宮記; Diary of Nishinomiya Sadaijin Minamoto no Takaakira]. 1953. Kojitsu sōsho 故実叢書 19 (Tokyo: Meiji Tosho Shuppan Kabushikigaisha; Yoshiokawa Kōbunkan)

SATŌ ATSUKO 佐藤厚子. 2003. *Chūsei no kokka gishiki : "Kenmu nenjū gyōji" no sekai* 中世の国家儀式「建武年中行事」の世界. (Tokyo: Iwata Shoin)

SATŌ, MASATOSHI [佐藤全敏]. 2008. *Heian jidai no tennō to kanryōsei* [平安時代の天皇と官僚制; Emperors and bureaucracy of the Heian period] (Tokyo: Tōkyō Daigaku Shuppankai)

SHIMURA, KANAKO [志村佳名子]. 2015. *Nihon kodai no ōkyū kōzō to seimu, reigi* [日本古代の王宮構造と政務・礼儀; Structure of the royal palace, government affairs and etiquette in ancient Japan] (Tokyo: Hanawa Shobō)

STEINECK, RAJI C. 2018. 'Chronographical Analysis: An Essay in Methodology', *KronoScope,* 18 (2): 171–98

YOSHINOUCHI, KEI [芳之内圭]. 2008. 'Higashiyama gobunko bon "nitchū gyōji" ni mieru Heian jidai kyūjū jikoku seido no kōsatsu: "naiju sōji no koto", "konoejin yakō no koto" no kentō o chūshin ni [「東山御文庫本『日中行事』にみえる平安時代宮中時刻制度の考察：「内豎奏時事」・「近衛陣夜行事」の検討を中心に〔含翻刻〕; Investigations of the time system at the Heian court as seen through *Daily Observances from the Higashiyama library* with a special focus on the time announcement of the Naiju and the night watch of the Konoe office (including a reprint)]', *Shigaku zasshi,* 117 (8): 36–56 (1414–34)

——. 2013. *Nihon kodai no dairi no un'ei kikō* [日本古代の内裏の運営機構; Administration mechanism at the imperial palace in ancient Japan] (Tokyo: Hanawa Shobō)

——. 2014. '*Nenjū gyōji 'Tenjō Daiban no koto'* [日中行事「殿上台盤事」; Meal at the palace in *Daily observances*]', *Historia,* 247: 56–81

YUASA, YOSHIMI [湯浅吉美]. 2015. 'Zenkindai Nihonjin no jikan ishiki [前近代日本人の時間意識; Time awareness of people in premodern Japan]', *Saitama Gakuen Daigaku kiyō (Ningen Gakubu hen)* 15 (December): 195–202

## Notes to Chapter 8

1. This project has received funding from the European Research Council (ERC) under the European Union's Horizon 2020 research and innovation programme (grant agreement no.

741166). I am very grateful for valuable comments on earlier versions of this article by members of the ERC Advanced Grant Project Time in Medieval Japan (TIMEJ) at the University of Zurich (PI Raji C. Steineck), as well as the reviewers and editors of this volume.

2. As the two works are attributed to the authorship or at least to the commission of emperor Go-Daigo (cf. Wada 1989 [1903]: 416), they are also known under the name of *Go-Daigo Tennō nitchū gyōji* 後醍醐天皇『日中行事』 (Daily observances of emperor Go-Daigo) and *Go-Daigo Tennō nenjū gyōji* 後醍醐天皇『年中行事』 (Annual observances of Emperor Go-Daigo). However, the work originally did not have a fixed title. '*Kenmu*' as well as '*Go-Daigo*' seem to be later additions from the Edo period.

3. In ancient and medieval Japan, time was recorded according to the Chinese twelve-hour system (*jūni shinkoku* 十二辰刻), by using the zodiac signs of the Chinese lunisolar calendar. One time unit (*shinkoku* 辰刻 or *toki* 時) corresponded to approximately two hours that were subdivided into four units (*koku* 刻 or *ten* 点) of approximately thirty minutes. Time was measured and announced by the Yin-yang Office (Onmyōryō 陰陽寮), the government office in charge of astronomical observations, divination, and calendar making, by way of water clocks (*rōkoku* 漏刻) (cf. Yuasa 2015: 199).

4. Board on which the timesheets (*hanachigami* 放紙) of the courtiers attending at court were affixed. It was placed in the Courtiers' Hall (*tenjōnoma* 殿上間), and was of approximately 160 cm in length, 26 cm wide at the top, and 23 cm wide at the bottom. For a detailed analysis of the custom of work time reporting at court, see Shimura 2015, see also Müller 2021: 101–02.

5. Matsuzono and Kondō (2017: 68, 73) date the work even earlier, on the grounds that the text includes details of the etiquette of cloistered emperors and regents despite the fact that Emperor Go-Daigo aimed to abolish the cloistered rule and regency government system during his reign. They therefore date the work to before Go-Daigo's enthronement in 1318.

6. Emperor Juntoku 順徳天皇 (1197–1242, r. 1210–1222), a son of Emperor Go-Toba, is the author of *Kinpishō* 禁秘抄 (Annotations of court secrets, 1221) another medieval compilation pertaining to court appointments and ceremonies. It seems to be no coincidence that two medieval emperors who strived to restore imperial power were fervid promoters of court etiquette.

7. Matsuzono and Kondō (2017: 45–46) point out that entries in ceremonial documents do not necessarily reflect practice at the time. They contain traditional as well as singular ceremonies. Therefore, their historicity needs to be verified by other sources. According to such comparisons they conclude that, whereas other *nenjū gyōji* such as *Gōke shidai* 江家次第 (1111) by Ōe no Masafusa 大江匡房 (1041–1111) are historically reliable, *Kenmu nenjū gyōji* is not (2017: 51).

8. We may also raise doubts about the factuality of the work's spatial descriptions. At the time of the text's production, Emperor Go-Daigo resided at the Nijō Tominokōji palace 二条富小路内裏, as the imperial palace had burned down in 1227, and the order to rebuild the palace was only made in 1334. Even though the Nijō Tominokōji palace was constructed after the model of the imperial palace, there remains some doubt regarding the accuracy of the texts' spatial descriptions. This is a point that would need to be verified, however, through time-consuming research, which is not within the scope of this article. For information about medieval palace architecture, see Kawakami (2002) and Ōta (2010).

9. The concrete time breakfast was eaten is not mentioned in the text, but it is placed between observances taking place from 7 to 9 am, and observances taking place between 11 am and 1 pm, so it can be inferred that the informal breakfast took place at the hour of the snake (c. 9–11 am). This is backed by other documents such as *Jichū gunyō* 侍中群要 (Cornerstones of Jichū officials), from the late eleventh century, *Higashiyama gobunkobon 'nitchu gyōji'* 東山御文庫本『日中行事』 (Daily observances from the Higashiyama library, 2013), written at the beginning of the eleventh century, and *Kinpishō*, from the early thirteenth century.

10. In other *nenjū gyōji* such as *Higashiyama gobunkobon 'nenjū gyōji'* this meal is called *hirugozen* (lunch). Cf. Yoshinouchi (2008: 53).

11. まづ四種まゐる。一盤に居る。陪膳すゝみて馬頭盤の左に居る。次にがいはん御ぜんを馬頭盤の北にすう [...]。あるひは四種のとほりの北のへりに居る。次に三の御盤くぼつき一、ひらもり四、二の御台の中におく。くぼつきの左右にひらもりすう。四の御盤くぼつき一、さきのくぼつきにむかへてすう。ひらもり二、もとのすゑに左右にすう。御しる二の御台の北のへりにならべてすう。五の御盤、御しゆさん、二の

御台東のへりの中ほどにすう。かいをとらず。六の御盤、御ゆのき、一の御台の北のへりに居る。あまがつ四種の中にすう。(あるひは四種の北のへり、或は四種のとほりにおける馬頭盤の前なり)。出御なき時は、二の御台の物は、役送におかしむ。陪膳、一の御台の前にゐたれば、景色をかうぶるなり。一二の御台まゐりて、[...]。さて、たかもり一盤、やきもの一盤まゐらす。蔵人もちてまゐる。陪膳とりて、馬頭盤の右に二行に居る。(高もりなり)。 やきもの、東南のへりに二かはらけづつ居る。陪膳、円座にしりぞきつく。蔵人、台盤所のすのこに高欄に手をかけて、おものまゐると奏す。(あるひはまゐりぬ)。主上、大床子につかせたまふ。大床子のはしにひざをかけてのぼりて、ゐざりよりて円座にうるはしく御座あるなり。陪膳、円座の上に居ながら、足をにがしてけいひつす。

12. I have slightly reformulated my published English translation of *Kenmu nitchū gyōji* in order to make it more easily accessible for readers without knowledge of the Japanese language.
13. According to Yoshinouchi (2013: 250), the duty to serve the official imperial meals shifted from ladies-in-waiting to officials between the Engi 延喜 (901–23) and Tenryaku 天暦 (947–57) eras.
14. ㊅床子御膳。時々必可有着御。其作法。蔵人奏御膳之時。御直衣自帳後着大床子(懸膝着之東向)。陪膳人警候。昔正食之。近代只立箸許也。取左波立箸。陪膳取其御箸。又立別御箸折出也。[...] 主上近代不着御。不着御之時。引懸御直衣。於朝餉御座供之。
15. The abolition of the meal at the dais also becomes apparent in the servants' increasing negligence at work (cf. Yoshinouchi 2013: 253).
16. Yoshinouchi (2013) convincingly shows through examples from diaries that as early as the beginning of the eleventh century the meals at the dais were already concentrated in one meal served in the evening, despite contradicting entries in *nitchū gyōji* documents. The simplification to one meal is also documented in *Chūji ruiki* 厨事類記 (Records about meals, ca. 1295) (cf. Yoshinouchi 2013: 269).
17. According to Yoshinouchi (2013: 259–60), the meal at night corresponds to the so-called *yūbe no saburai* 夜候 (夜侍), a small snack (cf. entries in *Jichū gunyō*, IV and V), and not to the meal at the Breakfast Room, since other documents of the time such as *Chūji ruiki* record only two meals a day at the Breakfast Room. As the *yūbe no saburai* was — like the breakfast — prepared by the palace kitchen office Mizushidokoro and taken in the Breakfast Room, she assumes that the authors of *Kinpishō* mistakenly treated it as a third meal in the Breakfast Room.
18. In another transcript of the *Kinpishō* it says: 'the chopsticks are taken three times' (三度取箸也). See *Kinpishō kōchū*, *Shūgaishō* (1952, 59).
19. 凡御膳大床子御膳。(上古朝夕近代一度供之)。朝餉ノ御膳。(朝夕夜供)。皆一度供之。此御膳等近代主上不着。又只御膳三度。是只女房サババカリ取之。只内々称小供御。御乳母沙汰供御三度可着也。
20. Instructive document presented from Emperor Uda 宇多天皇 (867–931, r. 887–97) to Emperor Daigo 醍醐天皇 (885–930, r. 897–930) on the occasion of the latter's enthronement in 897.
21. 朝巳時。夕申時之由。寛平遺誡也。但三度供之間。近代昼未時。夕入夜歟。
22. もとより出御あらば、陪膳円座にて、おものを奏するなり。うるはしくめすべきを、近代はよしばかりなり。ゆづけをめす事あり。陪膳まゐりて、御はんをわけて御ゆのきに入て出せば、蔵人、御ゆづけもちてまゐるなり。めしはてゝ、御はしを御飯にたていらせたまふ。うるはしくめさず、御さばをとりて、あまがつに入れてたてさせたまふ。
23. 朝餉のおものまゐる。とくせん女官、御だいをもちて、台盤所にまゐりておものだなにをく。あからさまにも台盤の上に公物は置かぬ事なり。陪膳の女房、朝餉のはしのたゝみに候す。御中の人、台盤所の両めんそへ障子のもとに候。下の人、そのつぎに有り。朝餉まゐる事、常のごとくうるはしくきこしめさぬおりは、ばいぜんの人、御はしをたてゝ、すゑを折かけて出だす。三度おしかさねてまゐる。心えぬ事なれど、いまは定れる事なり。中のたびは髪をあぐ。
24. もゝしきのうち、はたとせの春秋ををくりむかへて、今もかつ見るうちの事どもは、おぼつかなかるべきにもあらぬを、いまさらにかきつけんも、めづらしからぬ心ちすれど、おりにふれ時につけたる大やけごとども、行末のかゞみまではなくとも、をのづからまたその世にはかくこそ有りけれ、などやうの物語のたよりには成なんかし。
25. 春をむかふる程は、内わたりなべてことしげければ、いづくをはじめなるべしともわきがたき様なれど、所々の御装束ども、とのもり・かもりの女ずども、さはがしくいそぎとゝのへたるに、つゐなはてゝ、砌のともしびどもかすかに見えわたる程、四方拝の御装束いそがすめり。事行ふ蔵人、こどねりやうの者、声々ことにつきたるも、をりから所えたりがほなり
26. 追儺之後。蔵人召仰諸司御装束。掃部寮清涼殿東庭当第三間。去石階七尺許鋪葉薦。其上鋪長筵。南北行。其上立廻大宋御屏風八帖。其中設御座三所。[...] 寅刻御出

27. 追儺後主殿寮供御湯、[...] 鶏鳴掃部寮奉仕御装束、於清涼殿東庭、先敷葉薦、其上敷長筵、南北妻、其上立御屏風八帖[...] 設御座三所。
28. ひの御座の御簾、南のはし、北のがくの間をたれたり(此間に、承香殿の人、むかしは候ひけるとかや)。[...] 近頃、里内裏などにて、あたりの間一間中はんにあぐる事あり。ひが事なり。今の世には、本儀に任せて、常の時の如く、こうまろをにあぐ。
29. 卯の時に、とのもりの司あさぎよめするおとにおどろきて、蔵人、御殿の格子をあぐ。南の第二の間ををして見るに、いまださしたれば、鬼の間より入て [...]
30. 卯剋、主殿寮奉仕朝清事。[...]上格子事。蔵人一人入自鬼間、放昼御座御格子沾木、他蔵人等出自殿上東戸、始自南第二間[...]。
31. あしたのほど [...] 日給の事あり。[...] ひるの事どもはてぬれば、[...] 殿上の簡ふうず(ふくろにいるゝをいふなり)。
32. 辰剋、殿上日給事、(自三月至八月辰、自九月至二月巳)[...] 未刻封殿上簡事。

# CHAPTER 9

# The Construction of the Nation by Theatrical Fiction

*Charlotte Krauss*

*Université de Poitiers*

To the question 'can fiction change the world?' we can answer that it contributes to restructuring the world in which we live, and that it allows us to disseminate abstract ideas and concepts by illustrating them for sometimes very large audiences. In this chapter, I will consider an essential change in European political systems at the beginning of the nineteenth century and the educational effort provided by playwriting at the time — as well as its initially difficult reception. While it may seem curious to focus on theatrical fiction (rather than on the novel or another narrative genre), it is worth recalling the great prestige that the dramatic genre still enjoyed at the beginning of the nineteenth century. To this can be added the fact that the stage was then the place where a European author could hope to reach a wide audience — almost all strata of a society that was still predominantly illiterate. Paradoxically, the aspect of fictional narrative is relevant to the corpus of dramas that will be dealt with: I will show that the attraction of an epic ideal did indeed cause a major problem for dramatic texts dealing with national historical subjects at the beginning of the nineteenth century, making it impossible to stage them at the time of their creation — despite the aforementioned prestige of theatres. As for the adaptations made at later times, at the end of the nineteenth and the beginning of the twentieth century, and thanks to sometimes radical, and therefore inevitably reductive, choices, they raise the question of fidelity to the initial text. In order to be able to change the world, must fiction be clear, univocal, not very complex — or, failing that, must its interpretation be reduced to this simple level?

## 1. The Pedagogy of the Concept of the Nation

It all starts with the emergence of the concept of nation and the need to define national peoples. Even if the term 'nation' has been in circulation since the end of the Middle Ages (in particular to designate groups of students united by the same geographical origin within the first universities), sociologists, historians, and political scientists agree that the emergence of a new frame of reference took place between the end of the eighteenth century and the beginning of the nineteenth, following a questioning of the classical orders of the world — dynastic and religious.[1] Around 1800, it is first in theory, then in the reality of an increasing number of European countries, that the nation is established as the foundation of the state system; the subjects of an absolute sovereign become citizens, who, ideally, are convinced that they belong to a national people. Yet this conception of the State, which seems normal to us today, is in fact nothing natural: the nation is an abstract concept. This is reflected in the term 'imagined community' coined by Benedict Anderson in the 1980s and widely used since then (Anderson [1983] 2006). The nation makes it possible to organise life in society and to structure a complex world — but in order for the idea to be understood and adopted by the population, it must be filled with an imagination and a symbolism, which had yet to be created at the beginning of the nineteenth century.

Even though the thinkers of the time, the intellectuals, were quick to adopt the new concept, it proved more difficult to teach a whole population that they should feel unified and that they should constitute a nation. How did you explain to an inhabitant of one of the many small German-speaking states, subject to a more or less authoritarian sovereign and speaking one of the many German dialects, that he or she should feel German and belong to a people that did not correspond to any political reality? However, at the beginning of the nineteenth century, the problem became urgent, especially in the territories affected or even modified by Napoleonic policy. Faced with political crises and the prospect of imminent military conflicts, several European countries called for the defence of national territory. The need to justify these sacrifices made governments realise the urgency of creating a sense of belonging and collective identity among their entire population. This intellectual response can be observed in virtually all European countries. We can cite some different situations of the time, all of which lead to the same need for a pedagogy of the nation. The German-speaking countries, without political unity, see themselves as a united cultural space (with the notable exception of the Austro-Hungarian Empire, a multi-ethnic state in which the dynastic system was not called into question until 1848). Poland, for its part, has just been wiped off the European map by three successive divisions between its three neighbouring powers, the Russian Empire, the Kingdom of Prussia, and the Habsburg Empire. After the Congress of Vienna, 82% of the former Polish territory was officially part of the Russian Empire (Hoensch 1990: 192). The awakening of a Polish national consciousness and its dissemination through literature made it possible to gather protesters during uprisings, such as that of November 1830. Finally, France itself was shaken, especially in terms of the political conception of the State: it was basically since 1789 that the country had been balancing between several political systems, and the liberal camps in particular were rejecting hereditary nobility and relying on the adherence of the people to the idea of nationhood.

In agreement with the Czech historian Miroslav Hroch, a theorist of nation and nationalism, we can see that the spread of the national idea, at first purely elitist and intellectual, then moved on to a massive diffusion of the nation's identity conceptions among the population (Hroch 2005: 45–48) — and this second step relied heavily on writers and the powers of fiction. What is being told to the people? Stories — and history. In addition to incorporating a display of symbols (flags, songs, costumes, or customs — all identified as 'national'), literary creation revisits historical episodes, both distant and recent, identifying them as crucial moments in national history. For how better to bring the people together than by handing them a kind of mirror in which characters designated as ancestors (who speak the same language, have the same beliefs, and also the same human concerns) appear in their moments of glory (heroes), or sometimes of defeat (betrayed heroes)?

A solid groundwork was obviously established through the historiography of the time, by figures such as Jules Michelet. But more than factual texts do, fiction has the power to illustrate, to invent secondary characters and to accentuate divides; it helps to emphasise the emotional side of the action. In the episodes transposed into and transformed by fiction, the aim is to show the actions of one or more heroes and the cohesion of the people fighting an external enemy who is sometimes supported by traitors on the inside. Generally, the constellation suggests a parallel with the situation in the nineteenth century (e.g., the enemy can be identified as a predecessor of the 'evil' Napoleon Bonaparte). As for the historical moments chosen, we find a return either to the supposed, mythical origins of the nation, or to moments of crisis or revolutionary movements.

How does this pedagogical impulse come to playwriting? It is true that at the beginning of the nineteenth century, it is first of all the epic that is identified as the literary genre that can ensure the transformation of historical episodes into moments of glory (or crisis) of the nation. In the absence of rediscovered ancient texts identified as epics (the *Nibelungenlied* in Germany, the *Tale of Igor's Campaign* in Russia), new epics are created (such as the *Kalevala* in Finland) that offer historically inspired narratives. Epics also have the enormous advantage that they can, in turn, be identified as part of the national culture, as material evidence of the nation's existence. The problem is that reading a few pages of a long and complex epic poem in the evening by the fire is not the favourite pastime of the ordinary citizen. And this is where theatrical fiction takes over: the stages of the theatres could be the most appropriate place to show the national history to the people, in their own language, and thereby convince them of the existence of the nation.

## 2. Representing the Nation

In order to quickly sketch out the kind of dramatic texts to which this quest for nationhood leads, we can first mention the German production around the character of Arminius (or Hermann[2]) — and in particular Heinrich von Kleist's *Hermann's Battle* (*Die Hermannsschlacht*, published in 1821). Arminius, the Germanic victor of the Roman army commanded by General Varus in A.D. 9, had already inspired a significant number of literary texts since the rediscovery of the figure by German humanism. The nineteenth century sees him as the founder of the German nation, acting against an enemy who, thanks to the continuity from Latin to the Romance languages, goes from Roman to French.³ In a superficial way, Kleist's play, written in 1808, while the author is panic-stricken by the advance of Napoleon's army, reads as follows: Varus's (Napoleon's) army attacks the territory of the Germanic (German) peoples, Arminius the Cherusk (the German) proposes to Marbod, king of the Marcomanni (Austria) to unite against the aggressor. Once the battle is won, Arminius promises to attack Rome (Paris).

But on closer inspection, this reading turns out to be far too simple. One only has to read the epigraph with which Kleist preceded his play to grasp the antagonism that underlies it: 'Woe betide my fatherland, to strike the lyre for your glory is, faithful to thee, denied me, thy poet.'⁴ The desire to write for the nation thus comes up against an opposition whose nature is not specified, but probably reflects the desire to develop the story and to go beyond the unambiguity and platitude of a simple pamphlet. As a result, the play is indeed very complex: Hermann is an unscrupulous ruler who, in order to achieve his goal, accepts lying, the manipulation of others (including his own wife), and the pillaging and even rape of his own people (to make them believe atrocities were committed by the Romans). The play makes it clear that there is nothing heroic about these cruel acts. As for the famous battle, it simply does not take place, because Marbod can take Varus's army by surprise; Arminius arrives too late. And above all: as it stood, the work simply could not be performed in its time. The frequent changes of place, the large number of characters — the *Hermann* that Kleist wanted to 'give to the Germans'⁵ to be played in Vienna did not correspond to the possibilities of Italian-style theatre. For more than a generation, until 1860, the work remained a closet drama: the reader is reduced to imagining the fictional world imagined by the author.

★ ★ ★ ★ ★

Faced with limited possibilities and the requirements of theatres at the time, many authors gave up considering the performance of their dramatic works. This is the case, for example, of the French *scènes historiques*, an ephemeral literary genre that enjoyed some success in France in the 1820s. One of the authors who tried their hand at it was Prosper Mérimée, another the historian Ludovic Vitet who, in 1826, published *Les Barricades*. Some three hundred pages long, these *scènes historiques* are devoted to an episode during the (sixteenth century) Eighth War of Religion. The action is told in sixteen scenes of varying lengths, preceded by a brief prologue entitled 'The Return of Vincennes' that appears before the lengthy list of characters (about sixty). Focusing on the week of 6–13 May 1588, the work traces the people's uprising against Henri III, an unpopular king who had no heir — a movement initiated and led by Henri of Guise. The leader of the League allies himself with the people of Paris and returns to the city with his soldiers, despite a ban imposed by the king. The action focuses on the 'day of the barricades', 12 May: eight scenes show different stages of the day and attempt to probe the failure of both sides. In the end, Henri III has to flee Paris, but de Guise, unable to get his hands on his opponent, doesn't obtain the power he has hoped for: the queen mother announces that she is taking over the regency.

If the author presents himself as a historian and his work as a somewhat incoherent sequence of episodic scenes,[6] the structure of his work is, in reality, anything but random; on the contrary, it betrays a composition obviously aiming to give its rightful place to all the parties of the conflict. This implies representing the people: if the people of the third estate, unlike the nobles, lack an important place in historical sources, the desire to render a perfect local colour leads in *Les Barricades* to a broad representation of the popular masses, even if this requires a great deal of imagination based on meagre sources. This representation of the masses is introduced progressively into the work, bringing the reader closer and closer to the people; it reaches its climax in a staging of revolutionary events of rare violence, on the barricades and in the streets. The presence of the crowd reaches its peak in the middle of the *scènes historiques* and is undeniably the highlight of the work.

Confirming a general trend in the genre of *scènes historiques* and, more broadly, drama featuring national historical material, *Les Barricades* shows signs of a narrativity that betrays the appeal of the epic model. For Vitet's work, this fact is noted less at the level of action (there is no epic hero in *Les Barricades*) than at the level of form, and first of all in the intrusion of the epic narrative in the text — which is all the more surprising since it contradicts the historian's rejection of any fictionalisation in his preface.[7] But the stage directions are long, precise, and deliberately aimed at the reader: many of the details they reveal would not, in fact, be transposable to a theatre stage.[8] The scenes are also preceded by a historical account, 'Brief History of the League, from its Origin to the Day of the Barricades' ('Histoire abrégée de la Ligue, depuis son origine jusqu'à la journée des Barricades'), a richly commented presentation of the main characters, and finally a description of the costumes, taking into account the different classes of the population — all these narrative parts guide the reader in order to allow him to imagine scenes as close as possible to the historical reality.

As a representation of the French nation throughout its history and with respect for all social classes, *Les Barricades* has an eminently political significance. Although the work, later included in a complete trilogy entitled *La Ligue*,[9] was a great success in its time and influenced French Romantic theatre, particularly that of Victor Hugo,[10] it fell into oblivion in the twentieth century and is very little known today.

★  ★  ★  ★  ★

This brings me to my third example, which is Polish and little known to non-Polish speaking readers. In Poland, however, Adam Mickiewicz's *Dziady* (*Forefathers' Eve*) is not only regarded as the emblematic dramatic text of an epoch and of Romanticism (Miłosz [1969] 2013) but also, more widely, as a 'founding work'[11] of the entire Polish culture and national consciousness. The drama, which adapts contemporary subject matter, consists of four parts with a complicated genesis, spread over almost ten years, from 1823 to 1832, the year of the publication of the *Dziady* in Paris. It is only the third part that interests me here. This suite of nine scenes was written in 1832 in Dresden — supposedly in two weeks (which is not true): in reaction to the November Uprising (1830–1831), in which Mickiewicz, who had been banned from

Poland, had not taken part, the author revisits events he himself had experienced in Vilna a few years earlier (in 1823) and builds up a whole cult of martyrs to the Polish cause, oppressed by the Russian occupier.

The text itself is preceded by a dedication to the martyrs and a historical note introducing the figure of Senator Novosilcev:[12] depicted as the embodiment of evil, he persecutes Polish youth above all and turns Vilna into a 'huge prison' and 'the headquarters of the executioners.'[13] Faced with this diabolical machinery, the students gather in Polish-language poetic circles — until Novosilcev stops them, dissolves the circles and applies extremely harsh judgements, including exile to Russia and even imprisonment in Siberia. The only survivor is none other than Mickiewicz himself, who manages to obtain a passport to leave Russia in 1829. In publishing the third part of the *Dziady*, the author is thus also fulfilling a historical duty — which gives the literary text a value of peculiarity as well as its status as valuable testimony. At the same time, the text pursues the goal of consolidating the idea of the nation by means of a narrative of historical facts.

The national reference can be found, among other things, in the choice of the action's locations, which cover the geography of a large part of former Poland-Lithuania and especially three historical cities. The first scenes are located in Vilna, in the Basilian monastery transformed into a state prison,[14] then in the entourage of Senator Novosilcev. Scene four, which is very brief, is located in a village house, explicitly located near Lwów,[15] and scene seven in a living room in Warsaw. The last scene returns to an unspecified cemetery near a chapel, echoing the second part of the drama. The action, a sort of panorama, focuses first on the protagonist of the two previous parts, the poet Gustav. Imprisoned (for his poetry), he decides to change his name to Konrad. The night before Christmas allows him to meet other prisoners, former companions, for an exchange and to regain courage: Poland is not dead. In the most famous scene known as 'the great improvisation' (*wielka improwizacja*), Konrad defies God, then collapses and rises up, transformed into a hero: guided by his faith, he will fight for the national cause. His opponent, Novosilcev, is surrounded by several invisible devilish voices; his evil deeds are told (but hardly shown) and one of his assistants is killed by lightning (off-stage). Generally speaking, the drama makes the choice not to directly show the violence of the events.

As Michel Masłowski has pointed out, the path of the hero who, from Gustav, an introverted and sensitive poet, transforms himself into Konrad, a patriotic hero, corresponds to a path of initiation 'sufficiently suggestive to lead generations of Poles to identify with this pattern of personal development.'[16] This model of devotion to the national cause is supported by the vision of Father Piotr, who gives meaning to the martyrs by announcing to Poland an end to suffering: a saviour will succeed in leading the nation back on the road to freedom. The vision functions as 'a call to act in the same direction, to embody universal ethical causes, first and foremost that of the Freedom of Peoples.'[17] The spectator or reader of the *Dziady* is confronted with the spectacle of destiny experienced by young Polish patriots and revolutionaries. But at the same time as he observes their suffering, he is also called upon to imitate the gesture of Gustav/Konrad. The drama thus combines narrative and call to action.

Of the three examples cited, *Dziady*, though clearly received as a drama, is certainly the furthest from the stage: it is fragmented in the Romantic style and includes many narrative voices, some of which are more identifiable than others.[18] The impossibility of performing the play in the era of Italian-style theatre is therefore not only due to the political context: if it was impossible to perform any play in Polish, especially a work with political claims, *Dziady* is also far too complex and the voices are too undefined to be staged at the time of its publication. But despite this, the work displays dramatic form and was received as drama: its narrative character was therefore not fully accepted.

## 3. The Problematic Adaptation of Fiction on Stage

In his contribution to this volume, Claude Calame reminds us of the differentiation between diegesis (where the author is embodied by a protagonist) and mimesis (the representation) to conclude with the 'obviously' narrative character of fiction. It seems to me that this differentiation can help to understand the problems faced by the aforementioned plays: at a time when nation-building involves the imagination of a national past — and thus, initially, the sketching of fictional worlds inspired by History — authors easily succumb to an epic ideal. To varying degrees, the three examples above tell stories and guide the reader to explain the idea of a national people. However, these fictions are only compatible with theatre — with mimesis — if the staging strongly reduces them and therefore presents a truncated version. Narration allows the reader to discover an entirely new and complex fictional world; in theatre,[19] the spectator is accustomed to finding a less ambiguous, easily understandable world, allowing him or her to concentrate on the multiple facets of the artistic performance.

A glance at the subsequent reception of the aforementioned examples confirms this hypothesis. *Hermann's Battle* was first staged in Breslau in 1860, on the anniversary of the 'Battle of the Nations' (the Battle of Leipzig in 1813) (see Krauss 2014: 127–49). The theatre-maker Feodor Wehl adapted the play to the taste of the time, smoothing out the formulas and considerably reworking the scenes likely to offend the audience.[20] Although the reception was still lukewarm, the *Battle* soon became a national landmark in the German Empire. In 1871, the writer Rudolph Genée reinforced the nationalist interpretation by retouching the scenes, assuring the heroic Hermann of the reader's sympathy; he also replaced the desolation of the final picture with an expression of absolute confidence in the future of the German nation (Dörner and Vogt 2013: 293). The play was performed at the beginning of the First World War, and news of the French front was announced between acts (Seeba [1993] 2003), 358. Finally, in Hitler's Germany, *Hermann's Battle* quickly became the most performed play by Kleist (forty-six times during the 1933/1934 season) (see Reemtsma 2003: 149), and a 1940 edition presented the work as a 'Führerdrama' (Busch 1974, 127). The message of the text then became quite simple, as can be seen, for example, in a doctoral thesis on the myth of Arminius, defended in Greifswald in 1937:

> The main idea of this play is the following: a guide shows his people the way to liberation, leads them on the right path and inspires them with all his mind. Kleist wants all the German people to be inspired by this spirit. This is how the poet shows the way to the future. (Sydow 1937: 75)

Both the theatre industry and critics only rediscovered the complexity of Kleist's play when Claus Peymann directed it at the Bochum Theatre in 1982 — at that time the play was understood to denounce war in general (see Krauss 2014: 141–43).

If Ludovic Vitet's *Les Barricades* has never, to my knowledge, been adapted for the stage, other *scènes historiques* have had brief careers as opera or radio adaptations: *La Jaquerie* by Prosper Mérimée (1828), for example.[21] But this long play devoted to the peasant revolts of the fourteenth century was above all enthusiastically received in the very young Soviet Union of the 1920s, which identified *La Jaquerie* as a predecessor of communist literature and, again in a very truncated form, even made it into a play for children ('Detskij Teatr', in 1925) (Mérimée 1925). In view of the cruel and very explicit scenes in the original, this development seems rather astonishing.

It was not until 1901 that the first production of the complete *Dziady* was staged: Stanisław Wyspiański, himself a poet, an artist of the modernist *Młoda Polska*-movement ('Young Poland'), but also a renowned playwright, took up Mickiewicz's idea of a spectacular national drama and deduced from it the project of a 'teatr ogromny' ('monumental theatre'). By adapting *Dziady* to the stage, he pursues the goal of bringing all the fragments together in a single show while settling for a minimum of scenery. The reception of the public was extremely favourable, including for political reasons: the Austrian occupation zone in which Krakow was located at the time (in 'Galicia and Lodomeria') allowed theatrical performances, unlike the Polish provinces under Russian and Prussian occupation. Spectators therefore flocked from other parts of old Poland on 'more patriotic than theatrical excursions' to attend performances of *Dziady* that were celebrated as 'a kind of mass for the nation.'[22]

Unsurprisingly, it was after the First World War, when Poland regained its independence, that *Dziady*'s productions were particularly numerous. 'Every new premiere was celebrated as a theatrical festivity',[23] Wojciech Dudzik sums up. At that time, *Dziady*, as a national drama, was the very measure of the know-how of any Polish director (Dudzik 1999: 108). The political issue of the play became apparent again after 1945, in communist Poland under the control of Moscow. The climax was reached in the autumn of 1967 with a production by Kasimierz Dejmek at the National Theatre in Warsaw, planned to mark the fiftieth anniversary of the October Revolution. As Karl Dedecius explains, 'overnight the classic Mickiewicz became topical and highly explosive again. He turned into the beacon of a brief but symptomatic uproar.'[24] Dejmek's adaptation transposed Mickiewicz's dedication to his 'companions in study, prison and exile'[25] to the stage and suggested that the struggle for Polish independence was not over. The public approved and applauded every line it could understand as a message against Russia. The Polish Communist Party, out of fear of possible reactions from Moscow, then demanded the withdrawal of the anti-Russian passages and ended up limiting the number of performances[26] — which only increased public interest: all the remaining tickets were sold out. Finally, the First Secretary of the party, Władysław Gomułka, who, without having seen or even read the drama, judged it as 'a knife in the back of Polish-Soviet friendship' (Dudzik 1999: 118), decided to ban the performances of *Dziady* for good — a decision that led to a wave of protests that went far beyond the theatre and remained in the collective memory as 'March 1968.' The staging of Mickiewicz's national drama definitively became the catalyst that broke up discontent on the one hand, but also served as a pretext for the Communist Party to carry out ideological purges among intellectuals and Jews. Although it took five years for a new production of *Dziady* to be authorised,[27] the political and national character of Mickiewicz's drama was nevertheless reinforced by this crisis, whose collective memory now remains attached to the text as baggage that is as invisible as it is irremovable. Consciously or unconsciously, each new staging of the text, each reading is necessarily influenced by the political history of its reception. This reception has been based on the presentation of Polish history formulated by the work itself, it has developed the political statement over the decades and definitively confirmed *Dziady*'s status as a Polish national drama.

★ ★ ★ ★ ★

The examples of these three dramatic works illustrate the stakes but also the limits of theatrical fiction. In imagining the nation from historical material, Kleist as well as Vitet and Mickiewicz all use fictionalisation processes: they arrange historical details, add characters and invent scenes such that, according to the nineteenth-century vision, they could have happened. They also provide a national interpretation of historical facts, which is one of the factors explaining the epic tendency of the works, the addition of indeterminate voices, exhaustive stage directions and even commentary in notes. The three works thus turn out to be very complex and unperformable on the stages of nineteenth-century European theatres — closet dramas which, as Kleist admits in his epigraph, perhaps even miss the original intention of clearly explaining the nation to the people.

Now, if the reading of these closet dramas does indeed allow a reader to imagine all the details and the richness of the actions, their staging a few decades later inevitably involves an extreme reduction of the texts: whether these are national (or even nationalist) interpretations, communist or pacifist re-readings, the complexity of the works is necessarily reduced by the performance. Looking at the history of performances, the social impact of the works cited is nevertheless very real: it is probably the staging of theatrical fiction that changes the world.

## References

ANDERSON, BENEDICT. [1983] 2006. *Imagined Communities: Reflections on the Origin and Spread of Nationalism* (London: Verso)

BLAMBERGER, GÜNTER. 2011. *Heinrich von Kleist: Biographie* (Frankfurt: Fischer)

BUSCH, ROLF. 1974. *Imperialistische und faschistische Kleist-Rezeption 1890–1945: Eine ideologiekritische Untersuchung* (Frankfurt: Akademische Verlagsgesellschaft)

DEDECIUS, KARL. 1999. 'Adam Mickiewicz. Idol und Idee einer Nation', in *Von Polen, Poesie und Politik: Adam Mickiewicz 1798–1998*, ed. by Rolf-Dieter Kluge, 33–53 (Tübingen: Attempto)

DÖRNER, ANDREAS and LUDGERA VOGT. 2013. 'Ein Beispiel: Heinrich von Kleist, "Die Hermannsschlacht"', in *Literatursoziologie*, ed. by Andreas Dörner and Ludgera Vogt, 261–305 (Wiesbaden: Springer VS)

DRATWICKI, ALEXANDRE. 2015. 'Connaissez-vous la Jacquerie?', *Maison de la Radio*, 22 June <www.maisondelaradio.fr/-/article/connaissez-vous-la-jacquerie> [accessed 28 March 2020]

DUDZIK, WOJCIECH. 1999. 'Politik und Dichtung: "Die Totenfeier" (*Dziady*) — das polnische nationale Drama zwischen Beifall und Verbot', in *Von Polen, Poesie und Politik: Adam Mickiewicz 1798–1998*, ed. by Rolf-Dieter Kluge, 123–52 (Tübingen: Attempto)

HAGENAU, GERDA. 1999. *Adam Mickiewicz als Dramatiker: Dichtung und Bühnengeschichte* (Frankfurt: Lang)

HOBSBAWM, ERIC J. [1990] 2003. *Nations and Nationalism Since 1780: Programme, Myth, Reality* (Cambridge: Cambridge University Press)

HOENSCH, JÖRG K. 1990. *Geschichte Polens* (Stuttgart: Ulmer)

HROCH, MIROSLAV. 2005. *Das Europa der Nationen: Die moderne Nationsbildung im europäischen Vergleich* (Göttingen: Vandenhoeck & Ruprecht)

KLEIST, HEINRICH VON. 2001. *Sämtliche Werke und Briefe*, ed. by Helmut Sembdner. 2 vols (Munich: dtv)

KRAUSS, CHARLOTTE. 2014. 'Hermann. L'interprétation politique de textes littéraires — et ses conséquences', in *L'Interprétation politique des œuvres littéraires*, ed. by Carlo Arcuri and Andréas Pfersmann, 127–49 (Paris: Kimé)

MASŁOWSKI, MICHEL. 2001. *Le théâtre romantique polonaise*, in *Romantisme*, 111: 57–73

——. 2009. 'La structure rituelle des *Aïeux* et ses conséquences esthétiques', in *L'Âge d'or du théâtre polonais de Mickiewicz à Wyspiański, Grotowski, Kantor, Lupa, Warlikowski...*, ed. by Agnieszka Grudzińska and Michel Masłowski, 43–64 (Paris: Éd. de l'Amandier)

MÉRIMÉE, PROSPER. 1925. *Detskij Teatr* [La Jaquerie], trans. by B. Šapilov (Moskva: Gosudarstvennoe Izdatel'stvo)

MICKIEWICZ, ADAM. 2012. *Dziady drezdeńskie, część III*, ed. by Janusz Skuczyński (Wrocław: Zakład Narodowy Im. Ossolińskich)

MIŁOSZ, CZESLAW. [1969] 2013. *Geschichte der polnischen Literatur* [*The History of Polish Literature*] (Tübingen: Francke)

REEMTSMA, JAN-PHILIPP. 2003. *Unzeitgemäßes über Krieg und Tod* (Munich: Beck)

SEEBA, HINRICH C. [1993] 2003. 'Hermanns Kampf für Deutschlands Not: Zur Topographie der nationalen Identität', in *Arminius und die Varusschlacht: Geschichte, Mythos, Literatur*, ed. by Rainer Wiegels, Winfried Woesler, et al., 355–66 (Paderborn: Schöningh)

SYDOW, WOLFGANG. 1937. *Deutung und Darstellung des Arminius-Schicksals in seinen wesentlichen Ausprägungen seit Kleist* (Greifswald: Buchdruckerei H. Adler)

VITET, LUDOVIC. [1826] 1830. *Les Barricades : Scènes historiques, mai 1588* (Paris: Fournier Jeune)

YON, JEAN-CLAUDE. 1997. 'La révolution de 1830 au théâtre ou le triomphe de la Barricade imprimée', in *La Barricade*, ed. by Alain Corbin and Jean-Marie Mayeur (Paris: Publ. de la Sorbonne), pp. 85–96

## Notes to Chapter 9

1. For nation-theory and its history, see especially Anderson ([1983] 2006); Hobsbawm ([1990] 2003); Hroch (2005).
2. Arminius, the name given to the historical figure in the Latin sources (the only written sources transmitted), was Germanized into 'Hermann' in the era of humanism, in the entourage of Martin Luther.
3. See for example the famous Hermann Monument, erected near the city of Detmold in Germany and inaugurated in 1875 by the Emperor Wilhelm I: The statue's sword is clearly pointed at France.
4. 'Wehe, mein Vaterland, dir! Die Leier, | zum Ruhm dir, zu schlagen | Ist getreu dir im Schoß, mir | deinem Dichter, verwehrt' (Kleist 2001: 1, 533). All translations into English in this article are mine (C.K).
5. See a letter that Kleist sent to the Vienna theatre on 20 April 1809: 'Ich *schenke* [das Drama] den Deutschen; machen Sie nur, daß es gegeben wird' ('I give [the drama] as a gift to the Germans: just make sure that it is delivered to them') (Kleist 2001, II, 824).
6. In his preface, Vitet presents his work as the fruit of a spontaneity imposed by the material on the author, who is compared to a walker: 'Je me suis imaginé que je me promenais dans Paris au mois de mai 1588, pendant l'orageuse journée des Barricades, et pendant les jours qui la précédèrent; [...] chaque fois qu'une scène pittoresque, un tableau de mœurs, un trait de caractère sont venus s'offrir à mes yeux, j'ai essayé d'en reproduire l'image en esquissant une scène' ('I imagined that I was walking in Paris in the month of May 1588, on the stormy day of the Barricades, and during the preceding days [...] every time a picturesque scene, a tableau of manners, or a character trait offered themselves to my eyes, I tried to reproduce its image by sketching a scene') (Vitet [1826] 1830: v–vi).
7. In particular, he emphasizes the historical character of his work and rejects its classification as a dramatic genre with a clearly fictional character: 'Ce n'est point une pièce de théâtre que l'on va lire, ce sont des faits historiques présentés sous la forme dramatique, mais sans la prétention d'en composer un drame' ('It isn't a play that you are about to read; it is a set of historical facts presented in dramatic form, but without any claim to composing a drama') (Vitet 1830: 5).
8. An extreme example is the insertion of explanatory notes. For example, when (in scene 6) the queen asks her maid: 'Ma chère Camilla, va me chercher la liqueur de notre vieil arabe: on a dû la faire chauffer' ('My dear Camilla, go and fetch me the liqueur of our old Arab: it must have been warmed up by now'), a footnote specifies: 'C'est très probablement du café que demande Catherine: depuis 1545, le café était à la mode à Constantinople; en Italie on commençait à le connaître; mais en France c'était encore une liqueur mystérieuse: l'usage n'en devint public qu'au milieu du dix-septième siècle' ('Catherine is probably asking for coffee: since 1545, coffee was fashionable in Constantinople; in Italy it was beginning to become familiar, but in France it was still a mysterious liqueur: its use only became public in the middle of the seventeenth century') (Vitet 1830: 270). This footnote feigns the neutrality of a historian unrelated to the action, but it does little to hide the interference of a narrator who adds a few curious details about the period to the reading of the scene.
9. In addition to *Les Barricades*, this trilogy of *scènes dramatiques*, published in 1844, also included *Les États de Blois*, dating from 1827, and *La Mort de Henri III*, 1829.
10. Victor Hugo claims to have been inspired by Vitet's *Les Barricades* for his drama *Cromwell* and its famous preface. See Yon (1997: 86).
11. 'œuvre fondatrice' (Masłowski 2001: 59).
12. It is the Russian Nikolaj N. Novosilcev, who was the vice-governor of Poland from 1815 to 1832.
13. 'ogromne więzienie'; 'Założył główną kwaterę katostwa w Wilnie' (Mickiewicz 2012: 6).
14. There is a strong contrast with the indeterminacy of the places in the previous parts: the stage directions even indicate the name of the street (Ostrobramska) in which the convent is located.
15. Lviv (formerly Lvov), now located in Ukraine, at the time (from 1772 to 1918) officially Lemberg in Austria-Hungary (capital of the province of Galicia and Lodomeria).
16. 'suffisamment suggestif pour amener des générations de Polonais à s'identifier à ce schéma de développement personnel' (Masłowski 2009: 51).

17. 'un appel à agir dans la même direction, à incarner les causes éthiques universelles, celle de la Liberté des peuples en premier lieu' (Masłowski 2009: 51).
18. In the scene of the 'great improvisation', for example, the hero is torn between the forces of good and evil: the text gives no description of these characters, but only presents 'a voice on the left' (the devil) and 'a voice on the right' (the guardian angel). 'Spirits' are added, always without description or precision. This presence of indefinite voices, while not extraordinary in the theatre of the late twentieth or twenty-first century, is unthinkable in a play intended for the stage in the first half of the nineteenth century — several decades before the appearance of the stage director as a mediating authority in European theatre.
19. This consideration concerns traditional European theatre-forms and especially playwriting in the first half of the nineteenth century.
20. See Dörner and Vogt (2013: 290) as well as Blamberger (2011: 367).
21. The opera adaptation premiered at the Monte-Carlo Opera in March 1895 and was revived in December of the same year at the Opéra Comique de Paris. It is an opera in four acts: *La Jacquerie*, a project begun by Édouard Lalo in 1889 and completed by Arthur Coquard after the composer's death. The libretto (which greatly reduces the text of Mérimée) is by Édouard Blau and Simone Arnaud (Dratwicki 2015). There is also the manuscript of a sixteen-scene radio adaptation by Guy Favières, which was performed at the *Radiodiffusion française* on 8 November 1937 (BNF notice: FRBNF40888511, 4-YA RAD-2103).
22. 'Das waren eher patriotische als theatralische Exkursionen [...]. Im Fall der 'Totenfeier' wurde das Theater zur Kirche, d.h. es wurde dort statt einer Vorstellung eine Art Messe für die Nation gefeiert' (Dudzik 1999: 107).
23. 'Jede neue Premiere wurde zum Theaterfest: Schauspieler wie Zuschauer ergötzten sich an Mickiewicz' Worten, die endlich ohne jegliche Verstümmelung ausgesprochen werden durften' (Dudzik 1999: 107).
24. 'Der Klassiker Mickiewicz wurde über Nacht wieder brandaktuell und hochexplosiv. Er wurde zum Fanal eines zwar kurzen, aber symptomatischen Aufruhrs' (Dedecius 1999: 12).
25. 'Spółuczniom, spółwięźniom, spółwygnańcom' (Mickiewicz 2012: 3).
26. For a more complete account of the case, see Dedecius (1999: 12); Dudzik (1999: 116–19) and Hagenau (1999: 136–49).
27. By Konrad Swinarski in 1973 — a staging that was a major and lasting success (see Dudzik 1999: 121).

CHAPTER 10

# Feminist Resistance and the Powers of Fiction

*Anne Isabelle François*

Université Sorbonne Nouvelle

Can fiction change the world? In particular, can it put an end to patriarchy and sexism? Does it depend on the kind of fiction you read, or does *any* fiction, by definition, open itself up to feminist emancipation? Which mechanisms and types of engagement are at stake, and on what level? In order to examine these theoretical and pragmatic questions, this paper will proceed in two parts. I will begin in the first part by analysing a contemporary case study that exemplifies the power of a fictional universe and a creative use of fiction: Margaret Atwood's *The Handmaid's Tale*, embodied now in three planes (two novels, a TV series, and multiple real world protests). This case study will lead to the second part, comprising a general development of the intersection between feminist resistance and the powers of fiction, with a particular focus on the latest French academic research, as it is embedded in critical theoretical discourse with global relevance.

## 1. The Impact of Margaret Atwood's *The Handmaid's Tale*

On 21 January 2017, the day after Donald Trump was inaugurated as the forty-fifth President of the United States, the first major Women's March was held in Washington, D.C., across the country and around the world, in response to Trump's particularly violent and sexist campaign 'that insulted, demonized, and threatened many of us, leaving the communities hurting and scared' (Women's March, n.d.).[1] Two slogans then appeared, which were to take on a particular resonance: '*The Handmaid's Tale* is NOT an Instruction Manual' and 'Make Margaret Atwood Fiction Again.' If the second is a direct response to the Trump campaign's 'Make America Great Again', it has also become a rallying cry that problematises the issues of fiction, its status and power, re-actualising the discourse around fiction and its scope. Atwood's fiction's presence in the public sphere is all the more visible with the outfits worn by some participants, modelled on the costumes of the 'Handmaids', the characters in the novel, and the TV series adapting it, which at the time had yet to air. It was only three months later, in April 2017, that the first episode aired on Hulu, becoming the platform's most watched launch.

Bruce Miller, the showrunner, took full advantage of the visibility given to the fiction to publicise the adaptation, insisting on its topicality through the explicit comparison between the inaugural march and certain images from the TV series. He capitalised on these connections and the global dimensions of the march, explicitly comparing the anti-Trump Women's March with some of the visuals in the show: 'You're seeing *exactly the same* signs, *exactly the same* images, and you're also seeing Capitol police with guns, not firing them, thank God, but it's *the same thing*' (Lowry 2017; my emphasis). Just as the creator of the series encouraged and promoted the re-appropriation of the programme by political audiences and citizens, costume designer Ane Crabtree provided practical advice on how to fashion the famous 'Handmaid' costumes which have become globalised icons of protest and struggle:

> NARAL — a pro-choice charity — contacted me to ask for help because they wanted to protest in the senate. My jaw dropped open; I was so humbled by their strength. I had to say I cannot do this for you, but I can suggest how to do this quickly. From that moment, every time there was a protest in the US, or more recently in Poland, it's jarring and emotional to see them use these costumes. The thing that's so intensely poetic for me is that women are coming together and they're finding power in a uniform that was meant to hinder them and imprison them — that to me is the perfect outcome. (Morby 2017)

The method has spread widely, with protests around the world denouncing threats to women's rights or gender equality. In June 2017, women dressed as 'Handmaids' silently demonstrated in front of the Arizona Senate in Phoenix and on Capitol Hill in Washington D.C. to challenge various plans to repeal Obamacare and family planning subsidies; protests like them continued through September 2017 in Ireland, Argentina, Poland, Costa Rica, France, etc. Most of these demonstrations are linked to the problem of women's bodies being requisitioned by the state, as happens in the fiction, as well as to gender and sexual violence, as when the Alabama Senate passed the most restrictive abortion law in the country in May 2019, which prohibited abortion even in cases of rape or incest. Other 'Handmaids' greeted Vice-President Mike Pence on a visit to Philadelphia in July 2018 and challenged the appointment of alleged rapist Brett Kavanaugh to the US Supreme Court in the fall of 2018. The effectiveness and power of the strategy, a sort of polar opposite to Femen tactics of topless protest, is praised by Atwood herself, who comments: 'It's brilliant as a protest tactic. You're not saying anything, you're sitting very silently and modestly, and you can't be kicked out for dressing inappropriately, because you're all covered up. No frightful bare shoulders!' (Wagner 2019).

On 10 March 2017, two months after the inaugural Women's March, Atwood published an essay on 'What *The Handmaid's Tale* Means in the Age of Trump' in *The New York Times*. She also establishes an explicit link between current political events and her writing, further emphasising the principle of coincidence and superimposition between fiction and reality. This is especially relevant as, at the time, she was writing the sequel to the first novel, which was launched large-scale in September 2019:

> in the wake of the recent American election, fears and anxieties proliferate. Basic civil liberties are seen as endangered, along with many of the rights

for women won over the past decades, and indeed the past centuries. In this divisive climate, in which hate for many groups seems on the rise and scorn for democratic institutions is being expressed by extremists of all stripes, it is a certainty that someone, somewhere — many, I would guess — are writing down what is happening as they themselves are experiencing it. Or they will remember, and record after, if they can. Will their messages be suppressed and hidden? Will they be found, centuries later, in an old house, behind a wall? Let us hope it doesn't come to that. I trust it will not. (Atwood 2017)

Atwood has repeatedly stated that she decided to write *The Testaments*, the sequel to *The Handmaid's Tale*, in 2016 — the dark year of the vote on Brexit on 23 June and Trump's victory on 8 November. The publication of the second novel has given rise to a promotional device that is quite exceptional in its extension, once again bearing testimony to the importance of her fiction in our current public sphere: a first print run of 500,000 copies, more than 100,000 copies of which were sold in five days in the UK. The official launch at midnight on 9 September 2019 at Waterstones in Piccadilly, London, was followed on the 10th by a press conference at the British Library and a two-hour filmed conversation with a BBC journalist at the National Theatre, which was broadcast live to 1,300 cinemas around the world. This launch, worthy of a rock-star, earned Atwood the honour of covers in influential publications (*Time Magazine*, *Sunday Times Style*, *Maclean's*), and was followed and confirmed by the awarding of the Booker Prize for Fiction on 14 October 2019. The launch was organised jointly with the feminist association Equality Now, which documents instances across the world that make today's reality resemble that of Gilead, Atwood's fictional tyranny where women's bodies are enslaved. Atwood's press release (20 November 2018) announcing the publication of *The Testaments* centred on the explicit statement that it was inspired by contemporary events: 'Dear Readers: Everything you've asked me about Gilead and its inner workings is the inspiration for this book. Well, almost everything! The other inspiration is the world we've been living in' (Atwood 2018). Furthermore, in an exchange with readers on Reddit, Atwood prophesied that the current attacks against women's rights, particularly in the context of US health policy, will inevitably lead to 'dead bodies on the floor', and that if she were a young woman today, faced with the normalisation of misogyny, she would 'be taking a self-defence course' (Atwood 2017a). In general, the correlation between the American and global political situation and the broadcast of the TV series on the Hulu platform has, in fact, led to a re-actualisation of the discourse around fiction and its scope. Sales of Atwood's novel, published in 1985, have exploded: according to Amazon sales, *The Handmaid's Tale* was the best-selling novel in the US in 2017; it topped the Sunday Times bestseller list for sixteen consecutive weeks, just as the British publisher Vintage saw a 670% increase in sales between 2016 and 2017 (Liptak 2017).[2]

In addition, the broadcast of the first season of the TV series *The Handmaid's Tale* not only coincided with Trump's election, but also with the rise of the #MeToo movement, which grew after fall 2017. This was followed in January 2018 by the #TimesUp movement, the second Women's March, and the airing of the second season of the series, which started in April 2018. The year 2018 remains marked by these movements, which freed the voices of victims of sexual assault and harassment, and rapidly took on a viral dimension on social networks in the US and other countries (with the French version #Balancetonporc, hashtags #YoTambién in Spain, #quellavoltache in Italy or #MiraComoNosPonemos in Argentina).[3] The latest issue of the French journal *Mouvements* on 'Sexual Uprisings' (*Révoltes sexuelles*) aptly describes this development as a global mobilisation where millions of women are making 'a fundamentally revolutionary political gesture by speaking out publicly and breaking the isolation to which they were previously assigned in order to participate in a collective and international uprising' (Achin 2019: 99).[4]

These hashtags, as well as the dystopian fiction, in which women are deprived of their fundamental rights, are thus interpreted as vectors for women's mobilisation and empowerment: they give audience to women's words, which are so often questioned, and break the silence surrounding the different forms of heterosexist violence or aggression, thus serving as a banner for new alliances. Fiction is then celebrated for its capacity to innervate protest movements and, more broadly, to constitute a common political reference, providing a supplementary tool in the staging and visibility of public and social problems. The 'Handmaids' have indeed become a shared reference point: Kathleen Spencer, founder of Action Together Massachusetts (a protest group born after Trump's election) and the national association 'Handmaid Coalition', an activist movement created in the wake of the inaugural Women's March, points out that millions now have a common language and share a set of symbols to interpret and discuss what they see (Handmaid Coalition 2017). In August 2017, the activist group UltraViolet launched 'The Handmaid's Resistance', a programme providing instruction manuals, toolkits, and costumes for anyone who wants to hold an event in the style of the 'Handmaids', claiming: 'Now is the time to join together and loudly call out sexism and anti-women policies of Trump and politicians — or risk starring in a real-life version of *The Handmaid's Tale*' (a rephrasing of the slogan 'Make Margaret Atwood Fiction Again') (UltraViolet 2017). UltraViolet is also one of the founders of the 'Handmaid Coalition', which aims to respond to attacks 'targeting women, the working class, and minority groups' (Handmaid Coalition 2017) by supporting, lobbying, and coordinating peaceful demonstrations, offering a 'survival guide' or the possibility to sponsor a 'Handmaid' costume. Since fiction federates, aggregates, and constructs frameworks of experience (in the sense of Goffman's frame analysis) that can be transposed into reality, it is seen as offering a potent base of representations likely to be shared by a large audience and to be amplified. The characteristic and recognizable 'Handmaid' outfits (red robes and cloaks, white bonnets) are one such translation and transposition, a sign of feminist rallying around the world, an example of fiction providing creative tools that encourage citizen action (Kligler-Vilenchik 2016).

More generally, the question arises as to whether fiction can put an end to patriarchy and sexism. Its potential for change has become a postulate shared by those initiatives and activists who have made the 'Handmaid' into a political symbol and a symbol of women's empowerment — in short, into a fiction that is supposed to have provoked initiatives, epidemics of ideas, and large-scale collective movements, becoming a lever for thinking about actions and identifying strategies of combat. Empowerment is understood as an attempt to broaden the range and modes of intervention, both individually and collectively, in order to exert greater control over reality and one's well-being. This process is interpreted as a direct consequence of Atwood's fiction's ability to resonate with current events in the context of the decline in women's rights under the rise of populism. The TV adaptation (2017), in particular, stresses these echoes and the fiction's actuality: the world imagined by Atwood is transposed into the contemporary context (whereas in the novel, Gilead's regime belongs to the past, as indicated in the Final Historical Notes). It also facilitates the process of immediate identification with the heroine, whose real name we learn towards the end of the first episode of the first season ('My name is June'), while it remains a secret in the novel.

In fact, the blurring between reality and fiction is central to the fictional universe, the collective adaptations of which now cover a period of thirty-five years. Both novels present themselves as historical testimonies, miraculously recovered, showcasing one of the means of empowerment for women through voice and speech act, and share the same academic epilogue (*Symposium on Gileadean Studies*), suggesting that the world can change for the better.[5] The women narrators all take the risk to bear witness to the events and address their future audience expressly, such as Aunt Lydia, one of the narrators of *The Testaments*: 'If you are reading, this manuscript at least will have survived. [...] I'm aware of the risk I'm running: writing can be dangerous' (Atwood 2019: 5). Atwood began writing the first novel in Berlin in 1984, the year Orwell's dystopia was supposed to have become fact, observing at first-hand the effects of oppression, resistance, and constant surveillance. One of the main rules she imposed on herself was that every fact, from genocide to ritual rape, had to be attested and have a historical precedent, as is the case with the famous 'Handmaid' costume inspired by an advertisement (Old Dutch Cleanser) from the 1940s, which she was afraid of as a child. Atwood has repeatedly stressed this cardinal rule, making sure that every detail is real in the factual world, as in her *New York Times* essay in 2017: 'If I was to create an imaginary garden, I wanted the toads in it to be real.[6] One of my rules was that I would not put any event into the book that had not already happened in what James Joyce called the "nightmare" of history, nor any technology not already available. No imaginary gizmos, no imaginary laws, no imaginary atrocities' (Atwood 2017b).

The impression that the events described could happen in reality is even further accentuated in the TV adaptation, which increases its rallying power and audience. The action in the series is clearly shifted from the 1980s to the current context: we see the characters using mobile phones and the writers add contemporary references; for instance, Aunt Lydia references Tinder in a speech at the Red Centre.[7] The adaptation thus transforms the dystopia into a diagnosis of the present time, when reproductive rights are under threat throughout the world. Moreover, the heroine, Offred/June, is much more active in the TV series than in the novel:

she is a heroic figure who provokes social and political change, an empowered activist and militant, not an oppressed and passive victim. Her will to resist is expressed in particular in a number of catchphrases, which have now been displayed in a multitude of derivative products (T-shirts, pins, tattoos, etc.): 'They should've never given us uniforms if they didn't want us to be an army', 'I intend to survive', 'You are not alone', and the slogan in mock Latin '*Nolite Te Bastardes Carborundorum/* Don't let the bastards grind you down'.[8] In the series, Offred/June, who perfectly understands the spirit of these words, writes the sentence in large print on a wall in her room in the final episode of the second season. It is these phrases and slogans above all, expressing the wish to fight against patriarchy and male oppression through sororal solidarity, that have become the banners of identification through the series and perhaps the books.

Atwood's textual fiction, however, is much more ambiguous. Its heroine in particular is quite problematic from a feminist point of view: politically passive, even complacent and complicit in regime change. The novel shows to what terrifying extent one actually adapts to the most oppressive situations, stressing the resignation of an ordinary woman to an unspeakable fate in a world where there is little or no female solidarity — a central weakness identified by the Commander and one of the major reasons that allowed the imposition of Gilead's theocracy:

> Women can't add, he said once, jokingly. When I asked him what he meant, he said. For them, one and one and one and one don't make four.
> What do they make? I said, expecting five or three.
> Just one and one and one and one, he said. (Atwood [1985] 1996: 191)
>
> What the Commander said is true. One and one and one and one doesn't equal four. Each one remains unique, there is no way of joining them together. (197–98)[9]

In order to stay alive, both the female narrator and her scarlet 'sisters' take on the regime's ideology and internalise its imperatives, including the prevalent gender norms, in a paralysing acceptance of their fate; in particular, their reduction to mere reproductive functions, in a society where each individual is assigned a place exhibited by the obligatory dress colour. Offred's discourse remains decidedly contaminated by Gilead, the new regime, in a fictional world where the few women who are still fertile are forced to conceive children for the Puritan government that has taken control of part of the US. In particular, the reduction of identity to reproductive functions is expressed by the metonymy of the uterus as an empty organ, a passive receptacle. This is further reinforced by the recurrence of the sacralised motif of the chalice, which also reflects the docility that Offred wishes to make her own. The image she draws of herself ends up being almost completely conditioned: she no longer sees herself as anything more than an 'ambulatory chalice', a 'two-legged womb' (Atwood [1985] 1996: 142),[10] i.e., a person reduced to her uterus, enslaved to what Monique Wittig calls 'the category of sex', defined as 'the product of heterosexual society that turns half of the population into sexual beings, for sex is a category which women cannot be outside of' (Wittig [1980] 2001: 48).[11]

These textual ambiguities, which call into question the effective power of fiction in producing social change, have also attracted criticism, as in Esther Wang's chastising review of *The Testaments*, on the feminist website *Jezebel*. Wang stresses that the sequel's narrative (where Gilead is successfully overthrown because Aunt Lydia, amongst others, is secretly plotting its fall), however satisfying on a fictional level, appears quite simplistic when applied to the real world. She therefore forcefully reminds us that Atwood's Gilean novels are essentially an exercise in wishful thinking:

> Far from a prophetic warning of a possible, plausible future, I find myself more inclined to consider Atwood's novels of Gilead as the ultimate in wish-fulfilment — that totalitarian regimes can crumble so easily; that collaborators are secretly part of the resistance, chafing under the yoke. It is the pleasure of that idea that in part animates all those women who dress as handmaids in protest today, that drives much of the enjoyment of people who continue to tune in season after season of the television show (we don't watch something, after all, because it's a handbook for protest).
>
> At the inaugural Women's March protests in 2017, some carried signs that read 'Make Margaret Atwood fiction again'. We'd forgotten that Atwood's novels were always fiction. (Wang 2019)

Wang offers a (sobering?) reminder of fiction's limited powers in its scope, stating yet again the problem of translating fiction into actions and political programmes. Atwood's exemplary fiction calls into question the possibility of the return into action, what Ricœur names the time of action and suffering (*le temps de l'agir et du pâtir*) of *mimèsis 3*, the moment of intersection between the configured fictional world and the actual world in which action takes place, when the reader receives a fiction and thus changes his or her action (Ricœur 1983: 136).[12]

## 2. The Intersection of the Powers of Fiction and Feminist Resistance

Atwood's dystopian world offers a paradigmatic case study to consider the theories and questions raised by fiction, viewed as a means of feminist resistance, in general. What primarily prevails in the feminist discourses and analyses is the idea that divided receptions and partisan responses actually demonstrate the need to take fiction seriously, as it expresses reality and makes one see and feel the asymmetry of power relations. The fictional representations of sexuality and gender identities allow us to grasp the logics that organise the 'ideological territory' (Hall 1973) within which a stereotyped or counter-stereotyped discourse is developed; they offer a cognitive benefit, enabling us to decipher, in a critical perspective, the repressive gender norms and fictional codes that are expressed, and therefore, to respond to them with revisionist strategies. On the whole, feminist theories and discourses express an unfailing confidence, even faith, in the powers of fiction as a means of imposing gender norms (called 'gender fictions', *fictions de genre*) as well as a means of resistance, reconquest, and survival, a means to fight patriarchal society and its conception of naturalised gender bipartition. The postulate is twofold: first, that fiction contributes decisively to the fabrication and imposition of naturalised gender norms; and second, that these norms transfer from fiction into reality, constructing the very paradigm of reality and ultimately leading to concrete violence.

In the case of the *Handmaid's Tale*, the fiction is seen as providing an understanding of the regimes that seek to regulate, transform, and discipline bodies into 'docile' entities (Foucault 1976: 175–211; see also Devaux 1994). At the same time, fiction also becomes the very means of responding to these oppressive mechanisms by showing alternative representations, for instance, by enabling us to imagine other modes of procreation or models of parenthood. Against the naturalisation of femininity, based on a metonymic seizure of the uterus as the core of gender identity, fictions envision other configurations, defending the reappropriation of reproductive rights or deindexing the organ from the idea of a biological nature that regulates the categories of femininity and masculinity. This dissent invites us to imagine other readings of real and possible bodies, multiplied *ad infinitum* by the possibilities of fiction, as is the case in Emmanuelle Bayamack-Tam's *Arcadie* (2018), where the fact that the first-person narrator has no uterus appears to be the starting point for her metamorphosis (see Bujor 2022). Such fictions can be seen as exemplary of a fourth wave of feminism, which Aurore Koechlin defines as the synthesis between the materialist heritage and queer reinterpretations of identity (Koechlin 2019),[13] following a second wave linked to the conquest of reproductive rights, and a third focused on the redefinition of the subject of feminism, in particular the deconstruction of gender and sexual binaries. Such fictions thus state a gendered and sexual existence outside of the imposition of normative heterosexuality, clearly following a political agenda, as, for instance, in Paul Preciado's claim: 'we have the right to be boys without penises, girls without wombs, and even to be neither girls nor boys' (*nous avons le droit d'être des garçons sans pénis, des filles sans utérus, et même d'être ni fille ni garçon*) (Preciado 2019: 85).

What is at stake is always the belief in the power of fiction to deal with social issues relating to gender; its heuristic power (Allard 2007: 20),[14] whether be it to deconstruct the mechanisms of naturalisation through fiction or to fashion alternative visions to the common gender norms in order to trouble the binaries and hierarchies that derive from them. It is again the *Handmaid's Tale* that appears on the cover of Sandra Laugier's latest essay. Her argument is that fiction, and TV series in particular, take a decisive part in our ethical formation. It is therefore imperative to examine how we *experience* a fictional world, how profoundly we are affected by its representation of reality. Laugier states that the ordinary subject is empowered by this fictional experience and its 'capacity to understand, experience and appropriate the world, and to educate oneself' (Laugier 2019: 13).[15] Long-term attachment to serial characters who evolve in shared fictions that are accessible to all, that offer a wide range of ways for viewers to become invested, leads to what Laugier calls an 'augmented personal experience' (*expérience personnelle augmentée*) (2019: 356–67) and the possibility of transforming our personal lives and reality. Through fiction, we 'change not only our visions of the world, but also the world itself' (2019: 16).[16] In place of gender stereotypes, fiction substitutes a number of singular individuals, often heroines, struggling with the trials of ordinary life, building up a repertoire of situations, experiences, and forms of life through which alternative proposals are envisioned.

Feminist research therefore pays particular attention not only to models and representations of gender within fictional worlds, but also to the role of lived experience within or in relation to fiction: to 'experiential' parameters, including the possibility of collectivising one's personal experience in interpersonal discourse or shared action and the creative use of fiction. On the one hand, readers are faced with the power of 'gender fictions' (*fictions de genre*): the strength of social gender representations based on the major fundamental taxonomies that maintain the axiological systems with which they are linked, e.g., the fact that patriarchal society assigns each individual a sexual, social and political life programme based on his or her biological sex, on 'normative sexual categories' (*catégories sexuelles normatives*) and the 'heterosexual dogma' (*dogme hétérosexuel*) (Wittig [1980] 2001). On the other, fictions have the power to offer alternative social models and deconstruct the sexual traits traditionally attributed to women and men. Fiction is therefore understood as the site in which social relations, sexual identities, and modes of reproduction are reorganised, leading also to differentiated appropriations and readings, which is precisely ïan Larue's argument in her recent book *Libère-toi cyborg! (Free yourself, Cyborg!)*. For Larue, science-fiction in particular is, *per se*, endowed with feminist potential through its ability to 'project potential futures and [...] build worlds, a project that is specific to it and which is not that of general literature' (Larue 2018: 18)[17] — even if I heartily disagree with her distinction between general literature (thought to be submissive) and science-fiction (cast as emancipatory).

The question therefore arises whether *any* fiction could, by definition, be open to recuperation in the service of feminist emancipation. Here, feminist theories and critical studies are much more ambivalent. If the feminist potential of fictions that are understood as feminist is commonly accepted, what about a Harlequin novel, or fictions supporting patriarchal gender norms? What is at stake is the problem of *a priori* discrimination between good emancipatory fictions and the others, which would remain subservient to the dominant social gender ideology. In a text published in 1982, Angela McRobbie denounces the missionary, or what she terms 'recruitist' conception of the politics of feminist research, that is, researchers who see 'feminism' (i.e., their own) as a solution to the problems of all women, even if these women are excluded from it because of their class, race, or age (McRobbie 1982: 52). A number of theories and studies in the field of Cultural Studies aim not only to limit themselves to particular fictions with a feminist stamp, but also to focus on fictional practice as a whole. They examine the ways in which diverse audiences use fiction as a site for reproducing or contesting social norms, for expressing their identities, for conveying convictions and demands relating to the cause of women, their agency, and the means at their disposal to counterbalance patriarchal power or to accede to a political role.

Viviane Albenga, who has examined women's reading circles and clubs, thus states that the very practice of shared reading already constitutes a form of resistance and a source of empowerment (in the sense of gaining autonomy and the capacity to act) for women, which can lead to socio-political demands: 'Reading is endowed with a power of salvation, of survival in the face of the hazards of life, and even of emancipation from the social and political relations of domination' (Albenga 2017: 15).[18] Delphine Chedaleux reaches a similar conclusion: she rallied private Facebook groups of female *Fifty Shades of Grey* fans, dissecting their exchanges over several years. Against the hegemonically negative interpretations of E. L. James's trilogy of novels (2011–2012), Chedaleux shows that in these online groups, women readers are free to build their own value system together (Chedaleux 2018: 82–91).[19] Thus, by focusing on the diversity of fictional productions, including those that are postulated to be *a priori* non-emancipatory and non-feminist, these researchers stress the emancipatory virtues of the fictional imagination *per se* and are in line with classical reception studies, in particular Ien Ang's work on female spectators of *Dallas* (1985), published shortly after Janice Radway's study of Harlequin women readers (Radway 1984 and 1997). Ang's argument is that not only can one derive pleasure from a fictional situation without transposing it into one's own life (which seems evident, but is worth remembering: so many studies, even within feminist research, assume that women in particular are unable to read without doing so), but that the *content* of particular fictions ultimately matters less than the very act of consuming fiction and producing fictional experience, which in itself allows a liberating play with reality. Ang's hypothesis is stimulating because it shifts the terms of the debate: the issue is no longer so much to understand why a type of fiction (Harlequin novels, *Fifty Shades of Grey*, 'chick lit') appeals to women, but how the pleasure women derive from it influences the way they perceive themselves and evaluate their position within society (Ang 1985: 131–36). In short, it is a question not only of providing legitimacy to the cultural and fictional investments of these women, but also of grasping the way in which they participate in the construction of their subjectivity, understood in Foucault's sense as a site for exercising power and the capacity to act (Foucault 2001).

This paradigm of active reception and participatory engagement with fictions, without any *a priori* judgement or discrimination, is based in particular on the work of Stuart Hall, who distinguishes three possible positions for an individual 'decoding' a media message: hegemonic, negotiated or oppositional (Hall 1973). Hall provides a language for discussing the creativity and resilience of audiences around the notions of affiliation and participation: it is through situational practices of appropriation that groups or individuals create ways to challenge dominant ideologies and question institutions. Interpretive communities (in Stanley Fish's sense) or fandoms are then understood par excellence as an alternative space for debating political philosophies and envisioning social change. They thus do function 'as an alternative social community' (Jenkins 2013: 280) where questions relating to gender identity or sexual orientation can be raised and addressed, making it perhaps possible to conclude that *any* fiction may be the vector of feminist resistance.

## References

ACHIN, CATHERINE, VIVIANE ALBENGA, ARMELLE ANDRO, PAULINE DELAGE, SAMIRA OUARDI, JULIETTE RENNES, and SYLVIA ZAPPI. 2019. 'Éditorial', *Mouvements*, 99 (3): 7–10

ALBENGA, VIVIANE. 2017. *S'émanciper par la lecture : Genre, classe et usages sociaux des livres* (Rennes: Presses Universitaires de Rennes)

ALLARD, LAURENCE. 2007. 'À propos du *Manifeste cyborg*, d'*Ecce Homo* et de *La Promesse des monstres*, ou comment Haraway n'a jamais été post-humaniste', in Donna Haraway, *Manifeste cyborg et autres essais. Sciences — Fictions — Féminismes*, ed. by Laurence Allard, Delphine Gardey and Nathalie Magnan, 19–28 (Paris: Exils Éditeurs)

ANG, IEN. 1985. *Watching Dallas: Soap Opera and The Melodramatic Imagination* (London: Routledge)

ATWOOD, MARGARET E. (1985) 1996. *The Handmaid's Tale* (London: Vintage)

——. 2017A. 'I'm Margaret Atwood, author of *The Handmaid's Tale*, and executive producer of the Hulu original series based on the novel premiering April 26.' *Reddit*, 8 March 2017 <https://www.reddit.com/r/IAmA/comments/5y91f5/im_margaret_atwood_author_of_the_handmaids_tale/deo3pj1/> [accessed 24 June 2022]

——. 2017B. 'Margaret Atwood on What *The Handmaid's Tale* Means in the Age of Trump.' *The New York Times*, 10 March <https://www.nytimes.com/2017/03/10/books/review/margaret-atwood-handmaids-tale-age-of-trump.html> [accessed 24 June 2022]

——. 2018. 'Yes indeed to those who asked: I'm writing a sequel to The #HandmaidsTale.' Twitter, 20 November <https://twitter.com/MargaretAtwood/status/1067778206642683906> [accessed 24 June 2022]

——. 2019. *The Testaments* (London: Chatto & Windus)

BERNARD, ANDREAS. 2019. *Theory of the Hashtag* (Cambridge: Polity Press)

BIGEY, MAGALI. 2014. '*50 nuances de Grey*: Du phénomène à sa réception', *Hermès*, 69 (2): 88–90

BIGEY, MAGALI and SÉVERINE OLIVIER. 2010. 'Ils aiment le roman sentimental et alors? Lecteurs d'un "mauvais genre", des lecteurs en danger?', *Belphégor*, 9 (1). <https://dalspace.library.dal.ca/bitstream/handle/10222/47779/09_01_Magali_aiment_fr_cont.pdf?sequence=1&isAllowed=y> [accessed 19 July 2022]

BREDA, HÉLÈNE. 2019. 'Science-fiction féministe, des œuvres aux fans. Engagements expressifs et militants autour des romans d'Ursula K. Le Guin, Marion Zimmer Bradley, et Margaret Atwood', *Res Futurae*, 13 (June) <http://journals.openedition.org/resf/2271> [accessed 24 June 2022]

BUJOR, FLAVIA. 2022. 'L'utérus dans le récit contemporain: entre "expropriation" et "dénaturalisation" (1985–2018)', in *L'Utérus: De l'organe aux discours*, ed. by Morgan Guyvarc'h, and Véronique Mehl, 215–25 (Rennes: Presses Universitaires de Rennes)

CHEDALEUX, DELPHINE. 2018. 'Construire un regard sur la réception de "Cinquante Nuances de Grey": Les émotions de classe d'une ethnographie en ligne', *POLI — Politique de l'image*, 14: 82–91

DEVAUX, MONIQUE. 1994. 'Feminism and Empowerment: A Critical Reading of Foucault', *Feminist Studies*, 20 (2): 223–47

DOCKTERMAN, ELIANA. 2017. 'Margaret Atwood and Elisabeth Moss on the Urgency of "The Handmaid's Tale"', *Time Magazine*, 12 April <https://time.com/4734904/margaret-atwood-elisabeth-moss-handmaids-tale/> [accessed 24 June 2022]

FEDERICI, SILVIA. 2004. *Caliban and the Witch: Women, the Body and Primitive Accumulation* (New York: Autonomedia)

FOUCAULT, MICHEL. 1976. 'Droit de mort et pouvoir de vie', in *Histoire de la sexualité*, 1, 175–211 (Paris : Gallimard)

——. 2001. *Dits et écrits (1954–1988)* (Paris: Gallimard)

HALL, STUART. 1973. 'Encoding and Decoding in the Media Discourse', *Stencilled Paper*, 7: 90–103

Handmaid Coalition. 2017. <https://handmaidcoalition.org/> [accessed 19 October 2019]

*The Handmaid's Tale*. 2017. Created by Bruce Miller, directed by Reed Morano, Hulu series <https://www.hulu.com/series/the-handmaids-tale-565d8976-9d26-4e63-866c-40f8a137ce5f> [accessed 24 June 2022]

HOFFMAN, FREDERICK J. 1953. 'Marianne Moore: Imaginary Gardens and Real Toads', *Poetry* 83 (3): 152–57

HOGSETTE, DAVID S. 1997. 'Margaret Atwood's Rhetorical Epilogue in The Handmaid's Tale: The Reader's Role in Empowering Offred's Speech Act', *Critique: Studies in Contemporary Fiction* 38 (4): 262–78

HOUEL, ANNICK. 1997. *Le roman d'amour et sa lectrice, une si longue passion : L'exemple Harlequin* (Paris: L'Harmattan)

JENKINS, HENRY. 2013. *Textual Poachers: Television Fans and Participatory Culture* (New York: Routledge)

KELLER, EVELYN FOX. 1992. 'How Gender Matters, Or, Why It's So Hard for us to Count Past Two', in *Inventing Women: Science, Technology and Gender*, ed. by Gill Kirkup and Laurie Smith Keller, 42–56 (Cambridge: Polity Press)

KERGOAT, DANIÈLE. 2012. *Se battre, disent-elles....* (Paris: La Dispute)

KLIGLER-VILENCHIK, NETA. 2016. '"Decreasing World Suck": Harnessing Popular Culture for Fan Activism', in *By Any Media Necessary: The New Youth Activism*, ed. by Henry Jenkins et al., 102–48 (New York: New York University Press)

KOECHLIN, AURORE. 2019. *La Révolution féministe* (Paris: Éd. Amsterdam)

LARUE, ANNE. 2010. *Fiction, féminisme et postmodernité : Les voies subversives du roman contemporain à grand succès* (Paris: Classiques Garnier)

LARUE, IAN. 2018. *Libère-toi cyborg! Le pouvoir transformateur de la science-fiction féministe* (Paris: Cambourakis)

LAUGIER, SANDRA. 2019. *Nos vies en séries : Philosophie et morale d'une culture populaire* (Paris: Climats)

LIPTAK, ANDREW. 2017. 'Sales of Margaret Atwood's *Handmaid's Tale* Have Soared Since Trump's Win', *The Verge*, 11 February <https://www.theverge.com/2017/2/11/14586382/sales-margaret-atwoods-handmaids-tale-soared-donald-trump/> [accessed 22 June 2022]

LOWRY, RICH. 2017. 'No, "The Handmaid's Tale" Has Nothing to Do with Trump's America', *New York Post*, 18 September <https://nypost.com/2017/09/18/no-the-handmaids-tale-has-nothing-to-do-with-trumps-america/>

MCROBBIE, ANGELA. 1982. 'The Politics of Feminist Research: Between Talk, Text and Action', *Feminist Review*, 12: 46–57

MORBY, ALICE. 2017. 'My costumes are part of a "quiet uprising" among women, says Handmaid's Tale designer', *Dezeen*. 11 August <https://www.dezeen.com/2017/08/11/my-costumes-are-part-of-a-quiet-uprising-among-women-says-handmaids-tale-designer/> [accessed 22 June 2022]

PRECIADO, PAUL B. 2019. *Un appartement sur Uranus* (Paris: Grasset)

RADWAY, JANICE. 1984. *Reading the Romance: Women, Patriarchy and Popular Literature* (Chapel Hill: University of North Carolina Press)

———. 1997. *A Feeling for Books: Book-of-the-Month Club, Literary Taste and Middle-Class Desire* (Chapel Hill: University of North Carolina Press)

RICŒUR, PAUL. 1983. *Temps et récit I* (Paris: Seuil)

ULTRAVIOLET. 2017. 'The Handmaid's Resistance Toolkit' <https://weareultraviolet.org/about-us/> [accessed 19 October 2019]

WAGNER, ERICA. 2019. '"Writing is Always an Act of Hope": Margaret Atwood on *The*

*Testaments*. The Novelist explains how Trump's America shaped her bestselling sequel', *New Statesman*, 18 September <https://www.newstatesman.com/margaret-atwood-interview-the-testaments-handmaids-tale-sequel> [accessed 22 June 2022]

WANG, ESTHER. 2019. 'The Fictions of Margaret Atwood', *Jezebel*, 19 October <https://jezebel.com/the-fictions-of-margaret-atwood-1837878415> [accessed 22 June 2022]

WITTIG, MONIQUE. (1980) 2001. *La Pensée straight* (Paris: Balland)

WOMEN'S MARCH. N.D. 'Mission' <www.womensmarch.com/mission> [accessed 19 March 2018]

## Notes to Chapter 10

1. The Women's March was prompted in particular by the blatant misogyny of such Trump phrases as 'grab them by the pussy' and his systematic attacks on Hillary Clinton.
2. Atwood's novel is not the only case to have become a (belated) bestseller after Trump's election or Brexit; see also Orwell's *1984* (1949), Sinclair Lewis's *It Can't Happen Here* (1935), the *Narrative of the Life of Frederick Douglass, An American Slave* (1845), Jonathan Coe's *Middle England* (2018), and Ali Smith's *Autumn* (2016). A broader claim about the re-actualisation of the discourse around fiction and its scope in the current political context can be made here.
3. Still, one should not underestimate the pitfalls of the sign, especially its homogenising effect, changing how audiences bundle discourse and organize public discussion and debate. Clearly the hashtag, in activism, is used to meet specific needs and ends. See Bernard (2019).
4. 'Un geste politique fondamentalement révolutionnaire en prenant la parole publiquement et en rompant l'isolement auquel elles étaient assignées jusqu'alors pour participer à un soulèvement collectif et international.'
5. 'Offred fashions an alternative reality and forces it into the world, into history and thus makes possible social and political change' (Hogsette 1997: 270).
6. It is worth mentioning that Atwood here references Marianne Moore's 'Poetry'. See Hoffman 1953. My thanks to Alison James for pointing this out.
7. 'They made such a mess of everything. They filled the air with chemicals, and radiation, and poison. So God whipped up a special plague. The plague of infertility. [...] As birthrates fell, they made things worse: birth control pills, morning-after pills, murdering babies just so they could have their orgies; their Tinder' (*The Handmaid's Tale* 2017, season 1, episode 1, 'Offred').
8. Atwood comments: 'I'll tell you the weird thing about it: it was a joke in our Latin classes. So this thing from my childhood is permanently on people's bodies' (Dockterman 2017).
9. See also Keller (1992).
10. 'We are two-legged wombs, that's all: sacred vessels, ambulatory chalices.'
11. 'Le produit de la société hétérosexuelle qui fait de la moitié de la population des êtres sexuels en ce que le sexe est une catégorie de laquelle les femmes ne peuvent sortir.' Silvia Federici also links the politics of the uterus to the State's strategy to deprive women of the control over their own reproduction (Federici 2004).
12. 'la tâche de l'herméneutique est de reconstruire l'ensemble des opérations par lesquelles une œuvre s'enlève sur le fond opaque du vivre, de l'agir et du souffrir, pour être donnée par un auteur à un lecteur qui la reçoit et ainsi change son agir' (Ricœur 1983: 106-07).
13. The fourth wave, which comes from Latin America, also integrates the contribution of intersectional theories, which take into account the consubstantiality (Kergoat 2012) of power relations determining political subjects.
14. 'Puissance heuristique de la fiction.'
15. 'Capacité à comprendre, à expérimenter et à s'approprier le monde, et à s'éduquer.'
16. 'Changer non seulement nos visions du monde, mais le monde lui-même.'
17. 'Projeter des futurs potentiels et [...] construire des mondes, projet qui lui est spécifique et qui n'est pas celui de la littérature générale.' See Larue (2010).
18. 'La lecture est dotée d'un pouvoir de salut, de survie face aux aléas de la vie, voire d'émancipation à l'égard des rapports sociaux et politiques de domination.' See also Breda (2019).

19. See also Bigey (2014, 88–90), Bigey and Olivier (2010), and Houel (1997).

CHAPTER 11

# Engagement and Enchantment: Political and Ethical Uses of Fantasy Fictions

*Anne Besson*

*Université d'Artois*

The starting point of this paper is the important media presence, during the last years of the 2010s, of initiatives combining forms of political action — demonstrations, elections of representatives, struggles for human rights all around the world — and media franchises such as *Hunger Games*, *Harry Potter* or *Game of Thrones*. These phenomena are part of a widely shared generational, and sometimes transgenerational, culture (hence their efficiency and attractiveness) but also belong specifically to the fantasy genre. They involve the appropriation of certain gestures from fantasy fiction: the Rebellion's recognition gesture in *The Hunger Games* — three fingers raised to greet the Mockingjay, taken up by Thai protesters against the military coup of June 2014; 'Dumbledore's Army', a student union elected in 2015 and again in 2018 by the highly politicised French University of Rennes 2; placards showing typography and mottos taken from *The Game of Thrones* series ('Winter is not coming') brandished during the Global Climate Strikes in 2018 and 2019; scarlet 'Handmaids' marching in silence to defend the right to abortion, in the United States or in Poland.[1] This paper aims to provide theoretical insights about such uses of fantasy fictions, which seem paradoxical — how is it that dreaming about elsewhere and tomorrow manifests itself as ways of talking and acting here and now? Why is it that fantasy fictions are so well suited for these purposes, and how do their audiences relate to them?

## 1. Tomorrow, Elsewhere *vs* Here and Now

A prevalent preconception still associates fantasy literature (along with other cultural practices such as role-playing games, online universes, derivative works...) with escape routes far away from the harsh realities of existence, mixing illusions and delusions. Yet many examples from the past have already shown the opposite: a strong association of this cultural domain with ethical and political concerns.

Indeed, as any works of 'popular' or 'mass' culture, they embody the dominant ideological values of their time and space, but their specificities — the way they can project alternative worlds and ways — also make them forces of proposal, or supposition ('What if...?'). Within these fantasy texts, it is possible to 'imagine better',[2] to find models in order to subvert consensual standards.

The generations born since the turn of the century expect that fantasy franchises, as their shared cultural references, to give the best representations of gender, physical, social, and racial diversity, as much or even more than 'realistic' fictions, that they imagine what should be, what could be: hopes to look forward to, nightmares to avoid. Among those young people long thought to show little interest in political messages, some groups called 'fan-activists' thus find inspiration for their civic commitment in *Harry Potter*, *Avatar*, *Star Wars*, or *Hunger Games*. How can that be? We have to take a closer look at the past to answer this question.

Of course, different theories have long been and are still intensely discussed among scholars concerning the effectiveness, or the potential danger, of fictions — the ways they could really affect their consumers or not. It can be in positive ways, that range from cognitive gains to the development of empathy, from 'consolation' to 'reparation' (Gefen 2017), but also in negative ones, when fiction is seen as a force of contamination and is accused of promoting violence, lust, and stupidity. Since Plato, as we know, fictions have suffered this allegation, from epics and poetry, romances, to cinema and television, and finally, to modern-day video games and the Internet. On the same basis, fantasy fiction has long been suspected of encouraging a form of withdrawal from real life, often diagnosed as an addiction, from connected screens to 'binge-watching' TV series for young people today.

Without further inquiry, the path to save fiction, the only possible one for those who love stories, is quite clear: if we want to keep only the positive effects and not the negative ones, if we want to be able to say 'fictions are useful but they aren't dangerous', we have to postulate their indirect action. Jean-Marie Schaeffer shows in *Why Fiction?* (2010) that consumers' reactions to fictions are never direct imitations (if I kill zombies in my favourite videogames, what about doing the same in my college?). Rather, they operate through a particular kind of 'modelling', or 'global analogy' (Schaeffer 2010: 189) that causes 'partial disidentification', 'distancing', 'distance from ourselves to ourselves' (298), allowing us to question prejudices and preconceptions — and so doing, liberating the subversive potential of fiction which can change the way we spontaneously consider social norms.

Our fantasy genres can be understood as superfictions, not only because they more explicitly rely on world-building, or because they ask so clearly for our immersion, but also when it comes to evaluating their effects. The influential theorizations of science fiction pioneered in the 1970s by Fredric Jameson and Darko Suvin, both engaged in leftist politics,[3] show strong connections with Schaeffer's conception of fiction — even if their reference was more likely the work of Brecht on political theatre. For Suvin, the key words for defining science fiction are 'cognitive estrangement', putting reality at a distance by the way of a *novum*, so that the reader has to reconstruct a cognitive framework that makes sense of the storyworld (Suvin 1977 and 1979).[4] Far from taking us away from 'real life', the genre takes us back to it, its main purpose being, in Jameson's words this time, to 'defamiliarize and restructure our experience of our own *present*, and to do so in specific ways distinct from all other forms of defamiliarization' (Jameson 1982: 151).

If we go still further back in this history of criticism, Tolkien expressed a very similar line of thought in his 1939 conference, 'On Fairy-Stories', published in 1947: fantasy is described as a positive way of escaping the prison of so-called 'Real Life' ('How real, how startlingly alive is a factory chimney compared with an elm-tree: poor obsolete thing, insubstantial dream of an escapist!') (Tolkien [1964] 1988: 57) and regaining a clear view on what really matters:

> Why should a man be scorned if, finding himself in prison, he tries to get out and go home? Or if, when he cannot do so, he thinks and talks about other topics than jailers and prison-walls? The world outside has not become less real because the prisoner cannot see it. (Tolkien [1964] 1988: 56)

Tolkien gives a good example of ideological misuses (liberal empowerment coming from reactionary ideas, or the other way around) quite common today in the expanding field of ecology. It is striking today how his views, those of an Oxonian don, on escape and reaction, and his angry refusal of an ideology of progress he sees as a destructive force, foretell very contemporary discourses — radical ecology,[5] guilty conscience about Nature,[6] antispeciesism.[7] It is no coincidence, in this respect, if fantasy, in all its diversity, has established itself so strongly as the most important literary and media genre in the beginning of our twenty-first century.

Tolkien praises Faerie as a means of 'Recovery [...]: regaining of a clear view';[8] numerous works of youth fiction tell the story of a deep immersion from which the hero-reader comes back transformed and ready to transform the world around her (a good example of this scenario is given by Michael Ende's *The Neverending Story*, 1979). A well-known French author of youth fantasy, Pierre Bottero, popularised the metaphor of imagination as a 'step aside' ('pas de côté'), a swift move allowing a change of perspective on what life is supposed to look like (Bottero 2003).

By contrast, being too close to reality, too familiar, is not efficient for fantasy and science fiction, which need to preserve the adaptability and desirability of the message they convey: they take us 'back to the present' but through other spaces or times; they can relate to the dystopian genre, but not to the pamphlet. This is a lesson that was learnt in France with the failure of radical left science fiction towards the end of the '70s — the collection titled 'Here and Now', as an answer to the more famous 'Tomorrow, elsewhere', only lasted three years.[9] The right answer to political concerns was found in a middle way, a correct balance 'between narrow activism and blind escapism' (Huz 2018: 44),[10] which is well illustrated in *Gandahar* (novel by Jean-Pierre Andrevon, movie by René Laloux), a pro-ecology and anti-military *fable* full of colour and inventions.

Dystopias, which saw great public success in the 2000–2010s, followed by *cli-fi*, first in the US and soon afterwards in Europe, appear as such a genre: both entertaining and explicitly political, as well as aimed at the new marketing targets of teenagers and young adults, they invite the reader to dream of the collapse of repressive social systems. In future or parallel universes, which are more violent, more spectacular, and clearer in their boundaries and choices, it is possible to raise the alarm and to envision social threats already noticeable today — all forms of tyranny, even the most insidious; inequalities above all, as among the different Districts of Panem in *The Hunger Games* (Collins 2008–2010); racism in Mallory Blackman's *Noughts and Crosses* (2001–2008); eugenics in the *Divergent* series (Roth 2011–2013); or physical standardisation in Scott Westerfeld's *Uglies* (2005–2007). Respect for every individual's freedoms appears as a central value, along with a compassionate solidarity, an ethics of care, and the importance of taking minorities' rights into account, including nonhuman beings and the commons. Such ecofeminist and antispecist trends can be spotted, for instance, in the French novel *Sirius* by Stéphane Servant (2017).

Those messages are then taken up by readers. We will now provide some historical context and theoretical insight into their activities of appropriation and transformation, that bring imagination back to reality.

## 2. In Fantasy Kingdoms, Readers Rule.

To begin with an example, the most emblematic organisation when it comes to the emergence of fan-activism has long been the Harry Potter Alliance (HPA), already documented by fan studies works, by Henry Jenkins and his team in the US (Jenkins 2012 and 2014), or in France by Mélanie Bourdaa (2016). This powerful charity was founded in 2005 by fans of J. K. Rowling's work, with the ambition to channel the positive values shared by readers into collective actions for social change. For instance, they promoted a campaign to coincide with the *Hunger Games*'s franchise movies' release: it included a partnership with Oxfam to fight hunger in Africa, under the slogan 'HungerIsNotAGame' (2012), then a series of actions against social inequalities in 2013 and 2014, using 'Odds in our Favor' (at the time of the 'Fight for 15' strike by fast-food workers), the website 'We are the districts' and the hashtag #MyHungerGames for people to share their own experiences with poverty and exploitation in the US. Those quite fascinating actions have been studied from a sociological perspective as an example of new youth activism and as a success in terms of public communication (Jenkins 2016). For fiction and fictionality studies, however, their interest lies in two main aspects which we will successively explore: the reign of fantasy and the power of readers.

We first notice that *fantasy genres* are now at the centre of political debates, used as ideological arenas. Politically engaged works of fiction in our Western democracies can easily be debunked as propaganda. As they recall the instrumentalisation of narratives and medias by totalitarian or dictatorial regimes very often denounced in our dystopias; paradoxically, political readings and writings are deemed incompatible with democratic DNA. It has long been so, since the Cold War of the 1970s resulted in an ideological struggle often evaluated today in terms of 'excess.' If 'message fiction' remains suspect, attitudes appear to be changing recently: political agendas are back in the cultural world, and this leads to retrospective re-evaluations of 'engaged' stories. In our time, faced with many challenges and pitfalls, the rise of new social, economic, and ecological threats makes any universal value appear as a dangerous illusion; the shattering of socio-democratic consensus gives way to numerous anti-system or anti-capitalistic political positions, and once again, we witness fierce oppositions being played out around one of the hotspots of the debate, the one on which fiction has much to say: cultural liberalism. If we take a quick look at the causes advocated by the Harry Potter Alliance, 'literacy' was their first engagement, directly supported by J. K. Rowling ('Education and Libraries', 'Media Reform'), but they also promote, at the first ranks on their list, 'LGBTQIA+ Equality', 'Gender Equity', 'Youth Advocacy', and 'Racial Justice' (Harry Potter Alliance, n.d.) — probably because Rowling herself did not address those questions quite the way her readers would have wished.[11]

Fantasy genres and minorities' rights in fact shared a long history: because they were rejected from the heterocentric norm, gay and lesbian movements found shelter in the cultural margins, and they found a place of expression in SF and fantasy communities. For instance, the Free Amazons of Darkover, a science fantasy universe by Marion Zimmer Bradley, were among the favourites for feminist and/or lesbian readers in the pages of the fanzine *Moon Phases*, edited from 1981, and the fan club Gaylaxian Science Fiction Society was established in 1986 with the motto 'Out of the closet, and into the Universe'. Nowadays, huge public debates are taking place among online fandoms about equal and fair representations of diversity, beginning in 2009 (year of the 'RaceFail') and intensifying since 2014 (a year ironically labelled as the 'toxic turn') (Proctor and Kies 2018: 127). Those new cultural wars tend to be oversimplified as an opposition between 'good fan-activists' (also called Social Justice Warriors by those who do not approve, and think they are too eager to step up and fight for equity) and 'bad' fans, 'toxic fandom'.

Well-meaning producers decided to promote diversity, to multiply characters from non-white and non-Christian ethnic backgrounds, or to feminise scenarios because there was an economic interest to follow long-term evolutions of audiences towards ethical concerns. However, they faced brutal backlash from fans of Marvel comics, the *Star Wars* universe, or the *Ghostbusters* movies, mainly (but not only) voiced by white males crying out in protest, trying to hold onto the good old times of patriarchy and good conscience, and sometimes by Russian hackers taking advantage of their attacks on symbols of American cultural hegemony. In those complex online campaigns, the 'usual trolls' were not alone to resist change in the name of 'totemic nostalgia' (Proctor 2017: 1105–42). One of the most clear-cut examples in such muddy waters can be found with the 'Puppygate', a block-voting controversy concerning the Hugo Awards for science fiction works in 2015 and 2016: groups that called themselves 'Sad Puppies', then 'Rabid Puppies', who were close to Alt-Right politics, tried to overrun the votes for so-called 'message fiction' and stop progressive authors from winning awards.

Ideological uses of fantasy fictions have obviously expanded during these last years, whether in their interpretations by audiences, their transformations by producers, or their exploitation by activists. It is logical for conflicts that arise to escalate: though it has become commonplace to say that Tolkien's Ring and the atomic bomb should not be equated, the analogy between the Death Eaters and the Nazis feels inescapable. The plot of *Game of Thrones* is constantly read in terms of the 'political lessons' to be drawn from it — as per the title of a collection of essays edited by Pablo Iglesias, leader of the Spanish left-wing party Podemos (Iglesias 2014), who may now regret his identification with Daenerys Targaryen's positions. William Blanc, in his recent book, recalls how the interpretation of the White Walkers as a metaphor for climate change, requiring the union of all forces, has only recently emerged: George Martin did not think he had said that, and then the hermeneutic consensus somehow convinced him in retrospect (Blanc 2019: 71–75).

This social impact acquired by fantasy fictions does not originate from the works' messages, which can be forced in one direction or another, nor from the authors' will, which cannot do much about it; those who have taken charge are the communities of readers, of consumers/decoders, who are gaining weight in the balance of power. The momentum is strong and fast building, as we can see when turning once more to the example of *Harry Potter*. The evolution of the relationship between its author and readers over the last twenty years is very telling, since its durable success has notably rested on the choice soon taken on by the author to empower the readers. However, authority gradually slipped through the fingers of Rowling, and is contested today by fans who were at first happy and grateful that she had granted them some right of expression, small as it was, but now claim full ownership over the fiction they love and keep alive (Besson 2020).

Such an evolution can be understood as a long-term consequence of critical turns, with the parallel rise of theories of reception and cultural studies: the latter have contributed to highlighting and celebrating 'the role of the reader' in textual communication and the possibilities of resistant, subversive, 'oppositional' readings. We 'produce texts by reading them' (Eco 1984: 3), so they do not exist without being read; and we can challenge the coded meanings of texts, so they are ours, open to appropriation (Hall 1980). The perception of popular cultures as aesthetically illegitimate makes them even more available for ethical readings, and more limited to present-day relevance. They have always been ideological highways for the dominant thoughts of each time, but the contribution of Stuart Hall and the first cultural studies helped to counterbalance the powerful theories of cultural hegemony and alienated masses so as to give a more complete view of the different popular readings.

This empowerment of audiences, or at least this shifting balance between producers and consumers, combines with today's widely shared belief (discussed in the first part of this paper) in an effective use of fictions, and particularly fantasy fictions, which can make us 'imagine better'.[12] This eventually results in their use as tools of action in the real world, as in our first examples or in another media campaign showing young Israelis and Palestinians dressed as Na'vi characters from the movie *Avatar* (James Cameron, 2009) who marched through the occupied village of Bil'n, painted in blue, to protest against colonisation in February 2010.

The *Hunger Games* campaign mentioned earlier makes it easy to understand what the goal is and how it can be achieved — to make the cultural consumer a social player, to turn passive passion into action by becoming part of the story, 'turning fans into heroes' (Harry Potter Alliance, n.d.). One key principle in fandom invites each and every person to 'take back the narrative': make it yours, write your own story. The issues of a given text are taken one step closer — they are self-appropriated, shared universes that become individual expressions without severing their links with the solidarity and community values. We can read such a process in the choice of pronouns and possessive adjectives of the HPA campaign ('*My*HungerGames', 'Odds in *Our* Favor', '*We are the districts*'), or by looking at the 'Our values' list on the HPA website:

> We believe in joyful activism.
> We celebrate the power of community.
> We believe that heroes aren't born; they develop with practice and support.
> We believe in magic.
> We believe that the weapon we have is love.
> [...]
> We believe that unironic enthusiasm is a renewable resource.
> We know fantasy is not only an escape from our world but an invitation to go deeper into it. ('What We Do' 2019)

The same core idea appears each time: the belief ('We Believe', 'We celebrate', 'We know') that a symbolic power ('magic', 'love', 'unironic enthusiasm') can have a real impact: 'A creative and collaborative culture that solves the world's problems'. In other words, this is fundamentally utopian thinking that proves to be an important, dialectical result of the dystopian imaginary young readers grew up with.

To offer a broader conclusion on the renewal of fantasy fiction's political uses: the persistent instrumentalisation of the field of popular culture, doomed to ancillary positions, may certainly be regretted, but it is also to be welcomed insofar as it secures this culture's central position in contemporary debates, as the spearhead of a return to ethics and politics in our evaluation of the value of fictions. Massive changes are taking place in the way we relate to fictions: criteria such as relevance, utility, efficiency, and shared use among interpretive communities are now widely assumed to be necessary for a work of art to merit consideration. But when everybody agrees that we must 'take back the narrative' (as we would take back power), does this mean the exhilarating possibility of building other worlds together, or the much more threatening multiplication of competing stories? This is precisely why such phenomena, which are part of a deep range of shifts of authority in contemporary societies and too often cause perplexity, dismay, or even panic, must be thoroughly questioned, *considered*, from the perspective of their history, logic, and stakes.

## References

Blanc, William. 2019. *Winter is Coming: Une brève histoire politique de la fantasy* (Paris: Libertalia)

Besson, Anne. 2020. 'Fanthéories de Harry Potter: Part de l'auteur, part des lecteurs', in *Premier symposium de critique policière : Autour de Pierre Bayard*, Fabula, Les colloques <http://www.fabula.org/colloques/document4821.php> [accessed 22 June 2022]

Blackman, Mallory. 2001–2008. *Noughts and Crosses*, 4 vols (New York: Random House)

Bottero, Pierre. 2003. *La Quête d'Ewilan : D'un monde à l'autre* (Paris: Rageot)

Bourdaa, Mélanie. 2016. '"I Am Not a Tribute": The Transmedia Strategy of *The Hunger Games* vs. Fan Activism', in *The Rise of Transtexts: Challenges and Opportunities*, ed. by Benjamin L. Derhy Kurtz and Mélanie Bourdaa, 90–103 (London: Routledge)

Collins, Suzanne. 2008–2010. *The Hunger Games*. 3 vols (New York: Scholastic Press)

Eco, Umberto. 1984. *The Role of the Reader: Explorations in the Semiotics of Texts* (Bloomington: Indiana University Press)

Gefen, Alexandre. 2017. *Réparer le monde : La littérature française face au XXI$^e$ siècle* (Paris: José Corti)

Hall, Stuart. 1980. 'Encoding/Decoding', in *Culture, Media, Language*, ed. by Stuart Hall, Dorothy Hobson, Andrew Love and Paul Willis, 128–38 (London: Hutchinson)

Harry Potter Alliance. n.d. 'Our Commitments.' <https://www.thehpalliance.org/what_we_do> [accessed 2 June 2020]

Herman, David. 2005. 'Storyworld', in *Routledge Encyclopedia of Narrative Theory*, ed. by David Herman, Manfred Jahn, and Marie-Laure Ryan, 569–70 (London: Routledge)

Huz, Aurélie. 2018. 'L'Intermédialité dans la science-fiction française de *La Planète sauvage* à *Kaena* (1973–2003)' (unpublished doctoral dissertation, University of Limoges)

Iglesias, Pablo. 2014. *Ganar o Morir, Lecciones políticas en* 'Juego de Tronos', Pensamento Crítico (Madrid: Akal)

Jameson, Frederic. 1982. 'Progress Versus Utopia, or, Can We Imagine the Future?', *Science Fiction Studies*, 9 (2): 147–58

Jenkins, Henry. 2012. 'Cultural Acupuncture: Fan Activism and the Harry Potter Alliance', in 'Transformative Works and Fan Activism', ed. by Henry Jenkins and Sangita Shresthova, special issue, *Transformative Works and Cultures*, 10 <http://journal.transformativeworks.org/index.php/twc/article/view/305/259> [accessed 24 June 2022]

―――. 2014. 'Fan Activism as Participatory Politics: The Case of the Harry Potter Alliance', in *DIY Citizenship: Critical Making and Social Media*, ed. by Matt Ratto and Megan Boler, 65–74 (Cambridge, MA: MIT Press)

Jenkins, Henry, Sangita Shresthova, Liana Gamber-Thompson, Neta Kligler-Vilenchik, and Arely M. Zimmerman. 2016. *By Any Media Necessary: The New Youth Activism* (New York: New York University Press)

Knight, Damon. 1977. *The Futurians: The Story of the Science Fiction* (New York: John Day)

Proctor, William. 2017. '"Bitches Ain't Gonna Hunt No Ghosts": Totemic Nostalgia, Toxic Fandom and the Ghostbusters Platonic', *Palabra Clave* 20.4 (October): 1105–42 <http://palabraclave.unisabana.edu.co/index.php/palabraclave/article/view/1105/pdf> [accessed 24 June 2022]

Proctor, William and Bridget Kies. 2018. 'On Toxic Fan Practices and the New Culture Wars', *Participations: Journal of Audience and Reception Studies*, 15 (1): 127–42 <http://eprints.bournemouth.ac.uk/30957/1/on%20toxic%20fan%20practices.pdf> [accessed 24 June 2022]

Ross, Andrew. 1991. *Strange Weather: Culture, Science, and Technology in the Age of Limits* (New York: Verso)

Roth, Veronica. 2011–2013. *Divergent*, 3 vols (New York: Katherine Tegen Books/Harper Collins)

ROWLING, J. K. 2008. 'The Fringe Benefits of Failure, and the Importance of Imagination', Commencement address, Harvard University, in *Harvard Gazette*, 5 June <https://news.harvard.edu/gazette/story/2008/06/text-of-j-k-rowling-speech/> [accessed 24 June 2022]

SCHAEFFER, JEAN-MARIE. 2010. *Why Fiction?*, trans. by Dorrit Cohn (Lincoln: University of Nebraska Press)

SERVANT, STÉPHANE. 2017. *Sirius*, Epik (Arles: Le Rouergue)

SUVIN, DARKO. 1977. *Pour une poétique de la science-fiction : Études en théorie et en histoire d'un genre littéraire*, Genres et discours (Montreal: Presses de l'Université du Québec)

——. 1979. *Metamorphoses of Science Fiction: On the Poetics and History of a Literary Genre* (New Haven: Yale University Press)

TOLKIEN, J. R. R. (1964) 1988. *On Fairy-Stories*, in *Tree and Leaf* (London: Unwin Hyman)

WESTERFELD, SCOTT. 2005–2007. *Uglies*, 4 vols (New York: Simon Pulse)

'What We Do'. 2019. *Harry Potter Alliance*, November, <https://www.thehpalliance.org/what_we_do> [accessed 24 June 2022]

## Notes to Chapter 11

1. On the 'Handmaids', see also Anne Isabelle François's contribution to this volume (Chapter 10).
2. These are the key words of the Harvard commencement speech J. K. Rowling delivered on 5 June 2008: 'We do not need magic to change the world, we carry all the power we need inside ourselves already: we have the power to imagine better' (Rowling 2008).
3. This is no coincidence of course. From the very start, the North American SF fan communities, and the first theorists among them were, in large part, strongly engaged in leftist politics: notoriously the Futurians' Club — whose history has been told by one famous member, the writer Damon Knight — shared their first meeting place at the end of the 1930s with the Young Communist League of Flatbush (Knight 1977: 8). At the same time, the 'Committee for the Political Advancement of Science Fiction' (a group including Donald A. Wollheim and Frederik Pohl), from the 'Michelism' movement, advocated 'radical' change against the Nazi threat in Europe (Ross 1991: 114–16). SF and fantasy fans later became much warier of political dissent among their communities, but the emerging academic field on those subjects took over.
4. 'Storyworld' is used here in David Herman's definition of the word (Herman 2005: 569–70).
5. 'The escapist is not so subservient to the whims of evanescent fashion as these opponents. [...] And his opponents, so easily contemptuous, have no guarantee that he will stop there: he might rouse men to pull down the street-lamps. [...] For it is after all possible for a rational man to arrive, after reflection [...] at the condemnation of progressive things like factories, machine-guns and bombs' (Tolkien [1964] 1988: 57).
6. 'It is part of the essential malady of such days — producing the desire to escape, not indeed from life, but from our present time and self-made misery — that we are acutely conscious both of the ugliness of our works, and of their evil' (Tolkien [1964] 1988: 59).
7. 'The desire to converse with other living things largely founded the talking of beasts and creatures in fairy-tales [...]. A vivid sense of that separation is very ancient; but also a sense that it was a severance: a strange fate and a guilt lies on us' (Tolkien [1964] 1988: 60).
8. 'I do not say "seeing things as they are" and involve myself with the philosophers, though I might venture to say "seeing things as we are (or were) meant to see them" — as things apart from ourselves. We need, in any case, to clean our windows; so that the things seen clearly may be freed from the drab blur of triteness or familiarity — from possessiveness' (Tolkien [1964] 1988: 53).
9. 'Ailleurs et Demain' was a collection published by Robert Laffont Editions, created in 1969 and still active, with the same director, Gérard Klein. 'Ici et maintenant' only lasted from 1977 to 1980, directed by Bernard Blanc for Kesselring.
10. 'Une position intermédiaire et équilibrée, entre militantisme réducteur et dépaysement aveugle.'
11. In January 2020, the author was criticised for supporting a LGBTQIA+ offender, raising a

controversy among readers, still ongoing, as an example of so-called 'cancel culture', in 2022. Consequently, the HPA rebranded itself 'Fandom Forward' in June 2021.

12. See footnote 2 above.

CHAPTER 12

# Fiction or Death: The Latin American Tradition of Nonfiction

*Annick Louis*

Université de Franche-Comté/CRAL
(École des Hautes Études en Sciences Sociales–Centre national de la recherche scientifique)

This chapter examines a specific use of a certain kind of narrative, which positions itself at the boundary of fiction and nonfiction and seeks to produce some intervention into a reality that remains unpredictable; its purpose is to change the real world, but there are no specific indications concerning how and what is to be modified. For about twenty years, these narratives, which I call 'hybrids', have acquired visibility and have been highly successful; they seem to appeal to both common readers and social and human scientists. Other labels have been proposed: 'factual literature' (Genette 1993; Jeannelle 2007), 'document-works' (Bessière 2006), 'documentary narrative' (Ruffel 2012) 'factographies' (Zenetti 2014[1]), 'novel without fiction' (Cercas 2008, Volpi 2018), 'realityfiction' (Ludmer 2010), 'documentary realism' (Nash 2018), 'docufiction' — a word used by the media, particularly in the audiovisual realm; 'nonfiction' (Capote 1965); 'literature of investigation' (Coste 2017); 'inquiry' (Demanze 2019). Those terms have the advantage of not dividing the spectrum of such productions into two major groups — fictional and nonfictional — a division according to which everything in between would be an 'anomaly'. This does not correspond to my interpretation, because I contend that in literature there are no anomalies but conventions, traditions, established genres, and works that permanently challenge them. These terms also reflect the vast diffusion of this kind of narrative in the West, and the difficulty we have in establishing parameters to understand them.

Nevertheless, I consider — with the exception of Genette's 'factual literature' — that these terms define subcategories, and are related to narratives that present different characteristics and also belong to different periods and nations, although they share the blurring of boundaries between fiction and nonfiction.[2] I should point out that the term 'hybrid' is used here in a descriptive sense to indicate that the trait that defines them is the deliberate combination of heterogeneous elements, which readers and viewers can generally recognise — heterogeneous implying that they originate in different genres and narrative traditions. In other words, the term refers to the heterogeneity of the narrative mode; not to the genre, but to the fact that these narratives blur the borders between fiction and what is not fiction.[3] Lionel Ruffel has pointed out those characteristics, stressing also that these texts do not seek to conceal this heterogeneity, but on the contrary display and profess it. I would add that these texts display the narrative modes they combine, but, in fact, this exhibition is often accompanied by a movement of concealment of other elements and narrative traditions.[4] I should also point out that the formal elements combined are not necessarily innovative or new, whereas their combinations are — to the extent that their repetition allows them to be conventionalised and lead to the establishment of new literary traditions.[5] In order to understand these hybrid stories, let us bear in mind that the opposition between fiction and nonfiction ought not to be naturalised: in epistemological terms, it has no justification, but in terms of the history of fiction it is necessary to acknowledge it.

I will merely briefly mention here the parameters (temporarily) established to think about these narratives, for the lack of space to develop them: the paratextual device or readability device, called also reading protocol (editing context, publishing context, etc.); the narrative mode or structure (what structure is chosen, who endorses the narrative, on what type of narrative instance is the narrative constructed); the treatment of referential elements (reproduction, quotation, fragment, summary, etc.). Before examining the question of projection into reality, I wish to make two further observations. First, concerning the contemporary and international character of the phenomenon — the production of narratives where the boundaries between fiction and nonfiction are unclear — the contemporary is always evasive and unstable, but this should not prevent us from trying to think it through; for this very same reason it favours the urge for taxonomy, although it is not my intention to establish one here. The second observation concerns 'transnationality', which implies that it is impossible to address the phenomenon on the basis of national artistic productions or by isolating the phenomenon in one specific cultural area.[6] The question requires a broad comparative perspective from specialists from different areas or at least with a broad knowledge of these cultural areas. For this reason, even when this is not their intention, the works produced within one given cultural area seem to imply that the traits and meanings of its literature are specific to them — a perspective that a comparative analysis would most certainly contradict. Therefore, the underlying question is: what are the national specificities of this transnational phenomenon? And in this context: what is the specificity of Latin American literatures? The answer to this question depends, of course, on the critical choices and the corpus scrutinised.

## 1. The Latin American Tradition

While clearly contemporary in its visibility and presence, the process of blurring the boundaries between fiction and nonfiction is not entirely novel. Spanish-American literature has produced such pieces since at least the nineteenth century (although one could trace the tradition back to the chronicles of the discovery of America). One way to account for this tradition is to take into consideration specific historical characteristics, such as the colonial situation, the conditions for the development of independence, state violence, the complex and ambiguous relationship to European culture, or the material conditions for the publication and circulation of printed documents. All these traits not only gave rise to specific narrative modes, but also to particular reading regimes. In addition, literary criticism felt concerned by this kind of literature, and produced theories and conceptualisations for the last fifty years, trying to account for their effect on the literary system and on the relationship between literature and reality.

These texts were written and received at the same time — both as fictions and as narratives that contain a form of historical truth that is not necessarily referential. And while this tendency was far from dominant during the nineteenth and early twentieth centuries, it nevertheless raises the question of the relationship between 'knowledge literature' and 'power literature', which is found in De Quincey's writings, especially in 'Letters to a Young Man Whose Education has been Neglected' (De Quincey [1823] 1897), and in Jerónimo Ledesma's reading of these notions (Ledesma 2019). The expression used by De Quincey is 'literature of power', to designate a literature conceived from the perspective of the 'Belles Lettres', in order to differentiate it on a philosophical level from the literature in which what one wants to communicate dominates over the aesthetic effect. This is a literature of intervention in which the aesthetic effect prevails, and the knowledge it communicates is actually unimportant. What De Quincey proclaims to be novel is that this literature is not based on the conceptual antithesis of pleasure-knowledge, but on the antithesis of knowledge-power. The 'literature of power' is that which produces on the reader an activation of emotions dormant in daily life, through the artistic organisation of these emotions in the literary text. Power is a quality that is communicated through the text. In 1848, De Quincey reviewed this definition and stated that communicating power is one of the functions that the social organism called literature can perform. The two main functions, communicating knowledge and communicating power, are autonomous, and may present themselves in isolation, but they can also combine, and they often do. What is most common is therefore a mixed-function literature.

Among the corpus of texts that have positioned themselves on the boundary of fiction and document in Latin American literature, we will mention: *Facundo* by Domingo Faustino Sarmiento (1845), *Una excursión a los indios ranqueles* by Lucio V. Mansilla (1870), *Viaje al país de los matreros* by Fray Mocho (1897), *Operación masacre* by Rodolfo Walsh (1957), and *Oración: Carta a Vicky y otras elegías políticas* by María Moreno (2018). Most of them are canonical works and have become classics in Argentina, sometimes even school classics, but without losing their power of intervention, as David Viñas (1982 and 1986) evidenced in the case of *Una excursión a los indios ranqueles*. They are texts that, precisely, seek to question the boundaries and to intervene in reality by modifying it; that make writing an act and endow it with the ability to transform the conditions of what they denounce without relinquishing their fictional dimension. If these texts engage in the blurring of boundaries between fiction and nonfiction, it is not in order to create confusion in the reader's mind. They are not hoaxes or falsifications: they aim to trigger a reflection on the relationship between fiction and nonfiction. Hoaxes and confusion are avoided because they become the object of a specific reception, between fiction and nonfiction, but also because the aspects of the narrative that present such characteristics concern social and historical events on which there is a consensus.

If it seems obvious that the experience of a social reality which seemed to call into question the parameters of the real has played a role in the development of such a tendency, it is also undeniable that this type of experience can, on the contrary, prevent any literary transformation and fictional approach, as the literature on the Shoah shows (Mesnard 2017). In other words, historical events that seem to question reality, because they are excessive in their violence and their characteristics, do not necessarily lead to questioning the relationship between fiction and nonfiction. Nor do the excesses of the state necessarily create a fiction, as Ricardo Piglia proposes, considering, as he has it, that the Argentine dictatorship tried to impose a version of reality that denied factual events and built a real world that is not based on factual events (Piglia 2000). In the case of the latest Argentine dictatorship, the generation of fiction by the State has been studied, just as in the Mexican case, in relation to drug trafficking (Zavala 2018).

We need to add that this current in Latin American literature has often been identified with North American nonfiction, but this identification — which concerns primarily the work of Rodolfo Walsh, and more recently of María Moreno — was proposed by Latin American critics to legitimise a local production by resorting to an internationally recognised genre, and to endow Walsh's work with universalism (Amar Sánchez [1992] 2018). Because not only was Rodolfo Walsh's *Operación masacre* (1957) published before the development of the genre in the USA, it also appeared before the publication in book form of *In Cold Blood* by Truman Capote (dated 1965, while newspaper articles on which the book is based were issued in 1959).

Throughout the twentieth century, hybrid texts developed within the framework of the opposition between documentary/testimonial narrative and the novel (which marks the production of Walsh since *Operación masacre*). Testimony, in this case, is related to rumour, gossip, the flow of information that fails to become official news in times of state violence, and censorship. The testimonial narrative is not a document; it comes in the form of versions, rumours, variants, and sometimes has a fictional dimension. The dominant conception of the fictional novel in Latin America regarded it as a bourgeois genre, a temptation any engaged writer must overcome if their literature is to have an impact on the real. Miguel Barnet stated that 'the so-called fiction is losing more and more consistency' (Barnet 1969:

99–122), while Rodolfo Walsh claimed that 'fiction is likely to be reaching its splendid ending' (Piglia [1973] 1991: 18). Latin American testimony is therefore a *genre* postulated as a revolutionary literature, which challenges both the fictional novel and totalitarian states, and writes down truth and justice which the state dismisses (García 2014b). Nevertheless, the relationship of these writers to the novel remained ambivalent, as in Walsh's case: his revolutionary epic narrative rejected it, but it remained an object of desire for him as well as for other writers. It can be said that before the development of the ensemble named 'theories of fiction', initiated by Gérard Genette's *Fiction et diction* in 1991 (1993) and reinforced by the postulate of an anthropological conception of fiction (Schaeffer [1999] 2010) — which made it possible to sustain the 'truths of fiction' (Flahault and Heinich 2005) and afterwards the 'knowledge of literature' (Anheim and Lilti 2010), and, finally to conceive fiction as a restricted and autonomous phenomenon (Lavocat 2016) — it seemed impossible to think of fiction other than in terms of the opposition between 'literature of imagination' and 'engaged literature'.

The opposition between fiction and testimony is based on the assumption that certain events can only be rendered by the mode of testimony, because fiction would distort them. The case of *Yo, Rigoberta Menchú* in the 1980s (Burgos 1983; Stoll 1999; Arias 2001), led to a questioning of this opposition: the existence of non-referential elements (non-autobiographical in this case) seemed to challenge the totality of the testimony — as if literary testimony were to be confused with judicial testimony. Only recently, and thanks to the development of the theories of fiction, has it become possible to think that in the context of testimony, parts of the narrative can be fictional without thereby obliterating the truthfulness of the testimony. Thus, in the last twenty years, a change in the meaning of fiction and testimony has occurred, together with a resignification of the relations between these two genres, which highlights the fact that this tradition must lead to a conceptualisation of the functions of fiction. Theoreticians of Latin-American fiction have developed the notion that fictional narratives do not allow the restoration of historical truth, and that they do not necessarily oppose an official fiction; moreover, they have stated that fiction stages consensus and dissent regarding official and hegemonic discourses (Ferrer 2019).[7] We must take into consideration that between the 1990s and the beginning of the twenty-first century, these functions (to oppose or to supplement) have not always been dominant, but they are those on which critics insisted, giving them a visibility that carried also the impression that fiction was opposing official discourses. Most of the narratives that did so adopted traditional modes, and did not offer the kind of blurring between fiction and nonfiction that contemporary works have brought about, although some of them do oppose official discourse.

## 2. How to Do Things with Literary Works that Blur Borders between Fiction and Nonfiction

In the last part of my chapter, I would like to elaborate on three brief examples, one of which has already been mentioned: Lucio V. Mansilla's *Una excursión a los indios ranqueles* (*An Expedition to the Ranquel Indians*, Lola Arias's *Mi vida después* (*My Life Afterwards*, Teatro Sarmiento, [2009] 2016), as well as the book from which the title of my chapter is drawn: *Diario de una princesa montonera: 101 por ciento verdad* of Mariana Eva Pérez (*Diary of a Montonera Princess: 101 Percent Truth*, 2012).

*Una excursión a los indios ranqueles* by Lucio V. Mansilla (1870), is a work about which a contemporary, Eduardo Wilde, stated: '*Ranqueles* are fashionable since Lucio Mansilla invented them' (1931: 89) — a remark that illustrates the book's initial reception. The narrative, often considered as the first Argentinian ethnographic work, is the account of the expedition Mansilla undertook in the Argentine pampa between 30 March and 17 April 1870. That territory was at the time outside the control of Buenos Aires, and a peace treaty had just been signed with the *ranqueles*, while politicians debated the measures to be taken to end what was called the 'Indian problem', leading to the extermination campaign of 1878. It may be said that the book criticises these debates. Nevertheless, Mansilla, undoubtedly the most original and adventurous man of his generation, wished above all to recount his feats, enhance his reputation, and explore the borderland, that *no man's land* that was called the 'tierra adentro' (the territory outside the control of Buenos Aires in the Pampa). His goal was not to prevent the extermination of Indigenous people, but to *showcase* their world; like Walsh's *Operación Masacre*, the text relates what historians call a minor event (the expedition) destined to be forgotten, and transformed it into a major literary event. By doing so, it inserts itself into history (García 2014a).

*Mi vida después* (*My life after*) by Lola Arias (Teatro Sarmiento, 2009) stages six actors born in the 1970s and the beginning of the 1980s who engage in reconstructing their parents' youth through letters, photos, recordings, objects, clothes, stories, and forgotten memories. The performance adopts a radical form of autobiography-with-testimony, a 'real fiction'. Two of these actors, Horacio Speratti and Carlos Crespo, are children of the disappeared, and one, Vanina Falco, is the daughter of a policeman who illegally appropriated the child of a 'desaparecido', Juan Cabandié. The latter lodged a complaint against Falco and a trial ensued, whose record appears in the play. However, Vanina Falco could not testify, because in Argentina the law forbids children from testifying against their parents, unless they are the accusers. Two years later, Cabandie's lawyer argued that she had already been testifying for two years by means of the play, and the judge allowed Vanina Falco to give her official testimony. As we can see, the case illustrates how a work situated between fiction and nonfiction made it possible to amend legislation, which underlines the value of artistic performance.

Mariana Eva Pérez is the daughter of two 'desaparecidos' and was only a few months old when her parents were abducted. Initially, *Diario de una princesa montonera: 110 por ciento verdad*, was not a book, but a blog she wrote between 2009 and 2018. The book opens with her return from Europe, a time when she stays away from human rights organisations, and ends with her marriage and her travel back to Europe. As it has been pointed out, Mariana Eva Pérez's book is part of the movement of emergence of the children of the 'desaparecidos' in the literary and artistic sphere, those who have been called the 'post-orphans', the 'renegade monsters', the 'happy bastards' (Gatti 2008). As Jordana Blejmar observes in *Playful Memories* (2016), a new stage in post-dictatorship artistic production begins with the children of the 'desaparecidos', a generation that claimed the right to humour, fantasy, and playful narratives that stand on the boundaries of fiction and nonfiction, while questioning the economy of testimony as it had worked since the end of the dictatorship. Mariana Eva Pérez works essentially on language — by appropriating and inventing terms that give new meaning to the status of the children of the victims of the dictatorship. Blejmar recalls that there is no legislation in Argentina that considers the children of the 'desaparecidos' as victims. In the diary, it is difficult to differentiate between the public, the private and the intimate, while the blog sought to oppose the tradition of the *testimonio latinoamericano* and constantly dismisses the testimonial value of the blog, at the time of the hegemony of an official human rights policy.

Here are some examples of language usages in *Diario de una princesa montonera*. The question of the 'desaparecidos' is named 'el temita', which could be translated as 'the little matter', endowed with an ironic connotation; the children of the 'desaparecidos' become les 'hijis', instead of 'hijos', which is also the name of their association (Hijos e Hijas por la Identidad y la Justicia contra el Olvido y el Silencio/ Children for identity and justice against oblivion and silence), founded in 1993, a period of absence of justice. The word 'militante' becomes 'militonta', by phonetic association of 'militante' (activist) and 'tonta' (silly), to refer to a person without political awareness, with superficial interests. In addition, a series of political slogans for which the militants of the 1960s and 1970s fought, and died, sometimes in atrocious conditions, are rephrased: 'Perón o muerte' (Perón or death), a historical slogan, claimed by *guerrillas* and other armed movements, becomes 'Ficción o muerte' (fiction or death). The meaning of this transformation of the slogan remains uncertain: is it a parody, or rather does it create a distance from a slogan that had a political meaning for the parents' generation — which by the same token gives fiction a political dimension and a capacity for intervention into the real? We are therefore facing a new semantic field and the affirmation of a new functionality of fiction: blurring fiction/nonfiction boundaries becomes a new form of literary political activism. The slogan 'Fiction or death' indeed asserts the fact that these hybrid stories are the only literary (artistic) choice possible that can save us from a violent political history and allow literary production.

## 3. Borders and Reality

As stated earlier, what I call 'hybrid texts' turn writing into an act: they enable the challenging of borders, considering writing as an intervention into reality that can alter it. This is also how Lionel Ruffel interprets contemporary documentary writing, hybrid forms of docufictional inquiry, which often aim at intervening and engage in a quest for truth (2012: 14). These 'hybrid' texts combine literary strategies that the reader can recognise with the establishment of a pact of nonfiction like the one that testimony establishes, through paratextual elements such as dates, documents, and the biography of the writer. These texts do not discard fiction; they are not based on the impossibility of autonomous fictional narratives, as one might think from the perspective of European literary history and conceptualisation (in fact, French theory of fiction is formalist, and for this reason had difficulty conceptualising texts located on the boundaries of fiction and nonfiction).

In the twentieth century, Jorge Luis Borges's success transformed this kind of narrative, by establishing a regime of equivalence between fiction and other social discourses, and by focusing on the effect of fiction on reality — which is equivalent to postulating a relationship of complementarity between reality and fiction. His literary conceptions were endorsed by a host of writers, intellectuals, and critics, who often had a political ideology opposed to his own, and who used it to produce literature that displayed different characteristics. Borges embodies a triumphant and productive form at the international level of literature that postulates the relationship between fiction and reality as an enigma and leaves the reader to come up with the answers — as I have shown in my previous work (see Louis 1997, 2006, and 2007). I am referring to his two classic volumes, *Ficciones* (1944), and *El Aleph* (1949), as well as a series of notes from the 1930s and 1940s. In the conventionalisation of fiction/nonfiction, the blurring zones do not call into question historical reality or the achievements of historiography, but become zones of personal biography/autobiography that acquire a social dimension. Through the dissemination of Borges's writings, these trends have spread throughout Latin America and into literature worldwide; among those who have appropriated them are two 'globalised' Spanish-language writers, whose production has given rise to debates about the status of their works: Roberto Bolaño (1953–2003) and Javier Cercas (1962–).

My proposal is to relate the question 'are these texts fictions or documents?' to three other interrogations: Why should texts be submitted to this question? What critical conceptions does this entail? Why should we decide whether a narrative is fictional or nonfictional? I would add that these texts show that the essential question is not the status of the text but fictional immersion. Narratives such as Mansilla's allow us to put forward the hypothesis that this kind of writing seeks to provoke the intensity of fictional immersion and simultaneously to provoke an exit into the real world: the text preserves a form of referentiality that contains the potentiality of an unpredictable action. It is therefore not a question of provoking concrete and precise actions, such as induced by the traditional 'littérature engagée', by thematising social situations and proposing guidelines to confront them. In the texts I deal with, the mode of intervention is unpredictable, and depends both on their reception and on the subsequent development of events — that is, on the impact of the literary work in the social world.

Iuri Lotman described fictional immersion as a split state of mental abilities, which makes it possible to dive into the universe of a book, but without being out of one's depth, without disconnecting from the real conditions of our act of reading — because if we did, we would end up confusing fiction and reality (Lotman 1973). I propose a slightly different conception of fictional immersion: an incorporation of this split mental state into the act of reading. Within the book, we are immersed intensely, but this immersion implies our participation in a universe that we perceive simultaneously both as real and as fictional; the real universe may be ours or a universe that is alien to us, but the conditions of reading internalise the split pact of immersion.

For this reason, I would like to emphasise the potential of these texts and the unpredictability of their mode of intervention into reality. It was suggested that these texts call into question the powers of the discourses they tap into — journalism, social sciences, an idea of literature indexed to realism. I would like to suggest that in truth what they call into question is the separation, the compartmentalisation between spaces of social circulation, by putting forward writings that circulate between different zones of reception (even if this circulation is not immediate). The objective therefore is not political or social awareness, or to enhance the knowledge of unknown worlds or situations (on which Latin American testimonial literature focuses, but by opposing fiction). However, the objectives may vary. If it can be said that this type of text was defined in relation to social discourses and silences, or to the discourse of the state, or of journalists, my hypothesis is that in today's Latin-American writings these hybrid narratives seek to position themselves in relation to legal discourse, and often in opposition to it. Their function is to broaden the spectrum of laws, emphasising the insufficiency, corruption, deformation, or nonexistence of legislation.

## References

ANHEIM, ÉTIENNE and ANTOINE LILTI (eds.). 2010. 'Savoirs de la littérature', special issue, *Annales: Histoire, sciences sociales*, 65 (2)

AMAR SÁNCHEZ, ANA MARÍA. [1992] 2018. *El relato de los hechos: Rodolfo Walsh: Testimonio y escritura* (Buenos Aires: Random House/Literatura)

ARIAS, ARTURO (ed.). 2001. *The Rigoberta Menchú Controversy* (Minnesota: University of Minnesota Press)

ARIAS, LOLA. (2009) 2016. *Mi vida después y otros textos* (Buenos Aires: Reservoir Books)

BABY, HÉLÈNE (ed.). 2006. *Fiction narrative et hybridation générique dans la littérature française* (Paris: L'Harmattan)

BARNET, MIGUEL. 1969. 'La novela testimonio: socio-literatura', *Union*, 1: 99–122

BESSIÈRE, JEAN. 2006. 'L'œuvre document et la communication de l'ignorance', in 'Des faits et des gestes. Le parti-pris du document 2', ed. by Jean-François Chevrier and Philippe Roussin, special issue, *Communications*, 79: 319–35

BLEJMAR, JORDANA. 2016. *Playful Memories, The Autobiographical Turn in Post-dictatorship Argentina* (Switzerland: Palgrave, Macmillan)

BURGOS, ELISABETH. 1983. *Me llamo Rigoberta Menchú y así me nació la conciencia* (Guatemala: Arcoiris)

CAPOTE, TRUMAN. 1965. *In Cold Blood* (New York: Random House)

CERCAS, JAVIER. 2008. *Anatomía de un instante* (Barcelona: Mondadori)

CONIO, GÉRARD. 1987. *Le constructivisme russe*. Vol. II, *Le constructivisme littéraire* (Lausanne: L'âge d'homme)

Coste, Florent. 2017. 'Propositions pour une littérature d'investigation', *Journal des anthropologues*, 148–49: 43–62 <https://doi.org/10.4000/jda.6582>

Demanze, Laurent. 2019. *Un nouvel âge de l'enquête* (Paris: José Corti)

De Quincey, Thomas. (1823) 1897. *The Collected Writings*, x (London: Adam and Charles Black)

Ferrer, Lorena. 2019. 'La literatura como experiencia del disenso: Fracturas del imaginario en la Argentina menemista (1989–2001)' (unpublished doctoral dissertation, Universidad Autónoma de Madrid)

Flahault, François and Nathalie Heinich (eds.). 2005. 'Vérités de la fiction', special issue, *L'Homme*, 175–76 (July–September)

Garane, Jeanne M (ed.). 2018. *Hybrid genres/L'hybridité des genres* (Leiden: Brill Rodopi)

García, Victoria. 2014a. 'La obra testimonial de Rodolfo Walsh en el contexto argentino y latinoamericano de los años 1960–1970' (unpublished doctoral dissertation, Universidad de Buenos Aires)

——. 2014b. 'Testimonio literario latinoamericano: Prefiguraciones históricas del género en el discurso revolucionario de los años sesenta', *Acta Poetica*, 35 (January–June): 63–92.

Gatti, Gabriel. 2008. *Identidades desaparecidas: Peleas por el sentido en los mundos de la desaparición forzada* (Buenos Aires: Eduntref)

Genette, Gérard. 1993. *Fiction and Diction*, trans. by Catherine Porter (Ithaca: Cornell University Press). Originally published as *Fiction et diction* (Paris: Seuil, 1991)

——. 1994. *L'Œuvre de l'art, Immanence et transcendance* (Paris: Seuil)

——. 1997. *L'Œuvre de l'art: La relation esthétique* (Paris: Seuil)

Jeannelle, Jean-Louis. 2007. 'Les littératures factuelles', *Fabula*, Atelier littéraire <https://www.fabula.org/atelier.php?Les_litt%26eacute%3Bratures_factuelles>

Lavocat, Françoise. 2016. *Fait et fiction: Pour une frontière* (Paris: Seuil)

Ledesma, Jerónimo. 2019. 'X.Y.Z., la literatura entre De Quincey y Borges' (unpublished doctoral dissertation, Universidad de Buenos Aires)

Lotman, Iuri. 1973. *La Structure du texte artistique*, trans. by Anne Fournier, Bernard Kreise, Ève Malleret, Henri Meschonnic, and Joëlle Yong (Paris: Gallimard)

Louis, Annick. 1997. *Jorge Luis Borges: Œuvre et manœuvres* (Paris: L'Harmattan)

——. 2006. *Borges face au fascisme 1 : Les causes du présent* (Montreuil: Aux lieux d'être)

——. 2007. *Borges face au fascisme 2 : Les fictions du contemporain* (Montreuil: Aux lieux d'être)

Ludmer, Josefina. 2010. *Aquí América Latina: Una especulación* (Buenos Aires: Eterna Cadencia)

Mansilla, Lucio V. 1870. *Una excursión a los indios ranqueles* (Buenos Aires: Imprenta de Belgrano)

Mesnard, Philippe (ed.). 2017. *La littérature testimoniale, ses enjeux génériques* (Paris: SFLGC)

Nash, Mark. 2008. 'Reality in the Age of Aesthetics', *Frieze*, 114 (April) <https://www.frieze.com/article/reality-age-aesthetics> [accessed 24 June 2022]

Pérez, Mariana Eva. 2012. *Diario de una princesa montonera: 101 por ciento verdad* (Barcelona: Marbot Ediciones)

Piglia, Ricardo. (1973) 1991. 'Hoy es imposible en Argentina hacer literatura desvinculada de la política', in Rodolfo Walsh, *Un oscuro día de justicia*, 9–28 (Buenos Aires: Siglo XXI)

——. 2000. *Crítica y ficción* (Buenos Aires: Seix Barral)

Ruffel, Lionel. 2012. 'Un réalisme contemporain: Les narrations documentaires', *Littérature*, 166.2: 13–25.

Schaeffer, Jean-Marie. 2010. *Why Fiction?*, trans. by Dorrit Cohn (Lincoln: University of Nebraska Press)

Stoll, David. 1999. *Rigoberta Menchú and the Story of All Poor Guatemalans* (Boulder, CO: Westview Press.)

TOPUZIAN, MARCELO. 2017. 'Introducción: Entre literatura nacional y posnacional', in *Tras la nación: Conjeturas y controversias sobre las literaturas nacionales y mundiales*, ed. by Marcelo Topuzian (Buenos Aires: Eudeba), 9–65
VIÑAS, DAVID. 1982. *Indios, ejército y frontera* (Buenos Aires: Siglo veintiuno Editores)
——. 1986. 'Literatura argentina 1' (lectures) (Universidad Buenos Aires)
VOLPI, JORGE. 2018. *Una novela criminal* (Madrid: Random House)
WILDE, EDUARDO. 1931. 'Los ranqueles están de moda desde que los ha inventado Lucio Mansilla', *Tiempo perdido* (Buenos Aires: El Ateneo)
ZAVALA, OSWALDO. 2018. *Los carteles no existen: Narcotráfico y cultura en México* (Mexico City: Malpaso)
ZENETTI, MARIE-JEANNE. 2014. *Factographies: L'enregistrement littéraire à l'époque contemporaine* (Paris: Classiques Garnier)

## Notes to Chapter 12

1. The concept and the term appear already among the Russian constructivists, in relation to *LEF* (the Left Front of the Arts). See Conio (1987), Jeannelle (2007), and Zenetti (2014).
2. The choice of the term depends, of course, on what the critic wishes to emphasise, and on their training and the interpretive tradition in which they situate themselves. But also, on the aesthetic focus of the stories, which does not correspond to their reception: the activation of the work highlights certain elements and leaves others in the shadows and remains related to the articulation of phenomena and the sensitivity of our time (Genette 1994 and 1997).
3. Therefore, I depart from the traditional use of the term 'hybrid' in literary studies, which refers to contamination between genres. See Baby (2006); Garane (2018).
4. Ruffel states (2012, 3) that the documentary narrative differs from the realistic novel in that it displays itself as a document, integrates texts of various origins, and combines semiotic regimes; thus, it simultaneously produces a documentary effect and a real effect.
5. For Ruffel (2012, 3) the criteria that determine the emblematic character of a type of narrative are as follows: its form can be described by means of identifiable criteria; the whole appears more quantitatively represented in contemporary times than in other epochs; it attracts the attention of academic, journalistic, and public critics; it is represented at the global level; it is exported via translations; finally, it is the object of a contemporary fabrication that clearly inscribes it in public space and in the order of discourse.
6. I adopt the definition of Marcelo Topuzian, who considers the recent bibliography on the issue. For him, a transnational approach presupposes the radical questioning of the paradigm of history and the critique of national literatures which still dominates literary studies and their teachings (Topuzian 2017).
7. Ferrer points out that during this period of lack of justice (1987–2001/3), literature assumes the function of dissent, according to the conception of Jacques Rancière. The aim is to produce works that seek to push for justice, in part by researching historical events; the literature thus challenges political but also judicial power. The works nevertheless maintain 'classical' forms: fiction novel, historical novel. Yet, they also explore, within the framework of these classical forms, alternative modes of narrative, relatively new, such as the exploration of the consciousness of the executioner, in the tradition of Borges's 'Deutsches Requiem' (*L'Aleph*, 1949).

CHAPTER 13

# Fiction as Legal Authority? Orwell, Snowden, and State Cyber-Surveillance

*Henriette Korthals Altes*

*Maison Française d'Oxford/University of Oxford*

Does fiction change the world? I shall broach the question discussed at the first SIRFF/ISFFS conference through a narrower lens: can fiction have legal authority? My aim is to reassess to what extent references to Orwell's modern classic, *Nineteen Eighty-Four* ([1949] 2013), as they appear in American court rulings, progressed case law in the aftermath of Edward Snowden's disclosures concerning the NSA's mass surveillance programmes, and to what extent these literary references have contributed to the debate surrounding privacy, surveillance, and self-surveillance in the digital era. My title takes its cue from an article by John DeStefano (2007), 'On literature as legal authority', where he analyses how American courts have made use of literature more generally, rather than just fiction, and how literary references not only have a rhetorical value, as they underpin the persuasiveness of the legal argument, but also humanise the law. This is a now classical argument within the Law and Literature movement, which more generally claims that literature, as a cultural value, has a normative function. My aim in this essay is to re-examine this claim in the specific context of judicial references to *Nineteen Eighty-Four* and to evaluate their purpose in setting precedents. I will show how, in a limited number of cases, judicial reference to Orwell's classic did successfully progress case law. Legal scholars have indeed argued that references to Orwell provided a new cultural norm for the test of reasonable expectation that is embedded in the American privacy doctrine, even though the NSA surveillance practices remained unchanged. This supposed atypical direct legal effectiveness of literature on law invites several questions. Firstly, what prerogative do literature, fiction, and in particular Orwell's novel have over other types of cultural artefacts to set values and norms, especially over critical theory or the social sciences, for instance? Judicial reference to Orwell has been used as a warning against dystopian state surveillance and betrays how courts limit the debate about impinged privacy to physical or digital intrusion. My argument will be that judicial reference fails to engage with

Orwell's broader critique of surveillance. If *Nineteen Eighty-Four* was long perceived as a cautionary tale against totalitarian surveillance, I would argue that the novel is still relevant in the neoliberal era of digital surveillance, as it offers a stark warning against homogenised behaviour, the eradication of emotional ambivalence and complexity, and most crucially against the annihilation of independent thinking that surveillance entails. The novel, I therefore argue, advocates reading, writing, and literature as spaces of private interpretative freedom. My line of argument therefore will be that such limited harnessing of the literary reference points towards the failure to articulate privacy law and freedom of thought in novel ways, both of which are under high pressure in the digital era of mass cyber-surveillance and the self-surveillance it promotes.

Let me return to the use of the Orwellian reference in the larger context of state surveillance. Even Richard A. Posner, a legal scholar who has always been sceptical about the uses judges can make of literary references and the extent to which literature, as a cultural norm, can shape legal instruments, concedes that four hundred judicial quotations of Kafka had already been listed when he wrote his seminal *Law and Literature* (Posner [1988] 2009: 170). Yet he warns this may not say much about the literary sensitivities of the judge, who mostly will not have read the author: 'Like 'Orwellian', 'Kafkaesque' has become detached from the literary works that gave rise to the term, and is used mainly by persons who never read or have long forgotten those works' (Posner 2009: 179). With the title of his chapter, 'The Limits of Literary Jurisprudence', we already have adumbrations of the fact that limited knowledge will hamper the interpretative harnessing of the novel and rein in the authority of literature. In the case of Orwell, a search for *Nineteen Eighty-Four* on Westlaw, one of the most comprehensive legal databases worldwide, will return four hundred occurrences for all American courts, regardless of their appellate level or circuit, forty in the Supreme Court, and only one occurrence in an opinion of the Advocate General at the European Court of Human Rights. This should come as little surprise since the Common Law tradition evolves according to case law, which gives greater interpretive power to the judge. In the Napoleonic law tradition, the judge has little leeway when it comes to interpretation: his role is to apply the law that fits the case at hand *stricto sensu*, or as much as possible at least. As such the judge is 'the mouth of the law' ('la bouche de la loi'), to use the old saying that dates back to the French Revolution. What's more, where the European courts have at their disposal the European Convention of Human Rights as an unambiguous legal instrument, the American system seems to rely on an outdated apparatus compounded by the Fourth Amendment of the Bill of Rights which regulates warrant searches and torts based on trespassing and property law. It goes without saying that since 9/11 surveillance and cyber-surveillance have been deployed in ways that privacy rights could not have anticipated and rendered obsolete the American legal doctrine. With the Snowden scandal, when the full extent of the NSA's surveillance programme came to light, comparisons with Orwell haunted headlines on both sides of the Atlantic to condemn what the whistle blower had exposed, namely a so-called 'liquid' cyber surveillance that captures and capitalises on every computer click unbeknownst to citizens. These are the preliminary reasons that have brought me to examine how American courts use references to Orwell's *Nineteen Eighty-Four* when they rule on issues of surveillance and impinged privacy.

## 1. The Law and Literature Movement

To start, I will offer a few prefatory remarks about the Law and Literature movement and the ways it interweaves the two titular disciplines. The movement emerged in the seventies with a mission to harness literature and literary criticism as a way to provide a well-rounded but also more enlightened curriculum in law schools. The Law and Literature movement originally found its inspiration in the Wigmore list of legal novels, which was drawn up by the legal scholar in the early 1920s. Typically including novels by Dickens, Dostoevsky, and Dumas, it compounded fictional narratives about law, lawyers, and trials, that all question the fraught relation between law and justice. Today these texts are still seen to be fostering 'the attachment to democratic values conveyed by literature through its acute awareness of human needs' and to highlight 'the failure of great institutions to serve them' (Weisberg 2009; Wigmore 1922; Simonin 2007). Reading lists are now as diverse as the institutions offering a Law and Literature curriculum. They share the conviction that fiction can give insights into the complex emotional factors that the law and courtrooms deal with and shape, thus granting fiction and fictionality a heuristic value. Today the 'Law and Literature' movement is organised around two overarching research questions. The first has to do with the way law, justice, and the legal world is represented in literature — the legal or judicial imagination, in a way. As Alexandre Gefen has argued, this question is essentially the realm of the realistic novel (2013: 69). Hugo's *Dernier jour d'un condamné* (1829) or Camus's *L'Étranger* (1942) spring to mind as they have been quoted for instance by Robert Badinter (2000: 30, 266; Badinter in Morisi 2011: i–vi) as sources that shaped his convictions to abolish capital punishment in France in 1981. Concerning the absurdity of endless litigation, Dickens's *Bleak House* (1853) provides classically quoted references, while Kafka's *The Trial* (1925), in the modernist and absurdist vein, forms a cautionary tale against totalitarian (or not) bureaucracies that is now encapsulated in the adjective Kafkaesque. As for *Nineteen Eighty-Four*, which interests us here, it used to be classified as a science-fiction novel, a genre that depicts a counterfactual world and therefore allows the reader to explore alternative scenarios for what surveillance in a totalitarian state may bring. It may be useful to recall how Alain Badiou argues that the genre's fictional element, as it experiments with alternative worlds, invites comparisons with reality. Science-fiction functions as a 'metaphorical essay' that calls for the reader's discursive and analytical reading (Badiou 2003: 121; my translation). *Nineteen Eighty-Four*, as a piece of science-fiction, would therefore allow us to formulate counterpropositions when it comes to surveillance and privacy rights and, as such, it is 'counter-legal' ('contrejuridique'), to use Gefen's terminology (Gefen 2013: 69).

The second main preoccupation of the Law and Literature movement is to envisage law as literature, and thus foreground the textual and rhetorical nature not only of any form of legislation but the very practice of the judge and the lawyer. That any legislation, litigation, and courtroom judgement form performative statements goes without saying: they install a new order of law and a new state of things. What is more, this line of inquiry seeks out rhetorical elements that underpin the persuasiveness of legal arguments that aim to be generalizable. The Law and Literature movement has thus looked into how critical reading, inherent in all literary analysis, may be conducive to the judge's and lawyer's enhanced self-awareness. Peter Brooks has argued in favour of training lawyers to become critical readers, able to identify rhetorical strategies that underpin political agendas in legal texts or decisions (Brooks 2016: 262). Both the callings of judge and lawyer would gain from being fine narratologists, aware of what is at stake in the ambivalence of storytelling. In the same vein, Martha Nussbaum has advocated that literary reading, and the 'metaphorical imagination' it engages, is crucial to legal and political education (Nussbaum 1995: 37). Indeed, her ethics of reading rests on empathy and compassion, which allows the legal practitioners to understand human situations that don't belong to them and thus shape case law on that basis.

My inquiry will combine both questions. I will start by fleshing out what one may call the legal imagination of Orwell's *Nineteen Eighty-Four* and what it warns against. I shall then proceed to look at how and what elements of the novel were used by court rulings and if those judicial references did reshape case law and create precedents. Finally, I will discuss how, if *Nineteen Eighty-Four* as an emblem of totalitarian surveillance has served as a counter-cultural norm, judicial reference has failed to engage with the more sinister consequences of state surveillance, in particular, self-surveillance, the demise of independent critical thinking, and the internalisation of dominant discourses that cyber-surveillance brings along in the neoliberal digital era.

## 2. Why *Nineteen Eighty-Four*?

*Nineteen Eighty-Four*, like Kafka's *The Trial*, has often been considered as an Ur-Novel for surveillance studies. Surveillance studies emerged within the social sciences in the wake of Michel Foucault's account of panopticism given in *Discipline and Punish* ([1975] 1991). The Canadian sociologist David Lyon (1994, [2006] 2011, 2015) pioneered the field, which has since grown into various interdisciplinary sub-fields, including human rights law, international relations, and migration studies, to name the most obvious. More recently, literary studies have joined the debate and opened up new questions about the effects of surveillance on our sense of self, as well as about the conscious or unconscious conformism of thought, behaviour, and emotional life that self-surveillance inherent in the use of social media promotes. The enduring strength of Foucault's panopticism, a model based on Jeremy Bentham's project for a spherical prison with a single guard in a central watchtower, accounts for a surveillance society that no longer imposes discipline by means of force or violence but by the feeling of being observed. Indeed, in the panoptic prison, the guard is always visible but the inmate never knows if he is actually being watched, whether that gaze is real or imaginary. 'A real subjection is born mechanically from a fictitious relation', Foucault argues, and this fictitiousness is important because 'it automatizes and disindividualizes power' (Foucault ([1975] 2008: 183). The effectiveness of panopticism as a means of control rests on a simple psychological principle: the internalizing of the gaze of the guard, who embodied both law and possible punishment, and who no longer needs to be real. Whether the gaze is fictitious or not does not matter; fear ensures compliance.

So how does this play out in *Nineteen Eighty-Four*? As one knows, Oceania, the dystopian world the novel describes, has all the characteristics of a panoptic system that aims to homogenise society by eradicating deviance, and turning citizens into docile bodies and minds. Surveillance is indeed ubiquitous, as the proverbial 'Big Brother is watching you' has it. Interactive tele-screens ensure that his gaze is present in each household and that propaganda is continuously being dispensed. Whether the surveilling gaze in *Nineteen Eighty-Four* is real rather than imaginary in Big Brother's televisual presence is a moot question. Sébastien Lefait recalls how the novel fails to clarify how surveillance actually works: 'Surveillance may be palpable everywhere even if [...] no coherent explanation is given to demonstrate that it is actually in progress' (Lefait 2013: 23). Indeed Orwell's text, if erratic about the technological aspects of Big Brother's gaze, is explicit about the fact that surveillance is effective precisely because citizens do not know whether they are observed:

> There was of course no way of knowing whether you were being watched at any given moment. [...] You had to live — did live, from habit that became instinct — in the assumption that every sound you made was overheard, and, except in darkness, every movement scrutinised. (Orwell [1948] 2013: 5)

Surveillance can never be wholly ubiquitous; rather its effectiveness rests on the belief that you are constantly being watched. This becomes an 'instinct' to use Orwell's words, a second nature that echoes the internalised surveilling gaze of Foucault's panoptic model.

Yet, as David Lyon has underscored, the novel's visionary power stems not so much from the description of surveillance technologies, now outdated anyway, as from the mechanisms that underpin the surveillance society it describes (Lyon 1994: 58).[1] Indeed, ubiquitous surveillance is paired with a system of propaganda, the long-term establishment of Newspeak at the expense of English and thereby the eradication of independent thinking. What's more, dissent or any form of a counteraction or narrative is quelled, as the Resistance movement called the Brotherhood is none other than an undercover body of the regime set up to catch resisters. It is no surprise then that indoctrination and surveillance work so radically and that the vast majority of the proles are obedient.

Orwell, however, gives the reader a glimmer of hope that it is possible to escape Big Brother's eye, propaganda, and the thought police, as both protagonists embody forms of resistance. Winston indeed hides from the screen to write and read whereas

Julia romantically and idealistically reasserts that she belongs to herself, that she is her own thoughts and her own subjectivity. 'They can make you say anything — anything — but they can't make you believe it. They can't get inside of you' (Orwell 2003: 192). She fiercely denies the very principle of internalisation. It is by dint of torture and brainwashing that Winston ultimately gives in to sustaining the lie that 2 and 2 are 5, betrays his love for Julia, and eventually gives in to Big Brother.

Surprisingly, legal scholars do not appear to discuss *Nineteen Eighty-Four* in the light of panopticism and the principle of an internalised gaze. Posner, for instance, argues that privacy and loneliness are inimical to totalizing schemes, but he quotes Bentham rather than Foucault as a reference (Posner 2005: 459).[2] He indeed sees in the tele-screen a 'powerful metaphor of impinged privacy' (Posner 2009: 406). However, the novel for him revolves around the thought control that encompasses a whole array of insidious means, propaganda, education, denunciation, censorship, and lobotomy, warmongering and the manipulation of history and language, televisual or electronic surveillance representing a lesser ill. As a sceptic of the Law and Literature movement, Posner seems to take home rather contradictory lessons from *Nineteen Eighty-Four*. The novel, he argues, is a satire. It overdoes it in order to better function as a cautionary tale against totalitarian ills, the annihilation of thought, language, and history through Newspeak and the prevailing practices of doublespeak and doublethink. And yet his conclusion on the mechanisms underpinning Oceania are surprisingly naive when he asserts that the Internet makes political propaganda difficult. 'The internet is making it even more difficult for dictatorial regimes to conceal the truth about other societies from their subjects' (Posner 2009: 403). This assertion seems all the more simplistic in the post-truth era when the internet provides neoliberal democracies with surveillance and thought control strategies all the more insidious for coexisting with an apparent plurality of press.

Secondly, for Posner, total surveillance is not possible, and this is simply a matter of number. 'Suppose there are 100 million tele-screens, that would require 10 million watchers, and monitoring and coordinating their work and reading and acting on their reports would require millions more' (Posner 2005: 401). Interestingly, Posner's view on the inefficiency of surveillance echoes Slavoj Žižek's position, even though both men come from totally antagonistic critical and academic traditions. Žižek, when interviewed about surveillance and the NSA's bulk data extraction, argues, not without a hint of self-mockery, that, should he be placed under surveillance, there would be nothing but the banality of life to be seen. Tongue-in-cheek, he continues, the intelligence service may be introduced to philosophy watching him, in particular the Lacanian principle that the real is what escapes the gaze and language... (Žižek 2014). Žižek thus raises interesting questions about the accessibility of the real and its possible (mis)-interpretations. But problematically, the positions of both the lawyer and philosopher seem to limit surveillance to impinged privacy as a form of intrusion rather than considering its more sinister effects: compliance, homogenised behaviour, and ultimately the extinction of thought as the Appendix to *Nineteen Eighty-Four* compellingly describes.

Admittedly, *Nineteen Eighty-Four* has essentially been received as a cautionary tale against totalitarianism. Whether we see it as sci-fi or satire, what makes the novel relevant in today's prevailing neoliberal system is not so much the technological aspect of surveillance it describes as the underpinning power structures and the human consequences of surveillance it exposes. Surveillance, we know, has become digital and it operates even more effectively in a system where power structures are not totalizing but multiple and interlocking. The Internet and social media, presented as an instrument of freedom promoting free-market and multiple viewpoints, acts undercover so to speak, unlike the tele-screens that are manifest. And one can easily draw parallels between propaganda and fake news, all the more efficient for seemingly originating from a variety of sources, as well as between Newspeak, an impoverished language that eradicates complexity, with emojis and other emerging shorthands characteristic of the digital age. For *Nineteen Eighty-Four* is not only about the eradication of thought but also the killing off of the ability to acknowledge otherness, difference, and the ambivalence inherent in emotions, as Martha Nussbaum has argued (Nussbaum 2005: 280–99).

## 3. How Has *Nineteen Eighty-Four* Been Used in American Case Law?

It is against the backdrop of this reading that I would like to assess how American courts have used *Ninety Eighty-Four*, what function judicial reference played in the evolution of case law, and whether indeed the 'substance of literature' can or cannot help 'judges judge' (DeStefano 2007: 552). The question of judicial quotation of Orwell has indeed taken a more urgent turn in the aftermath of Edward Snowden's revelations made in 2013 about state surveillance and the ways in which the NSA and other national intelligence agencies captured personal data from emails, social media, and medical records (DNA dragnet) and exploited it for commercial and political purposes unbeknownst to citizens. The extent of state surveillance was immediately exposed as being 'Orwellian' in newspapers around the world (Crouch 2013; Foster 2013; Rusbridger 2013). Comparisons with Orwell then also made it into judicial statements, in particular when judges were asked to rule on the constitutionality of surveillance devices, the NSA, and other state cyber-surveillance programmes.

But first why would references to Orwell be needed at all? Contrary to the majority of European countries that are signatories to the European Convention of Human Rights, the American judicial system does not have a privacy law as such. Case law protecting against infringed privacy mainly rests on the Fourth Amendment to the Constitution, as part of the Bill of Rights, which regulates search warrants and seizures. There are furthermore four privacy torts, among which intrusion. It is thus in conjunction with property law and the notion of trespassing that infringed privacy has been remedied in the past. Unsurprisingly, these legal instruments are ill-fitted to respond to the rapid, often unpredictable development of surveillance technologies and even more so to combat the automatic capture of immaterial big data. To complicate matters further, case law also relies on the so-called 'Katz test' that dates back to 1967, that is, the notion of 'reasonable expectation of privacy.' The formulation is fuzzy enough and judges have had to interpret what reasonableness is by drawing on customary law and cultural norms.

One can see why Orwell's novel on surveillance has been enlisted precisely to provide such cultural norms. Among the vast body of judicial quotations, I have selected three emblematic cases that reflect the challenges posed by evolving surveillance technologies. For instance, in *Florida v. Riley* (1989), the dissenting judge invokes Orwell's *Nineteen Eighty-Four* in order to argue against the use of low hovering helicopters used to check evidence for tipped illegal marijuana plantations without a search warrant. Justice Brennan indeed argues that such a practice would go against the Fourth Amendment in the following terms:

> I hope it will be a matter of concern to my colleagues that the police surveillance methods they would sanction were among those described 40 years ago in George Orwell's dread vision of life in the 1980's:
> 'The black-mustachio'd face gazed down from every commanding corner. There was one on the house front immediately opposite. BIG BROTHER IS WATCHING YOU, the caption said... In the far distance a helicopter skimmed down between the roofs, hovered for an instant like a bluebottle, and darted away again with a curving flight. It was the Police Patrol, snooping into people's windows' *Nineteen Eighty-Four* (1949). Who can read this passage without a shudder, and without the instinctive reaction that it depicts life in some country other than ours? I respectfully dissent.[3]

Justice Brennan's argument implies that Orwell's novel should function as a counter cultural norm that provides a vision of 'dread' and therefore defines what is unacceptable. He explicitly associates the iconic quote 'BIG BROTHER IS WATCHING YOU' with the low-hovering helicopters. The literal identity between the real American surveillance techniques and fictional totalitarian ones leads to an emotional calling into question of American national identity. If this dissenting opinion did not progress case law, it showcases how the Orwellian reference serves to measure how surveillance risks becoming dystopian.

Orwell was called upon by dissenting judges in another landmark Supreme court ruling, *United States v. Jones* (2012), which held that placing a GPS tracking device on a car without the permission of the owner who was suspected of drug trafficking constituted a search in line with the Fourth Amendment. In the case in particular, again the 'reasonableness' of the warrant was assessed in light of the Katz test. Although Orwell was not referenced in the ruling itself, records of oral argument show that *Nineteen Eighty-Four* served to voice deep concerns about a ruling that would potentially give free reign to unfettered surveillance. The oral argument expressed a need to avoid 'an omen of 1984' 'a 1984-type invasion' of privacy, 'the so-called 1984 scenarios', and the '1984 [M]inistry of [L]ove, [M]inistry of--of [P]eace problem' (Hu 2017: 1868). As Margaret Hu argues, *Nineteen Eighty-Four* here serves as a touchstone to define the limit of what a reasonable and acceptable level of surveillance is without intruding on private life. When alluding to the '1984 [M] inistry of [L]ove,[M]inistry of--of [P]eace problem', the dissenting voices also raise concerns about doublespeak, the fact that a supposed protective institution — or in the case of *Jones*, a protective Amendment — serves exactly the contrary purpose. References to Orwell here once more point to not only the gaps in a legal doctrine that fails to adequately safeguard privacy, but more problematically, to the fact that an amendment protective of privacy is being used to violate it.

It is only after the Edward Snowden revelations that *Nineteen Eighty-Four* is quoted by the majority opinion in ensuing cases for infringed privacy. *Klayman v. Obama* (2013) did set a precedent and declared that the bulk collection of data operated under the NSA's mass cyber-surveillance programme was unconstitutional. In this case, again the adjective 'Orwellian' functioned as a touchstone or limit to the reasonableness invoked in the Fourth Amendment and the Katz test. Judge Richard J. Leon argued indeed that the bulk collection of data, operated automatically unbeknownst to citizens represented an 'almost-Orwellian technology that enables the Government to store and analyse the phone metadata of every telephone user in the United States' (*Klayman v. Obama*). He further warns against the collection of medical data, arguing that 'future technological advances in DNA testing... may empower the government to conduct wide-ranging "DNA dragnets" that raise justifiable citations to George Orwell.' To conclude, he sees in the NSA programme an arbitrary violation of privacy rights at odds with the fundamental freedoms upheld in the Bill of Rights, and in particular the degree of privacy ensured by the Fourth Amendment. The judge further does away with the national security justifications offered by the government as no imminent attack was shown to have been averted.

In the three cases above, which broadly reflect the evolution of surveillance techniques from small to big data, judicial reference to Orwell is mostly formulaic, with the adjective emblematizing totalitarian surveillance. It thus serves as a normative value when the legal doctrine presents gaps. In particular it offers a limit against which to set the 'reasonable expectation of privacy' of the Katz test. Of course, this formulation remains problematic because society's expectations concerning their privacy vary with circumstances. In the immediate aftermath of 9/11, for instance, opinion polls showed that the privacy infringements that surveillance entailed were by and large approved of because the terrorist threat was then perceived as real. Yet by 2005, when illegal phone hacking by the government had been brought to light and the memory of 9/11 started to fade, this approval also waned (Westin 2006). But expectations of privacy also evolve according to the extent to which it is granted so that the Katz 'reasonableness' test is not only culturally bound but also represents a vicious circle: the less privacy granted — whether for supposed security reasons or not — the less privacy is expected. Legal scholars such as Margaret Hu have therefore argued that judicial references to Orwell not only point to the obsoleteness and lacunae of the privacy doctrine in the era of big data and mass surveillance, they are also called upon to provide a cultural norm in the light of which the constitutionality of mass cyber-surveillance is assessed (Hu 2017: 1896).

## 4. *Nineteen Eighty-Four*: Beyond Case Law

Coming back to my titular question, does this mean, however, that *Nineteen Eighty-Four*, as a novel, has legal authority? If so, in what ways and to what extent? Literary scholars within the Law and Literature movement have been keen to grant fiction the ability to provide a counter-legal norm. Yet when it comes to judicial quotation of Orwell in the context of cyber-surveillance, we find ourselves in the rather unusual case of legal scholars conferring upon such quotations a practical function, that of providing a limit for an obsolete 'Katz test' of what is reasonable in terms of privacy. However, the idea that citation has legal authority needs to be nuanced considerably. With *Klayman* v. *Obama* (2013), the Supreme Court declared mass cyber-surveillance unconstitutional. Yet, this precedent did not mean that the NSA programme became illegal or was scrapped. Indeed, the USA's constitutional organisation has a strict divide between the judiciary and the legislative. And if the Supreme Court ruling on *Klayman* v. *Obama* may have formed a precedent, it remains that the judge is not the legislator. Only the government or Congress have the power to vote on a bill to modify the NSA programmes. So in practice, if case law can now protect citizens or groups against state cyber-surveillance and offers remedy against infringed privacy, the NSA programme persists in its robust existence.

Moreover, as the judiciary's role is to rule whether surveillance practices are constitutional, the use of language in court is foremost factual and referential rather than metaphorical or associative. Legal language, which relies on all terms being narrowly defined, functions much like a mathematical language that aims for unambiguous precision. Ambiguities are indeed meant to be resolved in the light of general interpretation rules, specific clauses, or technical legal doctrine, even if admittedly absolute unambiguity is an ideal rather than a reality (Brooks 2016: 268). Unsurprisingly, judicial quotation of Orwell in surveillance cases is often reduced to an adjective that functions as a clichéd pointer to dystopian surveillance. It betrays how the judge still conceives of surveillance as impinged privacy, narrowly defined as an intrusion, physical and now digital, a form of trespassing. So what the judiciary fails to engage with are the consequences of impinged privacy that Orwell's novel so poignantly exposes and which come sharply into evidence when it is read against Foucault's panopticism: the loss of political autonomy and individual conscience and the very conditions that make such loss possible, i.e., doublespeak.

It may be useful to recall that Winston Smith is resisting the regime by attempting to preserve a reading and writing space, however limited. The novel's Appendix ends on a sombre note when Newspeak ultimately prevails and literature as a space of interpretative freedom has been killed off. I have pointed out how *Nineteen Eighty-Four* exposed much more than the perverse effects of surveillance and impinged privacy: the loss of individuality, autonomy, freedom of speech and freedom of thought, but also and crucially so the mechanism of panoptic power, the effectiveness of a fictitious relation with a fictitious gaze, the dehumanizing effect of bureaucracy that treats individuals as mere data, doublespeak, and the reversal of meaning. Those are the elements that make *Nineteen Eighty-Four* still relevant to understanding the power relations of our liberal system rather than just the totalitarian regimes in place when it was published. Admittedly, some such aspects have been pointed to by judicial reference, notably doublespeak (in *Steelworkers v. Weber* 1979).

But by and large, judicial reference has been oblivious to further implications of surveillance in *Nineteen Eighty-Four*. This is a pity because a dialogue between law and literature on the matter would have opened up a much-needed debate about ways of protecting citizens against new invisible power structures inherent in the use of social media, structures that are far more insidious than totalitarian control but act as efficiently. Within the context of automatic and anonymous data collection, the Orwellian reference may still serve as a cautionary tale against a dehumanising bureaucracy where humans are reduced to numbers, pixels, and data, which has led legal scholar Viktor Mayer-Shönberger to advocate the need to protect what he calls 'the sanctity of the individual' (Mayer-Shönberger and Cukier 2013: 17).

It is of course not the function of judicial reference to open up such debate, which belongs to the remit of legislators. Such dialogue has taken place within surveillance studies in its variegated guises and disciplinary crossings. In that respect, lawyers working for the legislative power would gain, as Peter Brooks (2016) and Martha Nussbaum (2005) have suggested, from departing from strictly legal modes of reading to adopting interdisciplinary ones, and to live up to the full freedom of interpretation that literary and particularly close reading invites us to.

By way of conclusion, I would like to return to the right to privacy that appears so fragile in the light of mass cyber-surveillance. Privacy has always been a slippery cultural construct and, as Ariès and Duby's monumental *History of Private Life* (Ariès and Duby 1985–1987) testify to, it varies across cultures and evolves over time, even if anthropologists have identified a number of practices pertaining to the private sphere that remain a constant (Westin 1967a: 8–23). It is worth recalling that the American notion of privacy is very much tied to the Lockean notion of property (Westin 1967b: 330–64). For that reason, perhaps the legal doctrine that rests on the Fourth Amendment, tort, and property law seems obsolete and powerless in the face of mass cyber-surveillance. For that matter, judicial quotation of Orwell reveals how judges remain attached to the notion of impinged privacy as mere intrusion. By contrast, European privacy doctrine has a very different historical tradition. It is true that the *Déclaration des droits de l'homme et du citoyen* of 1789 did not mention it as such but jurisprudence held that it was subsumed under the inalienable right to freedom (art. 2), freedom of religion (art. 10), and freedom of thought and expression (art. 11). Tellingly, historians such as Philippe Ariès and Roger Chartier have traced how, as a result of the Gutenberg revolution, access to reading rapidly democratised. From the Renaissance, by way of the Reformation through to the Enlightenment, reading freed itself from the orthodoxy of a communal, religious, and public practice to silent and independent reading. Self-expression through diaries and memoirs thus became immensely popular in the eighteenth century (Ariès 1986; Chartier 1986; Chartier and Cavallo 1997). Incidentally, in *Nineteen*

*Eighty-Four*, Winston's resistance takes the form of reading shielded from Big Brother's eye. It is no surprise then that the parallel development of privacy and independent reading resulted in privacy rights being subsumed under freedom of thought. It is only a century and half later, in the context of the Holocaust, that privacy rights were formalised in the Universal Declaration of Human Rights in December 1948 — a few months before Orwell published *Nineteen Eighty-Four* — and then again in the European Convention of Human Rights in 1950.

The above historical detour thus highlights how privacy rights and freedom of thought have gone hand in hand. As such, it might be useful to better understand to what extent judicial reference to Orwell in the context of mass cyber-surveillance raises questions as to how the inalienable right to privacy or individuality would need to be rethought in relation to freedom of thought. Possible debate may be helped by the complexities of Orwell's fiction. Indeed, judicial references as well as discussion within surveillance studies have focused mainly on privacy issues and tended to overlook one of Orwell's key concerns, expressed in *Nineteen Eighty-Four's* Appendix: the destruction of thought. For what the novel cogently dramatises is how both infringed privacy and the annihilation of thought through Newspeak and propaganda are mutually self-reinforcing. Legal criticism on surveillance also seems to dodge the question of panopticism and the internalising of mendacious discourses, phenomena that have wide currency in neoliberal democracies despite the deceitful plurality of press they offer. And indeed, it is no coincidence that the era of cyber-surveillance coincides with the era of post-truth which has been characterised by much greater manipulation of language in the political sphere. Peter Brooks recalls how what he calls the 'perversion' of language became institutionalised under the Bush administration in ways reminiscent of doublespeak (Brooks 2016: 268). (In the aftermath of the Iraq war, French fries infamously became Freedom fries; the Patriot Act, hastily passed after 9/11, legalised surveillance practices; while untitled in-house memos, now known as 'Torture Memos', authorised torture while bypassing democratic legislative approval in the name of national security.) Education sociologists have been quick to identify how cyber-surveillance and social media foster conformism, self-surveillance, the rejection of dissidence, and the willing surrender of privacy rights, with the ubiquitous posting of selfies being only a lesser manifestation of it (Giroux 2015: 108–40). Peter Brooks (2016) and Martha Nussbaum (2005) suggested that the lawyer has much to gain from opening up to literary reading, reading that is empathic and compassionate and attends to the full interdisciplinary and interpretative potential of a text. Perhaps this may be the beginning of an urgent debate on how to protect both freedom of thought and privacy rights threatened by mass cyber-surveillance.

## References

ARIÈS, PHILIPPE. 1986. 'Pour une histoire de la vie privée', in *Histoire de la vie privée*, ed. by Philippe Ariès and Georges Duby, vol. III, *De la Renaissance aux Lumières*, ed. by Roger Chartier (Paris: Seuil), pp. 7–19

ARIÈS, PHILIPPE and GEORGE DUBY (eds.). 1985–1987. *Histoire de la vie privée*. 5 vols (Paris: Seuil)

BADIOU, ALAIN. 2003. 'Dialectique de la fable', in *Matrix, machine philosophique*, by Alain Badiou, Thomas Bénatouil, Elie During et al. (Paris: Ellipses), pp. 120–29

BADINTER, ROBERT. 2000. *L'Abolition* (Paris: Fayard, 2000)

BROOKS, PETER. 2016. 'Law's resistance to literature', in *Translating the Social World for Law: Linguistic Tools for a New Legal Realism*, ed. by Elizabeth Mertz, William K. Ford, and Gregory Matoesian (New York: Oxford University Press), pp. 261–69

CHARTIER, ROGER. 1986. 'Introduction', in *Histoire de la vie privée*, ed. by Philippe Ariès and Georges Duby, III, *De la Renaissance aux Lumières*, ed. by Roger Chartier (Paris: Seuil), pp. 22–25

CHARTIER, ROGER and GUGLIELMO CAVALLO. 1997. 'Introduction', in *Histoire de la lecture dans le monde occidental*, ed. by Roger Chartier and Guglielmo Cavallo (Paris: Seuil), pp. 7–46

CROUCH, IAN. 2013. 'So Are We Living in 1984?', *The New Yorker*, 11 June. <https://www.newyorker.com/books/page-turner/so-are-we-living-in-1984> [accessed 11 July 2022]

DESTEFANO, JOHN M. 2007. 'On Literature as Legal Authority', *Arizona Law Review*, 49: 521–52

FOSTER, PETER. 2013. 'NSA Spying "Likely Unconstitutional" and "Orwellian", Judge Rules', *The Daily Telegraph*, 16 December. <https://www.telegraph.co.uk/news/worldnews/northamerica/usa/10521703/NSA-spying-likely-unconstitutional-and-Orwellian-judge-rules.html> [accessed 11 July 2022]

FOUCAULT, MICHEL. [1975] 1991. *Discipline and Punish*, trans. by Alan Sheridan (London: Penguin)

FOUCAULT, MICHEL. [1975] 2008. 'Panopticism', in *The Routledge Critical and Cultural Theory Reader*, ed. by Neil Badmington and Julia Thomas (London: Routledge), pp. 178–201

GEFEN, ALEXANDRE. 2013. 'Théorie du droit et théorie littéraire', in *Imaginaires Juridiques et poétiques littéraires*, ed. by Catherine Grall and Anne-Marie Luciani (Paris: Presses Universitaires de France), pp. 67–77

GIROUX, HENRY A. 2015. 'Totalitarian Paranoia in the Post-Orwellian Surveillance', *Cultural Studies*, 29 (2): 108–40.

HU, MARGARET. 2017. 'Orwell's 1984 and a Fourth Amendment Cyber-Surveillance Non-Intrusion Test', *Washington Law Review*, 92 (December): 1819–1904

LEFAIT, SÉBASTIEN. 2013. *Surveillance on Screen: Monitoring Contemporary Films and Television Programs* (Lanham, MD: Scarecrow Press)

LESSIG, LAWRENCE. 2005. 'On the Internet and Benign Invasions', in *On Nineteen Eighty-Four: Orwell and our Future*, ed. by Abbot Gleason and Martha C. Nussbaum (Princeton, NJ: Princeton University Press), pp. 212–20

LYON, DAVID. 1994. *The Electronic Eye: The Rise of Surveillance Society* (Minneapolis: University of Minnesota Press)

——. [2006] 2011. *Theorizing Surveillance: The Panopticon and Beyond* (London: Routledge)

——. 2015. *Surveillance after Snowden* (Cambridge: Polity)

MAYER-SHÖNBERGER, VIKTOR and KENNETH CUKIER. 2013. *Big Data: A Revolution that will Transform How We Live, Work and Think* (London: Houghton Mifflin Harcourt)

MORISI, EVE, ed. 2011. *Albert Camus contre la peine de mort*. Preface by Robert Badinter (Paris: Gallimard).

Nussbaum, Martha C. 2005. 'The Death of Pity: Orwell and American Political Life', in *On Nineteen Eighty-Four: Orwell and our Future*, ed. by Abbot Gleason and Martha C. Nussbaum (Princeton, NJ: Princeton University Press), pp. 280–99

———. 1995. *Poetic Justice: The Literary Imagination and Public Life* (Boston: Beacon Press)

Orwell, George. [1949] 2013. *Nineteen Eighty-Four* (London: Penguin Classics)

Posner, Richard A. [1988] 2009. 'On the Limits of Literary Jurisprudence', in *Law and Literature* (Cambridge, MA: Harvard University Press)

———. 2005. 'Orwell Versus Huxley: Economics, Technology, Privacy and Satire', in *On Nineteen Eighty-Four: Orwell and our Future*, ed. by Abbot Gleason and Martha C. Nussbaum (Princeton, NJ: Princeton University Press), pp. 183–211

Rusbridger, Alan. 2013. 'NSA Surveillance Goes Beyond Orwell's Imagination', *The Guardian*, 23 September. <https://www.theguardian.com/world/2013/sep/23/orwell-nsa-surveillance-alan-rusbridger> [accessed 11 July 2022]

Simonin, Anne. 2007. 'Éloge de l'éclectisme : Penser le champ 'Droit et Littérature' à partir des listes de *Legal Novels* (1900–1987)', in *Textyles*, 31: 12–27

Weisberg, Richard H. 2009. 'Wigmore and the Law and Literature Movement', in *Law and Literature*, 21 (1): 129–45.

Westin, Alan F. 1967a. 'The Origins of Modern Claims to Privacy', in *Privacy and Freedom* (New York: Atheneum), pp. 8–23

———. 1967b. 'Privacy and American Law', in *Privacy and Freedom* (New York: Atheneum), pp. 330–64

———. 2006. 'How the Public sees the Security vs Liberty Debate', in *Protecting What Matters: Technology, Security, and Liberty since September 11* (Washington, DC: Computer Ethics Institute), pp. 19–41

Wigmore, John H. 1922. 'A List of One Hundred Legal Novels', *Illinois Law Review*, 17 (1): 26–41

Žižek, Slavoj. 2014. 'Surveillance and Whistleblowers', interview with Paul Holdengraber, International Authors' Stage, The Royal Library, Copenhagen, online video recording, *YouTube*, 19 May, <https://www.youtube.com/watch?v=PIPjmmmh_0s> [accessed 29 June 2022]

## Notes to Chapter 13

1. 'While *Nineteen Eighty-Four* has in many ways been superseded technologically, limited but important aspects of its account of a surveillance society still remain relevant today.'
2. See Lessig (2005), who does not discuss panopticism either. By and large, discussion of Orwell and panopticism within literary and surveillance studies has focused on new forms of power and compliance rather than on the articulation of privacy and freedom of thought.
3. Florida v. Riley, 488 U.S. 445 (1989), Page 488 U.S. 467.

CHAPTER 14

# Legal Revolutions as Fictions: Do they Change the World?

*Otto Pfersmann*

*École des Hautes Études en Sciences Sociales (EHESS)/Lier-FYT*

Legal systems seem *in a way* to be part of the objective world. They contain norms which are applied by courts or administrative agencies through decisions that have a very concrete impact on their addressees. Changes within a legal system may have a highly important incidence on those concerned, precisely because their 'legal situation' is changed. Changing the legal system *itself* through a set of revolutionary actions imposing a new order is generally seen as a set of events having the highest and most radical impact on people's lives. My claim, however, is that the element changing the real world can never be found in law itself, but rather resides in cognitive and practical attitudes related to merely fictional data — and that legal scholarship is perfectly unable to explain what *really* happens in such situations.[1] The reason lies in the normative nature of legal enactments and in particular in cases of legal discontinuity. Legal scholarship may explain such ruptures, but it is unable, when done seriously, to explain what happens in the world as it is. Developing this proposition requires looking first into revolutions as they seem to evolve in the real world (I), then into the nature of revolutions as specifically legal data (II). It will appear that what really happens is only indirectly related to legal discontinuity.

## 1. Events Reshaping the Real World

Revolutions are by standard understanding the most visible and violent changes a society may possibly undergo. And, still by standard understanding, such events happen in the real world. So, by definition and by hypothesis, if something is a revolution, then it has a relatively strong modifying impact on society, changing power relations and wealth distribution, but also the relevant conceptions of legitimacy determining these situations. Conceptually, it seems difficult to conceive of revolutions without any such large-scale turmoil in power relations, wealth distribution and modes of life.

This is what is usually invoked and represented when one thinks of revolutionary events: the assault on the Bastille, the storm of the Winter Palace in St. Petersburg, the decapitation of Louis XVI and a large part of the former elites, battles between competing factions, Bonaparte's violent intrusion into the Counsel of the Five-Hundreds, the delegates of the Second Continental Congress drafting and signing the Declaration of Independence, etc. But revolutions are not just events; a change of the relevant amplitude takes time and quite often it is difficult to say when such a modification starts and when it finishes. In their Declaration of 15 December 1799, the new Consuls stated, that 'the Revolution is bound to the principles by which it started, it is now finished',[2] but this proposition may have come too late or too early. A great deal of literature has been devoted to the question as to when this set of events really started and really ended, and if one certainly identifies particular events as belonging clearly to the core of the French Revolution, the debate concerning beginning and conclusion may simply be devoid of any clear-cut conclusion and perhaps simply of relevance.[3] In this sense, Revolution is a typically vague concept with a core meaning and unclear limits. The core meaning, however, turns around the fact that from the beginning to the end important changes occur in a given society and that these sets of events are by no means fictional.[4]

There may be, and there are, quite a lot of references to revolutionary events in fiction, and fiction may reframe the events in various narratives, romances, drama, films, games, and whatever media would be deemed appropriate. But revolutions in fiction are not real revolutions, except if some fictional work having a revolution as its subject matter were itself to be considered revolutionary in terms of its literary quality, but this is a different question and if that happens, it is still seen as an event in the real world, as would be the case for revolutions in other domains: science, the arts, behaviour, and customs, etc.

Some kinds of revolutions may be less noticeable than others as their identification requires possibly a certain expertise shared by only a small part of a given population. However, even metaphorically, it would seem conceptually inappropriate to talk about a revolution if there were strictly no set of events resulting in an important change in the relevant domain. And the metaphorical valence of the use of the concept in a domain different from politics in the largest acceptation resides precisely, or so it seems, in the fact that something similar to a political and social upheaval happens somewhere in the real world. The same criterion would evidently apply to revolutions in fiction, the fictional plausibility of which largely rests on their capacity to evoke a world outside the real world.

The problem to be raised here appears when we are asking ourselves which kinds of events we would consider as belonging to revolutions in the real world and in their core domain, namely political, social, and economic modifications of major magnitude as well as in the way of life within a given society. Quite often, it is less clear than ordinary understanding might suggest, and sometimes factual observation is unable to explain revolutionary events. On these we shall focus.

In many instances of developments usually qualifying as revolutions, the intent and scope of actions leading to upheaval is not simply enacted through physical violence, but also expressed through language in documents of high symbolic value, history referring to these as significant moments constituting the core events of these changes. The indictment of Charles the First (see Gardiner 1906, 371), the

British Bill of Rights, the American Declaration of Independence,[5] the French Tennis Court Oath of 20 June 1789,[6] the various declarations of the Petrograd Workers Soviet after the takeover of strategic institutions in November 1917[7] are typical examples of such acts by which a former legal order or some of its aspects, or at least certain of its implementations, is declared illegitimate and to be replaced either by something radically different, or by the return to something lost but to be more clearly established.[8]

The general view concerning these objects is that they played an important part in the course of events. Hence history retains them as relevant when qualifying a development as revolutionary. So does political science and quite often legal scholarship too. With all the difficulties in identifying a set of events as belonging to a revolutionary development, it may so far seem plausible to admit that within its very core one can find documents in which the scope of a contestation of legitimacy and the claim to an alternative legitimacy are forcefully outlined. Second, it can be plausibly admitted that some of these documents exercised a significant impact on the agents of the upheaval and that this element makes them indeed important causal factor in the real world and real history.

Some such documents continue to exercise such an influence. Suffice it to think of the status of the Declaration of Independence in present-day America or of the *Déclaration des droits de l'homme et du citoyen* (Declaration of the Rights of Man and the Citizen) in France.

All these elements taken together, we can admit so far: a) that revolutions happen in the real world — even though they may be subject matters of fictions; b) they consist of major changes in the distribution of power, wealth and in the ways of life; c) they consist of developments including events in which the main actors of the process express their aims and visions in declarations or other documents; d) these expressions constitute significant elements in the causal chain of events and are recorded as such in all fields of knowledge and communication related to the study as well as to a contemporary use of these statements. The facts that these texts were written and read are events, but their normative meanings are not.

This can be termed the thesis of revolution as originating in the real world. The fact that revolutions may and do appear in fiction does by no means weaken this thesis. When fiction refers to real or fictitious revolutions, i.e., when there is revolution in fiction, the author presents a development which answers the same properties in fiction, as with other kinds of events happening in fictional worlds and conceived with concepts referring to objects and events of the actual world, notwithstanding all possible narrative varieties in which such events would then be inserted.

## 2. Where Revolutions Really Happen

The problem with the revolution as originating-in-the-real-world-thesis is that it is misleading or at least insufficiently differentiated with respect to the nature of what is considered significant and constitutive of the meaning of a revolutionary development.

At this point, we may revert to the conceptual question as to what we would consider the core elements of a revolution. If we content ourselves with violent struggles, power relations, possession of goods and concrete ways of life in the meaning of behavioural observations, we may certainly gain important insights into the mechanisms of triggering conflicts, but we would not be able to integrate the elements, for instance, of the French Declaration into our inquiry or we could only retain those aspects which are strictly related to the exercise of effective power. But the interesting property of such documents, although being uttered in the real world and referred to as such, is that they are not related to the concrete exercise of effective power — but to statements as to how power should or may be or may not be exercised. They don't produce in and of themselves a different kind of behaviour. And quite often this was not even intended or foreseen. Sometimes it was thought to state simply the obvious. As norms are meanings of statements requiring that certain actions be performed, they are not themselves performing any action.

Let us take a few examples. The act known as the Tennis Court Oath or Oath of the *Jeu de Paume* or of real tennis (with respect to present-day lawn tennis) is related to an intimidation of the deputies of the Third State who found their meeting hall closed on 20 June 1789, then decided to meet in the neighbouring Tennis Hall where they famously promised not to separate until the Constitution of the Kingdom had been established. An oath is a normative act, a constitution is a set of norms concerning the production of other norms (at least this was what the Third Estate wanted to achieve: establish norms according to which competences to set laws, by-laws or judgements would have to be exercised). But neither oaths, nor constitutions — in this meaning — are facts or events, precisely because they are *normative* data and because such data as meanings of statements are not acts, the only acts being letters on paper or parchment, or words uttered in assemblies. What happened here, if something happened — and apparently something important happened — is in two ways related to something else then the real world.

The first aspect concerns the very fact that norms state that a certain set of actions ought to be realised or is authorised to be realised, not that such facts are effectively realised. Talking of such entities as if they were indeed to be followed requires that they be considered existing, even though they have no more existence than the utterance of the words. This point is highly contentious in theories of norms where two main models are in discussion. For the one mainly admitted in the English-speaking world, the highest norms, which have as their object precisely the identification, modification, and application of other norms, form a master-rule of recognition handled by the highest organic charges in a given system.[9] The other theory considers the ultimate origin of normativity as pertaining to fiction.[10] The Oath example shows, I contend, that the rule of recognition model does not work well in this, or in other cases. It indeed supposes a kind of soft continuity in the behaviour of those already in charge of setting norms at the highest level. But first, how do we know why and who those persons effectively are if we do not rely on facts of power — and doing so would be stepping outside the normative domain. But second, this model can hardly work when opposing claims to validity are at stake. And third in our concrete case, the deputies promise something which is precisely not recognised by those in the highest charge of norm-making. On 23 June, Louis XVI quashed all decisions taken by the Third Estate as unconstitutional. The Third Estate resisted, and Louis XVI finally admonished the Three Estates to join with the Third in common meetings on 27 June.

Now the very object of the Oath is the 'establishment of the Constitution of the Kingdom'. This can be understood in different ways. It may mean that the Constitution already exists and has only to be written down in order to exclude any doubt concerning its very content. This was most probably the understanding of many members of this first 'Constituent Assembly' as it later labelled itself. The other understanding would be that the Constituent Assembly drafts an entirely new Constitution from scratch. This is what was finally achieved by the rather short-lived Constitution of 1791, which lasted not quite one year — two years of drafting, one year of living — but again as a normative document. If one adopts the latter reading then one has indeed to suppose that something like the norms contained in the document named 'Constitution of 1791', had been valid as a normative order.

Interestingly, both readings seem to be present in the days of the Constituent Assembly. One can see this most clearly in another document which remains valid, we must suppose again, through the most confusing technicalities of French constitutional law, since we consider, still, that some such thing effectively exists. This document is the *Déclaration des droits de l'homme et du citoyen*, the Declaration of the Rights of Man (meaning human beings) and Citizen, which the Assembly elaborates until 26 August 1789. Again, the work of the Assembly is considered by many of its most active members a formulation of something, which exists in and of itself.

This shows the stronghold of theories of natural law even on those who made a legal system entirely different from the one hitherto existing. And this text, placed as a preamble before the Constitution of 1791 in fact had no real normative force, even though it was conceived of and drafted in normative terms. As a document stating the obvious, it was not considered to need any enforcement mechanism and certainly not against the new legislator who claims to express the voice of the nation itself. How indeed could such an organ possibly contain anything else then making concrete what the declaration promises as obvious?

We can take another example from the American experience, the longest seemingly in continuity since the eighteenth century. The American federal Constitution dates back to 1787 and is revered in the public as a nearly sacred document, beyond all partisan rivalries. But why should it be valid? And does it really exist in any continuity? The first question is not as simple as it seems. Certainly, the federal Constitution is elaborated and enacted against the clear exigencies of the then valid Articles of Confederation. If those were valid it was by fiction, and the Constitution could only be valid by an opposing fiction, finally shared by many, despite a fierce opposition by anti-federalists, which seems often forgotten in present-day scholarship. However, what is exactly valid under such a supposition? For instance, the Constitution doesn't say anything about constitutional review. All modern constitutions spell out rather precisely whether an organ, and if so, which one, may be entitled to annul formal primary legislation and which effects such annulment would have on the provisions so quashed. There is nothing concerning this rather fundamental question to be found in the American Constitution, the system which it instituted being nonetheless regarded as the inventor, first working example and model — i.e., the American model — of constitutional review. So, where does this judicial competence come from? It is often stated that the Court established it with its seminal decision *Marbury* v. *Madison* in 1803,[11] but a decision can hardly establish the competence which grants it its specific validity. Second, the American Constitution states that it can be amended according to a specific and rather difficult procedure. This is now fairly common in nearly all existing formalised constitutions. But in fact, some main amendments have not, it seems, been adopted according to this procedure, i.e., the civil war amendments putting an end to slavery and establishing a constitutional principle of equality among citizens of the United States.[12] If this reading is right, then there is obviously no continuity. But third, there is ongoing debate in American legal scholarship as to whether amendments are really binding and as to whether the Constitution cannot be modified by other means than this formal, all-too-difficult procedure. And fourth, it often happens that Supreme Court decisions do not exactly fit the exigencies of the text of the Constitution, developing rights the Constitution does not grant, providing powers, for instance to the President, to which this organ is not formally entitled, limiting other rights which may on the contrary seem protected. In other words, there is a highly paradoxical situation in which a normative text is revered as nearly sacred, but is constantly violated and possibly does not even constitute the text of the real Constitution, pushing for instance one author, a famous Harvard Law professor, to promote an *invisible Constitution* instead of the still readable document (see Tribe 2008). In this situation, it is probably not surprising that the debates are less concerned with a methodology for understanding this document than with the partisan question of who will be nominated to the Court.

This is the state of the debate, turning on entirely incompatible positions with reference to the same supposed entity, the Constitution of the United States. It raises the question as to what an uninvolved observer could tell about the United States, as the United States are by their very name a legal entity. The debates are dramatically real and the conflicts concerning these questions escalate at any new occasion.

Let us take another astonishing case: Germany. After the disasters of the Second World War, Germany made a new start by adopting the *Grundgesetz* or Basic Law entering into force on 24 May 1949. But as the name indicates, the *Grundgesetz* should not be a Constitution, as it was thought that the Reich still existed and that the Weimar Constitution had never been formally abrogated. Two theses were and are still proposed concerning this question: according to a view elaborated by Hans Kelsen, the Reich ceased legally to exist with the Unconditional Surrender of 8 May 1945 (Kelsen 1944 and 1945); according to the opposing view taken by the majority of German constitutional scholars, the Reich did not cease to exist, but lost its capacity to act. Even the German Federal Constitutional Court took this view in a famous decision dated 31 July 1973.[13] This debate confuses, in my view, two highly distinct questions. One problem is the continuity of the legal entity 'Germany' bearing rights and duties in public international law. Another question is the continuity of the German Constitution. It can be retained for certain that the Basic Law of 1949 has not been produced and adopted in accordance with the relevant rules of the Weimar Constitution of 1919. However one may think about the continuity of the Reich as a subject of public international law, the *Grundgesetz* creates a new legal order from scratch, not foreseen by any previous provision of the formerly valid Constitution. But then the question is until what point this formerly valid Constitution was really valid. And next, it appears that the enactment of the *Grundgesetz* was legally preceded by acts of the Allied powers and the Länder. After the London Conference of 1948, the Prime ministers of the western Länder were handed a First Document calling on them to establish a new federal state. Neither this act, nor the following convocation of a Parliamentary Council in Bonn, was foreseen by any previous legal norm — except for, precisely, the Unconditional Surrender, without which the Western Allies could not have empowered the Prime Ministers to start a constitutional procedure.[14]

Germany remembers the hundred years of the Weimar Constitution and the seventy years of the Basic Law. The Weimar Constitution is commonly considered a revolutionary act with respect to the Constitution of the then existing German Empire. But when does Weimar cease to exist? And is the Basic Law assumed as a revolutionary act or the concretisation of a previous revolutionary act? Or, is it, on the contrary, considered that there is a continuity from Weimar to the Nazi constitution, from there to Unconditional Surrender and from there to the Basic law? Can one really sustain that Germany has not known any revolution since 1919? But again, as in other countries, the Constitutional Court considered it its duty to discreetly restate the Constitution rather than to simply implement it. If this were indeed the case, then there would be another kind of revolution and the question is: to what extent would we be admitting such events as constituting a development answering the conceptual requirements of a revolution?

Another example may make the case more visible. The French constitutional laws of 1875 take their origin in the revolutionary overturning of the Second Empire after the battle of Sedan and the proclamation of the Republic on 4 September 1870. It would thus be an error to make the so-called Third Republic start in 1875. But when does the Third Republic exactly end? One usually thinks and generally reads that it was 28 October 1946, with the promulgation of the Constitution of the 'Fourth Republic'. But this Republic in fact starts much earlier, and in a somewhat surprising way. Indeed, the provisional Government of the French Republic, victorious in its fight against the Vichy Government, proclaimed on 9 August 1944 that the Republic had never ceased to exist.[15] If this were legally correct, then the Third Republic still existed (on this day of 1944) and its rules had to be obeyed. However, the Government called for elections on 5 October 1945 and asked whether the so elected Assembly should be 'constituent'. But this is not foreseen by the Constitution of 1875, and therefore the Fourth Republic starts in October

1945 with a legal revolution of the Government that claims to restore republican legality.

The Fifth Republic is generally considered to be the legal order that succeeds the Constitution of 1946. However, the Constitution of 4 October 1958 is a revision of the Constitution of 1946, thus there is continuity tracing back to 1945. But then, in 1962, de Gaulle called for a referendum in order to change the rule governing the election of the President of the Republic. The legal problem is that this referendum is not foreseen in the rule of constitutional revision (which would require a previous vote of the two Chambers on an identical text). Thus, there is discontinuity as of 1962 and the legal Fifth Republic starts only then.

But again, on 16 July 1971, the Constitutional Council reviews a law with respect to the preamble of the Constitution and all the texts to which the Preamble refers,[16] although the Preamble had been clearly excluded from any reference in constitutional review in 1958; hence the Declaration of 1789, the paradigm of the French Revolution, has existed legally only for 49 years. Thus there is a rupture in continuity which goes entirely unnoticed until the decisions of the Constitutional Council exceed a certain threshold in making the Declaration prevail on statutes adopted by both Chambers of Parliament. These events of 1971 were totally deprived of any violence, even verbally.

Many years after the decision handed down in 1971, legal scholars started to call it 'revolutionary', but stated at the same time that it only gave voice to something already present but not really visible to lawyers trained in the spirit of the Third and Fourth Republics. Is this something like a retrospective revolution?[17]

A case of prospective revolution can probably be found in Israel. The Constituent Knesset elected after Independence did not draft a Constitution, but declared instead all subsequent Knessetim to be also constituent and that the Constitution would be drafted in chapters. Legal scholarship then engages in a campaign asking for a 'constitutional revolution' (Barak 1993; Navot and Peled 2009) and finally the Supreme Court, strictly not entitled to review legislation — it would be difficult in the absence of a clearly formalised Constitution — states that it has indeed the duty to control formal legislation against the hitherto enacted fundamental laws.[18] This can again be understood in different manners. Either one admits that from that point on the Court has indeed the competence to review legislation and the fundamental laws indeed form a formal Constitution, then this act certainly introduces a discontinuity in the system. Or one takes the view, with the Court, that it is a duty of any Supreme court to be the Supreme court in a clear-cut constitutional system where it is in and of itself the duty and competence of such a court to control the formal primary legislator. But if so, then there would be no discontinuity, let alone anything revolutionary.

In all these various cases, we find events leading to the drafting of texts the meaning of which is not entirely understandable without reference to fiction — i.e., the fiction, that prescriptive sentences are objectively valid norms and not mere utterances of private individuals — providing normative validity to a set of provisions aiming at setting how future developments should be settled in avoidance of conflict. On some occasions, they accompany developments qualifying as revolutionary; sometimes the application of the concept may be questionable, sometimes strictly counterfactual. What they all do have in common is one or another variety of normative discontinuity.

These and similar events may be termed revolutions-originating-in-fiction. The real world may be peaceful and continuous, it may be in turmoil and upheaval, it may take notice and refer in conflict to these documents, or conflicts may evolve without any effective mention of such expressions. As normative orders exist by virtue of fiction — the fiction that the statement that something ought to be performed is considered as binding, whereas it has not and cannot have any causal impact whatsoever — the only thing which makes a difference does not lie in the norms, but in the attitude the addressees take towards such statements, whether related to old traditions or to newly and surreptitiously imposed claims to validity. To put it in other words: there is no difference between 'established' or not-established norms, because norms exist only by virtue of fiction and cannot be established, except by other norms (a Constitution can establish the validity of ordinary legislation, but a Constitution is a paramount fiction insofar as it is a normative statement).

My point is then the following: first, one has to distinguish changes in power relations, economic wealth and ways of life from their normative framing and the question of its continuity. Constitutions, well or badly drafted, do not in and of themselves change powers and lives; effective modifications in real life may happen completely besides or outside a constitutional framing. As far as this is concerned, the question as to whether there is continuity or discontinuity cannot be settled without fictional elements (the fiction that a new normative order is in place or the fiction that a previous normative order is still in place, while most people seem to follow a different way of acting) and thus with the help of theories promoting a better knowledge of legal ruptures. They may be *legally* violent, when the departure from the hitherto existing setting is beyond any doubt, they may be *legally* soft, when measures operating normative discontinuity are taken in order to make these events less clearly, if at all visible — which doesn't make them less legally vicious.

All of this happens, however, outside the empirically observable world. What happens within this world is the way people do *refer* to these events and settings. And this may be subject to the most opposing varieties. Legal normativity may be ignored, falsely sacralised while effectively violated, slavishly followed, or explicitly challenged, openly asked to be overturned while largely implemented within the same organic structures, and so forth.

In order to study these developments, one has to acquire the relevant knowledge of inner-legal events, which can sometimes raise, as our examples amply show, daunting interpretative challenges. But without understanding that the law does not change the world in and of itself, but only its own inner structure which it sometimes simply destroys, one will have difficulties identifying beliefs, attitudes, or social movements referring to these strictly normative data. And one may have difficulties distinguishing attitudes, beliefs, and acts that effectively refer to *legally* normative elements from others, where reference points to other normative settings, like *moral* extra-legal beliefs or political activism.

## References

ACKERMAN, BRUCE. 2000. *We the People*, II: *Transformations* (Cambridge, MA: Harvard University Press)

ALEXY, ROBERT. 2009. *The Argument from Injustice: A Reply to Legal Positivism*, trans. by Stanley Paulson and Bonnie Paulson (Oxford: Oxford University Press)

'Assemblée nationale'. 1789. 'Procès-verbal de la séance de l'assemblée tenue dans la salle du Jeu de paume le 20 juin 1789, suivi du serment dit du Jeu de paume', Paris, Archives nationales, AE.I.5.3bis <http://www2.culture.gouv.fr/public/mistral/caran_fr?ACTION=RETROUVER&FIELD_98=MOTS%2dMAT&VALUE_98=%20Etats%20g%e9n%e9raux%20de%201789%20&NUMBER=13&GRP=0&REQ=%28%28Etats%20g%e9n%e9raux%20de%201789%29%20%3aMOTS%2dMAT%20%29&USRNAME=nobody&USRPWD=4%24%2534P&SPEC=&SYN=1&IMLY=&MAX1=1&MAX2=1&MAX3=100&DOM=All> [accessed December 2019]

BARAK, AHARON. 1993. 'A Constitutional Revolution: Israel's Basic Laws', Faculty Scholarship Series, Yale Law School, paper 3697 <http://digitalcommons.law.yale.edu/fss_papers/3697> [accessed 29 June 2022]

BENEDICT, MICHAEL LES. 1999. 'Constitutional History and Constitutional Theory: Reflections on Ackerman, Reconstruction, and the Transformation of the American Constitution', *Yale Law Journal*, 108: 2011–38

BONE, ANN. 1974. *The Bolsheviks and the October Revolution: Central Committee Minutes of the Russian Social-Democratic Labour Party (Bolsheviks) August 1917–February 1918* (London: Pluto Press)

BRÉGEON, JEAN-JOËL. 2011. *Écrire la Révolution française : Deux siècles d'historiographie* (Paris: Ellipses)

BUNYAN, JAMES, and HAROLD HENRY FISHER. 1934. *The Bolshevik Revolution, 1917–1918: Documents and Materials* (Palo Alto, CA: Stanford University Press)

CONSEIL CONSTITUTIONNEL. 1971. 'Decision no. 71-44 DC of 16 July 1971', English version, *Journal officiel*, 18 July 1971, p. 7114 <https://www.conseil-constitutionnel.fr/en/decision/1971/7144DC.htm> [accessed 20 December 2019]

DWORKIN, RONALD. 1999. *Freedom's Law: The Moral Reading of the American Constitution* (Oxford: Oxford University Press)

FURET, FRANÇOIS. 1978. *Penser la Révolution française* (Paris: Gallimard)

FURET, FRANÇOIS and DENIS RICHET. 1965. *La Révolution française* (Paris: Larousse)

GARDINER, SAMUEL RAWSON, ed. 1906. *The Constitutional Documents of the Puritan Revolution, 1625–1660* (Oxford: Clarendon Press)

*Gazette nationale ou le Moniteur universel*. 1789. 20 June.

*Gazette nationale ou le Moniteur universel*. 1799. 16 December.

GOUVERNEMENT PROVISOIRE DE LA RÉPUBLIQUE FRANÇAISE. 1944. 'Ordonnance du 9 août 1944 relative au rétablissement de la légalité républicaine sur le territoire continental', *Légifrance* <https://www.legifrance.gouv.fr/affichTexte.do?cidTexte=LEGITEXT000006071212> [accessed 29 June 2022]

HARRISON, JOHN. 2001. 'The Lawfulness of the Reconstruction Amendments', *The University of Chicago Law Review*, 68: 375–462

HARTS, HERBERT. 1961. *Concept of Law* (Oxford: Clarendon Press)

KELSEN, HANS. 1944. 'The International Legal Status of Germany to be Established Immediately Upon Termination of the War', *The American Journal of International Law*, 38: 689–94

——. 1945. 'The Legal Status of Germany According to the Declaration of Berlin', *The American Journal of International Law*, 39: 518–26

——. 1991. *General Theory of Norms*, trans. by Michael Hartney (Oxford: Clarendon Press), originally published as *Allgemeine Theorie der Normen* (Vienna: Manz, 1979)

MICHELET, JULES. (1847–1853) 1939. *Histoire de la révolution française*, ed. by Gérard Walter (Paris: Gallimard)
MUSSGNUG, REINHARD. 2003. 'Zustandekommen des Grundgesetzes und Entstehen der Bundesrepublik Deutschland', in *Handbuch des Staatsrechts der Bundesrepublik Deutschland: Historische Grundlagen*, 1, ed. by Josef Isensee and Paul Kirchhof (Munich: Beck), pp. 315–54
NAVOT, DORON and YOAV PELED. 2009. 'Towards a Constitutional Counter-Revolution in Israel?', *Constellations*, 16 (3): 429–44
PFERSMANN, OTTO. 1995. 'Pour une typologie modale de classes de validité normative', *La Querelle des normes — Hommage à Georg Henrik von Wright*, ed. by Jean-Luc Petit, *Cahiers de philosophie politique et juridique de l'Université de Caen*, 27: 69–113
——. 2019A. 'Comparative Hermeneutics of Constitutional Revision Clauses and the Question of Structural Closure of Legal Systems', *Cardozo Law Review*: 3191–3216
——. 2019B. 'Révolutions constitutionnelles, analyses doctrinales et justifications jurisprudentielles', in *Émergences de nouveaux modèles de démocratie constitutionnelle Afrique, Proche-Orient*, ed. by Patrick Charlot, and Claude Klein, Collection Néo-rétro constitutionnalisme (Paris: Mare & Martin), pp. 29–51
RITZ, WILFRED J. 1986. 'The Authentication of the Engrossed Declaration of Independence on July 4, 1776', in *Law and History Review*, 4: 179–204
——. 1992. 'From the *Here* of Jefferson's Handwritten Rough Draft of the Declaration of Independence to the *There* of the Printed Dunlap Broadside', in *Pennsylvania Magazine of History and Biography*, 116: 499–512
SOBOUL, ALBERT. 1981. *Comprendre la Révolution* (Paris: Maspero)
TRIBE, LAURENCE H. 2008. *The Invisible Constitution* (Oxford: University Press)
TOCQUEVILLE, ALEXIS DE. (1856) 1986. *L'Ancien Régime et la Révolution* (Paris: Gallimard)
TSESIS, ALEXANDER. 2012. *For Liberty and Equality: The Life and Times of the Declaration of Independence* (Oxford: Oxford University Press)
VILLANI, GIOVANNI. (1348) 1991. *Nuova Cronica*, ed. by Giovanni Porta (Parma: Fondazione Pietro Bembo, Ugo Guanda Editore)

## Notes to Chapter 14

1. Norms are the meaning of statements that certain actions *ought* to be performed (or that they are authorised or prohibited). 'Law' stands here for an organised set of explicitly stated norms presenting a certain degree of efficacy and comprehending mechanisms of enforcement in case obligations set forth in the first place are not complied with. As used in the present paper, it excludes mere moral norms as well as facts (of compliance or non-compliance). Such systems are made up of a variety of norm-types defined by the system itself (constitutional law, ordinary legislation, executive orders, judicial decisions and so on). The exact nature of norms and especially *legal* norms as retained here constitutes the main object of debate in legal theory. Some authors, like Ronald Dworkin (1999) in the American literature on the subject, or Robert Alexy (2009) in Germany, try to show that Law contains moral elements, whereas other schools (dubbing themselves 'realists') claim that Law is nothing else than certain specific social facts. The position retained here is opposed to both moralist and factualist conceptions of *legal norms*. It sees them as stating that something *ought* to be performed (or is authorised or prohibited from being performed) (see e.g., Pfersmann 1995). Norms are not interpretations, but their formulation requires interpretation.
2. This is at least the vision purported in the Proclamation by the Consuls of the Republic from Frimaire 24 year VIII: 'Citoyens, la Révolution est fixée aux principes qui l'ont commencée: elle est finie.' *Gazette nationale ou le Moniteur universel* (1799, 1).
3. Since the days of the Revolution, there has been a heated debate concerning its timeline and nature: is there a revolution before the Estates-General are convened, is there a first revolution, ended by the Terror or is the Terror an indivisible part of the Revolution, where exactly does the

Revolution come to an end etc. See for instance Michelet ([1847–53] 1939); Tocqueville [1856] 1986) Furet and Ricet (1965) and Furet (1978), Soboul (1981). These controversies concerning both the nature and timeline of the French Revolution are presented and discussed in Brégeon (2011).
4. This is at least the idea already expressed in the *Nuova Cronica,* written during the first half of the fourteenth century by the Florentine historian Giovanni Villani, whose thirteenth book begins with the following observation: 'Here we should begin the thirteenth book, as the style of our treatise requires; because it is new matter, and great changes and different revolutions occurred during this time in our city of Florence due to our discord between citizens as well as the bad regime of the Twenty Officials, as already mentioned; and these things were so many, that I the author, who was present, doubt that our successors will believe it to be true; and yet it all happened just as we will say below' (translated by Alison James and Otto Pfersmann). ('Convienne cominciare il XIII libro, però che richiede lo stile del nostro trattato; perch'è nuova materia, e grandi mutazioni e diverse rivoluzioni avennero in questi tempi alla nostra città di Firenze per le nostre discordie tra' cittadini, e male reggimento de' XX uficiali, come adietro fatto avemo menzione; e fieno sì diverse, ch'io autore, che fui presente, mi fa dubitare che per li nostri successori apena fieno credute di vero; e fu pur così, come diremo apresso.') ([1348] 1991: 291)
5. The Declaration, aimed at *performing* independence, had obviously no previously defined legal status, even after being printed under the supervision of Jefferson and sent to the states. Even though its language and political thought may still be of influence, it is not quoted by any presently valid constitutional document (See for instance Ritz 1986 and 1992; Tsesis 2012).
6. See 'Assemblée nationale' (1789). However, the fact that the document is conserved in archives does not confer it any particular *legal* status.
7. The October Revolution is particularly interesting in this respect as even the purportedly legal decrees (on peace, on land, and on the election of a constituent assembly) are in fact overturned by the decree on transfer of power to the soviets. See Bunyan and Fisher (1934); Bone (1974).
8. The Tennis Court Oath, stating 'We swear never to separate ourselves from the National Assembly, and to reassemble wherever circumstances require until the constitution of the realm is drawn up and fixed upon solid foundations' (*Gazette nationale ou le Moniteur universel* 1789, 1), can be interpreted as meaning that the Constitution already exists, but has to be 'fixed'. The *Déclaration des droits de l'homme et du citoyen* (Declaration of the Rights of Man and Citizen) seems even more committed to mainly set forth in writing something which already exists.
9. This is the view famously presented in Harts (1961).
10. This view was first developed by Hans Kelsen (1991).
11. U.S. Reports: *Marbury v. Madison,* 5 U.S. (1 Cranch) 137 (1803).
12. See Ackerman (2000), and Harrison (2001). Benedict (1999) urges a historicisation of constitutional interpretation in the wake of Ackerman's theory. Against historicisation of *legal* analysis and especially Ackerman's approach, see Pfersmann (2019a).
13. BVerfGE 36, 1–37 (LT1–9). Its main statement concerning the legal existence of the German Reich is the following: 'It is maintained (cf. e.g., BVerfG, 1956–08–17, 1 BvB 2/51, BVerfGE 5, 85 <126>), that the German Reich has survived the breakdown of 1945 and has not disappeared with the surrender nor with the exercise of foreign state power in Germany by Allied forces; it still has legal capacity, but lacks any power to act as a state in the absence of organisation. The Federal Republic of Germany is not "legal successor" of the German Reich, but identical with the state "German Reich". It is, however, partly identical with respect to its territorial extension.'
14. For a comprehensive account, see Mußgnug (2003: 315–54).
15. See 'Gouvernement provisoire' (1944), article 1: 'La forme du Gouvernement de la France est et demeure la République. En droit celle-ci n'a pas cessé d'exister.' ('The form of the Government of France is and remains the Republic. By law, this Republic has not ceased to exist.' Translation by Alison James.)
16. See 'Conseil constitutionnel' (1971). The issue as to whether this decision constitutes a revolution or an accomplishment of the Constitution is still the matter of debate (see also Pfersmann 2019b).
17. Concerning the French and Israeli cases, see for instance Pfersmann (2019b).
18. *Bank Mizrahi v. Migdal Cooperative Village,* November 9, 1995, CA 6821/93.

PART IV

# Changing Fictions:
# Metafictional Effects

CHAPTER 15

# Quixotism as a Humorous Reflection on Fiction's Effects

Yen-Mai Tran-Gervat

*Université Sorbonne Nouvelle*

An old, bored Spanish *hidalgo* starts reading romances of knight-errantry and loses his mind through too little sleep and too much reading; soon convinced that his mission in life is to embody knight-errantry in modern Spain, he goes out of his village to confront those he sees as giants disguised as windmills and to defend his Lady Dulcinea's honour against villains pretending to be mere travellers. The story invented by Cervantes in the two parts of *Don Quixote* (1605 and 1615 respectively) assumed legendary status almost immediately, and the many subsequent imitations and adaptations have been extensively studied, as has quixotism itself as a critical and theoretical statement.

This paper does not aim at travelling on already well-trodden critical paths at length: starting from well-known facts about quixotism, I wish to examine them anew through the scope of humour, favouring its narrower, historical meaning as it was first defined in the eighteenth century, with reflexivity and empathy at its core. I shall distinguish the notion from close terms like satire and parody, which are regularly present in the analysis of *Don Quixote* and its imitations, and examine how humour is less a characteristic of the eighteenth-century understanding of quixotism than a potential of quixotism which some authors choose to highlight as part of a specific type of reflexive fiction. Case studies on a Woody Allen film and on a recent novel by Salman Rushdie will show that the relevance of a humorous reading of quixotism is not period sensitive.

## 1. A Quick Survey of Quixotism through Literary History and Theory

Jean Canavaggio, in *Don Quichotte, du livre au mythe* (2005), coins three useful expressions to characterise the three dominant readings of Cervantes' novel from the seventeenth to the nineteenth century. Cervantes's *hidalgo* (nobleman) first appeared as 'une plaisante figure' (a pleasant figure) (Canavaggio 2005: 45–81) in the decades following the book's publishing: in what was generally received as a comic book and a satire on the books of chivalry, the pseudo-knight was initially derided for his folly.

In the eighteenth century, Canavaggio shows that the reception of *Don Quixote* was characterised by 'un rire éclairé' (an enlightened laughter) (2005: 83–120): Don Quixote was still mainly ridiculous, but he was seen as both a comic *and* a likable figure, whose ideals could be used to satirise an increasingly materialistic and selfish society.[1] In such a reading, the literary parody coincides with a social satire.[2] During the Romantic period, Don Quixote lost most of his ridicule and was seen as what Canavaggio terms 'un messager d'idéal' (a messenger of ideals) (Canavaggio 2005: 121–65): the self-proclaimed knight, whose battle against imaginary giants resulted in a defeat against mere windmills (Cervantes [1605] 2011: I, ch. 8), was seen as a precursor of the Romantic hero in pursuit of greater ideals whose quest is thwarted by the triviality of everyday reality.

Those readings are presented by Canavaggio as successive phases in the reception of Cervantes's novel, but they can also be considered as the main possible tendencies in interpreting the broader notion of quixotism and how it reflects on fiction's effects at any given time.

In the early 1960s, in *History of Madness* (*Histoire de la folie à l'âge classique*), Michel Foucault began his inquiry into late Renaissance forms of literary madness with a phenomenon that he did not call quixotism, but rather 'madness by romantic identification':

> Let us begin with the most important, and the most durable — since the eighteenth century will still recognize its only just erased forms: *madness by romantic identification*. Its features have been fixed once and for all by Cervantes. But the theme is tirelessly repeated: [...]. The chimeras are transmitted from author to reader, but what was fantasy on one side becomes hallucination on the other; the writer's stratagem is quite naively accepted as an image of reality. In appearance, this is nothing but the simple-minded critique of novels of fantasy, but just under the surface is an enormous anxiety concerning the relationships, in a work of art, between the real and the imaginary, and perhaps also concerning the confused communication between fantastic invention and the fascinations of delirium. (Foucault [1961, 1972] 2001: 25–26)

In line with the Romantic reading of *Don Quixote*, Foucault insists on the tragedy underlying all forms of madness, including quixotic madness, as conceived at the end of the Renaissance. His analysis points to a double meaning of the quixotic 'theme': a superficial one which has to do with satirising the fantasy at work in fiction, and a deeper one that reveals a grave preoccupation with fiction itself as a relationship between reality and imagination. This points to what we shall study as satiric quixotism later on, as well as to a philosophical reflection on fiction that goes beyond the aims of this paper.

A decade later, in 1970, Harry Levin published an influential article entitled 'The Quixotic Principle: Cervantes and Other Novelists'; it is mainly this text that coined the adjective 'Quixotic' in later English-language literary criticism. Levin analyses:

> Cervantes made his vital innovation when he elevated this mock-hero to a sphere of excessive literacy. [...] In the Knight of the Rueful Countenance we behold a full-length portrait of a single-minded reader for whom reading

is believing, and whose consequent distortions of reality help to sharpen our apprehension of it. (Levin [1970] 1972: 229)

Here, Levin insists on the effects of what Jean-Marie Schaeffer later called fictional immersion (Schaeffer 2010: 153–73),[3] as they are thematised through the fictional excesses of the 'quixotic principle': in Levin's view, quixotism[4] presents the reader of fiction with a fun-house mirror. Howard Mancing shows in the 'Quixotic novel' entry and bibliography of his *Cervantes Encyclopedia* (2003) that literary theory and criticism have not stopped exploring the notion of Quixotism since the 1960s and 1970s.

An instance of these explorations is Scott Paul Gordon's *The Practice of Quixotism* (2006): in its introduction, the book foregrounds what the author calls 'the quixotic trope', in order to re-read various quixotic fictions by eighteenth-century English women from a postmodern point of view (Gordon 2006: 1–10).[5] Gordon's book develops the notion of 'orthodox' quixotism, based on the common meaning of what a 'quixote' is[6] and on the relationship of quixotic madness with social orthodoxy. Although the book is centred on eighteenth-century England and takes into account the reception of Don Quixote at the time,[7] Gordon's interpretation of quixotism is more along the lines of satire (because of foregrounded social issues) than along those of humour, which interest me.[8]

## 2. Defining 'Humour'

In its common use in English, as well as within the specific range of Humour Studies, the word 'humour' is usually understood as an 'umbrella term' (Attardo 2014: xxxi) that covers every notion that has to do with laughter or comedy. Will Noonan has stressed the importance of 'reflecting back' on the word's history for humour studies, and particularly on what its reception and adoption by the French as being closely linked with 'the sense of humour' and 'English humour' can bring to the field (Noonan 2011). Paul Gifford (1981) has commented on the diverging evolutions of the English word 'humour' and of the French word *humeur* in the seventeenth and eighteenth centuries, thus explaining how the French language had to adopt the recently anglicised *humour* to denote the new phenomenon that the word had come to evoke in English. Referring to Stuart M. Tave's *The Amiable Humorist* (1960), Gifford establishes that what *humeur* could not express anymore was 'that dimension of reflexive self-awareness which was decisively to shape the English notion of humour as established by the theorists of the late seventeenth century' (Gifford 1981: 536).

Among those theorists, Corbyn Morris is of particular interest here, since his book, *An Essay Towards fixing the True Standards of Wit, Humour, Raillery, Satire and Ridicule* (1744), gives a prominent place to Don Quixote.[9]

The best-known part of Morris's essay is when he establishes contrastive definitions of 'humour' (as opposed to 'wit'), 'a man of humour' and 'a humourist':[10]

> HUMOUR is any *whimsical Oddity* or *Foible*, appearing in the *Temper* or *Conduct* of a *Person* in *real Life*.

> [...]
> A *Man* of HUMOUR is one, who can happily exhibit a weak and ridiculous *Character* in real Life, either by assuming it himself, or representing another in it, so naturally, that the *whimsical Oddities*, and *Foibles*, of that *Character*, shall be palpably expos'd.
> Whereas an HUMOURIST is a *Person* in real Life, obstinately attached to sensible peculiar *Oddities* of his own genuine Growth, which appear in his Temper and Conduct.
> In short, a *Man* of *Humour* is one, who can happily exhibit and expose the Oddities and Foibles of an *Humourist*, or of other *Characters*. (Morris 1744: 15–20)

A hundred and fifty years after Ben Jonson's 'Comedy of Humour', Morris's definition of humour is still closely linked with bodily humours, whose imbalance can be observed through humorous 'oddities'. In Morris' terms, 'a man of humour' is an author or an actor: someone who excels at representing or enacting humour. His 'humourist' would be, for us, a self-conscious humorous character; someone who has a sense of humour.[11]

## 3. From Don Quixote as a 'Humourist' to Humorous Quixotism

Although Morris's specific terminology did not last, his effort at defining what is at stake in humour in his time continues to help us shape the historical meaning of the word 'humour.'

The second part of Morris's essay is centred on 'An Analysis of the Characters of an Humourist, Sir John Falstaff,[12] Sir Roger De Coverley,[13] and Don Quixote'. In the ensuing analysis, one readily understands that Morris's references to 'real life' are actually what we would call 'a realistic context'. Let us focus on his analysis of humour in the character of Don Quixote:

> Quixote is a Character, wherein *Humour* and *Ridicule* are finely interwoven; [...]. The *Humour* appears, in the Representation of a Person in real Life, fancying himself to be, under the most solemn Obligations to attempt hardy Atchievements; and upon this Whimsy immediately pursuing the most romantic Adventures, with great Gravity, Importance, and Self-sufficiency; To heighten your Mirth, the hardy Atchievements to be accomplish'd by this Hero, are wittily contrasted by his own meagre weak Figure, and the desperate Unfierceness of his Steed Rozinante; — The *Ridicule* appears in the strange Absurdity of the Attempts, upon which the Knight chuses to exercise his Prowess; Its Poignancy is highly quicken'd, and consequently the Pleasure it gives you, by his miserable Disasters, and the doleful Mortifications of all his Importance and Dignity;--But here, after the Knight, by diverting you in this manner, has brought himself down to the lowest Mark, he rises again and forces your Esteem, by his excellent Sense, Learning and Judgment, upon any Subjects which are not ally'd to his Errantry; These continually act for the Advancement of his Character; And with such Supports and Abilities he always obtains your ready Attention, and never becomes heavy or tedious. (Morris 1744: 38)

In this analysis, humour resides precisely in Quixote's madness and romantic illusions: the reader's pleasure is heightened by the ridiculous contrast between his fantastic attempts and his predictable failures. Significantly, however, he continues to be admirable in other respects and 'obtains your ready attention'.

Ten years later, Sarah Fielding and Jane Collier confirm this humorous reading of *Don Quixote* in the prologue to the fifth part of their novel, *The Cry* (1754), in a very famous (but often abridged) quotation. A lengthier quotation is necessary here, because the humorous reading of *Don Quixote* expressed is itself closely linked with a specific conception of fiction's effects on the reader of *Don Quixote*, and, more broadly, of any quixotic novel or character:

> That the chief personage of the comic should be endued with virtue and excellence, seems most palpably evident, in order to gain the attention of the reader; as also to give him the opportunity of energising the pleasing sensation of love and affection. [...]
>
> To travel through a whole work only to laugh at the chief companion allotted us is an insupportable burden. And we should imagine that the reading of the incomparable piece of humour left us by Cervantes can give but little pleasure to those persons who can extract no other entertainment or emolument from it than laughing at Don Quixote's reveries, and sympathising in the malicious joy [of his tormentors]: and that strong and beautiful representation of human nature, exhibited in Don Quixote's madness in one point, and extraordinary good sense in every other, is indeed thrown away on such readers that consider him only as the object of their mirth. (Fielding and Collier 1754: 168–69)

This detailed analysis leads us to view humour as a double effect of fiction, in which a character elicits in the reader both mirth *and* affection, laughter *and* empathy, ridicule *and* admiration. In this particular case, as the most famous part of the quotation sums it up, 'Don Quixote's madness in one point and extraordinary good sense in every other'.

In 1782, Joseph Warton, when commenting on Alexander Pope's parodic *Memoirs of Scriblerus*,[14] underlines 'the rich vein of humour that runs through [it]' and compares it with 'the serious manner of Cervantes', which is explained in a lengthy footnote:

> *Don Quixote* is the most original and unrivalled work of modern times. The great art of Cervantes consists in having painted his mad hero with such a number of amiable qualities, as to make it impossible to despise him. This light and shade in drawing characters, shews the master. [...] How great must be the native force of Cervantes' humour, when it can be relished by readers even unacquainted with Spanish manners, with the institution of chivalry, and with the many passages of old romances, and Italian poems, to which it perpetually alludes. (Warton [1782] 1806: 398)

From these three representative analyses of Don Quixote as the model of the eighteenth century 'amiable humourist', a definition of humorous quixotism can be drawn: if a Quixote presents a literary madness 'in one point' and admirable qualities 'in every other', he or she can be considered a humorous Quixote. Likewise, we can arrive at a definition through reader response theory if we consider the effects of fiction: quixotism can be interpreted as humorous when the case of madness through fictional identification simultaneously provokes the reader's distancing through ridicule *and* some kind of empathy through respect, admiration, attachment, or identification.

However, humorous quixotism must be distinguished from the first-degree reading of quixotism as a satire against fictions of fantasy: mocking laughter as the sole reaction of the reader to the quixotic character was reproved by Sarah Fielding, but such a reading was in a sense endorsed by Cervantes himself through a statement by the author's friend at the end of the novel's Prologue:

> This book of yours doesn't need any of the things you say are lacking, because it's all a censure of the books of chivalry [...]. And since the intention of your writing is to destroy the favour and influence the books of chivalry have in the world and hold over the common folk. (Cervantes [1605; 1998] 2011: 8–9)[15]

Among the imitators of Cervantes, many wrote satirical quixotic novels: in Charles Sorel's *Le Berger extravagant ou l'Anti-roman* (1627), the author essentially mocked the contemporary vogue of pastoral romances through a would-be shepherd's ridiculous fantasies; a century later, Father Bougeant derided the popular oriental tale, ridiculing its principles in *Voyage merveilleux du prince Fan-Férédin dans la Romancie* (1735).

Charlotte Lennox's *The Female Quixote* (1752) is harder to define: apparently, Arabella's excessive reading of (badly) translated seventeenth-century French heroic romances puts her in undoubtedly ridiculous situations that would dismiss any consideration for such fiction in the eyes of both the author and reader, and the satirical purpose explains Arabella's eventual recovery. However, the heroine's passion for truth and virtue, as she has conceived them from her books, is still what makes her a true heroine for the reader, and the woman that Glanville wishes to marry. Lennox's novel alternates between the satirical and the humorous.

The distinction between satirical and humorous quixotism depends not only on the character's ridicules and qualities, but also on the status of what Gérard Genette identified as the 'hypotexts' or 'hypogenres', which are exhibited in the parody that is developed through the fictional mad reader's imperfect imitation (Genette 1997).[16] If the hypotext is obviously mocked by the author, the other characters, and the reader through obvious ridicule attached to the literary reference, satire is the main motivation of the quixotic principle. If a degree of affection or attachment for the hypotext appears in the narrative, it could lead to a respectful interpretation of the parody, and consequently to a humorous reading of the attached quixotism.

In *Don Quixote* itself, the very beginning of Quixote's madness is clearly ironic and satirical:

> And of all of them [his books], none of them seemed as good as those written by the famous Feliciano de Silva, because the clarity of his prose and those obscure words of his seemed to be pearls, and more so when he came to read those flirtatious remarks and letters of challenge, where many times he found items such as these: 'The reason of the unreasonableness which against my reason is wrought, doth so weaken my reason, as with all reason I do justly complain of your beauty.' And also when he read: 'The high heavens, which with your divinity doth fortify you divinely with the stars, and make you deserveress of the deserts that your greatness deserves.' (Cervantes [1605; 1998] 2011: 20)[17]

However, most of the time, after Don Quixote leaves his village, his ridiculous first-degree imitations of chivalric actions and language do not debase Cervantes's main 'hypotexts': in Chapter 6, when Quixote's household decide to burn the books that made him lose his mind, the curate spares those he considers the best ones, among which are *Tirant lo blanc* and *Amadís de Gaula*.

When entering the Sierra Morena later in part I, Don Quixote is still delusional as he wishes to imitate the amorous despairs of Amadís and Ariosto's Orlando. His own version of madness through unrequited love is hilarious (e.g., Cervantes [1605; 1998, Part I, Ch. XXV] 2011: 252–53), but Cervantes's parody of those two great literary models is still mainly respectful (see Tran-Gervat and Duché 2019: 46–67): the result is humorous rather than satirical.

These distinctions can be summed up in a table:

| Quixotic character \ Literary reference | Ridiculed | Admired |
|---|---|---|
| Ridiculed | Satiric parody and quixotism | Humorous parody through quixotism |
| Admired | Satiric parody through humorous quixotism | Heroic imitation |

## 4. The Paradox of Quixotic Fiction: Mocking *and* Acknowledging Fiction's Effect

As far as fiction's effects are concerned *within* quixotism, the same distinctions can be made when considering how an author of fiction represents fiction's effects in the quixotic character who acts or speaks unreasonably through literary or cultural identification and imitation. In cases of satirical quixotism, the fool's unmitigated ridicule illustrates the absurdity and sometimes the dangers of fiction through the excesses of a given genre, or even through the pleasantness of fiction itself, which is then condemned as a deceitful medium: it depicts fiction as a reliance on the charms of fantasy to derail readers from a more sensible and reasonable view of the world and of their place in it. However, such a reading supposes the establishment of a clear distance between the satirised object and the judgemental or dismissive actor. In quixotism, such a satiric distance is always created by unmitigated ridicule.

However, in quixotism as well as in parody in general, the distance is always compromised by the inner reflexivity of the device, due to the presence of the criticised reference *within* the critical discourse itself.

Drawing on Bakhtin's reflections on medieval carnival, Linda Hutcheon (1985) has highlighted the paradox at the heart of parody: as subversive as parody wishes to be, it will always remain partially conservative by definition, like medieval carnivals themselves, which are a form of authorised subversion:

> This paradox of legalised though unofficial subversion is characteristic of all parodic discourse insofar as parody posits, as a prerequisite to its very existence,

> a certain aesthetic institutionalisation which entails the acknowledgement of recognizable, stable forms and conventions. (Hutcheon 1985: 74–75)

Quixotism is closely linked with parody, because from the moment the Quixote decides to emulate fictional characters or writings, he or she starts to imitate the discourses and actions that he or she so admires, but with an incongruity that transforms the imitation into parody (from the author's point of view); whether it is done 'on a lower social scale', thus creating a burlesque effect;[18] or simply in a context that clashes with the original cultural reference. The paradox of quixotism resembles the paradox of parody: it mocks a behaviour that has been necessarily experienced, on one level or another, by each of its readers: fictional immersion.[19] A Quixote is a reader who is unable to come out of fictional immersion: although it is represented as unreasonable and excessive in its comic, fictional version, immersion is a familiar and often delightful experience for the critical reader of the quixotic narrative. The immersive effect of fiction is both thematised *and* used by quixotic fiction.

In satirical quixotism, the argument for using this paradoxical device is usually that quixotic fiction uses fictional immersion to lead its reader towards the truth, as opposed to romance and fantasy, which pose an inherent danger by drawing readers towards chimeras. Humorous quixotism, however, is not logically challenged by its own paradoxical principle: our expected identification with the Quixote's experience of fictional immersion (minus the delirium due to excess) is part of the created humour. The quixotic character is ridiculous, but we know what fictional immersion is, even if we are not familiar with fiction theories. Even as fiction amateurs, every reader of quixotic novels has experienced how one can momentarily be engrossed by a book, a TV programme, or a film to the point of obsession. The only difference between the Quixote and myself (as a reader who laughs at his or her misadventures) is the degree and length of said passion: quixotism is continuous and extends its effects into the mad reader's 'real' life, whereas 'normal' fictional immersion is temporary and ceases when I exit the fictional experience. Between these two extremes of madness and reason is the contemporary phenomenon of 'fandom', which is an excess that usually stops before becoming madness.

Wherever the real reader places himself or herself on the scale of fictional immersion (from reason to fandom), he or she shares this experience with the quixotic character, so that the fictional excesses of the invented romantic misadventures reflect a part of the reader's own experience: the reflexive aspect of quixotism is what usually favours a humorous interpretation of its comic effects, rather than a satiric one.

Humorous and satiric quixotisms are not definitive or exclusive categories: we have seen that their identification may depend on the reader's or critic's perspective, and that they can coexist within a given work of quixotic fiction. However, sometimes humorous quixotism can clearly be identified as being the author's intended creation: I shall try to point out some objective markers of humour in two case studies of the twentieth and twenty-first centuries.

In Herbert Ross's film *Play it Again, Sam* (1972), adapted by and starring Woody Allen, the main character, Allan, is a film critic who is fascinated by Michael

Curtiz's film *Casablanca* (1942), starring Humphrey Bogart and Ingrid Bergman. He is also very unlucky in his attempts at seduction and regularly tries to correct his own clumsiness with women by taking advice from a vision of 'Humphrey Bogart', who appears only to his eyes and ears (and to the audience's). The film is a delightful comedy with a quixotic character that is mainly humorous: fiction's effects are not satirised here, they are taken for granted and used as a device of reflexive humour. The audience is addressed both as a comedy audience, who are ready to laugh at Allan's clumsiness and hilarious dialogues with 'Humphrey Bogart', and as film lovers, who are expected to share Woody Allen's and his character's admiration for *Casablanca* and its main actor.[20] The respectful parody of the closing scene of *Casablanca*,[21] at the end of *Play it Again, Sam* confirms the reading of Allen's quixotic film script as a humorous reflection on cinema itself and on its possible effects on one's life: although ridiculous most of the time, Allan's passion for *Casablanca* and Humphrey Bogart's fictional characters eventually plays a decisive role in his life (which is otherwise depicted in a realistic setting), allowing him to recognise and declare his love for his best friend's wife (played by Diane Keaton). The possible effects of fiction on one's life are not dismissed through satire, but embraced through humour.

The most recent addition to quixotic fiction is Salman Rushdie's novel, *Quichotte* (2019). It deploys the metafictional possibilities of any quixotic fiction to an impressive degree, engaging the reader in a third-degree narrative whose complexity appears as partly ironic, as if Rushdie wanted to write a playfully self-conscious post-post-modern quixotic novel.

'Quichotte' is the name that Rushdie's Quixote chooses at the beginning of the novel, in memory of Jules Massenet's opera, which he discovered while he lived in Paris as a child with his father. When the novel starts, the ageing Indian-American pharmaceutical salesman has just lost his job and has decided to engage in a quest for the love of his life, TV star Salma R. (who became famous through a spy TV show adapted from a series of spy novels and then reached stardom when becoming America's Indian-American equivalent of Oprah). However, we quickly understand that this story is itself a novel that is being written by a fictional author within the fiction we are reading. The novel also tells the story of the author of *Quichotte*, a second-rate Indian-American writer, who earned a living under a French-sounding pseudonym (Sam Duchamp) by writing spy novels and who decided to write something radically different, this time more personal. Every character in both levels of fiction is carefully drawn, and all of them are of Indian descent, like Salman Rushdie himself, who amusingly inserts parenthesis that are supposed to allow the reader to discern which are the 'real' references and which are 'fictional' ones in his characters' biographies.

Within the quixotic story of Quichotte, humour is central: the ageing salesman has spent most of his life in seedy motels, watching television. His canon is that of the American television and his motto is 'everything is possible'; he is convinced that the TV star he worships will fall in love with him. His TV references are partly satirised, but every reader, even when not entirely familiar with American TV programmes, knows what reality TV is, what fictional series are, what talk shows are, and has even maybe had the guilty pleasure of watching and liking some of them.

Moreover, Quichotte (who is very close to Don Quixote himself in age and intellectual finesse) is developed by Rushdie as a very appealing character, no matter how ridiculous his mad obsession with perfect romantic love. The quixotic fiction within the novel even goes as far as allowing Quichotte's fantasies to become 'real': feeling lonely, the character wishes he had a son with him that he could call Sancho; the actual apparition of said son is not due to a joke played on him by people he has met and who take advantage of his folly, but a chosen fantastic development of the novel itself, which for the occasion re-writes *Pinocchio*. The chapters written from Sancho's point of view, the character that came directly out of his father's imagination and paternal desire, are humorous developments on fiction writing itself. Humour here is mainly due to the explicit affinity between author and characters, which the reader is kindly asked to share in through laughter and emotions. Salman Rushdie's quixotic novel keeps its satirical piques for political considerations on British, Indian, and American societies: fiction, imagination, and fantasy are benevolently mocked, their positive effects on their beholders' world far exceeding the negative ones and the calamities of the 'real world'.

Although Allen's *Play it Again, Sam* and Rushdie's *Quichotte* clearly display many features of post-modern fiction, their uses of quixotism do not stimulate their audience's intellect as much as they resonate with their emotions: the comic situations born from the character's excessive form of fictional immersion create an effect that is not strictly fictional immersion, but what we could call fictional appreciation. The Quixotic characters ridiculous acts make us aware of the mechanisms of fictional immersion, thus impeaching it for us, but the fact that the character is depicted as a likable, endearing fool allows us to recognise and embrace his folly as a reflection of, rather than on, our own moments of fictional oblivion.

As I approach the conclusion of this paper, I am reminded of a specific critical anecdote. Over thirty years ago, when the film *Dead Poets Society* (Peter Weir, 1989) was released, it was considered enough of a social phenomenon (students started to read more poetry, or stood on the tables of their classroom when their literature teacher came in...) for various debates to take place. One of these was broadcast on the French public radio channel France Culture, between two female literature professors, one of whom was my own teacher at the time; their discussion was about the professor played by Robin Williams in the film, an unorthodox teacher in a very strict 1950s private school, who encourages his students to 'make [their] lives extraordinary' through the Horatian phrase '*Carpe diem*' and the reading of poetry. Professor A considered such a teaching dangerous, since it could create devastating ideals and illusions in the young minds of impressionable students (in the film, one of the fictional students commits suicide); Professor B rejoiced that a fictional teacher could elicit an enthusiasm for poetry in real-life students. At one point, Professor A said: 'But you know how the Chinese saying goes: 'When the wise man points at the moon, the fool looks at the finger'; to which Professor B answered: 'Yes, it may be so, but at least, the fool gets the opportunity to look up!'

Using 'humour' in its historical meaning is not only about reconstructing the eighteenth-century reception of *Don Quixote* or tracing back the origins of a specific word: the resulting notion is a useful tool for literary analysis, and for the purposes of this paper, it was best suited to approaching the emotional element of quixotic reflexivity. Humorous quixotism is about a fool who obstinately looks at the finger that is pointed by fiction towards imaginary things and is convinced that by going in the pointed direction, he or she will experience the same adventures. It is about the ridiculous actions the fool takes to reach unreachable goals, and about the reader who laughs at them, but who at the same time knows how pleasurable it is to follow the roads of fiction; or how pleasurable it is for the author to create the stories that capture our fantasies; so that, by laughing at the fool who has been trapped by fiction's effects, one acknowledges one's own pleasure in willingly entering the same enticing traps.

## References

ATTARDO, SALVATORE. 2014. Introduction, *Sage Encyclopedia of Humor Studies* (Thousand Oaks, CA: Sage Publications)

CANAVAGGIO, JEAN. 2005. *Don Quichotte, du livre au mythe : Quatre siècles d'errance* (Paris: Fayard)

CERVANTES, MIGUEL DE. [1605] 1998. *El ingenioso hidalgo de la Mancha*, ed. by Francisco Rico (Centro Virtual Cervantes) <https://cvc.cervantes.es/literatura/clasicos/quijote/edicion/default.htm> [accessed 19 July 2022]

——. 2011. *Don Quixote*, trans. by Tom Lathrop (New York: Signet Books)

CLOSE, ANTHONY. 1977. *The Romantic Approach to Don Quixote: A Critical History of the Romantic Tradition in 'Quixote' Criticism* (Cambridge: Cambridge University Press)

ESCARPIT, ROBERT. 1960. *L'Humour* (Paris: P.U.F.)

FIELDING, SARAH, and JANE COLLIER. 1754. *The Cry: A New Dramatic Fable*, II (Dublin: George Faulkner)

FOUCAULT, MICHEL. [1961] 1972. *Histoire de la folie à l'âge classique*, rev. edn (Paris : Gallimard)

——. 2001. *Madness and Civilization: A History of Insanity in the Age of Reason*, trans. by Richard Howard (London: Routledge)

GENETTE, GÉRARD. 1982. *Palimpsestes : La littérature au second degré*, Poétique (Paris : Seuil)

——. 1997. *Palimpsests. Literature in the Second Degree*, trans. by Channa Newman and Claude Doubinsky (Lincoln: University of Nebraska Press)

GIFFORD, PAUL. 1981. 'Humour and the French Mind: Towards a Reciprocal Definition', *The Modern Language Review*, 76: 534–48

GORDON, SCOTT PAUL. 2006. *The Practice of Quixotism: Postmodern Theory and Eighteenth-Century Women's Writings* (New York: Palgrave)

HUTCHEON, LINDA. 1985. *A Theory of Parody: The Teachings of $20^{th}$-Century Art Forms* (New York: Methuen)

LEVIN, HARRY. [1970] 1972. 'The Quixotic Principle: Cervantes and Other Novelists', in *Grounds for Comparison* (Cambridge, MA: Harvard University Press), pp. 224–43

MANCING, HOWARD. 2003. 'Quixotic Novel', in *The Cervantes Encyclopedia*, II (Westport, Greenwood Press)

MORRIS, CORBYN. 1744. *An Essay Towards Fixing the True Standards of Wit, Humour, Raillery, Satire and Ridicule* (London: J. Roberts and W. Bickerton)

NOONAN, WILL. 2011. 'Reflecting Back, or What can the French tell the English about Humour?', *Sydney Studies in English*, no. 37: 92–115

PAULSON, RONALD. 1997. *Don Quixote in England: The Aesthetics of Laughter* (Baltimore and London: Johns Hopkins University Press)

PAVEL, THOMAS. 2010. 'Immersion and Distance in Fictional Worlds', *Itinéraires. Littérature, Textes, Cultures*, 2010–11 (May): 99–109 <https://doi.org/10.4000/itineraires.2183>

ROBERT, MARTHE. 1963. *L'Ancien et le nouveau : De Don Quichotte à Franz Kafka* (Paris: Grasset)

ROSS, HERBERT (dir.). 1972. *Play it Again, Sam* (Paramount Pictures)

RUSHDIE, SALMAN. 2019. *Quichotte* (London: Jonathan Cape)

SCHAEFFER, JEAN-MARIE. 2010. *Why Fiction?*, trans. by Dorrit Cohn (Lincoln: University of Nebraska Press)

TAVE, STUART M. 1960. *The Amiable Humorist: A Study in the Comic Theory and Criticism of the Eighteenth and Early Nineteenth Centuries* (Chicago: The University of Chicago Press)

TRAN-GERVAT, YEN-MAI. [2001] 2006. 'Pour une définition opérationnelle de la parodie littéraire', in 'L'Intertextualité', special issue, *Narratologie*, Centre de narratologie appliquée de l'Université de Nice-Sophia Antipolis, 4: 65–78. Online version in *Cahiers de narratologie*, 13 <https://journals.openedition.org/narratologie/372>

——. 2011. '"Humour cervantique" et "roman parodique": Réflexions sur le rire et le roman au XVIII$^e$ siècle, à partir du cas de *Tristram Shandy*', in *Études françaises*, 47(2): 55–70 <http://id.erudit.org/iderudit/1005649ar>

——. 2014. 'Le *learned wit* dans l'Angleterre du XVIII$^e$ siècle, du *Scriblerus Club* à *Tristram Shandy*: L'ombre portée de *Don Quichotte*', in *Savoirs ludiques. Pratiques de divertissement et émergence d'institutions, doctrines et disciplines dans l'Europe moderne*, ed. by K.Gvozdeva, A. Stroev and L. Millon, Colloques, congrès et conférences — Littérature comparée, 21 (Paris: Honoré Champion), pp. 207–20

——. 2015. 'La marginalité paradoxale de l'excentrique : Réflexions sur la figure de l'"humouriste' anglais au XVIII$^e$ siècle', in *Étrangeté de l'autre, singularité du moi : Les figures du marginal dans les littératures*, ed. by Feuillebois-Pierunek et Z. Ben Lagha, Rencontres (Paris: Classiques Garnier), pp. 369–82

——. 2016. 'Translating Quixotism and its Terminology in the 17th Century', in *Hermeneutics of Textual Madness: Re-Readings*, ed. by M. J. Muratore, 1 (Fasano: Schena Editore), pp. 193–209

—— and VÉRONIQUE DUCHÉ. 2019. 'Topoï paysagers et réécriture parodique: Don Quichotte dans la Sierra Morena', in *Natura in fabula : Topiques romanesques de l'environnement*, ed. by I. Trivisani-Moreau and P. Postel (Leiden: Brill Rodopi), pp. 46–67

WARTON, JOSEPH. (1782) 1806. *Essay on The Genius and Writings of Pope*, II (London: Thomas Maiden)

## Notes to Chapter 15

1. As is the case in Henry Fielding's 1731 comedy *Don Quixote in England*, which Canavaggio quickly studies in that chapter, among other eighteenth-century works inspired by Cervantes (Canavaggio 2005: 106–07).
2. See Tran-Gervat ([2001] 2006: para. 37) on parody as 'a playful rewriting of a recognizable literary system (text, style, stereotype, generic norm...), that is exhibited and transformed so as to create a comic contrast, with an ironic or critical distancing'.
3. For an English development of the notion of immersion, see Pavel (2010).
4. The French equivalent could be the neologism that Marthe Robert uses throughout her book on Kafka and Cervantes (1963): '*donquichottisme*'.
5. Among the books Gordon focuses on is Charlotte Lennox's *The Female Quixote* (1752), which I am currently translating into French for Classiques Garnier under the title *Lady Quichotte*. Gordon studies this novel in his first chapter, as a prominent example of what he calls 'orthodox

quixotism', due to the fact that Arabella's 'madness through literary identification' (Foucault) with the heroines of seventeenth century French romances is clearly shown as ridiculous and bound to be cured in order for her to get properly married.

6. 'Quixotism [...] is a discourse that describes — or establishes — a stark difference between an "us" [who are rational] and a "them" [who are delusional]' (Gordon 2006: 3).
7. As it was established in critical landmarks such as Close (1977) and Paulson (1997).
8. I have already studied in different contexts some of the issues that will be developed here: see for example Tran-Gervat (2011 and 2014).
9. From a slightly different perspective, I have studied this in a yet unpublished paper given at the 2018 International Society for Humor Studies (ISHS) conference, entitled 'Don Quixote as a Prototype of Humour in Eighteenth-Century England'.
10. These definitions are quoted and translated by Robert Escarpit in his French historical and theoretical landmark essay, *L'Humour* (1960).
11. On this subject, see Tran-Gervat (2015). I developed a critical approach to the humoral reading of Don Quixote's madness in Tran-Gervat (2016). More recently, I gave a conference paper in a 'Literature and Medicine' research seminar in Dijon ('Nommer le corps, nommer la maladie', June 4, 2018) on 'La folie de Don Quichotte est-elle humorale ou humoristique?'
12. The comic character created by Shakespeare in *Henry IV,* parts I and II (1598–1600), as well as in *The Merry Wives of Windsor* (1602).
13. A character created by Addison in *The Spectator* (1711–1712).
14. Composed with Swift's and Arbuthnot's contributions in 1713–14, published in 1741.
15. In the original: 'este vuestro libro no tiene necesidad de ninguna cosa de aquellas que vos decís que le falta, porque todo él es una invectiva contra los libros de caballerías [...]. Y, pues esta vuestra escritura no mira a más que a deshacer la autoridad y cabida que en el mundo y en el vulgo tienen los libros de caballerías'.
16. Studying various forms of 'hypertextuality' (when a literary work alludes to, quotes, rewrites, parodies a previous work), Genette identifies the source text as the 'hypotext' and the new resulting text as the 'hypertext'. In the case of parody in *Don Quixote,* the hypertext is Cervantes' novel, the hypogenre is the romance of knight-errantry, and some hypotexts can be clearly identified (*Amadís de Gaula* is alluded to in the first chapter, when Don Quixote de la Mancha choses his new name after Montalvo's hero). Strictly speaking, Genette allows the notion of 'hypogenre' only when speaking of pastiche (which is predominantly imitative), but I have argued in favour of the validity of the notion even in cases of parody (Tran-Gervat 2001).
17. 'y de todos [sus libros], ningunos le parecían tan bien como los que compuso el famoso Feliciano de Silva, porque la claridad de su prosa y aquellas entricadas razones suyas le parecían de perlas, y más cuando llegaba a leer aquellos requiebros y cartas de desafíos, donde en muchas partes hallaba escrito: *La razón de la sinrazón que a mi razón se hace, de tal manera mi razón enflaquece, que con razón me quejo de la vuestra fermosura.* Y también cuando leía: *[...] los altos cielos que de vuestra divinidad divinamente con las estrellas os fortifican y os hacen merecedora del merecimiento que merece la vuestra grandeza*' (Part I, Chapter 1).
18. This is how Channa Newman and Claude Doubinsky chose to translate Genette's more metaphorical 'mais à l'étage au-dessous', in chapter 24 of *Palimpsests* (Genette 1982: 158; Genette 1997: 144), in which the French critic's analysis of Marivaux's *Télémaque travesti* (1714) introduces this youth playful parody of Fénelon's *Aventures de Télémaque* before distinguishing it, in the following chapter, as a singular and masterful instance of 'antiromance' or 'mixed parody' (Genette 1997: 153–56).
19. See note 3 above.
20. As in any parody, failing to recognise the hypotext would ruin most of the audience's potential interest in the film; and who would be able to identify the *Casablanca* quotations without reliving the pleasure of watching it?
21. The airport scene between Ingrid Bergman's Ilse and Bogart's Rick is featured in the opening scene of the film, which shows a fascinated Allen in a theatre where the 1942 film is playing.

CHAPTER 16

# Metafiction in Japanese and Western Literature: *Chô-kyokô* and Meta-Mystery

*Masahiro Iwamatsu*

*Kwansei Gakuin University*

The term *metafiction*, coined in 1970 by American novelist William Henry Gass, became popular in Japan in the second half of the 1980s. But around 1980, a Japanese novelist, Yasutaka Tsutsui, had already invented the word *chô-kyokô* (sur-fiction). In his criticism and in his novel experiments, Tsutsui shows the possibility of self-referential fiction.

At the end of the 1980s, another metafictional movement appeared in Japanese literature: meta-mystery, a detective novel that takes on a metafictional and often playful consciousness, with its self-referential narrative, nested structure, narrative tricks, and challenge to realism. This movement continued through the following decade and exerted a remarkable influence on manga, animation, and video games.

We will first take a quick look at some examples of metafictional experiments in Japan. We will not so much emphasise the particularity of these examples as, on the contrary, their points in common with Western metafiction. The example of a short story by Katsuhiko Otsuji will invite us to re-examine the works of Paul Auster, Agota Kristof, and Italo Calvino by shedding light on what the modern reader unconsciously expects from fiction.

These examples will show how Japanese fictional writing is haunted by reflection on the nature of fiction.

## 1. Metafiction, Surfiction, and *Chô-kyokô* (Sur-Fiction)

In the 1970s and '80s, researchers and writers paid attention to self-referential fictional works by naming various types, as illustrated in Table 1. William Henry Gass originally proposed the term metafiction, which would take some time to become widely known to anyone interested in literature. Today, the term is so popular that it is almost surprising that most of these writers and scholars proposed these neologisms of kinship without any mention of the word metafiction.

| | | |
|---|---|---|
| metafiction (1970) | Gass (1980, 24–25) | cf. logico-mathematical 'metatheorem' |
| | redefinition 1970 Scholes (1995, 29) | assimilates all perspectives of criticism into the fictional process itself |
| | redefinition 1983 Hutcheon (1983, 1) | includes in itself a commentary on its own narrative and/or linguistic identity |
| | redefinition 1984 Waugh ([1984] 1988, 2) | conscious of itself, systematically draws attention to its status as an artifice in order to ask questions about the relationship between fiction and reality |
| | redefinition 1992 Lodge (1992, 206) | calls attention to its fictional status and its own compositional processes |
| surfiction (1973) | Federman (1975, 10) | tries to explore the possibilities of fiction beyond its own limits |
| introverted novel (1976) | Bradbury and Fletcher (1991) | draws attention to the narrator (eighteenth century) and to the autonomy of the structure itself of fiction (twentieth century) |
| récit spéculaire (1977) | Dällenbach (1977) | takes the reflexive/recursive modality cf. "*mise en abyme*" (Gide) |
| récit poétique (1978) | Tadié (1994, 8) | conflict between the referential function and the poetic function of language |
| self-begetting novel (1980) | Kellman (1980) | self-productive and autotelic |
| chô-kyokô (sur-fiction) (1981) | Tsutsui (1985b, 216) | cf. Robbe-Grillet 1989 |
| chô-shishôsetsu (sur-autofiction) (1989) | Otsuji (1989) | calls into question the framework of the work/text itself |
| texte conflictuel (1989) | Calle-Gruber (1989, 26) | the effects of meaning (of representation) nourished by the self-representation of the mechanisms that give rise to them |
| writerly novel (1990) | Alexander (1990, 167) | brings to the forefront both language and the activity of writing, refusing to treat it or use it as a transparent window on the world cf. '*scriptible*' (Barthes [1970] 1994, 558) |

| roman métareprésentatif (1990) | Ricardou (1990b) | cf. *mise en cause du récit* ('questioning the narrative') Ricardou 1990a) (1973) |
| --- | --- | --- |
| roman scriptural (1992) | Korthals Altes (1992, 195) | cf. *scripturalisme* (Ricardou 1967, 54) |
| meta-mystery (first half of 1990s) | | Japanese fandom slang |

TABLE 1. List of metafictional notions

Around the year 1980, the Japanese novelist Yasutaka Tsutsui invented a word *chô-kyoko* (literally, hyper-fiction or sur-fiction), also ignoring the notion of metafiction, as well as 'surfiction', another name proclaimed by Raymond Federman (1975) in 1973.

Like Alain Robbe-Grillet,[1] Tsutsui proclaims that there is no reason for the novel to represent reality:

> In plays, authors may give his character lines as if he is aware of his fictional status. For example, in Ibsen's 'Peer Gynt', a character is made to say 'don't be alarmed — one doesn't die | right in the middle of Act Five!'[2] In the case of novels, however, such occurrences are rare. Even if there are any examples, The author advocates that the entire novel is a 'joke' or 'parody'. (Tsutsui 1984: 314)

This consideration resulted in his novel *Fictional People*, completed in 1981. Here, all the characters become aware that they are characters in a novel. This playful trait reminds us of Raymond Queneau's *Witch Grass* (*Le Chiendent*, 1933) and *The Flight of Icarus* (*Le Vol d'Icare*, 1968), Felipe Alfau's *Locos: A Comedy of Gestures* (1936), or *Mahu or The Material* (*Mahu ou le matériau*, 1952) by Robert Pinget.

At the beginning of the novel, as the author has not yet mentioned his name, the hero goes out the front door to look at the nameplate at his door and finds his surname for the first time. He is always thinking about how characters should act in his situation, how they should react (in a novelistic way) to the actions of the other characters, and whether the author is foreshadowing something in his actual situation.

In a conventional novel, the flow of time would not be constant: the narrative would omit the duration of the characters' sleep or their moving from a point A to point B. In contrast, Tsutsui's novel unifies the duration of the narration and the story. Before the spread of word-processing machines, Japanese writers used sheets of manuscript paper with grids, for example of four hundred letters, i.e., twenty letters, twenty lines. In this novel, a sheet of manuscript paper is equivalent to one minute in the diegetic world; the description continues without ellipsis even when the hero goes to the toilet, and the blank pages continue during his fainting.

From this novel to the present, Tsutsui continues the metafictional experiments in his works.

## 2. Meta-Mystery or Self-Referential Detective Story

At the end of the 1980s, another metafictional movement appeared: meta-mystery, a detective story that takes on a metafictional and playful consciousness, often accompanied by the challenge to realism. This movement continued through the next two decades.

One of its characteristics is the play of narrative levels. In *Paradise Lost in the Box* (Takemoto 2015), one of the predecessors of experimental crime novels, written by Kenji Takemoto and published early in 1978, a character named Niles (after Thomas Tryon's novel *The Other*) writes a detective novel entitled *How was the Room Sealed?* The characters in this embedded novel and those in the embedding novel share the same names and attributes, which makes it difficult to distinguish between reality and fiction in this novel.

In addition, each chapter begins with the comments of the characters who have just read the entire text of the previous chapter. A character who has been found dead is alive in the next chapter and comments on the death of his double. After reading the first three chapters, we think of a nesting structure, a multiple embedding like Matryoshka dolls or Chinese boxes.

But if we follow the text, we find a coherence between chapters of odd numbers, and another coherence between chapters of even numbers. According to the odd-numbered chapters, the even-numbered chapters are those of the novel written by Niles; however, according to the even-numbered chapters, the odd-numbered chapters are those of his novel. Such a structure of the Ouroboros with two snakes, each biting the tail of the other, is also found in Seikô Itô's experimental novel *The Beetle on the Waves* (1995) and can be traced back to Christine Brooke-Rose's novel *Thru* (1975). These examples remind us of Escher's lithograph, *Drawing Hands* (1948), where two hands draw each other.

Narrative tricks are another feature of the new wave of Japanese crime fiction. They invite readers to misinterpret the story by using their own tacit assumptions. Here is a basic example of the type of narrative trick found in Douglas Hofstadter's work:

> A father and his son were driving to a ball game when their car stalled on the railroad tracks. In the distance a train whistle blew a warning. Frantically, the father tried to start the engine, but in his panic, he couldn't turn the key, and the car was hit by the onrushing train. An ambulance sped to the scene and picked them up. On the way to the hospital, the father died. The son was still alive but his condition was very serious, and he needed immediate surgery. The moment they arrived at the hospital, he was wheeled into an emergency operating room, and the surgeon blanched and muttered, 'I can't operate on this boy — he's my son.'
>
> What do you make of this grim riddle? How could it be? (Hofstadter 1985: 136)

Hofstadter is not talking about a male surgeon but about a female surgeon who is the wounded boy's mother.

In Japan, many detective novels make the reader misunderstand the chronological order of the events told or the identity of the characters such as their names, sexes, ages, etc. Yasutaka Tsutsui's *The Lautrec Villa Murders* (1990), a crime novel narrated in the first person, actually has two narrators who share the same family name. These examples are contemporary with Brigitte Aubert's *Les Quatre fils du Docteur March* (1992) and could be influenced, for example, by Fred Kassak's *Nocturne pour assassin* (1957), an astonishing novel that makes us misunderstand the sex of a character even though it is written in French, with that language's system of gender inflections.

Takemaru Abiko's 1992 third person novel *The Sickness unto Massacre* (Abiko 2017) takes the points of view of three characters:

> 1) Retired detective Higuchi is investigating a series of lust murders whose victims are young girls, with the help of a victim's sister.
>
> 2) Minoru Gamou is absent from the university the day after his first murder. He is a psychopathic assassin who seduces girls at the campus, at the arcade, or at the bar, to take them to the hotel where he slaughters them, absorbs himself in necrophilia, and removes part of their corpses.
>
> 3) Masako Gamou, a housewife, finds something strange in the attitude of her son who is a university student, and she discovers a plastic bag containing something bloody in his room.

At the end of the novel, the reader will be informed that the psychopathic murderer Minoru Gamou is not a student but a professor at a university. His son who suspected him found the horrible bag in his father's room and hid it. The housewife Masako is not Minoru's mother anymore but his wife, and she had suspected her son, just like the reader.

The preference for narrative trickery in Japanese crime novels at that time was so enthusiastic that it invited critics to reread the classics of the genre. They found the metafictional qualities not only of the *mise en abyme* (which closely resembles Gide's *The Counterfeiters* [1925]) in Ellery Queen's *The Tragedy of Y* (1932), but also of the manipulation of the detective prepared by the criminal who uses false clues — red herrings — in order to steer him towards a false story and to make him collaborate in the crime unconsciously, for example in his *Siamese Twin Mystery* (1933) and his *Ten Days Wonder* (1948) (see among others Norizuki 2007; Kasai 2005; Iiki 2010).[3]

## 3. Katsuhiko Otsuji's 'Short Story'

Here is another example which, in turn, foregrounds the narrative condition of the text itself. Katsuhiko Otsuji (also known as an avant-garde artist Gempei Akasegawa) published a short story entitled 'Short story' in a monthly literary magazine *Gunzo*, March 1991. The beginning of this short story is completely self-referential:

> I've been asked to write a short story of some kind. (Otsuji 1991: 213)

'I', a writer who bears a complete resemblance to the author, tells us how he has received the request to write the short story itself.

At the beginning of the story, the present date is January 15th, 1991. The March issue of *Gunzo* magazine comes out around February 8th, so the writer started writing the short story just three weeks from the day it went on sale, if we take his statement to be true. January 15th 1991 was the last day that the United Nations Security Council had presented to Iraq the year before as the deadline for the evacuation of Kuwait. The narrator raises this international problem in real time as if he is inflating the letters in his manuscript:

> It's almost two o'clock [Japanese local time]. The Arab Gulf crisis is looming, and the US and Iraq are facing each other in a tentative position. This time today is the time limit. I turned on the radio in front of me, but the fact that it was two o'clock didn't mean that anything would happen in a minute or two, so I turned it off immediately. The first thing I had to do is to write this short story. (Otsuji 1991: 214–15)

I asked the editor Mr. Fuji about the scale of the work and he replied, 'Well, usually at least thirty sheets [of manuscript paper with grids of four hundred letters].' (Otsuji 1991: 215)

The narration goes back and forth from the narrative micro-situation to the situation of the narrator's daily life, and to the international macro-situation. It seems as if the author has nothing to write and adds the letters only to satisfy the minimum length of a short story. He bargains, as if he wants to reduce the letters he has to write:

> It's already two o'clock. There are countless ammunitions around Iraq waiting to be detonated, but is it possible to finish a short story within fifteen sheets? (Otsuji 1991: 216)

The change of aspect, from macro- to micro-situation, thus emerges even in such a short sentence:

> He tells me that while the last deadline for the redaction is January 23rd, he needs at least the title of the story by January 20th for the table of contents of the magazine. In that case, I will have to decide it prematurely, but the deadline in general has some leeway. It will extend if you want it and force it to, and it can be put off even for about ten days if you stretch it out slowly and carefully like rubber. [...] Also in the gulf, it is said that missiles have not been launched as of 0:00 [local time of the Gulf] of January 15th. (Otsuji 1991: 218)

He calls the 'deadline' the cut-off date for his short story, which he is reluctant to write, as well as the time limit for the evacuation of Kuwait presented by the UN.

The short story turns out to be *chô-shishôsetsu*, sur-autofiction (Otsuji 1989), which does something that only fiction can do:

> anyway, I sent him the short story. One by one, the manuscript papers slipped through the facsimile machine. In the end, thirty-five sheets went under, and finally, the lamp went out with an electric scream. I wrote 'went out' because it went out, but I'm still writing this, even though the short story should have been finished before that. I'm a little confused about this mystery. The more I write, little by little, the more the short story inches along. (Otsuji 1989: 237)

## 4. Three Western Examples: Auster, Kristof, and Calvino

This example invites us to reread the outcome of three novels written in the second half of the twentieth century,[4] just as the vogue for meta-mystery invited readers and critics to re-examine the classics of detective stories.

First, the year following the publication of Otsuji's short story, Paul Auster published his novel *Leviathan*. One day, narrator-writer Peter Aaron finds a newspaper's story about the 'explosive' death of a man. Aaron realises that it is his old friend Benjamin Sachs. Then, two FBI detectives visit him.

Aaron writes his recollection of Sachs in chronological order; his chronicle finally catches up with the first FBI visit, and he explains the narrative situation of the text himself that he began writing 'the next morning' (Auster 2005: 380) after the two inspectors' visit, which he has continued to write now for 'two months' until now, when he will finish:

> As it is, *these past eight weeks* are all I will ever have. Three-quarters of the way into the second draft (in the middle of the fourth chapter), I was forced to stop writing. That was *yesterday*, and I'm still trying to come to grips with how suddenly it happened. *The book is over now* because the case is over. If *I put in this final page*, it is only to record how they found the answer, to note the last little surprise, the ultimate twist that concludes the story. (Auster 2005: 380; my emphasis)

Finally, Inspector Harris visits him again, having deduced the relationship between Sachs and the successive terrorist attacks in the United States; here are the last sentences of the novel:

> Then I pointed to the studio, and without saying another word I led Harris across the yard in the hot afternoon sun. We walked up the stairs together, and once we were inside, *I handed him the pages of this book*. (381–82; my emphasis)

If it was 'yesterday' (380) that Harris visited Aaron and if Aaron 'handed him the pages of this book' (381), how could he write this sentence at the end of the pages of this book? The closing sentence, 'I handed him the pages of this book', undermines the reliability of the entire text in one fell swoop.

Another example can be found in Agota Kristof's *The Notebook* (*Le Grand Cahier*, 1986), which tells the story of infant twins who take refuge with their grandmother in a small town near the border. The novel consists of about sixty short compositions in which they record their experiences in 'the notebook' (Kristof [1986] 1997: 28). In the original French text, they call it 'le Grand Cahier' (the Big Notebook) with capital letters in the initial, which is the original title of the novel itself.

In their first-person narrative, the twins do not use the word 'I'. Here is a highly self-referential passage in the twelfth composition (chapter):

> We are sitting at the kitchen table with our sheets of graph paper, our pencils, and the notebook. We are alone.
> One of us says: 'The title of your composition is: "Arrival at Grandmother's."'
> The other says: 'The title of your composition is: "Our Chores."' (Kristof 1997: 28)

These titles of two compositions coincide respectively with the first and the fourth chapters of the novel.

> At the end of two hours we exchange our sheets of paper. Each of us corrects the other's spelling mistakes with the help of the dictionary and writes at the bottom of the page: 'Good' or 'Not good'. [...] If it's 'Good', *we can copy the composition into the notebook.*
>
> To decide whether it's 'Good' or 'Not good', we have a very simple rule: the composition must be true. We must describe what is, what we see, what we hear, what we do.
>
> For example, it is forbidden to write, 'Grandmother is like a witch'; but we are allowed to write, 'People call Grandmother the Witch.' [...]
>
> Similarly, if we write, 'The orderly is nice', this isn't a truth [...]. So we would simply write, 'The orderly has given us some blankets.' (Kristof 1997: 29; my emphasis)

At the end of the novel, the heroes sacrifice their father in order for one of them to cross the mined border:

> Yes, there is a way to get across the frontier: it's to make someone else go first.
>
> Picking up the linen sack, walking in the footprints and then over the inert body of our Father, one of us goes into the other country.
>
> The one who is left goes back to Grandmother's house. (Kristof 1997: 183)

So, did this 'notebook' itself cross the border or did it stay in the country? The text avoids pronouncing which of the twins writes each chapter, but when we take seriously the assertion that their composition must be true, it is absolutely not possible that the final chapter is written by the one who went to the other country, since he has no clear proof that his brother has precisely returned to Grandmother's house.

Moreover, the reader may also conjecture that this last chapter, which tells of their separation can never have been corrected by the brother of the one who wrote it, because he had already separated from his brother at the time of its writing, which poses a paradox undermining the reliability of the statement itself regarding the truth of the entire text.

Finally, Italo Calvino's *The Nonexistent Knight* (*Il Cavaliere inesistente*, 1959) begins as the story of Agilulf, a knight in the service of Charlemagne. But in Chapter 4 the narrator, or rather the writer, Sister Theodora of the Order of St. Columban, begins to intervene. She recounts not only the adventures of Agilulf, of the young warrior Bradamante who loves him, of the young knight Raimbaud who is in turn in love with Bradamante, but also her own efforts in writing this story, which she is 'writing in a convent, from old papers unearthed or talk heard in our parlour here or a few rare accounts by people who were actually present' (Calvino 1998: 308). The story about the knights is interrupted immediately after she describes Bradamante's escape from Raimbaud's love.

In the last chapter, the narrator suddenly hears a horse galloping and Raimbaud knocking on the door, asking the sister at the door if Bradamante is there, and she unexpectedly sets herself into action, which she describes in the present tense:

> But *now* I run to the window and cry, 'Yes, Raimbaud, I'm here, wait for me, I knew you'd come, I'll be down, I'll leave with you.' [...]
> Yes, book. Sister Theodora who tells this tale and the amazon Bradamante are one and the same. (1998: 381; my emphasis)

Here, the story about the knights in the past time catches up with and breaks into the description of the narrative situation in the present. She knew that Raimbaud would catch her, just as Aaron in *Leviathan* knew that one day the FBI would come back to him, and the narrator of Otsuji's short story that the magazine would go on sale. All three narrator-writers are well aware that they have a writing deadline in the near future.

Logically, however, the simultaneous description of the writing situation cannot suddenly gain what Gérard Genette calls 'total transparency' (Genette 1980: 219) of Hemingwayesque simultaneous narration, or 'live coverage'. How can the narrator continue writing after running to the window? This paradox would invite us to think of this warrior nun in love as the next Disney princess to follow Elsa and Anna: we would see her on the screen running to the window, throwing the pen, which in turn automatically continues to engrave the letters of the story on the parchment.

## 5. Conclusion

In his letter to Louise Colet on 9 December 1852, Flaubert wrote that 'An author in his book must be like God in the universe, present everywhere and visible nowhere' (Flaubert 1980: 173). What Flaubert and his followers had tried to exclude from fiction was the trace of the narrator's own enunciation. This is why they aimed at a simultaneous, unmediated reporting of the state of affairs in the fictional world, including the consciousness of the characters. Modern narrative fiction had to conceal its self-referential elements, which Roman Jakobson would have called 'phatic' (cf. Jakobson 1960: 355–56).

But the phatic reference to one's own act of enunciation is essentially a rather banal and even necessary phenomenon in nonfiction texts such as essays, notes, letter-writing, blog posts, and oral communication in general.

And this self-referentiality is also the necessary condition for the metaleptic paradox of narrative levels of which we have cited examples. This 'self-reference, or the Strange Loop' (cf. Hofstadter 1989) in the tangled narrative hierarchy of post-realist writers is close to Kurt Gödel's Proposition VI, via the analogy of Epimenides's paradox, called the 'liar' or 'Cretans's paradox'.

Bringing invisible conventions to the forefront by transgressing the very conventions of narrative fiction reveals the difference between what we expect from fiction and what we expect from nonfiction.

## References

ABIKO, TAKEMARU. (1992) 2017. *Satsuriku ni Itaru Yamai* [The Sickness unto Massacre] (Tokyo: Kodansha)

ALEXANDER, MARGUERITE. 1990. *Flights from Realism: Themes and Strategies in Postmodernist British and American Fiction* (London: Edward Arnold)

AUSTER, PAUL. (1992) 2005. *Leviathan*, in *Collected Novels*, II (London: Faber & Faber)
BARTHES, ROLAND. (1970) 1994. *S/Z*, in *Œuvres complètes*, ed. by Éric Marty, II, *1966–1973* (Paris: Seuil)
BRADBURY, MALCOLM and ANGUS FLETCHER. 1991. 'The Introverted Novel', in *Modernism: 1890–1930*, ed. by Malcolm Bradbury and James Walter MacFarlane, 394–415 (London: Penguin)
CALLE-GRUBER, MIREILLE. 1989. *L'Effet-fiction: De l'illusion romanesque* (Paris: Alfred G. Nizet)
CALVINO, ITALO. 1998. *The Non-Existent Knight*, in *Our Ancestors*, trans. by Archibald Colquhoun (London: Vintage), pp. 285–381
DÄLLENBACH, LUCIEN. 1977. *Le Récit spéculaire: Essai sur la mise en abyme* (Paris: Seuil)
FEDERMAN, RAYMOND. [1973] 1975. 'Surfiction: Four Propositions in Form of an Introduction', in *Surfiction: Fiction Now... and Tomorrow*, ed. by Raymond Federman (Chicago: Swallow), pp. 5–15
FLAUBERT, GUSTAVE. 1980. *The Letters of Gustave Flaubert: 1830–1857*, ed. and trans. by Francis Steegmuller (Cambridge, MA: Bellknap Press/Harvard University Press)
GASS, WILLIAM HENRY. (1970) 1980. 'Philosophy and the Form of Fiction', in *Fiction and the Figures of Life* (Boston: David R. Godine), pp. 3–26
GENETTE, GÉRARD. (1972) 1980. *Narrative Discourse: An Essay in Method*, trans. by Jane Lewin (Ithaca, NY: Cornell University Press)
HOFSTADTER, DOUGLAS R. 1985. *Metamagical Themas: Questing for the Essence of Mind and Pattern* (London: Penguin)
———. 1989. *Gödel, Escher, Bach: An Eternal Golden Braid* (New York: Vintage)
HUTCHEON, LINDA. 1983. *Narcissistic Narrative: The Metafictional Paradox* (London: Routledge)
IBSEN, HENRIK. (1867) 1970. *Peer Gynt*, trans. by Peter Watts (London: Penguin)
IIKI, YUSAN. 2010. *Ellery Queen*. [Ellery Queen] (Tokyo: Ronsôsha)
JAKOBSON, ROMAN. 1960. 'Closing Statement: Linguistics and Poetics', in *Style in Language*, ed. by Thomas A. Sebeok, with a foreword by John W. Ashton (Cambridge, MA: MIT Press), pp. 350–77
KASAI, KIYOSHI. 2005. *Tantei Shôsetsu to Nijisseiki Seishin: Minerva no Fukurou wa Tasogare ni Tobitatsuka* [*The Detective Story and the 20th Century Spirit: Does Minerva's Owl Fly at Dusk?*] (Tokyo: Tôkyô Sôgensha)
KELLMAN, STEPHEN G. 1980. *The Self-Begetting Novel* (London: Macmillan)
KORTHALS ALTES, LIESBETH. 1992. *Le Salut par la fiction? Sens, valeurs et narrativité dans Le Roi des aulnes* (Amsterdam: Rodopi)
KRISTOF, AGOTA. (1986) 1997. *The Notebook*, trans. by Alan Sheridan, in *The Notebook, The Proof, The Third Lie* (New York: Grove Press)
LODGE, DAVID. 1992. *The Art of Fiction: Illustrated from Classic and Modern Texts* (London: Penguin)
NORIZUKI, RINTARÔ. (1995) 2007. 'Shoki Queen ron' ['Early Ellery Queen'], in *Fukuzatsu na Satsujin Geijutsu: Norizuki Rintarô Mystery Juku* [*The Complex Art of Murder: Rintarô Norizuki's Mystery School*] (Tokyo: Kôdansha, 2007)
OTSUJI, KATSUHIKO. 1989. *Chô-Shishôsetsu no Bôken* [Adventure of Sur-Autofiction] (Tokyo: Iwanami Shoten)
———. 1991. 'Tampen' ['Short Story'], in *Deguchi* [Exit] (Tokyo: Kôdansha), pp. 211–37.
RICARDOU, JEAN. 1967. 'Un Ordre dans la débâcle', in *Problèmes du nouveau roman* (Paris: Seuil), pp. 44–55
———. 1990A. *Le Nouveau Roman* suivi de *Les Raisons de l'ensemble* (Paris: Seuil)
———. 1990B. 'Les Raisons de l'ensemble' in *Le Nouveau Roman* suivi de *Les Raisons de l'ensemble* (Paris: Seuil), pp. 225–48

Robbe-Grillet, Alain. (1955/63) 1989. 'From Realism to Reality', trans. by Richard Howard, in *For a New Novel: Essays on Fiction* (Evanston, IL: Northwestern University Press), pp. 157–68

Scholes, Robert. [1970] 1995. 'Metafiction', in *Metafiction*, ed. by Mark Currie (London: Longman), pp. 21–38.

Tadié, Jean-Yves. [1978] 1994. *Le Récit poétique* (Paris: Gallimard)

Takemoto, Kenji. [1978] 2015. *Hako no naka no Shitsuraku* [Paradise Lost in the Box] (Tokyo: Kôdansha)

Tsutsui, Yasutaka. (1979) 1984. 'Kyokô to Genjitsu' ['Fiction and Reality'], in *Tsutsui Yasutaka Zenshû* [The Complete Works of Yasutaka Tsutsui], XX (Tokyo: Shinchôsha), pp. 304–45

——. [1981] 1985A. *Kyojin-tachi* [Fictional People], in *Tsutsui Yasutaka Zenshû*, XXIII (Tokyo: Shinchôsha), pp. 7–152

——. [1981] 1985B. 'Chô-Kyokô Sengen' ['The Sur-Fictional Manifesto'], in *Tsutsui Yasutaka Zenshû*, XXIV (Tokyo: Shinchôsha), pp. 216–17

Waugh, Patricia. (1984) 1988. *Metafiction: The Theory and Practice of Self-Conscious Fiction*. (London: Routledge)

## Notes to Chapter 16

1. Robbe-Grillet wanted 'to make something out of nothing, something that would stand alone, without having to lean on anything external to the work' (Robbe-Grillet 1989: 162), blaming the surrealists for claiming that their works were more realist than the realist works: 'All writers believe they are realists. [...] Realism is [...] the quality which each believes he possesses for himself alone. [... T]his was the watchword of the romantics against the classicists, then of the naturalists against the romantics; the surrealists themselves declared in their turn that they were concerned only with the real world' (1989: 157–58).
2. Originally 'Act Three' (Tsutsui's misquote). We cite it from Ibsen (1970: 178).
3. On other ways of ensnaring readers and making them complicit in crime novels, see Maxime Decout's contribution to this volume (Chapter 17).
4. The choice of the following three examples is completely arbitrary in all respects except for their period (late twentieth century) and their paradoxical self-reference to their own narrative act at the end of the text.

CHAPTER 17

# Killing the Reader? On Some Unfortunate Side Effects of Reading

*Maxime Decout*

*Sorbonne Université/Institut Universitaire de France*

The idea is well known: a book could have such an impact on its reader that it would come to influence his or her existence. It is possible to study this imaginary in which the action of the works, taken to extremes, becomes a particularly disturbing theme. The reader's death or guilt because of a text have become recurring elements in the self-reflexive experiments of modernity. This situation is at the origin of what I will call *murderous fictions* that impose themselves at a time when the boundaries between reality and fiction are attacked, without being abolished (see Lavocat 2016). The aim is to ask if and how a fiction can transform its reader into an assassin or kill him/her — excepting the not very glorious case where it makes him or her die of boredom. One genre in particular is ideally suited to such an undertaking: the detective novel. Detective fiction hides the essential clues and prevents us from solving the case, so that it destroys the good and competent reader in us, puts them to death symbolically, and makes us responsible for our own failure to interpret. This is even more evident when the text portrays reader-investigator characters who are trapped by fiction.

The incrimination of the reader by murderous fictions is thus a site where the power of books is both constructed and questioned. Without ever attaining this power completely, these texts allow it to be seen and to be imagined. They make the reader feel its possibility. But while the reader-character can be the victim of the text, the causes of our own inability to unravel the mystery can never be the same as they are for the reader-character. The pragmatic effectiveness of fiction is thus asserted only in order to challenge it all the more forcefully. This paradox appears to be the main limit to the dream of completely manipulating the reader's existence. It is for this reason that Oulipo co-founder François Le Lionnais describes the case of the guilty reader as an ambition that the detective novel has never realised, despite its many attempts to do so (Le Lionnais [1973] 1988a: 65).

## 1. Death by *Mise en Abyme*

The first means of incriminating the reader is a *mise en abyme* in which a reader character is driven to commit or be the victim of a murder. This crime stems from a confusion between the real and the fictional reader-character, as in Michel Butor's *L'Emploi du temps* (*Passing Time*), Jean Lahougue's *Non-lieu dans un paysage* (Non-place/Case Dismissed in a Landscape) and Georges Perec's *'53 jours'* (*'53 Days'*). In these three novels, a character reads a fascinating text which presents a certain number of similarities with the one we hold in our hands, most often indicated by a kinship of their title or author: in Butor, it is a detective novel signed by Burton, *Le Meurtre de Bleston*; in Lahougue, a novel entitled *Non-lieu dans un paysage* signed by L.; and in Perec a manuscript entitled *53 jours*.

*L'Emploi du temps* tells the story of Jacques Revel's stay in the town of Bleston, during which he becomes passionate about a detective novel, *Le Meurtre de Bleston* (Murder in Bleston), signed by J.C. Hamilton. The book deciphers the mysteries of the town of Bleston for him, so much so that Revel uses it as a guide to explore this labyrinthine space. Gradually bewitched, Revel makes the author 'an accomplice against the city, a wizard accustomed to this kind of peril who could provide [him] with charms powerful enough to defy them' (Butor [1956] 1995: 57, (my translation).[1] A man named Burton (not unlike the name Butor), finally confides in him that he is the author of this novel. *Le Meurtre de Bleston* is a distorted version of the novel *L'Emploi du temps*. However, Burton asks Revel not to expose his secret. The narrator has only one idea: Burton's pseudonym is a sign that his book hides a secret about a crime that was actually committed, leading the novelist to disguise himself. From that moment on, *L'Emploi du temps*, as if contaminated by *Le Meurtre de Bleston*, is transformed into a kind of detective novel where it is difficult to untangle what is factual and what is merely the fruit of Revel's projections from what he reads in the novel.

It is by revealing Burton's identity that Revel then completes the metamorphosis of the text into a detective novel, as Burton subsequently meets with an accident that the narrator assumes to be an assassination attempt. However, Revel will never succeed in proving this, nor in finding a culprit. In fact, the only culprit is Revel himself, who may have endangered Burton's life by his indiscretion. But his fault is of a singular nature: it stems from his total and unconscious immersion in fiction, from the certainty that fiction says something about reality. Fiction thus realises the fate that awaits every investigator in revealing the identity of a culprit whom he thus puts to death, literally or symbolically, as Burton had explained: to become a new Oedipus who discovers, at the end of his investigation, his own guilt. The only nuance is that Revel is the victim of a book (a fact that Burton carefully concealed from him). This is perhaps the fate reserved for the modern Oedipus, for investigators who decipher texts instead of reality.[2]

In Lahougue's work, which is strongly reminiscent of *L'Emploi du temps*, the reader's enchantment does not begin with the novel *Non-lieu dans un paysage*, but rather with a mysterious manuscript received by the narrator, a professional reader for a publishing house. The text's author has chosen as a pseudonym the name of a painter, Desiderio.[3] The manuscript, barely more than twenty pages long, is a sort of imperfect sketch that paints a portrait of a woman written 'in a casual, sometimes faulty but roué style' (Lahougue 1977: 17, my translation).[4] It reminds the narrator of 'certain detective novels' since the woman described almost looks like a corpse, despite the fact that her death is not explicit. Faced with this unpublishable manuscript, the narrator suspects a hoax but also a strange form of appeal: thus begins the investigation of its author, on the basis of the book. To do this, the narrator goes to 11 rue Nazareth, the address from which the manuscript was posted, where he meets the owner who confesses that her tenant has suddenly disappeared. The narrator then moves into the vacant apartment, and begins his immersion in the life of the supposed author and his text.

The narrator is aware, however, that he is gradually being deceived: 'I thought I had taken *too much pleasure* in my reading. And how could I admit that it was now this pleasure [...] that clearly marked me out to solve an unknown drama?' (Lahougue 1977: 47).[5] The manuscript produces an excess of pleasure that in turn arouses the need to perpetuate and renew this pleasure in the real world. It will be read and reread eagerly, fanning the flames of mystery, the reader noting, for example, that 'all the gestures of the narrator were now as obvious to me as my own presence' (Lahougue 1977: 131).[6] The name Desiderio, which connotes the omnipotence of this desire for fiction, even comes to empower itself and to function in the narrator's language as an adjective: a 'Desiderio curiosity', a 'Desiderio meaning', 'my Desiderio curiosities', a 'Desiderio duty', 'a Desiderio revelation' (Lahougue 1977: 98, 129, 127, 147, 151).[7] These impulses become the elementary principles and attitudes that govern the reader's investigation, revolving around a single, hidden centre. Inside a villa, the narrator then finds a book, *Non-lieu dans un paysage*, written by L. and signed at the end by a character named Desiderio. The narrator then writes a text of the same name and sends it to the publishers he works for, as if he had metamorphosed into Desiderio. Lahougue's novel concludes by quoting the last words of this mysterious book that plans the murder of Desiderio, without it being known whether the reader-character will act in accordance with what he has just read — whether he will murder this Desiderio that he has somehow become.

Perec's '*53 jours*' ([1989] 1993) shares several common points with *L'Emploi du temps* and *Non-lieu dans un paysage*, but utilises a more complex device. In the first part of the novel, the consul asks the narrator to investigate the disappearance of a crime writer, Serval, using his latest manuscript called *La Crypte* (The Crypt). The narrator is convinced that clues are hidden in this text, where several other books appear. The narrator gradually gets lost in a labyrinth of fictions, in which it becomes difficult to differentiate between reality and illusion. At the end of the first part, the narrator becomes certain that the consul has set a trap for him, but he finds his corpse and is arrested by the police. It is in fact Serval, the novelist aware of the power of fiction, who has manipulated his reader into accusing him of the consul's murder through his text. The second part, however, tells us that this whole story is just another manuscript, by someone called Serval, and investigated by another reader called Salini. A new *mise en abyme* appears so that Salini finds himself 'in the same position as the narrator'[8] of the first part (Perec 2000: 118). He sometimes 'feels the need to reassure himself by going through all the features that distinguish him from the narrator-character' (Perec 2000: 119),[9] and 'almost wonders if he hasn't been explicitly designated by the author' (Perec 2000: 118).[10] His attitude is both more immersive and more conscious than that of the narrator of the first part, since he is confronted with a greater number of echoes between fiction and reality, but also warned by the hero's setbacks of the dangers of losing oneself in the text.

A brief comparison of *L'Emploi du temps*, *Non-lieu dans un paysage* and '*53 jours*' is now necessary to understand the differences between the texts beyond a scenario with many similarities. *L'Emploi du temps* does not solve the mystery: we will never know if Burton was indeed the victim of an attempted murder and if his text concealed some secret or not. The reader is overcome by doubt and anxiety about the powers of fiction. *Non-lieu dans un paysage* also ends ambiguously. It quotes the last lines of L.'s novel, which bears the same title as Lahougue's and which commands the reader character to kill Desiderio. In this way, the end of Lahougue's story is textually identical to that of L.'s book: the real reader reads the same text as the character and almost tends to merge with him. In '*53 jours*', on the contrary, the mysteries are solved, but the presence of four different novels that figure the work 'en abyme' leads to the complete disorientation of the reader. At the same time, however, the powers of fiction also seem to diminish in intensity due to the multiplication of the work's doublings and reflections. The majority of the *mises en abyme* in '*53 jours*' do not affect the reader's universe, but rather take place between texts within the plot. They therefore concern the reader only indirectly. Only the *mise en abyme* of the first part within in the second reflects the reader's universe, which is therefore perceived as more threatening: the reader has the feeling that he or she could be included in the world of fiction.

## 2. Metaleptic Vertigo

In any case, Lahougue and Perec go further than Butor: the ends of their novels discreetly move from the *mise en abyme* to metalepsis, the crossing of the border between reality and fiction. The difference between these two notions is sometimes difficult to distinguish. It lies in the fact that the *mise en abyme* proceeds by including one fictional universe in another, whereas metalepsis moves from one universe to another. The surest way to make the reader guilty of a crime, or to murder him, would be to bring a murderer or a corpse from the book he is reading into his living room or through the front door. But this is doubtless no easy task....

The conclusion of '*53 jours*', for example, extends the *mise en abyme* of the first part into the second via a striking metalepsis: we learn that a writer called Georges Perec was hired to write the manuscript that is the first part and to accuse Salini, the reader, of the murder of Serval. This emergence of the author's name is what forces readers to project themselves completely into the place of the reader-character for the first time — a move that the previous *mise en abyme* had only laid the ground for. In Lahougue's work, the *mise en abyme* comes about through the discovery of L.'s novel, *Non-lieu dans un paysage*. L.'s book and Lahougue's book, which are nevertheless different, merge at the denouement as the novel ends by quoting the final lines of L.'s text:

> Climb those few more steps that separate you from my last refuge, it is finally daylight there. Open the door, it isn't locked... It will be enough for you to close this book before me, before you, under the lamp, to make me disappear [...]. Then look at the time on your wrist: it will always be the time of my death. (Lahougue 1977: 183–84, my translation)[11]

These sentences are imperative, perhaps programmatic. They move from *mise en abyme* to metalepsis. More precisely, this metalepsis functions on two levels: it is both an internal metalepsis (for the character of Lahougue confronted with L's book) and an external one (for the real reader confronted with Lahougue's book). It is frightening in that it removes the barriers between fiction and reality within the novel as well as in the reader's universe. In this way, it enjoins Lahougue's reader character, and certainly the actual reader as well, to go upstairs and perhaps find Desiderio ready to be killed. It is only in these last lines that we, as readers, are incited to take action, and that our fate as murderous readers and victims of the powers of fiction is confirmed in the extreme. It is the gesture of closing the book that puts both the character and his reader to death.

Several stories have recourse to this same phenomenon of the second-person character's interpellation, but according to a more generalised metalepsis. This happens, for example, in Max Dorra's short story 'Vous permettez que je vous dise tue?' ([1999] 2000) or Peter Lovesey's 'Youdunnit' [1989] 1994 — the latter title replacing the detective's and reader's usual interrogation: 'who [has] done it?' with a categorical and accusatory answer. This second-person address to the reader within the text is based on their excessive consumption of crime novels: as they finish the story, they realise with dread that they are simply dead and awaiting judgement in a kind of afterlife, having committed suicide after actually committing a murder.

The fact remains that, in the case of these two stories, the 'you' character is guilty in the same way as any other character. This type of metalepsis, as in Butor's *La Modification* or Perec's *Un homme qui dort*, is, in Genette's words, more economical than effective (Genette 2004: 77–78). Indeed, contrary to the apostrophe that concludes *Non-lieu dans un paysage*, or to the character of Perec at the end of *53 jours*, the generalisation of the process soon makes 'you' simply a sort of protagonist in the reader's mind, just as distinct from him as any other character.

These examples therefore demonstrate that this kind of incriminating metalepsis should be used sparingly. 'Continuidad de los parques' ('Continuity of Parks'), a famous short story by Cortázar, is able to achieve maximum effect with minimum effort. The plot begins with a rather imprecise *mise en abyme* that does not directly concern the actual reader: 'He had begun to read the novel a few days before' (Cortázar 1967: 63).[12] This book is not characterised and does not immediately reflect the one you are reading. But little by little, the character, who sits in a green velvet armchair with a splendid view of a park, also settles into his reading as you do into the short story: 'the novel spread its illusion over him almost at once. He tasted the almost perverse pleasure of disengaging himself line by line from the things around him' (Cortázar 1967: 64, translation modified).[13] This immersion begins simultaneously for you, the actual reader, as well, but the second paragraph allows for a trick that is likely to go unnoticed:

> Word by word, licked up by the sordid dilemma of the hero and heroine, letting himself be absorbed to the point where the images settled down and took on color and movement, he was witness to the final encounter in the mountain cabin. The woman arrived first, apprehensive; now the lover came in, his face cut by the backlash of a branch. (Cortázar 1967: 64)[14]

You didn't notice any trick? That is to be expected. The text does not point out anything abnormal and focuses henceforth on this couple who, we are given to understand, are preparing to murder the husband. The man then leaves the woman and walks towards a house, enters it, bursts into the living room, approaches a green velvet armchair and the man reading a novel. Through this sudden metalepsis, it becomes clear that 'you', the reader, are going to be murdered by one of the characters magically emerging from the text.

A rational explanation of the phenomenon is nevertheless possible. The text led you to believe that the story of the couple was the one being read by the main character. However, it did not assert anything of the kind. If you reread the previous excerpt, you will see that the story moves on to the story of the man and the woman after having evoked the novel being read — but without stipulating that they are indeed the protagonists of this book.

It is only you, dear reader, who read badly, who made the connection because you trusted the text — because, like the character, you were immersed in the plot and seized by the referential illusion that blinded you. You may still think that the murderer has magically escaped from the pages of the book, but nothing proves this. The fact remains that this last interpretation has a strong consequence: like you, the reader-character has been a victim of his reading. He is punished because he has allowed himself to be fooled by the referential illusion. Contrary to the other reader incriminations we have talked about, this one operates a real metalepsis whose success is guaranteed by the skilful setting up of two plots that you believe to be separate, and which, when they come together, continue to be so in your mind. This is why you feel that the boundary between the book and the real has actually been transgressed — to your great misfortune.

## 3. Culpable Reading

It is possible, however, to incite you to commit murder or assassinate yourself not by metaphorically compromising you, as previous *mises en abyme* and metalepses do, but by directly incriminating your activity as a reader. From that moment on, reading itself becomes a violent act. It is no longer a question of killing as any murderer would do, but of putting to death by reading or because you read.

We can see this in 'Une nouvelle policière en arbre' (A Tree-form Detective Story) by François Le Lionnais, wherein the reader reads a participatory text in which various alternatives are left at his disposal ([1973] 1988b: 272). This schema could lead to a text where the real reader can be held responsible for the crime because of his choice of direction for the story. This time, however, it is not the reader as a character but as an actor in the construction of the text who would be at fault.

Benoît Peeters's *La Bibliothèque de Villers* (The Villers Library, [1980] 2017.) offers another solution. The narrator is working in the Villers library on archives recounting a series of unsolved murders, dating back to 1905, when a new series of four murders occurs. The narrator comes to believe that the fifth victim can only be himself. Without any real *mise en abyme*, the reader character is in mortal danger. But in the end it is the library curator, Lessing, who dreamed of writing a total crime novel and whom the narrator had suspected, who is found murdered.

Rereading a letter from Edith, Lessing's secretary and the narrator's mistress, who is also one of the victims, the narrator experiences a sort of epiphany at the end of the story: according to him, the truth lies 'under every sentence', 'almost in every word' (Peeters 2017: 56). Edith 'died because she didn't know how to read this evidence', the narrator himself almost died, and you yourself, dear reader, were hoodwinked. The novel ends by declaring that this truth will be recorded in the story that the narrator will write. The key to the mystery is therefore hidden within the text that we have just deciphered and that you are now summoned to reread. Rereading, you then find several troubling clues that transform the enigma into a textual one; in particular, the fact that when the victims' initials are put together the name Villers appears, itself an anagram of *livres* (books). It is as if the text itself is the source of the murders.

But above all, this investigation leads you to a revelation close to that of Oedipus: you may well be the culprit. There are two possible interpretations: either you didn't solve the case when no one else could, as you learn at the end; in that case, you are the artisan of your own failure and perhaps also of the massacre. Or else, you unravel the mystery and discover that, since the culprit that everything points to, Lessing, has also been murdered and all other characters are dead, the only remaining suspect is the one who has the least chance of being called into question, as in *The Murder of Roger Ackroyd*: the narrator. The latter could have been bewitched by Lessing's criminal text, either simply by following its content and principle, or by reading it. Whatever you do, it is the reader here who is inevitably the culprit, by dint of his reading.

## 4. The Murderous Text

Nevertheless, even in *La Bibliothèque de Villers*, you may still think you are safe from any real involvement since, in most of the cases observed so far, readers kill a character or get murdered because of a given situation. There are almost always contextual reasons for the effectiveness of a book on its reader — which is good news for you.

To get out of what we must call a dead end (at least, from the point of view of a novelist who wishes to incriminate you), some have adopted a final and very practical solution: imagining a murderous text that functions outside the plot data.

When there is no longer anything to legitimise the deadly power of a book within a story, you, dear reader, may really have the impression of being on the verge of death or prison. There is no protective distance that holds for you: you risk your skin on every page.

Vila-Matas's *La asesina ilustrada* (*The Lettered Assassin*) is particularly representative of this desire to emancipate a criminal text little by little from all the reasons that inform its action. Elena Villena, at the beginning of the novel, finds the body of Vidal Escabia lying next to the manuscript she had sent him shortly before, *La asesina ilustrada*. As in *L'Emploi du temps*, *Non-lieu dans un paysage*, and '*53 jours*', the murderous mechanics are set in motion by a *mise en abyme* that contaminates the reader's universe. But the rest of the text will gradually abandon this scenario and prove its insufficiency in provoking the fear of the reader. For the moment, there is no proof that the manuscript has anything to do with the death of Vidal Escabia.

Then you learn that Elena Villena gave her manuscript to her husband, Juan Herrera, a writer who died shortly afterwards. Ana Cañizal, his secretary, supposes that the parallels with the writer's life caused him a mortal shock. Compared to this death, that of Vidal Escabia can no longer be rationalised. How, indeed, could the same text cause a devastating concussion for two different readers because of its content? Vila-Matas thus uses Juan Herrera's death to better highlight the inexplicable character of Vidal Escabia's death, and also of the subsequent death of Ana Cañizal who also succumbs shortly afterwards without any explanation. Among the three deaths that appear to be due to the text, only one can be explained by a specific situation. One conclusion alone can be drawn from this: quite apart from any particular relationship it establishes with the reader, and in an almost magical way, the reading of the text itself is lethal.

This case is not unique: Perec's *La Disparition* (*A Void*), for example, can be interpreted in the same way. In this novel, Anton Voyl's friends disappear one after the other. We learn that the crimes were committed by Inspector Swann himself. We do have a murderer, then, but we are missing one essential piece of information: how did he do it? Nothing tells us this. This is why the murders, each one more fanciful than the last, seem to follow no logic at all. This arbitrary character of death must be put in relation to the constraint of the text: *La Disparition* is a lipogram in *e*. Yet each executed protagonist is associated with a letter of the alphabet, as if the murderer were following the author in cutting them out of the story. Two murders are particularly exemplary: that of Ottavio, who is struck down after reading a text written by Swann and which is a lipogram in *a* (and, obviously, in *e*); that of Savorgnan, killed with a Smith-Corona which, although not a revolver as one might expect, is a typewriter that crosses the protagonist out of the text as if by a strikethrough. These two crimes are clearly perpetrated by the text itself. In case you still have any hesitations on this score, the postscript removes them: it makes the 'Scriptor', i.e., the author, the person responsible for the murders, because of the writing law that he conscientiously applied throughout the novel's pages. It is the text that is the murderer and that, to attain this end, does not need you to have any particular connection with it.

\* \* \* \* \*

Murderous fictions thus represent a turning point in the affirmation of the power of fiction over the reader's existence, paradoxically striving to base their relationship with the reader on his or her elimination. In this way, they envisage completely fulfilling the fantasy of a text's influence via the very negation of an essential component of the way literature works. Nevertheless, murderous fictions almost always reach a dead end by admitting their inability to completely rule out your existence: they have indeed, unless I am mistaken, not yet killed you. This is why, faced with the inadequacies of *mise en abyme* and metalepsis, and with the difficulties of making the act of reading guilty in itself, texts such as *La asesina ilustrada* and *La Disparition* have recourse to a more radical option: to imagine an inherently murderous text. In these works, the reasons given by the plot are established only to be better challenged by an almost supernatural arbitrariness that frees the text from any guardianship. Language becomes autonomous in a text whose contact alone would cause death, for reasons that are impossible to understand. It is in this way that the fantasy of killing the reader bursts forth in all its excessiveness and, paradoxically, gives almost complete life to the book itself through this murderous gesture. As long as the effectiveness of the work depends on circumstances outside of it, and in particular on the singular reader who reads it, it remains under the latter's control. But, as soon as it is in a position to assassinate any reader, it metamorphoses into a kind of entity or living being in its own right, over which no one any longer has control. Fiction thus asserts that it can change life; moreover, that it can suppress it, to the point of taking the risk of making its very foundation, the reader, disappear — and thus denying itself. But maybe it's worth the risk. This leaves you, dear reader, with only two options. The safest thing is to stop reading for good. The other is to continue to do so, trembling at the thought of stumbling, one day or another, upon a murderous text.

## References

Butor, Michel. [1956] 1995. *L'Emploi du temps* (Paris: Minuit)
Cortázar, Julio. 1967. 'Continuity of Parks.' In *End of the Game and Other Stories*, trans. by Paul Blackburn (New York: Pantheon Books)
——. [1964] 1995. 'Continuidad de los parques', in *Final del juego*, ed. by Jaime Alazraki (Madrid: Anaya and Mario Muchnik)
Decout, Maxime. 2015. *En toute mauvaise foi* (Paris: Minuit)
——. 2018. *Pouvoirs de l'imposture* (Paris: Minuit)
Dorra, Max. [1999] 2000. 'Vous permettez que je vous dise tue ?', in *La Machine à déplier le temps* (Paris: Flammarion)
Genette, Gérard. 2004. *Métalepse : De la figure à la fiction* (Paris: Seuil)
Lahougue, Jean. 1977. *Non-lieu dans un paysage* (Paris: Gallimard)
Lavocat, Françoise. 2016. *Fait et Fiction: Pour une frontière* (Paris: Seuil)
Le Lionnais, François. [1973] 1988a. 'Les structures du roman policier: Qui est le coupable? (avant-projet de classification)', in *La Littérature potentielle. Créations, re-créations, récréations* (Paris: Gallimard)

LE LIONNAIS, FRANÇOIS. [1973] 1988B. 'Une nouvelle policière en arbre' in *La Littérature potentielle. Créations, re-créations, récréations* (Paris: Gallimard)
LOVESEY, PETER. [1989] 1994. 'Youdunnit', in *The Crime of Miss Oyster Brown and Other Stories* (New York: Little, Brown, and Company)
PEETERS, BENOÎT. [1980] 2017. *La Bibliothèque de Villers*, suivi de *Tombeau d'Agatha Christie* (Brussels: Les Impressions Nouvelles)
PEREC, GEORGES. [1989] 1993. *'53 jours'* (Paris: Gallimard)
——. 2000. *'53 Days'*, ed. by Harry Mathews and Jacques Roubaud, trans. by David Bellos (Boston: David R. Godine)

## Notes to Chapter 17

1. 'Un complice contre la ville, un sorcier habitué à ce genre de périls qui pût [le] munir de charmes assez puissants pour [lui] permettre de les défier'.
2. The comparison of the detective with Oedipus is frequent and it is at the centre of *L'Emploi du temps*, as if deciphering signs were always a guilty activity, for the character as well as the reader. For more details, please refer to Decout (2015: 146–60; and 2018: 45–47).
3. Monsù Desiderio is already a pseudonym that was adopted by the Lorraine painters François de Nomé and Didier Barra in the seventeenth century.
4. 'dans un style désinvolte, parfois fautif mais roué'.
5. 'J'avais pris à ma lecture, pensais-je, *trop de plaisir*. Et comment admettre que c'était désormais ce plaisir [...] qui me désignait clairement pour résoudre quel drame?'
6. 'Tous les gestes du narrateur m'étaient désormais aussi évidents que ma présence.'
7. '[Une] curiosité Desiderio', 'une signification Desiderio', 'mes curiosités Desiderio', un 'devoir Desiderio', 'une révélation Desiderio'.
8. 'dans la même situation que le narrateur' (Perec 1993: 157).
9. '[Il a] parfois besoin de se rassurer en énumérant tous les traits qui le distinguent de ce personnage' (Perec 1993: 158).
10. 'en vient presque à se demander s'il n'a pas été explicitement *désigné* par l'auteur' (Perec 1993: 157–58).
11. 'Monte encore ces quelques marches qui te séparent de mon dernier refuge, il y fait enfin clair. Ouvre la porte, elle n'est que poussée [...]. Il te suffira de refermer ce livre devant moi, devant toi, sous la lampe, pour que je disparaisse [...]. Alors regarde l'heure à ton poignet, ce sera toujours celle de ma mort'.
12. 'Había empezado a leer la novela unos días antes' (Cortázar [1964] 1995: 23).
13. 'la ilusión novelesca lo ganó casi en seguida. Gozaba del placer casi perverso de irse desgajando línea a línea de lo que lo rodeaba' (Cortázar 1995: 23).
14. 'Palabra a palabra, absorbido por la sórdida disyuntiva de los héroes, dejándose ir hacia las imágenes que se concertaban y adquirían color y movimiento, fue testigo del último encuentro en la cabaña del monte. Primero entraba la mujer, recelosa; ahora llegaba el amante, lastimada la cara por el chicotazo de una rama' (Cortázar 1995: 23).

CHAPTER 18

# When Fiction Changes the World... of Fiction

*Frank Wagner*

*Université Rennes 2*

## 1. Can Fiction Change the World?

As observed by the editors of a recent volume titled *Pouvoir de la littérature: De l'energeia à l'empowerment* (Power of Literature: From *Energeia* to *Empowerment*), to ask what literature — and within it, fiction — *can do* seems to come back to 'asking an old question' (Bouju, Parisot, and Pluvinet 2019: 7). However, despite the multiple responses that this question has already elicited over the centuries, I cannot help but notice that it is being posed again today with renewed insistence and in renewed terms. This is thanks to the diversification of media forms that offer fictions, as well as to the renewal of critical methods brought to bear on them — above all in the area of cognitive sciences.

However, even if the present inquiry implies a larger reflection (whether posed in new terms or not) on the general powers of fiction, it is also more precise and specific, since it introduces the hypothesis of an action (*pragma*) by fiction on the world where it is produced and received. '*Does* fiction change the world?' Upon closer examination, we find that this formula also contains two questions in one: that of the transformative capacities of fiction; and that of the effectiveness of the resulting modifications. Of course, these two aspects are undoubtedly intertwined. For the sake of economy, however, and without entirely neglecting the verdict of *praxis*, I will focus on the first. This brings an inflection of the initial question, now reformulated as follows: '*Can* fiction change the world?' and, above all, 'according to what modalities?'

In order to address these questions, this study will be broken down into two stages. First, I will offer a theoretical reflection, synthesising various opinions on the nature, degree, conditions of possibility, and specific modalities of a transformative action (or not) of fiction on the world. Next, from a more empirical perspective and in accordance with the title of this contribution, we will review some examples of literary texts in which the possibility of an *effective* action by fiction (whether positive or negative) is represented within fiction itself. From the confrontation between theorists' hypotheses and writers' own 'proposals', there will emerge a kind of panorama of the presumed pragmatic capacities of fiction, as well as of the hopes and fears that they continue to fuel today. Finally, it remains to be noted that for reasons of space, only the *reception* aspect of fiction will be considered here, without drawing conclusions on possible transformations experienced by its creators.

## 2. How Can Fiction Change the World?

To start out on this path, let us begin by recalling an obvious fact that is often overlooked but can hardly be contested. 'Does fiction change the world?': in one sense at least, an affirmative answer goes without saying. Fiction indeed modifies the world by the mere fact of its appearance, since it is *added* to the world. On either side of 1932, there is thus a world without (before) and a world with (after) Céline's *Voyage au bout de la nuit* (*Journey to the End of the Night*) (1932). This observation is at least partially in line with Jean-Marie Schaeffer's point, if we extend its meaning slightly: 'as a result of concentrating on its relationship with reality we run the risk of forgetting that fiction is also a reality, and therefore an integrating part of reality' (Schaeffer 2010: 186). While such a reminder is important, it nevertheless seems difficult to be satisfied with it, as Schaeffer's subsequent remarks attest: 'the essential question is not [therefore] that of the relations that fiction maintains *with* reality; it is more a matter of seeing how it operates *in* reality, that is, in our lives' (186). We note here the adoption of a clearly pragmatic perspective, as well as the final 'equation': in order to operate in reality, fiction must, according to particular modalities that Schaeffer details in *Why Fiction?*, affect *our lives*. Here is the first element of our answer...

Still, however widespread the idea, the hypothesis that fiction acts on our lives is nonetheless posed in axiologically contrasting terms. The question of the powers of fiction thus opposes pessimists to optimists; let us say, at the risk of being over-schematic, Plato versus Aristotle,[1] as well as the more or less conscious or willing heirs to their apparently antagonistic positions. In the first camp stand all those who are frightened by the mimetic foundations of fiction, perceived as vectors of harmful illusion(s); in the other, all those who, on the contrary, salute fiction's capacity to serve as a model. But perhaps the endless resurgence of the debate between them can largely be attributed to misunderstanding, since, on the theoretical level, the conception of fiction as mimetic feint is not a priori opposed to its possible modelling capacities.

Indeed, a number of theorists have set out to dissolve precisely this presumed incompatibility, starting with Yuri Lotman ([1970] 1973), whose attribution of certain functions to 'ludic simulation' has rightly enjoyed considerable posterity:

> — 'to learn a behaviour without being submitted to the immediate sanction of reality'
> — 'to teach us to modelise situations susceptible to presenting themselves in the future'
> — '[it] permits us to get used little by little to the dysphoric situations that we have to confront in real life.' (Lotman, summarised in Schaeffer 2010: 106)

These intuitions obviously influenced Schaeffer's *Why Fiction?*, first published in French in 1999, which cites them in support of its analyses of 'mimesis as a means of knowledge' (Schaeffer 2010: 95–108). This last idea seems to be decisive, insofar as recognising that fiction possesses a *cognitive* function makes it possible to avoid opposing it, in caricatural fashion, to conceptual knowledge of a rationalist and philosophical type, perceived as the only possible mode of knowledge. We can thus consider that one of the great merits of *Why Fiction?* lies in its author's insistence on the modelling capacities of fictional *mimesis*, whatever the media involved. In taking this stance, moreover, Schaeffer answers at least partially the question at hand here, since his detailed examination of 'mimetic modelling' (2010: 186) leads him to affirm that 'fiction gives us the possibility to continue to enrich, to remodel, to readapt all along our existence the original cognitive and affective base thanks to which we have acceded to our personal identity and to our being-in-the-world' (Schaeffer 2010: 300). By virtue of the 'permanent mental makeshift' (*bricolage*) that can result from its use (Schaeffer 2010: 301), it does not seem excessive to believe that fiction has the capacity to 'change' the subject-reader — or rather to help him/her to change through successive experiences of fictional immersion. This is no doubt only a first step on the path that would lead to 'changing the world', but it seems far from negligible.

We find the same hypothesis, moreover, in the work of several recent analysts of fiction who, like Schaeffer, draw on the cognitive sciences to enrich their reflection. Raphaël Baroni, for instance, in *Les Rouages de l'intrigue* (The Cogs of the Plot), underlines 'the adaptive and ethical functions of mimetic narratives' (Baroni 2017: 52). In particular, he presents the mimetic narrative as 'a laboratory of simulated practical and moral experiences' (Baroni 2017: 53), whose benefits are not limited to the sole sphere of contact with fiction but extend to 'our natural and cultural environments' (2017: 58) — that is, to the world in which we live and read. As for the ethical dimension, it derives in this case from the postulated link between intrigue and the 'decentring of the self' (2017: 184), which favours the development of a 'reflection on complexity open to an encounter with otherness that compels us to a permanent mental makeshift' (2017: 184).[2] Without ignoring the potential dangers of mimetic narratives, induced by certain manipulative uses of their 'cogs', Baroni thus clearly insists on their capacity (particularly in the case of literary texts) to broaden our possibilities thanks to the work of unveiling to which they invite us. According to this view, aesthetic experience thus favours a cognitive, affective, ethical, and more broadly existential 'profit.' Like Schaeffer, Baroni puts forth a form of apology for fiction, albeit a nuanced one, highlighting its possible transformative virtues — at least at the individual level of the reader or spectator.

Finally, a few minor differences aside, we encounter similar ideas in Vincent Jouve's recent book *Pouvoirs de la fiction: Pourquoi aime-t-on les histoires ?* (Powers of Fiction: Why Do We Love Stories?) (2019). Among 'the virtues of fiction' (111), three main functions are listed. First of all, a compensatory or consoling capacity, which is in line with Schaeffer's reflections on the novelistic as the vector of an 'existential utopia' (Schaeffer 2004). In this respect, fiction has virtues that are in a sense therapeutic, favourable to the development of the human being; it is therefore anthropological. Here we should doubtless distinguish between the properties of *fiction* and those of *narrative*, which as such 'responds to the anguish of contingency' (Jouve 2019: 119) by elaborating a concerted form. But we may consider that, in the case of *fictional narrative*, these virtues ultimately reveal themselves to be convergent, and thus guarantee an all the more effective 'consolation.'

However, the interest of fictional narrative does not lie entirely in its ability to satisfy our 'need for security' (Jouve 2019: 120) but rather in the tension it establishes between this aspiration and our 'desire for novelty' (2019: 120). Indeed, it rests both on the appeal to and the overcoming of 'anthropological, cultural and aesthetic models' (2019: 123), offering its receiver a most enriching experience. Next, according to Jouve, fiction can be perceived as a laboratory of experiences — in reference both to Lotman's intuitions and to the 'thought experiments' of cognitivists.[3] With fewer psychological, emotional, or existential risks, we are thus able to confront situations that we did not previously know or would never even have considered. As a 'life simulator', fiction thus favours a potential confrontation with otherness, as well as a salutary opening of the field of our possibilities. Finally, in addition to this beneficial 'existential training' (2019: 133), Jouve believes that fiction offers us the opportunity to 'exercise our minds' (2019: 142) thus refining our cognitive capacities. This revitalisation of our mental life results from the intense interpretative activity in which fiction invites us to engage. In this regard, whether it unfolds diachronically and/or synchronically, the interpretation prompted by fiction proves to be both formative and — at least potentially — liberating, by involving us in dialogue and critical feedback.

From Lotman to Jouve, via Schaeffer and Baroni, to cite but a few cases,[4] a certain number of common elements can be observed: as many plausible virtues of fiction, brought to light by cautious and measured apologists. With equal measure and caution, let us say that we can reasonably suppose that fiction possesses the capacity to 'change' its receptors on the affective, cognitive, and even ethical level — a fact that is not insignificant. However, we may hesitate to take the further step from this point to inferring that changing the reader (his or her worldview) changes the world *ipso facto*. For there is a distance between the virtual and the actual, as well as between the individual and the collective. *Does changing the reader (or the spectator) amount to changing the world?* For reasons as numerous as they are varied, the elucidation of which would require, at the very least, the services of a psychologist, a sociologist, and a philosopher, the equation can still appear overly optimistic — even if certain precedents (*Uncle Tom's Cabin* [Stowe 1852], *Germinal* [Zola 1885]) can undoubtedly be identified.[5]

## 3. When Fiction Changes the World of Fiction

On the other hand, there exists a universe where fiction undoubtedly changes the world: *its own world, that of fiction*. Even if we might seem to be neglecting the initial question, let us draw on a few examples to briefly investigate what these phenomena of *mise en abyme* can teach us about the transformative capacities of fictional narrative. My first observation is a purely empirical one that is perhaps subject to doubt, since I am unsure of the extent to which it is conditioned by the limitations or orientations of my own personal cultural background: in a fictional regime, the intradiagetic representations of such transformative capabilities appear much more often to be negative rather than positive. In fact, praise for the powers of fiction is found much more frequently in the works of writer-readers who choose the essay form — Michel Tournier's *Le Vol du Vampire* (*The Flight of the Vampire*) (1981), Alberto Manguel's *A Reading Diary* (2004), etc. This apparent disproportion can easily be understood, both for historical reasons (the importance of negativity in modern literature) and for structural reasons (the superior potential of the negative in terms of narrative effectiveness and the production of novelistic interest).

Still, it is of course possible to identify literary examples that show, in a *mise en abyme*, the benefits that readers can derive from the company of fiction, in terms of individual or collective enrichment. We might think of the pages where the narrator-character of Proust's *Recherche* ([1913–1927] 1987) evokes the renewed apprehension of the world that he gains from his readings, especially from his discovery of the work of Bergotte. This is partly due to the generic ambiguities of the work and to the autodiegetic narrator's notorious propensity to *excursus*, but such occasions offer a prefiguration of Nelson Goodman's reflection that upon leaving an encounter with a work of art, 'the world we step into is not the one we left [...]; we see everything in terms of those works' (Goodman 1984: 192). It does not seem excessive to assert that Proust's work is for some of his readers what Bergotte's is for 'Marcel': an optical instrument that modifies their perception of the world and the beings who move through it.

Another, very different example should be mentioned here: Philip K. Dick's *The Man in the High Castle* (1962). This dystopian novel is based on the following hypothesis: in 1947, the Allies surrendered to the Axis forces, so that the United States is under German-Japanese control. Yet most of the characters in this fiction read a novel within the novel by the writer Hawthorne Abendsen (a character in the main diegesis), *The Grasshopper Lies Heavy*, some excerpts of which are 'reproduced', and which represents a universe where, as in ours, the Allies won the Second World War. The story reaches its climax when the heroine (Juliana) points out to Abendsen that, unknowingly, he has written not fiction but a factual text revealing historical reality — as a few occasional waverings of the dystopian universe had already led us to suspect.[6] Learning lessons from such a novel is no simple task, all the more so since the text is burdened with abundant pseudo-philosophical dross, and soaked in a 'New Age' jargon characteristic of Sixties counterculture. But with a bit of good will, and beyond the ambiguities that after all give the novel its spice, it is possible to read it as a eulogy in action of fiction's powers of *unveiling*, playing out this time on a supra-individual scale.

To complete this all-too-brief list, my readers will be able to find other examples (Volodine,[7] Bello,[8] etc.) by drawing on their personal encyclopaedias. But it is clearly much easier to find examples of *mises en abyme* of negative transformations induced by encountering fictions; even if, in these matters, the axiological polarisation is trickier to establish than it seems. In any case, two emblematic characters come immediately to mind here, Don Quixote and Emma Bovary, whom critics often tend to conflate. However, on closer inspection, the postures they exemplify should be distinguished (see Wagner 2012: 392–93). Indeed, at the diegetic level, under the ill-digested influence of his readings of novels of chivalry, Don Quixote takes the 'real' for the imaginary, for example windmills for giants (Cervantes 1605–1615). On the other hand, Emma seems to take the imaginary for the 'real', for example the thrilling loves of fictional heroes for authentic interpersonal relationships, which she thinks are reproducible in her own existence. But beyond this difference, the essential point lies in the common inability of these two characters to conform to the fictional pact that is supposed to govern the reading of novels. Consequently, even if the respective positions of Cervantes and Flaubert ([1857] 1972) require recontextualisation and further distinctions, we may still wonder whether their novels denounce certain reading pathologies rather than the dangers of fiction as such. What unites the sad-faced knight and the dissatisfied bourgeois woman is in fact their shared inability to perceive and adopt the relationship of 'shared ludic feint' (Schaeffer 2010: 121) that underpins the harmonious (and therefore happy) relationship to fiction.[9] Furthermore, by virtue of the literary narrative's complex scenography, it is both possible and probable that these misunderstandings of the reading pact promote, by contrast, respect for this pact on another level. Taught by these intradiagetic counterexamples, real readers, outside of the diegesis, are then encouraged not to make such a mistake — if ever they had been inclined to do so. From Sorel's *Le Berger extravagant* (The Extravagant Shepherd) ([1627] 1972). to Marivaux's *Pharsamon* ([1737] 1972), there is no shortage of examples that are similar in their premise and implications. Closer to our own time, we can also think, *mutatis mutandis*, of the psychotic reader in Stephen King's *Misery* (1987), whose emotional dependence on the adventures of Misery Chastain leads her to imprison and torture her favourite writer; or of the monomaniacal narrator of Tanguy Viel's *Cinéma* (1999), whose life 'hangs on a film' ('ne tient qu'à un film', back cover), Joseph Mankiewicz's *Sleuth* (1972).

All these examples, among many others, therefore carry a representation of the negative transformations that fiction can provoke in reader-characters. But precisely, the very phenomenon of the *mise en abyme* of reading activity makes them into as many obliquely self-denouncing fictions (see Schaeffer 2010: 136 and 324 n29). The resulting dialectic of immersion and emersion brings a specific kind of pleasure, since the properties of the same shared ludic feint in which we are indulging become the object of more or less subtly deformed representations. Far from being reducible to a wearisome metalectoral lesson in which all dissonance is explicitly resolved at the end, such texts play with the phase shift between levels of meaning as well as with ambiguity, and precisely in this way stimulate our capacity for critical distance and our interpretative ingenuity. In this sense, in addition to the aesthetic satisfaction they offer (and which remains their essential quality in my view), they paradoxically represent as many practical illustrations of the positive powers of fiction as analysed by Schaeffer, Baroni, Jouve, and others.

\* \* \* \* \*

Since questions have been asked, we might as well conclude by trying to answer them. At the end of the day, can fiction change the world? And according to what modalities? We have seen that fiction can only act by changing its readers or spectators, that is, by helping them to constantly make affective, cognitive, and ethical readjustments. On a personal level, as will by now be clear, I am completely willing to acknowledge and delight in this power. As to whether, on a supra-individual scale, a modification of the world in which we consume these fictions can or must result, let me leave it to those more competent than I am in these matters to answer this thorny question...

*Translated from the French by Alison James*

## References

BARONI, RAPHAËL. 2017. *Les Rouages de l'intrigue: Les outils de la narratologie postclassique pour l'analyse des textes littéraires* (Geneva: Slatkine)
BELLO, ANTOINE. 2007. *Les Falsificateurs* (Paris: Gallimard)
———. 2009. *Les Éclaireurs* (Paris: Gallimard)
———. 2015. *Les Producteurs* (Paris: Gallimard)
BOUJU, EMMANUEL, YOLAINE PARISOT, and CHARLINE PLUVINET (eds.). 2019. *Pouvoir de la littérature. De l'energeia' à l'empowerment* (Rennes: Presses Universitaires de Rennes)
CÉLINE, LOUIS-FERDINAND. 1932. *Voyage au bout de la nuit* (Paris: Denoël & Steele)
CERVANTES, MIGUEL. 1605–1615. *El ingenioso hidalgo Don Quixote de la Mancha*, 2 parts (Madrid: Francisco de Robles)
DICK, PHILIP K. 1962. *The Man in The High Castle* (Boston: Mariner Books)
ELGIN, CATHERINE Z. 1992. 'Comprendre: L'art et la science', in *Lire Goodman* (Combas: Éditions de l'Éclat), pp. 49–67
FLAUBERT, GUSTAVE. [1857] 1972. *Madame Bovary* (Paris: Gallimard)
GOODMAN, NELSON. 1984. *Of Mind and Other Matters* (Cambridge, MA: Harvard University Press)
JOUVE, VINCENT. 2019. *Pouvoirs de la fiction: Pourquoi aime-t-on les histoires?* (Paris: Armand Colin)
KING, STEPHEN. 1987. *Misery* (New York: Viking)
LAVOCAT, FRANÇOISE. 2016. *Fait et fiction: Pour une frontière* (Paris: Seuil)
LEICHTER-FLACK, FRÉDÉRIQUE. 2012. *Le Laboratoire des cas de conscience* (Paris: Alma)
LOTMAN, YURI. (1970) 1973. *La Structure du texte artistique*, trans. by Anne Fournier, Bernard Kreise, Ève Malleret, Henri Meschonnic, and Joëlle Yong (Paris: Gallimard)
MANGUEL, ALBERTO. 2004. *A Reading Diary* (New York: Farrar, Straus, and Giroux)
MARIVAUX, PIERRE DE. [1737] 1972. *Pharsamon, ou les nouvelles folies romanesques*, in *Œuvres de jeunesse* (Paris: Gallimard)
PROUST, MARCEL. [1913–1927] 1987. *À la recherche du temps perdu*, 4 vols (Paris: Gallimard)
SCHAEFFER, JEAN-MARIE. 2010. *Why Fiction?*, trans. by Dorrit Cohn (Lincoln: University of Nebraska Press)
———. 2004. 'La catégorie du romanesque', in *Le Romanesque*, ed. by Michel Murat and Gilles Declerq (Paris: Presses Sorbonne nouvelle), pp. 291–302
SOREL, CHARLES. [1627] 1972. *Le Berger extravagant* (Geneva: Slatkine)
STOWE, HARRIET BEECHER. 1852. *Uncle Tom's Cabin*, 2 vols (Boston: John P. Jewitt)
TOURNIER, MICHEL. 1981. *Le Vol du Vampire* (Paris: Gallimard)

VIEL, TANGUY. 1999. *Cinéma* (Paris: Minuit)
WAGNER, FRANK. 2012. 'Des coups de canif dans le contrat de lecture', *Poétique*, 172: 387–407
ZOLA, ÉMILE. 1885. *Germinal* (Paris: Charpentier)

## Notes to Chapter 18

1. See Claude Calame's contribution to this volume (Chapter 1) for a reconsideration of Plato's and Aristotle's accounts of mimesis and diegesis.
2. We note in passing the use of the formula 'permanent mental makeshift', previously encountered in Schaeffer.
3. Jouve quotes Elgin (Jouve 2019, 126n1; Elgin 1992). We might also mention Leichter-Flack (2012), even if she does not explicitly lay claim to a cognitivist approach.
4. See also Lavocat 2016.
5. It has been claimed that Harriet Beecher Stowe's *Uncle Tom's Cabin* (1852) favoured the emergence of the abolitionist cause, leading to the U.S. Civil War (on this point see the editors' Introduction to this volume). Émile Zola's novel *Germinal* (1885) is thought to have alerted the public to the condition of underground miners.
6. Particularly in Chapter 14, under the troubled gaze of the character Nosubuke Tagomi.
7. Within the dystopian universe elaborated by Antoine Volodine, 'post-exotic' works create community cohesion as well as having other functions.
8. See in particular the fictional postface of *Les Producteurs* (Bello 2015), the third and final part of the *Falsificateurs* trilogy (which also includes *Les Falsificateurs* [Bello 2007] and *Les Éclaireurs* [Bello 2009]), where fiction, and literature more generally, are credited with a significant ability to appease conflicts.
9. For an alternative reading of quixotism, see Yen-Mai Tran-Gervat's contribution to this volume (Chapter 15).

# ABSTRACTS

Chapter 1. Poetic Forms of Narrative and Pragmatic Fiction: *Poiein — Plattein — Prattein*

*Claude Calame, École des Hautes Études en Sciences Sociales (EHESS)*

Taking a distant, anthropological approach to another culture can shed light on our own aporias and, in a differential and critical way, challenge the concepts by which we try to break out of aporia when we attempt to define the forms of literary and artistic creation. In this case, (narrative) fiction has recently been defined as shared playful pretence, or as a result of metaleptic effects that create a possible world requiring interpretation. A return to Plato's *Republic* shows that approaching fiction implies, first, an exploration of enunciative strategies referring to the instance of discourse and the author (the *poiein* — making, poetic creation); second, a semio-narrative semantics (an investigation into the *plattein* — crafting or fashioning); and ultimately, via pragmatics (taking into account the *prattein*, or doing), a cultural and social anthropology of fiction.

Chapter 2. The Fiction of Factuality (Some Perspectives from Pre-Modern Japan)

*Judit Árokay, Heidelberg University*

In Japan, given the religious (Buddhist) and political (Confucian) setting that has been fundamentally hostile to fiction, the boundaries between fact and fiction are constantly challenged and examined, showing a keen awareness of the interrelatedness of reality and fiction. An analysis of exemplary texts from the genre of Japanese medieval histories shows the ambiguity of the modern concept of fiction if applied to pre-modern Japanese writing. In medieval history writing, e.g., in the genre of *kagami mono* (called *rekishi monogatari*, historical tale, in modern terms) historical claims to factuality are made via fictional means. Although these texts are not intended as theoretical treatises, they show a keen awareness of different functions and effects of fiction. This analysis of different rhetorical methods (used to repudiate the slightest appearance of fictitiousness of historical fact) offers a sense of the effects attributed to fiction and factuality in a medieval Japanese setting.

Chapter 3. For a Theory of Fiction as *Show, Performance, Entertainment*

*Yasusuke Oura, Kyoto University*

Definitions of fiction have tended, until now, to take as a model the novel or written narrative. This sometimes distorts our overall view of fictional products.

One may even wonder whether this definition, which is often too literary or even essentialist, does not lead to theoretical rigidity. Taking as a model unwritten, theatrical, cinematographic, or televisual fiction allows the development of a resolutely unorthodox approach to those phenomena called show, performance, or entertainment — phenomena that have not been explored much in terms of fiction, and whose fictional status remains ambiguous. A theory of fiction centred on show and performance is a theory of the *actor*: a flesh-and-blood being who plays an imaginary character. The case of Bunraku, a form of Japanese puppet theatre, provides a paradoxical illustration of this account, allying overt artifice (the visible presence of the puppeteer) and fictional immersion. This approach to fiction has two advantages: it broadens the notion of fiction by adapting it to the reality of our current cultural consumption; and it displaces and thus freshens up all our theories of fiction.

### Chapter 4. The Moral Problem of Fiction: Rethinking the Emotional Effects of Fictional Characters
*Mario Slugan, Queen Mary University of London*

As originally formulated, the paradox of fiction involves three assertions. Separately they all appear intuitively correct but taken together they cannot all hold simultaneously: 1) fictional objects and entities cause genuine emotions, 2) only objects and events which we believe truly exist can cause genuine emotions, 3) we do not believe that fictional objects and emotions truly exist. The present-day view is that the paradox is not really a paradox, i.e., proposition 2 is considered to be false. An alternative solution can be proposed, however. Without denying the idea that non-existent objects can cause genuine emotions, the view that we actually fear monsters in horror films does not accurately describe the standard spectatorial response. Rather, what we fear is the possibility, however minute or irrational it might be, that in actual life there might be some monster-like entity which might do us harm. This is not only applicable to horror and fear but can be generalised to numerous other emotional engagements with fictional objects and entities.

### Chapter 5. Lucianic Fictions and the Rise of Unbelief
*Nicolas Correard, Nantes Université*

The rediscovery of Lucian of Samosata (c.125–80 CE), 'who spares neither men nor gods', and the vogue of Lucianic writing in the Renaissance, have long been recognised as one of the driving forces in the development of religious incredulity in the humanist elites, but we still lack a full assessment of Lucian's impact in the history of ideas and beliefs. Lucian's irony was used by Erasmus and Rabelais in their campaign for a radical brand of evangelism, but his works were also favourites among thinkers like Alberti, Bruno, La Mothe le Vayer, Voltaire, Hume, and Wieland. The massive wave of censorship that struck Lucianic writings at the end of the sixteenth century was a desperate reaction to what was felt as a real political challenge. Lucianic fictions, when written in vernacular languages, spread subversive ideas to a wide audience. Staging unrepentant unbelievers who poke fun at the creed of hell in dialogues of the dead; exposing religious fanatics acting out of perverse and obscure motivations on earth; or imagining a comical Jupiter confronted with his own incapacity to manage the skies: these were some ways in which early modern European authors could think about and express what was still barely imaginable: the idea that modern religious creeds, just like ancient ones, were merely fictions.

## Chapter 6. Fiction and the Modelling of Chance
*Anne Duprat, Université de Picardie Jules Verne/Institut Universitaire de France*

Scholarship on the relationship between fiction and chance has led to new approaches over the past twenty years, particularly in France, Germany, and the United States. Postclassical narratology, cognitivist approaches to literature, or applications of the logic of possible worlds to literary fictions are some of the areas that have brought unprecedented attention to the role played by fiction in conceptions of contingency and human attitudes to risk. During the same period, several studies have taken up the question of the historical transformations of these relationships since the beginnings of modernity, but on a new basis. At the intersection of these new proposals, a question arises: by simulating chance, does literary fiction merely imitate the behaviour of contingency in reality and thus propose a more or less credible substitute for it, reflecting the history of different discourses on the world? Or do fiction's own productions operate differently, as projections that are then integrated by its audience into the different models we build in order to understand, predict, and act in the world? Faced with such situations as climate change and the global pandemic, fictional representations of chance have their own heuristic value, helping us to model, manage, and respond to the experience of complex phenomena.

## Chapter 7. Pygmalion's Virtual Doll: The Case of a Real Metalepsis?
*Nathalie Kremer, Université Sorbonne Nouvelle/Institut Universitaire de France*

A man's marriage to the virtual singer Hatsune Miku in Tokyo and Professor Ishiguro's creation of the android Geminoid HI in Osaka are recent cases that seem to realise the dream of the 'living copy'. This technological achievement is the result of expertise at the forefront of engineering and modern digital technology, but it also reveals the persistence of the ancestral dream of the automaton becoming a living being, a dream dating back at least to the myth of Pygmalion. These ancestral fictions, where the artificial becomes real, can be read as fictional dramatisations of a form of metalepsis: a boundary crossing between narrative levels or universes. But in the case of Geminoid and its avatars, when fiction becomes reality, can we speak of a real metalepsis, a transgression of ontological boundaries? On the one hand, from an ontological point of view, the separation is maintained, since imaginary objects cannot actually intrude into reality. On the other hand, from a pragmatic point of view, we can view those moments when fiction has a tangible impact on the world and on human behaviours as metaleptic.

## Chapter 8. Etiquette to Change the World? Fictional Time-Order and Imperial Power at the Court of Emperor Go-Daigo

*Simone Müller, University of Zurich*

Court manuals from classical and medieval Japan describe the daily and annual routines at the imperial court, known as *nitchū gyōji* and *nenjū gyōji* respectively. They provide the image of an integral system in which time and space interweave to form a dense and refined mechanism. *Nitchū gyōji* and *nenjū gyōji* also had an important political function, however: they aimed to confirm the emperor's authority and to prescribe court etiquette for future generations. This raises the question of the extent to which these prescriptive and politically motivated texts corresponded to court reality. Were they really followed strictly, or did they have a merely symbolic function? Did they reflect the court's real practice or were they representative? By comparing the two medieval works *Kenmu nitchū gyōji* and *Kenmu nenjū gyōji*, written in the first half of the fourteenth century, with other court documents from the time, this article traces both the interrelation and the gap between the fiction and the reality of temporal procedures at the medieval Japanese court to show that *Kenmu nitchū gyōji* and *Kenmu nenjū gyōji* are semi-fictitious narratives, that aim at construing a temporal ideal of court routine in order to consolidate imperial power and thus to impact the world.

## Chapter 9. The Construction of the Nation by Theatrical Fiction

*Charlotte Krauss, Université de Poitiers*

To the question 'Can fiction change the world?', we can answer that it contributes to restructuring the world in which we live and allows us to disseminate abstract ideas by illustrating them, sometimes for very large audiences. A case in point is the educational effort provided by the theatre in response to changes in European political systems at the beginning of the nineteenth century. After 1800, the concept of the nation gradually replaced that of the monarchies of divine right as the basis of the state: the subjects of an absolute ruler become citizens, who, in ideal circumstances, are convinced that they belong to a national people. The construction of a whole national imaginary owes a great deal to literary fiction and especially to historical episodes transposed into and transformed by fiction. If the epic was identified as the ideal narrative, it was through stage performance in particular that intellectuals aimed to reach the population. An analysis of German, French, and Polish examples shows how history was fictionalised in order to depict it as national. Yet the influence of the epic ideal contributes to making these dramatic projects unperformable, turning them into closet dramas that appeal to the individual imagination of their readers, at least at the time of their publication.

## Chapter 10. Feminist Resistance and the Powers of Fiction

*Anne Isabelle François, Université Sorbonne Nouvelle*

Feminist theories engage intensely with fiction as a space that allows the exploration and unmasking of the asymmetry in power relations, of the 'ideological field' (Stuart Hall) where stereotypical discourses and gender norms emerge.

These norms cross over into reality, make inroads into it, and participate in its construction, perpetuating inequalities and leading to very real acts of violence. Fiction therefore also becomes a means of resisting individual as well as collective normative imperatives, or regimes that aim to transform bodies into 'docile' entities (Foucault), via an act of empowerment, reconquest, or even survival, in a struggle to oppose patriarchal society and naturalised gendered conceptions. It is therefore crucial to take fiction seriously, to decipher critically repressive codes and resist them by revisionist strategies, which also lead to divided receptions and partisan responses. The dystopian world of Gilead imagined by Margaret Atwood (in her novels and their television adaptation), for instance, has provided the impetus for multiple protests in the real world. But it is not only such overtly feminist fictions that have emancipatory potential; shared reading practices may allow participatory and empowering engagement with any work of fiction.

## Chapter 11. Engagement and Enchantment: Political and Ethical Uses of Fantasy Fictions

*Anne Besson, Université d'Artois*

A widely accepted idea still associates the literatures of the imaginary (science-fiction, fantasy) and the cultural practices associated with them (roleplay or online games in 'universes', fanfiction, etc.) with 'escapism', away from the harsh realities of existence. However, many examples show on the contrary a strong association of this cultural field with ethical and political uses. If they are vectors of values and ideology, as is the case more generally for 'popular' or 'mass cultural' products (for instance, the colonialist, scientistic, or collectivist discourses present in science-fiction during the twentieth century), their projection of other possible worlds also associates them with new claims for rights that are likely to circumvent or subvert norms. Now at the forefront of the cultural benchmarks shared by the generations born since the turn of the twenty-first century, fantasy fictions are expected (perhaps even more than 'realistic' fictions) to give the fairest representation of diversity (whether physical, social, racial, or gendered), and to imagine their desirable extensions or the stumbling points to avoid. Today, numerous 'fan-activists' lay claim to *Harry Potter*, *Hunger Games*, or *Avatar* as inspiration for their commitment. These references allow them to reach an audience that does not adhere to traditional forms of political communication.

## Chapter 12. Fiction or Death: The Latin American Tradition of Nonfiction

*Annick Louis, Université de Franche-Comté/CRAL (EHESS-CNRS)*

'Hybrid' texts, which deliberately combine heterogeneous elements and position themselves between fiction and nonfiction, have acquired global visibility and success in the last twenty years. This transnational phenomenon, however, has national specificities. Latin American literature has a longer tradition of such narratives at the boundary of fiction and document, which date back to the nineteenth century, develop through the twentieth century in the framework of the opposition between the novel and testimonial narrative, and turn in recent years to audio-visual media, Facebook, and blogs. Some examples from Argentine literature reveal the specific historical conditions that give rise to these narrative modes as well as the particular reading regimes that develop in response to them. These narratives seek to produce some intervention into reality that remains unpredictable. Their aim is to change the real world by questioning social discourses and silences, but there are no specific indications concerning what exactly is to be modified, and by what means.

## Chapter 13. Fiction as Legal Authority? Orwell, Snowden, and State Cyber-Surveillance

*Henriette Korthals Altes, Maison Française d'Oxford, University of Oxford*

Does judicial citation of literature help progress case law? Quotation of Orwell's *Nineteen Eighty-Four* in American courts has served to fill in the lacunae of American privacy law, especially in the context of Snowden's revelations about mass cyber-surveillance. This example offers some support for claims by the Law and Literature movement that literature may provide a counter-cultural norm or 'counter-legal' propositions. In *Klayman v. Obama* (2013), however, it was legal rather than literary scholarship that argued that *Nineteen Eighty-Four* served as a counter norm, with a direct practical impact: it served to refine a legal instrument, the 'Katz test' of reasonableness of privacy, in the age of big data. If citation of Orwell succeeded in progressing case law, it nevertheless failed to change legislation, as the NSA programme still operates. Furthermore, judicial citations reference the idea of a totalitarian world but fail to engage with the broader issues raised by Orwell's novel, which warns against the sinister effects of surveillance: infringed privacy, homogenised behaviour and the destruction of thought and feeling. A more holistic discussion, as advocated by Martha Nussbaum and Peter Brooks, would engage fully with Orwell's demonstration that surveillance leads to destruction of thought and the impoverishment or annihilation of emotion. Surveillance should be rethought not only in terms of infringed privacy but also infringed freedom of thought, which in the digital era has been put under pressure in insidious ways.

## Chapter 14. Legal Revolutions as Fictions: Do they Change the World?

*Otto Pfersmann, École des Hautes Études en Sciences Sociales (EHESS), Lier-FYT*

Legal systems seem *in a way* to be part of the objective world. They contain norms which are applied by courts or administrative agencies through decisions having a very concrete impact on their addressees. A modification within a legal system may have a highly important incidence on those concerned, precisely in that it changes their 'legal situation'. Changing the legal system itself through a set of revolutionary actions imposing a new order is generally seen as a set of events having the highest and most radical impact on people's lives. However, a consideration of several examples from European and American history shows that the element changing the real world can never be found in law itself, but rather resides in cognitive and practical attitudes related to merely fictional data — since normative orders exist by virtue of fiction — and that legal scholarship is entirely unable to explain what really happens in such situations.

## Chapter 15. Quixotism as a Humorous Reflection on Fiction's Effects

*Yen-Mai Tran-Gervat, Université Sorbonne Nouvelle*

Since the publication of *Don Quixote* (1605–1615), many authors have explored what Harry Levin, in his 1970 essay, called 'the Quixotic principle'; that is, the fact that a character reads so much fiction that he or she develops a form of madness consisting in no longer being able to tell reality from fiction. Offering an alternative reading of this phenomenon, this chapter examines how, from Cervantes to Salman Rushdie (*Quichotte*, 2019), with a detour via Woody Allen's *Play it Again, Sam* (1972), what is usually seen as satire (of romance fiction in realistic contexts) could instead be considered a humorous reflexion by fiction on its own effects. Humour is understood here in its historical, eighteenth-century meaning, as distinct from satire and parody, and with reflexivity and empathy at its core. Its use in quixotic fictions induces a pleasurable acknowledgement of the enticements and illusions of fiction.

## Chapter 16. Metafiction in Japanese and Western Literature: *Chô-kyokô* and Meta-Mystery

*Masahiro Iwamatsu, Kwansei Gakuin University*

The term *metafiction*, coined in 1972 by the American novelist William Henry Gass, became popular in Japan in the second half of the 1980s. In 1979, however, the Japanese novelist Yasutaka Tsutsui had already invented the word *chô-kyoko* (surfiction), without knowing either the notion of metafiction or that of 'surfiction', another term used by the French-American novelist Raymond Federman in 1973. In his criticism and fiction experiments, Tsutsui shows the full potential of self-referential fiction. At the end of the 1980s, another metafictional movement appeared in Japanese literature: the meta-mystery, a form of detective novel that became metafictional and often playful, with self-referential narrative, nested structures, narrative faking, and a challenge to realism. Anticipated by the work of Kenji Takemoto, this movement continued in the following decades (with works by Tsutsui and Takemaru Abiko, among others). Finally, Katsuhiko Otsuji's 'Short Story' (1991) emphasises the fictional communication between narrator and reader, and can be compared to texts by Italo Calvino, Agota Kristof, and Paul Auster that refer in similar fashion to their own narrative act. The resulting metaleptic paradoxes invite reflection on the nature of fiction precisely by transgressing its conventions.

## Chapter 17. Killing the Reader? On Some Regrettable Secondary Effects of Reading

*Maxime Decout, Sorbonne Université/Institut Universitaire de France*

The fantasy is well known: a book might have such a strong influence on its reader that it would come to influence his or her existence. In its most extreme form, the reader is the victim of a book. Can a fiction turn its readers into assassins or kill them? This situation both posits and calls into question the power of books. In the twentieth century, it gives rise to *murderous fictions* that often exploit the genre of the detective novel. In works by Michel Butor, Jean Lahougue, and Georges Perec, the means of incriminating or victimizing the reader is a *mise en abyme*. Also employed by Lahougue and Perec, and to even greater effect by Julio Cortázar, metalepsis goes even further, suggesting the intrusion of a fictional universe into reality. Finally, reading itself may be cast as a murderous act (François Le Lionnais, Benoît Peeters), or a book made into a murder weapon (Enrique Vila-Matas, and Perec once again). It is clear that when the reader (in the text) becomes a victim of the text, the power of fiction triumphs. But since the reasons for this situation can never apply exactly to us, these texts also implacably affirm fiction's lack of pragmatic efficacy.

## Chapter 18. When Fiction Changes the World... of Fiction
*Frank Wagner, Université Rennes 2*

Fiction necessarily adds to the world by virtue of its very existence, but the question remains: how exactly does it operate in our lives? The hypothesis of fiction's transformative action, whether harmful or beneficial, on the world that contains it has long interested philosophers as well as sociologists and literary theorists. Lotman, Schaeffer, Baroni, and Jouve are among those who have plausibly argued that fiction has benefits on an individual level, but making the leap to the collective may seem overly optimistic. Fiction itself has delved into the question of its own transformative capacities, representing through *mise en abyme* the virtues or dangers of fiction (in textual, cinematic, or some other form). Praise for the powers of fiction, whether on an individual or supra-individual level, can be found in works as different as Proust's *À la recherche du temps perdu* and Philip K. Dick's *The Man in the High Castle*, as well as in fictions by Volodine, Bello, and others. Still, it is much more common to find representations of negative transformations induced by fiction, from the well-known cases of Don Quixote and Emma Bovary to more recent works by Stephen King or Tanguy Viel. Yet even these self-denouncing fictions, through the aesthetic satisfactions that they offer, can serve as illustrations of the positive powers of fiction.

# FURTHER READING

BARONI, RAPHAËL. 2017. *Les Rouages de l'intrigue: Les outils de la narratologie postclassique pour l'analyse des textes littéraires* (Geneva: Slatkine)

BOOTH, WAYNE C. 1988. *The Company We Keep: An Ethics of Fiction* (Berkeley: University of California Press)

BOUJU, EMMANUEL, YOLAINE PARISOT, and CHARLINE PLUVINET (eds.). 2019. *Pouvoir de la littérature: De l'energeia à l'empowerment* (Rennes: Presses Universitaires de Rennes)

CAÏRA, OLIVIER. 2011. *Définir la fiction* (Paris: Éd. de l'EHESS)

COHN, DORRIT. 1999. *The Distinction of Fiction* (Baltimore, MD: Johns Hopkins University Press)

CURRIE, GREGORY. 1990. *The Nature of Fiction* (Cambridge: Cambridge University Press)

——. 2020. *Imagining and Knowing: The Shape of Fiction* (Oxford: Oxford University Press)

FELSKI, RITA. 2008. *Uses of Literature* (Oxford: Blackwell)

GEFEN, ALEXANDRE. 2017. *Réparer le monde: La littérature française face au XXI$^e$ siècle* (Paris: José Corti)

GENETTE, GÉRARD. 1980. *Narrative Discourse: An Essay in Method*, trans. by Jane Lewin (Ithaca, NY: Cornell University Press). Originally published as 'Discours du récit' in Genette, *Figures III* (Paris: Seuil, 1972)

GENETTE, GÉRARD. 1993. *Fiction and Diction*, trans. by Catherine Porter (Ithaca, NY: Cornell University Press). Originally published as *Fiction et diction* (Paris: Seuil, 1991)

GENETTE, GÉRARD. 2004. *Métalepse: De la figure à la fiction* (Paris: Seuil)

HAMBURGER, KÄTE. 1993. *The Logic of Literature*, trans. by Marilynn J. Rose, rev. edn (Bloomington: Indiana University Press). Originally published as *Die Logik der Dichtung* (Stuttgart: E. Klett, 1957)

JOUVE, VINCENT. 2019. *Pouvoirs de la fiction: Pourquoi aime-t-on les histoires?* (Paris: Armand Colin)

KEEN, SUZANNE. 2007. *Empathy and the Novel* (Oxford: Oxford University Press)

LAMARQUE, PETER, and STEIN HAUGOM OLSEN. 1994. *Truth, Fiction, and Literature: A Philosophical Perspective* (Oxford: Oxford University Press)

LANDY, JOSHUA. 2012. *How to Do Things with Fictions* (New York: Oxford University Press)

LAVOCAT, FRANÇOISE. 2016. *Fait et fiction: Pour une frontière* (Paris: Seuil)

NÜNNING, VERA. 2014. *Reading Fictions, Changing Minds: The Cognitive Value of Fiction* (Heidelberg: Universitätsverlag Winter)

NUSSBAUM, MARTHA C. 1995. *Poetic Justice: The Literary Imagination and Public Life* (Boston: Beacon Press)

OATLEY, KEITH. 2011. *Such Stuff as Dreams: The Psychology of Fiction* (New York: John Wiley & Sons)

PAVEL, THOMAS G. 1986. *Fictional Worlds* (Cambridge, MA: Harvard University Press)

——. 2013. *The Lives of the Novel: A History* (Princeton: Princeton University Press). Originally published in French as *La Pensée du roman* (Paris: Gallimard, 2003)

RORTY, RICHARD. 1989. *Contingency, Irony, and Solidarity* (Cambridge: Cambridge University Press)

Ryan, Marie-Laure. 1991. *Possible Worlds, Artificial intelligence, and Narrative Theory* (Bloomington: Indiana University Press)

Sartre, Jean-Paul. 1988. *What Is Literature? and Other Essays*, trans. by Steven Ungar (Cambridge, MA: Harvard University Press). Originally published as *Qu'est-ce que la littérature?* (Paris: Gallimard, 1948)

Schaeffer, Jean-Marie. 2010. *Why Fiction?*, trans. by Dorrit Cohn (Lincoln: University of Nebraska Press). Originally published as *Pourquoi la fiction?* (Paris: Seuil, 1999)

Searle, John R. 1975. 'The Logical Status of Fictional Discourse', *New Literary History*, 6 (2): 319–32 <https://doi.org/10.2307/468422>

Walton, Kendall L. 1978. 'Fearing Fictions', *The Journal of Philosophy* 75 (1): 5–27 <doi:10.2307/2025831>

———. 1990. *Mimesis as Make-Believe: On the Foundations of the Representational Arts* (Cambridge, MA: Harvard University Press)

Zunshine, Lisa. 2006. *Why We Read Fiction: Theory of Mind and the Novel* (Columbus: Ohio State University Press)

# INDEX

Abiko, Takemaru, *Sickness unto Massacre* 223, 255
activism 8, 144, 146, 153, 156, 157, 158, 161, 171, 199, 253
actor(s) 3, 9, 28, 39, 46, 47, 48, 49–50, 51–52, 103, 107 n. 16, 170, 193, 208, 211, 213, 237, 250
Aeschylus 20
aesthetics xii, 4, 18, 26, 32, 77, 91, 160, 167, 175 n. 2, 212, 243, 244, 246, 256
Agrippa, Heinrich Cornelius 76, 77
Albenga, Viviane 149–50
Alberti, Leon Battista, *Momus* 72, 73–74, 75, 78, 81, 250
Alexander, Marguerite ('writerly novel') 220
Alfau, Felipe, *Locos: A Comedy of Gestures* 221
Alighieri, Dante, *Inferno* 80
allegory 73, 77, 81
Allen, Woody 1, 99, 205, 213, 214, 217 n. 21, 255
  *The Purple Rose of Cairo* 1, 2, 98–99
  *see also* 'Play it Again, Sam'
Almodóvar, Pedro 48
Amadís (fictional character) 1, 211, 217 n. 16
*Ancien Régime* 70
Anderson, Benedict, *Imagined Communities* 130
Anderson, Wes 48
Andrevon, Jean-Pierre 157
Ang, Ien 150
anthropology x, xi, 9, 18, 19, 20, 27, 28, 30 n. 20, 70, 169, 187, 244, 249
Anna Karenina (fictional character) 63, 67 n. 7
anticlericalism 3
antiquity, classical world 7, 9, 21, 24, 71, 87, 93, 99, 100, 130
  *see also* Greece
Arias, Lola, *Mi vida después* 170
Aristotle, *Poetics* 27, 242
Arminius 131, 132, 136, 139 n. 2
Árokay, Judit x, 9, 31, 249
artifice 50, 220, 250
atheism 9, 72–75, 76, 81, 84 n. 3
Attardo, Salvatore 207
Atwood, Margaret, *The Handmaid's Tale*, *The Testaments* 10, 141, 142–48
Aubert, Brigitte, *Les Quatre fils du Docteur March* 223
audience response 9
Austen, Jane 1
Auster, Paul, *Leviathan* 225, 227, 255
autobiographical pact 34
*Avatar* (James Cameron, 2009) 156, 160

Badiou, Alain 179
Badinter, Robert 179
Bakhtin, Mikhail 211
Baldwin, James 4
ballet 47
Barak, Aharon 198
Barclay, John 78
Barbusse, Henri, *Le Feu* 4
  pacificism 4
Barnet, Miguel 168
Baroni, Raphaël, *Les Rouages de l'intrigue* 243, 247, 256
Baudrillard, Jean 2
Bayamack-Tam, Emmanuelle, *Arcadie* 148
Bayle, Pierre 80
Béguin, Guillaume, *Titre à jamais provisoire* 102
Bello, Antoine 245
Bentham, Jeremy 8, 180, 182
Bergman, Ingrid 213
Bernard, Jean-Frédéric, *Dialogues critiques et philosophiques* 80
Bessière, Jean 165
Besson, Anne x, 10, 155
Bialock, David 37, 38
Bible, the 75–77
Blackman, Mallory, *Noughts and Crosses* 157
Blanc, William 160
Blejmar, Jordana, *Playful Memories* 171
Boccacio, Giovanni, *Decameron* 77, 84 n. 8
body, the 22, 23, 45, 47, 51, 52, 238
Bogart, Humphrey 213
Bolaño, Roberto 172
Bollywood 49
Bonaparte, Napoleon 131, 132, 192
  Napoleonic law tradition 178
Borges, Jorge Luis 172, 175 n. 7
Bottero, Pierre 157
Bougeant, Guillaume-Hyacinthe, *Voyage merveilleux du prince Fan-Férédin* 210
Bouju, Emmanuel, Yolaine Parisot and Charline Pluvinet 241
Bouleau, Nicolas 90, 91, 93, 96 nn. 6, 7 &12
Bourdaa, Mélanie 158
*bovarysme*, *see* Flaubert
Bracciolini, Poggio 73
Bradbury, Malcolm, and Angus Fletcher ('introverted novel') 220
Brecht, Berthold 156
Brennan, William J. 184

Breton, André 4, 14 n. 6, 94
Brooke-Rose, Christine, *Thru* 222
Brooks, Peter 180, 186, 187, 188
Brown, Dan, *The Da Vinci Code* 4
Bruno, Giordano, *Spaccio della bestia trionfante* 72, 75
Bunraku (puppet theatre) 49–51, 250
Butler, Kenneth D. 39
Butor, Michel, *L'Emploi du temps* 232, 234, 235, 256

Cabandié, Juan 170
Calame, Claude x, 8, 9, 17, 135, 248 n. 1, 248
Calle-Gruber, Mireille ('texte conflictuel') 220
Calvin, Jean 76, 77
    Calvinism 79
Calvino, Italo, *Il Cavaliere inesistente* 219, 225, 226–27, 255
Cameron, James, *see Avatar*
Cammelli, Antonio 74
Canavaggio, Jean, *Don Quichotte, du livre au mythe* 205–06
Capote, Truman, *In Cold Blood* 165, 168
Carroll, Noël 55, 56, 60, 62, 63, 67 n. 10
*Casablanca* (dir. Michael Curtiz) 213
Cavaillé, Jean-Pierre 71, 75
Cavell, Stanley 5
Céladon (fictional character), *see* Urfé, Honoré d'
Céline, Louis-Ferdinand, *Voyage au bout de la nuit* 242
censorship 6, 52, 74, 76, 80, 81, 168, 182, 250
Cercas, Javier 165, 172
Cervantes, Miguel de, *Don Quixote* 1, 2, 10, 69–70, 78, 103, 205–17, 246, 255, 256
    Don Quixote (fictional character) 1, 2, 103, 206, 207, 208, 209, 210, 211, 212, 213, 214, 246, 256
    quixotism 2, 205–17, 248 n. 9, 256
chance:
    causality 70, 87, 88, 89, 94
    models and modelling (outcomes) 9, 85–86, 87, 89, 90, 91, 93–94, 251
    probability, Bayesian networks 86, 90, 91, 92
    relationship between fiction and chance 86
Charlton, William 59, 63
Chedaleux, Delphine 150
Chinese culture 32, 35, 37, 42 n. 3, 48, 116, 119, 120, 126 n. 3, 214, 222
Christianity 76, 79
Church 4, 70, 72
cinema xiv, 1, 5, 6, 18, 45, 46, 48, 69, 87, 88, 92, 99, 104, 143, 156, 213, 246, 250, 256
Citton, Yves, *Mythocratie* 105
Claireville, Onésime Somain de 78
clandestine (literature, treatise, etc.) 74, 76, 77, 80
climate change 9, 85, 86, 160, 251
cognitive sciences 5, 241, 243
Cold War 158
Coleridge, Samuel Taylor ('willing suspension of disbelief') 50, 56
colonialism 160, 167, 253

Commedia dell'Arte 47, 49
comedy 5, 22, 23, 27, 47, 87, 207, 208, 213, 216 n. 1, 221
consciousness (also the unconscious) 40, 78, 81, 99, 113, 130, 133, 137, 163, 175, 180, 208, 213, 219, 220, 222, 223, 227, 232, 234, 242
Constitution, the (American, French, German) 13, 183, 185, 186, 194–99
convention(s) (literary) 4, 9, 31, 33, 41, 80, 114, 118, 119, 165, 166, 172, 212, 221, 227, 255
Correard, Nicolas ix, 10, 69, 72, 74, 77, 78, 79, 84 n. 6, 250
Cortázar, Julio, 'Continuidad de los parques' 235–36, 256
Coste, Florent 165
COVID-19 pandemic 9, 85, 90, 96 n. 1, 251
Crabtree, Ane 142
Crespo, Carlos 170
crime 1, 3, 6, 57, 222–23, 232, 233, 234, 235, 237, 238
critical distance 37, 246
culture x, 4, 7, 9, 15, 17–18, 19, 31, 39, 41, 48, 69, 82, 99, 116, 131, 133, 155–56, 160–61, 167, 187, 214, 245, 249
    cultural liberalism 159
    popular culture(s) 160, 161
Currie, Gregory 5, 96 n. 5, 107 n. 10
Cyrano de Bergerac, *Les États et Empires de la Lune* 72, 75–76, 78
cyberculture 4
    cybernetics 89, 102
    cyber-surveillance, *see* surveillance
    *see also* Internet culture

Dällenbach, Lucien ('récit spéculaire') 220
Dante, *see* Alighieri, Dante
Dawes, James 5–6
*Dead Poets Society* (dir. Peter Weir) 214
Decout, Maxime xi, 11, 229 n. 3, 231, 255
Dedecius, Karl 136
De Gaulle, Charles 198
Dejmek, Kasimierz 136
Demanze, Laurent 165
democracy, democratic values 5, 70, 143, 158, 159, 179, 182, 187, 188
    pre-democratic societies 70
Depp, Johnny 46
De Quincey, 'Letters to a Young Man Whose Education has been Neglected' 167
DeStefano, John 177, 183
detective fiction 1, 219, 222–23, 225, 231, 232–33, 235, 236–37, 240 n. 2, 255, 256
Detienne, Marcel 30 n. 12
Dick, Philip K., *The Man in the High Castle* 245, 256
Dickens, Charles, *Bleak House* 179
digital media 4, 8, 177–78, 180, 183, 185–88, 251, 254
Disney 2, 227
docufiction 10, 47, 165, 171
Dorra, Max 235

Dudzik, Wojciech 136, 137, 140 nn. 22, 23, 26, 27
Duprat, Anne xi, 9, 85, 251
dystopia (dystopian worlds, novels) 10, 144, 145, 147, 157, 158, 161, 177, 181, 184, 186, 245, 248 n. 7, 253

Eco, Umberto 160
Einstein-Bergson debate (1922) 92
Einstein-Bohr controversy (1927, 1930) 92
emotion 3, 5, 6, 8, 26, 33, 53, 55–60, 63–65, 86, 94, 131, 142, 167, 178–80, 183, 184, 214, 215, 244, 246, 250, 254
Emperor Go-Daigo 111–14, 120, 121, 123, 126 nn. 2 & 8, 252
  *Kenmu nitchjū gyōji* and *Kenmu nenjū gyōji* 111–14, 119–20, 121–23
Ende, Michael, *The Neverending Story* 157
enlightenment (Buddhism) 39–40
Enlightenment, the 70, 78, 79, 80, 81, 99, 100, 187
  Christian counter-offensive 80
  see also *separate entries for* Voltaire, Hume
enunciative strategies, modes 17–19, 27, 28, 249
environment:
  global warming 70, 155
  see also climate change
epic narrative xii, 10, 20, 23, 24, 27, 87, 129, 131, 133, 135, 137, 156, 169, 252
epistemology, theory of knowledge 56, 57, 59, 72, 89, 90, 91, 92, 93, 100, 166
erotic books 3
Erasmus, Desiderius 72, 76, 77, 78, 79, 80
escapism 2, 157, 253
Espinel, Vicente 78
essay form 245
ethics 77, 158, 161, 180
  see also morality
Euripides 18, 24, 26, 27
  *Hippolytus* 27

fact and fiction 4, 8, 19, 32, 34, 40, 41, 47, 102, 164, 165–68, 171–72, 231, 249, 251
Falco, Vanina 170
fandom 150, 159, 161, 212, 221
fantasy fictions, fantasy genres 8, 10, 155, 156, 159, 160, 161, 253
Federman, Raymond 220, 221, 255
feminism 148, 149
  female empowerment 144, 145, 149, 241
  'gender fictions', *fictions de genre* 147, 149
  'Handmaid Coalition' 144
  women's marches, Washington DC 141, 142
Ferraris, Antonio de, known as Galateo 74
fiction(s): see also fact and fiction, nonfiction *and* paradox
  action on emotions, beliefs, and feelings 3, 5, 9, 53–108 *passim*
  as beneficial or harmful 6, 7, 10, 242, 256
  as critique 89, 90–92
  conception of 26, 27, 28, 107 n. 14, 156, 169, 173, 209, 242
  effects on law 177, 179–80, 186, 254
  as force of contamination 156, 238
  and empathy 5–6, 10, 51, 57, 64, 156, 180, 205, 209, 210, 255
  'gender fictions', *fictions de genre* 147, 149
  influence on public opinion 3, 4, 10
  influence on lives, identities and social practices 2, 9, 10, 27, 28, 109–201 *passim*
  as laboratory of experiences 243
  as escapism or wish-fulfilment, see escapism
  mimetic feint 242
    see also shared ludic feint
  and murder 6, 11, 56, 88, 103, 223, 231, 233–39
  and novelty 244
  paradox of 55, 58, 59, 61, 63, 64, 65, 67 nn. 5 & 6, 211, 212, 227, 250
  and patriarchy 141, 144, 146, 147, 149, 253
  as philosophical tool 81
  pragmatic value of world they create 86, 94
  and reality 102, 103, 105, 142, 172, 173, 220, 234, 235
  self-denouncing 246, 256
  as shaping societal reforms and political events 3
  as show, entertainment 9, 40, 45–46, 51–52, 107 n. 16, 209, 249, 250
  as testing ground for human behaviour 87
  therapeutic virtues of 243–44
  theories of x, 5, 7, 8, 51, 169
    see also fictionality, fiction studies
fictional:
  characters 1, 6, 9, 49, 51, 55, 57, 59, 61, 63, 64, 67 nn. 8 & 13, 72, 119, 139 n. 7, 212, 213, 250
  immersion 4, 18–19, 28, 19, 49–51, 98–99, 156–57, 172–73, 207, 212, 214, 232, 236, 243, 250
  universe x, 2, 89, 104, 107 n. 19, 141, 145, 234, 256
fictionality, fiction studies x, xii, 7, 9, 31, 32, 33, 40, 41, 46, 48, 49, 50–51, 78, 92, 93, 114, 119, 123, 158, 179
Fielding, Henry, *Don Quixote in England* 216 n. 1
Fielding, Sarah and Jane Collier, *The Cry* 209, 210
First World War 135, 136
Flahault, François 169
Flaubert, Gustave 227, 246
  author like God in the universe 227
  Charles Bovary (fictional character) 2
  *bovarysme* 2
  Emma Bovary (fictional character) 1, 2, 246, 256
Fontenelle, Bernard Le Bouyer de, *Nouveaux dialogues des morts* 80
Fortin de la Hoguette, Pierre 3
Foucault, Michel 148, 150, 180, 181, 182, 186, 206, 217 n. 5, 253
  *History of Madness* (*Histoire de la folie à l'âge classique*) 206

France, French 3, 4, 5, 6, 18, 48, 69, 70, 74, 75, 77, 78, 80, 82, 84 n. 1, 97, 130, 132, 133, 135, 139 nn. 3 & 8, 141, 142, 144, 155, 157, 158, 172, 178, 179, (188), 192, 193, 194, 195, 197, 198, 201–02 nn. 3, 15 & 17, 207, 210, 213, 214, 216 nn. 4 & 5, 251, 217 nn. 10 & 18, 223, 225, 243, 252, 255
Franco, Niccolò 75
François, Anne Isabelle xi, 10, 141, 163 n. 1, 252
Fray Mocho (Álvarez, José Sixto) 167
free speech 73, 78
freedom (reader, individual, expression, etc.) 4, 5, 7, 14 n. 5, 22, 52, 80, 118, 122, 134, 158, 178, 183, 185–88, 254
Friend, Stacie 55, 56, 58, 64
Fukuda, Yasunori 42 n. 1
Furetière, *Dictionnaire universel* 69

Gabriel, Markus 102, 104,
*Game of Thrones* 10, 57, 58, 155, 160
   Daenerys Targaryen (fictional character) 160
   Tyrion Lannister (fictional character) 57, 58, 59, 61, 63, 64, 65
*Gandahar*, novel by Jean-Pierre Andrevon, film by René Laloux 157
Garasse, François 77
Gass, William Henry 219, 220, 225
Gatten, Aileen 33, 37
Gefen, Alexandre 5, 156, 179
gender, *see* feminism
Genée, Rudolph 135
Genette, Gérard xii, 14 n. 1, 30 n. 3, 48, 101, 103, 123, 165, 169, 175 n. 2, 210, 217 nn. 16 & 18, 227, 235
   *Figures III* 101
*Genji monogatari* (*The Tale of Genji*, Murasaki Shikibu) 1, 14 n. 1, 32, 34
Germany 131, 135, 139 n. 3, 196, 197, 201 n. 1, 202 n. 13, 251
   Constitution 196, 197
   German humanism 72, 131
   *Grundgesetz* 196, 197
Gide, André 220, 223
Gifford, Paul 207
Giovio, Paulo 76
Goble, Andrew 113
Goffman, Erving 144
Gomi, Fumihiko 42 n. 1
Gomułka, Władysław 137
Goodman, Nelson 69, 245
Gordon, Scott Paul, *The Practice of Quixotism* 207, 217–18 n. 5
Gore, Al, *An Inconvenient Truth* 86
Gorgias, 23
Greece, Ancient x, 8, 9, 18, 19, 22, 71
   Ancient Greek poetics 9, 20, 27
   Muses (Hesiodic) 20, 21, 22, 23, 24, 25
   *see also* antiquity *and separate entries for ancient Greek authors*

Greenblatt, Stephen, *The Swerve* 73
Gueudeville, *Dialogues des morts d'un tour nouveau* 80

Haga, Yaichi 35, 37, 42 n. 7
Hall, Stuart 150, 160
harm (caused by fiction) 6, 7, 10, 242, 256
   *see also* fiction
*Harry Potter* (J.K. Rowling) 10, 155, 156, 158, 159, 160, 163 n. 1, 256
   Harry Potter Alliance 158, 159, 160, 161
Harweg, Roland 119
Hasumi, Shigehiko 46
Heinich, Nathalie 169
Hesiod 20, 21, 23, 24, 27
   *Theogony* 24
   *see also* Greece
history of ideas x, 71, 250
Hitchcock, Alfred 6, 88, 107 n. 21
Hofstadter, Douglas 222, 227
Homer, *Iliad* and *Odyssey* 20, 21, 22, 23, 27
   *see also* Greece
*homo fingens* 51
horror (genre) 56, 59–60, 61–63, 64, 250
Hroch, Miroslav 130–31
Hu, Margaret 184, 185
Huet, Pierre-Daniel, *Traité de l'origine des romans* 70
Hugo, Victor 87, 133, 139 n. 10, 179
human rights, see *rights*
humanism 73, 131, 139 n. 2
   humanist(s) 69, 71, 72, 74, 76, 77, 78, 81, 250
   *see also* Renaissance
Hume, David 80–81
humour, humourists xiv, 10, 14 n. 3, 47, 48, 171, 205, 207–08, 209, 212, 213, 214, 215, 255
   evolutions of the word 207
   as double effect of fiction (mirth and affection) 209
*Hunger Games, The* 155, 158, 160
Hutcheon, Linda 211–12, 220
Huz, Aurélie 157

Iglesias, Pablo 160
imagination 5, 7, 17, 26, 27, 28, 56, 62–63, 70, 75, 93–94, 96 n. 12, 130, 133, 135, 150, 157, 158, 169, 179, 180, 206, 214, 252
imitation 4, 6, 71, 82, 100, 156, 205, 210–11, 212, 245
   *see also* mimesis
Indian classical theatre 47
internationalism, transnationality 10, 144, 153 n. 4, 166, 168, 172, 180, 197, 224
Internet culture 69
   Hatsune Miku 97–105
   virtual technology 98
   *see also* cyberculture
interpretation 9, 10, 19, 69, 75, 76, 77, 81, 87, 89, 91, 92, 107 n. 10, 129, 135, 137, 148, 150, 159, 160, 165, 178, 182, 186, 187, 201 n. 1, 202 n. 12, 207, 210, 212, 236, 237, 249

irony 72, 77, 78–79, 80, 81, 82, 250
Ishiguro, Hiroshi 100–01, 102, 104, 251
Itô, Seikô, *The Beetle on the Waves* 222
Iwamatsu, Masahiro xi, 10, 219, 255

Jakobson, Roman 227
Jameson, Fredric 156, 157
Japan (Japanese culture, scholarship, fictional practices)
   x, xi, xiii, 5, 7–8, 9, 10, 31, 32, 34–35, 36–37, 38,
   39, 40–41, 45, 46, 47, 48–49, 51, 97, 103, 111, 113,
   119, 123, 219, 221, 222–23, 224, 245, 249, 234,
   250, 252, 255
   Akazome, Emon 36
   and Buddhism 37–40
   Bunraku (puppet theatre) 49–51, 250
   and Chinese culture 32, 35, 37, 42 n. 3, 48, 116, 119,
      120, 126 n. 3, 222
   and Confucianism 38, 249
   etiquette 10, 32, 111–24, 252
   Fujiwara no, Michinaga 36–38, 40
   Fujiwara no, Takamitsu 42 n. 5
   *Fushimi tennō shinki* 114
   *Gōke shidai* (Ōe no Masafusa) 121, 126 n. 7
   *Hanazono tennō shinki* 114
   *Heike monogatari* 38–39, 43 n. 8
   *Higashiyama gobunkobon 'nitchū gyōji'* 116, 117, 118,
      119, 121–22, 126 nn. 9 & 10
   *Genji monogatari* 1, 14 n. 1, 32, 34
   historical tales, historiography 31, 32, 33, 35, 36, 40,
      43 n. 8, 249
   itinerant storytellers 38, 39
   *Izumi Shikibu nikki* (Izumi Shikibu) 34–35
   Kabuki, *see main entry* Kabuki
   *kagami mono* 249
   *Kagerō nikki* (Fujiwara no Michitsuna no haha) 34–35
   *Kamo ujibito Yasutaka nenjū gyōji* 120–21
   *Kenmu nitchjū gyōji* and *Kenmu nenjū gyōji* 111–15,
      117–18, 126 n. 2, 127 n. 12
   *Kinpishō* 116–17, 126 nn. 6 & 9
   *Kojiki* 35, 42 n. 2
   meta-mystery 219, 221, 222, 225, 255
   *monogatari* and *nikki*, difference 34
   nation-building 40
   *Nihonshoki* (*Chronicles of Japan*) 32, 35, 39, 42 n. 2
   Nō theatre 39, 47, 49
   *Ōkagami* 33, 36–41, 42 n. 7, 43 nn. 10 & 11
   *rekishi monogatari* 31, 33, 35, 37, 43 n. 9, 249
   ritual 39, 113, 114, 121, 123
      and Taoism 39
   *Saikyūki* 116, 119
   *Shiji* (Sima Qian and Sima Tan) 35
   *Tosa Nikki* (Ki no Tsurayuki) 34
Jeannelle, Jean-Louis 165
Jenkins, Henry 150, 158
Jonson, Ben 'Comedy of Humour' 208
Jouve, Vincent, *Pouvoirs de la fiction: Pourquoi aime-t-on
   les histoires?* 243–44, 247, 256

Kabuki 47, 51
Kafka, Franz 178, 179, 180, 216 n. 4
   *The Trial* 179
Kassak, Fred, *Nocturne pour assassin* 223
Kavanaugh, Brett 142
Keaton, Buster, *Sherlock Jr.* 1, 2
Kellman Stephen G. ('self-begetting novel') 220
Kelsen, Hans 196
King, Stephen 246, 256
Kleist, Heinrich von, *Die Hermannsschlacht* 131–32,
   135–36, 137
Koechlin, Aurore 148
Köhler, Erich 87
Kondô, Akihiko 97, 98, 99, 102, 103, 105
Korthals Altes, Henriette xii, 10, 177, 221, 254
Krauss, Charlotte xii, 10, 129, 135, 136, 252
Kremer, Nathalie xii, 9, 97, 251
Kristof, Agota, *Le Grand Cahier* 225–26, 255
Kukkonen, Karin 93

Lahougue, Jean, *Non-lieu dans un paysage* 232–33,
   234–35, 256
Laloux, René 157
La Mothe Le Vayer, François de 78, 250
Landy, Joshua 6
Lang, Fritz 88
Lavocat, Françoise xii, 3, 8, 19, 27, 28, 30 n. 19, 47, 96
   n. 2, 98, 101–02, 103, 104, 105, 107 nn. 10, 11, 13,
   18, 20 & 21, 169, 231, 248 n. 4
Larue, Ïan, *Libère-toi cyborg!* 149
Latin America xiii, 10, 153 n. 13, 165, 166–67, 168,
   169, 173, 253
   Argentina 142, 144, 167, 170, 171
   Brazil 2
   Mexico 168
Laugier, Sandra 5, 148
law xiii, 8, 10, 22, 23, 50, 73, 76, 142, 145, 170, 173,
   177, 178, 179–80, 181, 183, 183–84, 186, 187, 188,
   191, 194, 195, 196–97, 198, 199, 238, 254
   Human rights law 180
   Law and Literature Movement 179
   legal discourse 10, 173
*Lazarillo de Tormes* 77, 78
Ledesma, Jerónimo 167
Lefait, Sébastien 181
Lejeune, Philippe 34
Le Lionnais, François 231, 236, 256
Lennox, Charlotte, *The Female Quixote* 210, 216 n. 5
Leon, Richard J. 185
Levin, Harry 206–07, 255
Lévy-Leblond, Jean-Marc 93
*Lights Out* (dir. David F. Sandberg) 60, 61
literacy 69, 159, 206
Lodge, David 220
*logos* 20, 22, 23, 24, 25, 30 n. 5
Lotman, Yuri / Iuri 172, 173, 242, 244, 256
Louis, Annick xiii, 10, 165, 253

Louis XIV 192, 195
Lovesey, Peter 235
Lucian of Samosata (c. 125–80 CE) x, 69–82, 250
　Menippean satire x, 71, 77, 78, 81
　influence on Renaissance Europe 71, 72, 78
　'fictions of unbelief' 71, 74
Ludmer, Josefina 165
Luther, Martin 77, 84 n. 7, 139 n. 2
　Lutheranism 75, 79
Lyon, David 180, 181
Lyons, John 87

Machiavelli, Niccolò 75
Mallarmé, Stephane 94
Manckiewicz, Joseph 246
Mancing, Howard, *Cervantes Encyclopedia* 207
Manguel, Alberto, *A Reading Diary* 245
Mansilla, Lucio V., *Una excursión a los indios ranqueles* 167, 170, 172
Marbod 132
Marivaux, Pierre de:
　*Le Télémaque travesti* 217 n. 18
　*Pharsamon* 246
Marx, Karl, *Thesis on Feuerbach* 69
Masłowski, Michel 134
mass culture and media 4, 69, 253
　media franchises 155
Massenet, Jules 213
Matsuzono, Hitoshi and Yasukazu Kondō 112, 113, 114, 119, 120, 122–23, 126 nn. 5 & 7
Mayer-Shönberger, Viktor 187
McCormick, Peter 59, 63
McCullough, Helen C. 36, 37, 38, 39, 40
McRobbie, Angela 149
Meiner, Carsten 87
Mérimée, Prosper, 132
　*La Jaquerie* 136, 140 n. 21
metafiction 10, 203, 213, 219–27, 255
　list of metafictional notions 220–21
　surfiction 219, 220, 221, 255
metalepsis 9, 10, 14 n. 2, 19, 28, 30 n. 3, 97–105, 234–36, 239, 251, 256
metaphor 22, 28, 36, 89, 157, 160, 179, 180, 182, 186, 192, 217 n. 18, 236
metonymy 19, 146
Michelet, Jules 131, 202 n. 3
Mickiewicz, Adam, *Dziady* (*Forefathers' Eve*) 133–34, 136, 137
Middle Ages, medieval (times, audiences, histories) x, 9, 31, 33, 35, 36, 37, 38, 41, 42 n. 7, 77, 93, 111, 119, 129, 211, 249, 252
Milner, Jean-Claude 88, 96 n. 4
mimesis 6, 7, 22, 25, 27, 100, 135, 147, 243, 248 n. 1
*mise en abyme* 10, 11, 220, 223, 232–35, 236, 238, 239, 245–46, 256
Moix, Yann, *Orléans* 17, 27
Molière, *Tartuffe* 3

morality (moral) 3, 4, 5, 6, 7, 16, 18, 20, 21, 22, 24, 36, 55–65, 71, 72, 87, 90, 102, 199, 201 n. 1, 243, 250
　moral persuasion (role of imagination and arts in) 56
　moral problem of fiction (MPF) 55–65, 250
Moreno, María 167, 168
Morita, Tei 116
Morris, Corbyn, *An Essay Towards fixing the True Standards of Wit, Humour, Raillery, Satire and Ridicule* 207
Müller, Simone xiii, 10, 111–24, 252
Murakami, Haruki 98
Murasaki Shibuku, *see* Genji Monogatari
*Murder of Roger Ackroyd, The* (Agatha Christie) 237
music x, xii, 22, 23, 24, 25, 26, 45, 48, 49, 50, 60, 70
myth, mythology x, 18, 20, 21, 22, 25, 33, 35, 38, 39, 42 n. 1, 43. n. 11, 72, 99, 100, 105, 119, 131, 136, 205, 251

narrative:
　diegesis 19, 22, 27, 96 n. 10, 135, 245, 246, 248 n. 1
　testimonial 168, 171, 173, 253
　storytelling 20, 21, 22, 31, 38, 39, 180
　nesting structure 222
　tricks 222
　*see also metalepsis, mimesis, mise en abyme*
narratology x, xiv, 93, 251
Nash, Mark 165
Nashe, Thomas 78
nation xii, 8, 40, 129–37, 143, 165, 195, 224, 252
　conception of the State 130
　national ceremonies as form of art 113
　'imagined community' (Anderson) 130
　national consciousness 133
　national drama 136, 137
　national history 40, 131
　national identity 10, 40
　nationalism 130
Netherlands 80
Nicole, Pierre 3
Nietzsche, Friedrich 73
Nolan, Christopher, *Inception, Interstellar* 92
nonfiction 164–73, 253
　'hybrids' 5, 10, 27, 164, 165, 166, 168, 171–72, 173
　'factual literature' 164, 165
　form of literary political activism 171
　*see also* fact and fiction
Noonan, Will 207
novel(s) 1–4, 5, 10, 14 n. 3, 17, 27, 33, 37, 40, 46, 48, 51, 59, 69, 70, 76, 79, 87, 94, 96 nn. 3 & 10, 98, 100, 101, 104, 129, 141–43, 145–47, 149–50, 158, 167–69, 175 nn. 3 & 7, 177–78, 179, 180–83, 184, 186, 188, 205–07, 209–10, 212–14, 219, 220–21, 222–26, 231–38, 243, 245–46, 248 n. 5, 249, 253, 255, 256
Nussbaum, Martha 5, 180, 183, 187, 188, 254

Obama, Barack 4, 70

Obsopoeus, Vincent 72
Oedipus 232, 237, 240 n. 2
Olivier, Laurence 46
opera 47, 48, 49, 51, 136, 140 n. 21, 213
Orikuchi, Shinobu 39
Orwell, George, *Nineteen Eighty-Four* 10, 145, 153 n. 2, 177–88, 254
Otsuji, Katsuhiko (Akasegawa Gempei) 219, 220, 223, 224–25, 227, 255
Oulipo xi, 31
Oura, Yasusuke xiii, 8, 9, 44–52, 249
Ovid, *Metamorphoses* 99, 100, 104, 107 nn. 6 & 17
    Pygmalion (fictional character) 99, 100, 104, 107 n. 6
Ozon, François 48

panfictionalism 47
paradox (of fiction) 49, 55, 58, 59, 61, 63, 64, 65, 67 nn. 5 & 6, 250
parody 10, 73, 171, 205, 206, 210, 211–12, 213, 216 n. 2, 217 nn. 16, 18 & 20, 221, 255
Paskins, Barrie 59, 63
Pausanias 25
Peeters, Benoît 237, 256
Peking opera 47
Pence, Mike 142
Perec, Georges xi, 232, 233–34, 235, 238, 256
Pérez, Mariana Eva, *Diario de una princesa montonera: 101 por ciento verdad* 170–71
performance 3, 8, 9, 18, 22, 24, 26, 27, 39 45–52, 103, 132, 135, 136–37, 170, 249–50, 252
performativity 8, 25, 26, 45, 48–49, 50, 180
Pfersmann, Otto xiii, 8, 10, 190–99, 201 n. 1, 254
philosophy x, xiii, 5, 8, 9, 19, 69, 71, 72, 73–74, 75–76, 78, 79–80, 81, 87, 89, 90, 99–100, 150, 163 n. 8, 167, 182–83, 206, 243, 244, 245, 256
    ontology 1, 5, 8, 19, 27, 98, 101–02, 103, 104, 105, 107 n. 11, 251
Pier, John 19, 101
Piglia, Ricardo 168, 169
Pinget, Robert, *Mahu ou le matériau* 221
*Pinocchio* (Carlo Collodi) 214
Plato 4, 6, 18, 20, 22, 24, 25, 27, 30 nn. 5 & 9, 71, 156, 242, 248 n. 1, 249
playfulness 7, 11, 28, 46, 48, 98, 171, 213, 216 n. 2, 217 n. 18, 219, 221, 222, 249, 255
*Play it Again, Sam* (dir. R. Herbert) 212, 213, 214, 255
pleasure 2, 10, 14 n. 3, 18, 47, 49, 50–51, 58–59, 70, 99, 107 nn. 8 & 12, 147, 150, 167, 209, 214, 215, 217 n. 20, 233, 235, 246
plot 24, 27, 30 n. 17, 67 n. 9, 88, 89, 92–93, 160, 234, 235, 236, 237, 239, 243
poetics x, xii, xiv, 9, 18, 20, 27, 69
poetry x, 21, 22, 23, 27, 33, 35, 36, 94, 134, 153 n. 6, 156, 214
    post-symbolist and surrealist poetry 94
    poetic forms of narrative 17–29, 249
    *see also* epic

Poland, Polish drama 130, 133, 134, 136, 142, 155
politics xii, 4, 70, 77, 86, 122, 149, 153 n. 11, 156, 159, 161, 163 n. 3, 192
    political action 8, 144–45, 146, 155–59, 161, 171, 199, 253
    *see also* activism, revolution
Polkinghorne, Donald 113
polysemy 19, 28
Ponnau, Gwenhaël 100
Pontano, Giovanni 74
Pope, Alexander 209
Posner, Richard A. 178, 182
post-modern fiction 89, 213, 214
pragmatics, pragmatism (pragmatic fiction) x, 6, 8, 9, 17–28, 45, 86, 90, 92, 94, 98, 101, 105, 141, 231, 242, 249, 251, 256
Preciado, Paul 148
pretending 18, 28, 46, 51, 75, 119, 205
    *see also* shared ludic feint
Prior, Matthew, 'A Dialogue between Thomas More and the Vicar of Bray' 80
privacy, invasion of 177–78, 179, 182, 183–88, 254
product, productivity 46, 70, 77, 78, 79, 93, 94, 98, 105, 146, 220, 249, 253
Prometheus 100
Proust, Marcel, *À la Recherche du temps perdu* 245, 256
psychology 4, 5, 6, 9, 59, 79, 113, 181, 244
    and social cognition 5
puppet theatre, *see* Bunraku
Pygmalion myth, *see* Ovid

Queen, Ellery, *The Tragedy of Y, Siamese Twin Mystery, Ten Days Wonder* 223
Queneau, Raymond, *Le Chiendent, Le Vol d'Icare* 221
quixotism, *see* Cervantes

Rabelais, François 72, 77, 79, 80, 250
Radford, Colin 55, 56, 57, 58, 62, 63
Radway, Janice 150
Rai, San'yō 42 n. 3, 43 n. 5
reader, the (readers) 2–8, 10, 14 n. 3, 19, 31–38, 40, 41, 42 n. 4, 70, 77–80, 82, 98, 132, 133, 135, 143, 147, 149, 150, 156, 158–59, 160, 161, 165, 166, 167, 168, 172, 179, 180, 181, 207–15, 222, 223, 225, 226, 229 n. 3, 231–39, 241, 243, 244–47, 252, 255, 256
    freedom of 4
    reader-characters 231, 232, 233, 234, 236, 246
    reading activity 246
reception 9, 11, 26, 28, 71, 77, 81, 129, 135, 136, 137, 147, 150, 160, 168, 170, 172
religion 18, 21, 26, 28, 30 n. 15, 39, 70–81, 130, 132, 187, 249, 250, 251
    religious troubles, quarrels 74
    theology 2, 23, 72, 75, 76, 78, 80, 81
Renaissance 7, 70, 71, 72, 73, 76, 78, 187, 206, 250
representation xi, xii, 3, 4, 6, 7, 9, 10, 11, 18–19, 22, 24, 26, 27, 28, 30 nn. 15 & 17, 46, 52, 55, 61, 70,

76, 78, 81, 85–87, 89, 90–94, 101, 104, 105, 133, 135, 144, 147, 148, 149, 156, 159, 208, 209, 220, 245, 246, 251, 253, 256
revolution(s), revolutionary literature 10, 69, 77, 82, 131, 133, 134, 136, 144, 169, 178, 187, 191–99, 254
   *Déclaration des droits de l'homme et du citoyen* (1789) 187, 193, 195, 198, 202 n. 5
Ricardou, Jean 221
Richardson, Brian 87
Ricœur, Paul 27, 147
rights 5–6, 142–43, 144, 145, 148, 155, 159, 171, 178, 179, 180, 183, 185, 188, 193, 195, 196, 197, 253
   of nonhumans, 158
ritual 18, 24, 25, 26, 27, 39, 71, 88, 113, 114, 121, 123, 145
Robbe-Grillet, Alain 220, 221, 229 n. 1
Romanticism 3, 133
   'Werther effect' 3, 70
   Don Quixote as precursor of Romantic hero 206
Rowling, J. K., *see* Harry Potter
Ruffel, Lionel 165, 166, 171
Rushdie, Salman, *Quichotte* 205, 213, 214, 255
Ryan, Marie-Laure 8, 101, 103

Sarmiento, Faustino, 167
Sartre, Jean-Paul 4
satire 10, 71, 72, 75, 76, 77, 78, 80, 81, 182, 183, 205, 206, 207, 210, 213, 255
Satō, Atsuko 113, 114, 120
Satō, Masatoshi 116
Schaeffer, Jean-Marie xii, 4, 7–8, 11, 18–19, 26, 46, 48, 98, 101, 103, 156, 169, 207, 242–43, 244, 246, 247, 248 n. 2, 256
   *see also* shared ludic feint
Scholes, Robert 220
science-fiction x, 86, 92, 94, 96 n. 10, 149, 156, 157, 159, 179
Scott, Walter 1
Searle, John 5, 8, 46
Second World War 4, 70, 196, 245
self-reflexivity 10, 17, 19, 231
semantics 19, 28, 45, 91, 171, 249
Servant, Stéphane, *Sirius* 158
shadow theatre, *see* Bunraku
Shakespeare, William:
   Desdemona (fictional character in *Othello*) 87
   Hamlet (fictional character) 3, 14 n. 4, 46
   play-within-the-play 3
   *Romeo and Juliet* 87
shared ludic feint 7, 8, 18–19, 26, 98, 246
Sheffield, John, 'A Conversation between Mahomet and the Duc de Guise' 80
Sheppard, Fleetwood, *Calendar Reformed* 80
simulation 2
Slugan, Mario xiv, 6, 9, 55–65, 250
Smith, Adam 81
Smith, Murray 56

Snowden, Edward 176–88, 254
society 1, 2, 7, 70, 129, 130, 146, 147, 149, 150, 159, 180, 181, 185, 191, 192, 206, 214, 253
   social forces and cultural products 69, 70
   social change 70, 147, 150, 158
sociology, sociologist 5, 7, 129, 158, 180, 188, 244, 256
Socrates 20, 23
   *Phaedrus* 23
Sorel, Charles, *Le Berger extravagant ou l'Anti-roman* 78, 210, 246
Soviet Union 136, 137, 193, 202
Sparrow, Jack (fictional character)
Spencer, Kathleen 143–46
Speratti, Horacio 170
Spinoza, Baruch 80
Staquet, Anne 71
Stendhal 103
stereotypes (fictions perpetuating) 4, 6, 49, 70, 147, 148, 216 n. 2, 252
Stoichita, Victor, *The Pygmalion Effect* 100
story(telling), *see* narrative
Stowe, Harriet Beecher, *Uncle Tom's Cabin* 3, 4, 244, 248 n. 5
Sue, Eugène, *Le Juif errant* 3
Suits, David B. 56
surveillance xii, 145, 176–88, 254
Suvin, Darko 156, 157
sympathy 4, 55, 63, 64, 65, 135

Tadié, Jean-Yves ('récit poétique') 220
Takemoto, Kenji, *Paradise Lost in the Box* 222, 255
Tave, Stuart M., *The Amiable Humorist* 207
technology 8, 47, 90, 91, 98, 99, 100, 101, 102, 105, 145, 181, 183, 184, 185, 190 n. 1, 251
television x, 4, 5, 8, 9, 10, 45, 46, 47, 147, 156, 213, 253
testimony 2, 3, 17, 120, 134, 143, 145, 168, 169, 170, 171, 172, 173, 253
theatre, playwriting, drama xii, 3, 8, 10, 18, 25, 26, 27, 39, 45, 46, 47, 48, 49, 128–37, 140 n. 19, 143, 156, 192, 217 n. 21, 250, 251, 252
   French *scènes historiques* 132
   closet drama 132
theories of fiction, *see* fiction
Tolkien, J. R. R. x, 157, 160, 163 n. 5
Tomita, Mayu 103
Tournier, Michel, *Le Vol du Vampire* 245
tragedy 18, 20, 22, 23, 24, 27, 30 n. 15, 206, 223
Tran-Gervat, Yen-Mai xiv, 10, 205–15, 255
Trump, Donald 141, 142, 143, 144, 151, 152, 153 n. 1
truth 5, 20, 21, 22, 23, 24, 25, 32, 33, 34, 35, 39, 40, 47, 63, 64, 81, 86, 92, 93, 114, 167, 169, 170, 172, 173, 182, 188, 210, 212, 226, 237
Tsuda, Sokichi 33, 42 nn. 2 & 3
Tsutsui, Yasutaka ('chô-kyokô') 219, 220, 221, 223, 255
   *The Lautrec Villa Murders* 223
   *see also* metafiction

Urfé, Honoré d', *L'Astrée* 3
utopia 10, 161, 243

Varus 131, 132
Vegio, Maffeo 73
Velasco, López de 77
Verne, Jules 87
Viau, Théophile de 78
video games 6, 47, 87, 97, 219
Viel, Tanguy, *Cinéma* 246, 256
Vila-Matas, Enrique 238, 256
Villiers de l'Isle-Adam, *L'Ève future* 100, 104
Viñas, David 168
virtual world 96–105, 244, 251
Vitet, Ludovic 132, 133, 136, 137, 139 nn. 6, 7, 8, 9 & 10
Volodine, Antoine 245, 256
Volpi, Jorge 165
Voltaire 72, 79, 80, 250
 *Conversation dans les Champs-Elysées* 80
Vuillème, Jean-Bernard 17

Wagner, Frank xiv, 11, 14 n. 7, 142, 214–47, 256
*Wall-E* (dir. A. Stanton) 86
Walsh, Rodolfo, *Operación masacre* 167, 168, 169, 170
Walton, Kendall 46, 55, 56, 59, 60, 61, 62, 63, 67 n. 5, 107 n. 10

Wang, Esther 147
Warton, Joseph 209
Waugh, Patricia 220
Wehl, Feodor 135
Westerfeld, Scott, *Uglies* 157
Weston, Michael 59, 63
Wieland, Christoph Martin 79, 250
 *Geheime Geschichte des Philosophen Peregrinus Proteus* 79
Wilde, Eduardo 146, 149
Williams, Robin 214
Winfrey, Oprah 213
Wittig, Monique 146, 149
women 3, 6, 21, 34, 35, 50, 70, 141, 142–45, 146, 147, 149–50, 207, 213
Wyspiański, Stanisław 136

Xenophanes 22, 24, 25

Yanal, Robert J. 63, 67 n. 13

Zenetti, Marie-Jeanne 165
Zimmer Bradley, Marion 159
Žižek, Slavoj 182
Zola, Émile, *Germinal* 96 n. 3, 244, 248 n. 5

www.ingramcontent.com/pod-product-compliance
Lightning Source LLC
Chambersburg PA
CBHW080439170426
43195CB00017B/2823